A HISTORY
OF
BOGNOR REGIS

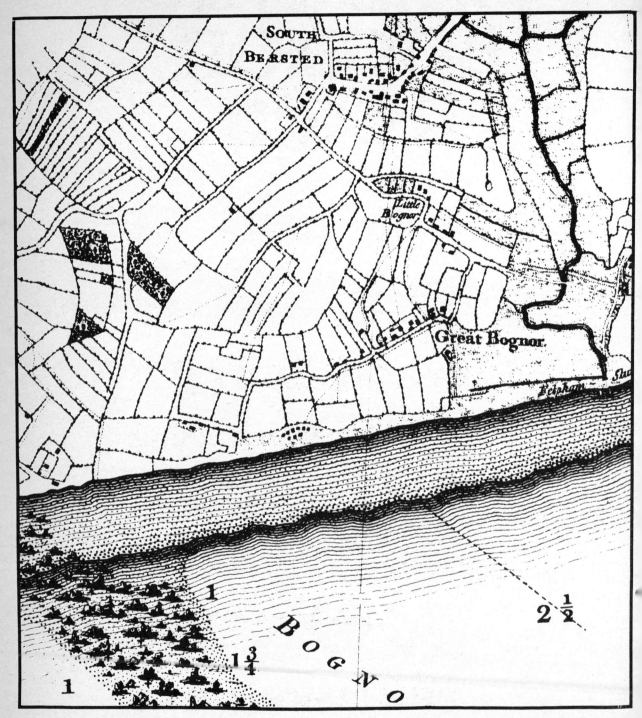

Detail from Thomas Yeakell and William Gardner's map of southern Sussex, 1778, showing Bognor before the arrival of Sir Richard Hotham.

A History of
BOGNOR REGIS

Gerard Young
Completed by Derek Young

PHILLIMORE

1983

Published by
PHILLIMORE & CO. LTD.
Shopwyke Hall, Chichester, Sussex

ISBN 0 85033 487 X

Typeset in the United Kingdom by:
Fidelity Processes - Selsey - Sussex
Printed and bound in Great Britain by
THE CAMELOT PRESS LTD.
Southampton, Hants.

CONTENTS

LIST OF PLATES

(between pages 140 and 141)

1. Sir Richard Hotham, 1722-1799
2. Merton Grove, Hotham's house at Wimbledon
3. Sir Richard Hotham and his wife
4. South Bersted church, 1790
5. South Bersted parish register extract
6. Hothamton Crescent: The North Wing
7. Hothamton Crescent: Dome House
8. Hothamton Crescent: The South Wing
9. Hotham's last resting place, South Bersted churchyard
10. Early Bognor trade card
11. Early Bognor trade card
12. Rock Buildings, later Rock Gardens
13. William Blake's cottage at Felpham
14. The *Fox Inn* at Felpham
15. Turret House, Felpham
16. Princess Charlotte, 1796-1817
17. Dome House
18. The Jubilee School, High Street
19. Chapel House, sale particulars, 1815
20. Sudley Cottage
21. The *White Horse Inn*, South Bersted
22. The *Sussex Hotel*, High Street
23. Waterloo Square
24. Steyne Place, West Street
25. Bognor from the sea, 1857
26. The coal ketch, *Annie*
27. The library and bazaar, High Street
28. The Bognor Improvement Company's plan, 1835
29. Arthur Smith's view of proposed Victoria Park Estate, 1870s
30. Robert Knapton's view of Bognor, 1823

(between pages 172 and 173)

31. Bognor's first Town Hall and Assembly Rooms
32. Laurel Cottage, Church Path
33. The *Norfolk Hotel*
34. The opening of the new Pier, 1865
35. An early view of the Steyne
36. Bath House, the Steyne
37. The library, Waterloo Square
38. Barnham station, 1864

xi

LIST OF TEXT FIGURES

Frontispiece: Early Bognor from Yeakell and Gardner's Map, 1778

ACKNOWLEDGEMENTS

Grateful thanks, for the illustrations in the text and plate-section of this book, are due to:

Mr. Robert Hamlin, Librarian and Information Officer at the West Sussex Institute of Higher Education (Bognor Regis College) for access to original material in the Gerard Young Collection, housed in the College Library; The West Sussex County Council Library and Archives Service, for access to photographs, microfilms, prints and drawings at the West Sussex Record Office and Chichester and Bognor Regis Libraries, and for the generous help given by their staff; The Rev. H. Pruen, vicar of South Bersted, for permission to reproduce the extract from the parish register of 1787, held by the West Sussex Record Office; Mrs. Seymour, for the loan of photographs from the collection of the late Mr. R. J. and Mr. H. W. Seymour; Mr. Derek Young, Mr. R. Iden, Mr. J. M. Hawkins, Mrs. C. D. May, Mrs. E. Pollington and Bognor Regis Local History Society, for the loan of material from their collections, and for original photographs and line drawings by Mr. C. Butler, Mr. P. Iden, Mr. R. Iden, and Miss Ann Hewitt of Phillimore.

The sources for the illustrations in the plate section are as follows:

Gerard Young Collection: Plates 7, 10-15, 18-24, 27, 29, 31, 34, 39, 43-6, 54-5, 60-2, 66, 68, 72, 75-6, 79, 88-9, 94-7, 100; Derek Young: Plate 2; West Sussex Record Office: Plates 5, 30, 33, 35, 37, 47, 53, 63, 77-8, 80-1; Bognor Regis Library: Plates 50, 73, 82-3; Seymour Collection: Plates 26, 38, 45, 48-9, 58, 70-1, 87; R. Iden collection: Plates 9, 25, 28, 40, 42, 51, 56-7, 59, 64, 69, 90-3 (nos. 40, 51, 64, 69, 92 and 93 are photographs taken by R. Iden); John Hawkins collection: Plates 17, 41, 65, 67, 98-9; Plates 6, 8, 32, 36, 85 were all photographed by Mr. C. Butler; Mrs. C. D. May: Plate 86; Mrs. E. Pollington: Plate 84; Phillimore & Co. Ltd.: Plates 74 and 101 were photographed by Miss Ann Hewitt; Miss G. M. Muddle, author of *A Methodist Tapestry*: Plate 52; Lindsay Fleming, author of *History of Pagham*: Plates 1, 3, 4, 16.

The sources for the line illustrations are as follows:

Gerard Young Collection: End-papers, Figs. 10 (taken from Dally's 1828 Bognor Guide), 14-17, 19-21, 23; West Sussex Record Office: Figs 2, 7-8, 11, 13, 25; Chichester Library: Figs. 5, 22 (from Visitor's Guide, 1856); J. M. Hawkins collection: Figs. 3, 26; R. Iden collection: Figs. 4, 9, 12, 18; Fig. 24 drawn by R. Iden; Fig. 27 drawn by Peter Iden.

PREFACE

In completing my brother's book, I made extensive use of the valuable files containing the results of his own researches; but I wish here to express my thanks to all who assisted me in gathering the additional information I found necessary as the work progressed—in particular to Robert Hamlin, Librarian of the Bognor Regis College, who so patiently and efficiently filled the gaps in my knowledge by dealing with the numerous queries which I addressed to him over a period of years. My warmest thanks are also due to Ronald Iden who, in my absence from Bognor, shouldered the important task of researching and compiling the plates and illustrations in accordance with my list of selected subjects.

I have been greatly encouraged by the close interest shown in the progress of the book by the members of the Bognor Regis Local History Society, who have, I feel, inherited from my brother the work of exploring Bognor's past which he started on his own many years ago.

DEREK YOUNG
1983

INTRODUCTION

IN 1787 builders were at work on two commodious residences both destined to play important rôles in the history of the British seaside holiday. Indeed, as far as Sussex was concerned, 1787 was the *annus mirabilis* in which were laid the early foundations of its future prosperity.

At Brighton the contractors had reached the final stages in the transformation of the farmhouse, recently bought by the Prince of Wales, into a mansion, or even palace, better suited to the substantial requirements of the heir to the throne. The completion of Brighton House — later, as the Royal Pavilion, to be orientalised by Nash's domes and minarets — set the seal on the fortunes of Brighton, for it guaranteed to the town the frequent presence of its biggest social asset. Once securely anchored to Brighton by his expensive new Pavilion, the Prince was hardly likely to transfer his patronage elsewhere. Rival resorts, of course, might take a different view. They could at least nurture the hope of winning the favours either of the Prince himself or of another member of the Royal Family, and the newest resort on the Sussex coast started hoping along these lines as soon as it was born.

Twenty-six miles to the west of Brighton, while the finishing touches (for the time being) were being applied to the Prince's seaside residence, work was beginning on a curiously similar project: the reconstruction of another Sussex farmhouse to provide a suitable home for another rich and distinguished visitor. Sir Richard Hotham had made an exploratory journey to the South Coast, had liked what he saw of it and had decided to buy a convenient property for conversion into a permanent marine retreat. The work of rebuilding Sir Richard's farmhouse, soon to be dignified by the name of Bognor Lodge, began in January 1787.

And so, to all intents and purposes, did the story of Bognor, which is the subject of this book. The local historian who aims to extend his researches into the pre-Hotham era might well spare his energies, for most of what he would be looking for is now under the sea. The original settlement of Bognor (*Bucgrenora*, the borderland of Bucgren) was engulfed by the English Channel, as was the first cathedral of the diocese now ruled from Chichester — its bells, according to the old legend, can still be heard ringing under the waves on stormy nights — and the same fate would certainly have befallen the land now occupied by modern Bognor if Hotham had not embarked on the creation of a new holiday resort on this section of the coast. For a seawall had to be built and gradually extended to protect the town, and the vital importance of this defence was demonstrated time and time again. For instance, in the course of a single January storm in 1890 the coastline on either side of the wall was eroded to a depth of six feet; and

Bognor's fight to preserve itself from its greatest attraction, the sea, has continued ever since.

There have been other forms of depredation since Hotham's time, and it is not the sea that must take the blame for the fact that nothing now remains of Bognor Lodge. Fortunately, much else of late 18th-century and early 19th-century Bognor has survived and as you enter the town from the east you can still catch something of the spacious aristocratic atmosphere intended by its founder. Fine mansions stand among trees — including the Dome House, the one which, in Hotham's dreams, would become a seaside residence of the Prince of Wales or even of George III.

He was disappointed in this, as he was in so many of the ambitious plans he evolved for the resort which he fondly hoped would always bear his name. And yet, in one sense, he triumphed in the end. Brighton today, in spite of the long and faithful patronage of the Prince who became Regent and King, is still just Brighton — but Bognor is *Bognor Regis*.

BERSTED LODGE, BOGNOR.

Fig. 1. Sir Richard Hotham's Chapel House, re-named Bersted Lodge, where the future William IV was entertained at house-parties.

Chapter I

HOTHAM THE HATTER

WHO WAS Sir Richard Hotham? It is a question that has never been fully answered, possibly because few people asked it. No biography was written about him, he left no memoirs and his name is absent from the *Dictionary of National Biography*. What fame he has is due simply to the fact that he created a popular watering-place out of an obscure fishing settlement on the West Sussex coast.

Richard Hotham was born into a peaceful England on 5 October 1722, with the German-speaking George I on the throne, the country run by land-owning gentry and Robert Walpole just recently in office as the first Prime Minister. Hotham was of Yorkshire stock and may well have been born in that county, but it was in London that he began his career, probably as an apprentice to a hatter. On 3 December 1743, when he was 21, he married Miss Frances Atkinson, who was also a northerner (from the parish of Stockton-on-Tees) and, by one account, was the daughter of his employer. The wedding took place at Chelsea Hospital, with the Rev. Thomas Sampson officiating. Paintings of Hotham depict him as a handsome man of some character, with a very firm jaw and clear eyes. If this should be suggestive of kindly force, then the portraits marry well with the accounts of the vigour of his activities throughout his life. It is perhaps, all over again, the customary tale of an enterprising Yorkshireman's rise to commercial success.

Hotham soon launched himself on his own account as a hatter. His shop was in Searle Street, which is a byway leading from the south-east corner of Lincoln's Inn Fields into Carey Street. His business sense was strong. He made it a rule to sell only high-quality articles, so that new customers soon became old ones, and he attracted lively attention by distributing copper discs all over London and the provinces. They were the size of a penny. On one side was stamped: 'Rd. Hotham, Searle Street, Lincoln's Inn, London sells hats'; and on the reverse: 'and stockings of his own manufacturing wholesale & retail'. This advertising device caught the public fancy — a 'durable document' was one description — and Hotham was quickly on his diligent way to success.

He was now living in an exhilarating age. The Jacobite rebellion of 1745 had failed, faith in the Government was strengthened, London trade was flourishing and the Empire expanding. By 1752, he had moved to better premises at the corner of Old Hungerford Market in the Strand (where Charing Cross Station stands today) and eight years later he had prospered to the extent of taking on a Mr. Jackson as partner and joining his father, Joseph Hotham, in the business of shipping for the East India Company. His fortune grew and, with it, his social status. He built himself a country house to the south of London, in the fashionable

1

Winbledon area that knew ·Pitt, Wilberforce, Lyde Brown, the collector of antiques, the Marquis of Rockingham, Earl Spencer and Benjamin Bond Hopkins.

His house was not in Wimbledon itself — which was then a village fringing the common and clustered near St Mary's church on the hill — but some distance to the east, where there was a tollgate into the parish of Merton. Here, in spacious grounds adjacent to a cross-roads, stood the first house which Hotham built for himself, a picturesque white residence which he called Merton Grove. Its most prominent feature was a semi-hexagonal porch with round-arched niches on each side and an ogee-arched window above the doorway. The front of the house also had ogee windows on the upper floor, with Venetian windows below. Today the site of Merton Grove is occupied by the houses in Balfour Road, and South Wimbledon Underground Station stands on the opposite corner of the cross-roads. But when Hotham lived there it was a rural spot with shady groves and views over fresh, unbroken country. The river Wandle flowed through the meadows not far away, and Hotham used to stroll the short distance along the London Highway to the *King's Head* inn by Wandle Bridge. There he would board one of George Hoath's daily coaches for London, often with Richard Thornton, a founder-director of Lloyds Bank, as a fellow-passenger.

Hotham entered into the life of a country gentleman with the same unabashed enterprise with which he had built up his business in London. He had a good eye for the main chance and he had his reward on 12 April 1769. On that day he was knighted by George III. There had been an undercurrent of anarchy in the king-dom, whipped up by the democratic agitations of John Wilkes; and various districts, eager to dissociate themselves from these radical goings-on, were presenting expressions of their loyalty to the King. On behalf of the people of Surrey, Hotham and Mr. Timothy Waldo of Clapham handed the King an address embodying their county's loyalty and Hotham returned to South Wimbledon as Sir Richard, while it was as Sir Timothy that Waldo went home to Clapham. In the following year, as if to demonstrate that he had won the county's esteem as well as the King's, the people of Surrey made him their Sheriff.

As a knight, he was entitled to display a coat-of-arms and it is in this connec-tion only that his name can be associated with the old titled family of Hotham in the East Riding. This Yorkshire title began with Sir John Hotham, M.P. for Beverley, who was created a baronet in 1621 and died in 1645. Hotham is a common enough name in Yorkshire and it is probable that all its bearers share a common origin. Richard Hotham, therefore, decided to adopt the same coat-of-arms as the titled Beverley branch. The holder of the baronetcy at this time was Sir Beaumont Hotham, who was a barrister in the Middle Temple and became a Baron of the Exchequer and M.P. for Wigan. He was living in Stratton Street, Piccadilly, where Sir Richard called on him one day with an interesting proposal. It was to the effect that, although he had no claim, he would like to carry the Hotham arms if the family had no objection. In return, he would have great pleasure in putting Sir Beaumont and his son in his will for a handsome legacy. To this generous if somewhat naive offer Sir Beaumont acquiesced, but he suggested that it might be as well if the arms were slightly altered for Sir Richard's use. This was done and the sequel to this courteous little meeting follows in another chapter.

Sir Richard was now 48 and it is in his dealings with the East India Company that one gets the full flavour of his personality. Robert Clive had by now laid the foundations of the British Empire in India, and the Honourable East India Company — a sovereign power — was busy creating a new world of commerce at the far end of the sea lanes. The Company chartered ships from private owners, such as Hotham himself now was, and back they came, after a year or so away, bringing new, rich, spicy smells into the London docks.

Hotham, however, saw little to praise in the Company's methods of handling this huge trading concern; and in a pamphlet of 32 pages, entitled *Reflections on East India Shipping*, he addressed himself to the allegedly duped holders of East India stock. In a righteous preface he wrote:

> Anonymous writers sometimes mean, by concealing their names, to take unwarrantable liberties in treating their subject, and also to prevent personal attack. As I mean no improper freedom, but to keep close to facts, and the most probable Truths, I think myself as much entitled to address the proprietors of East India stock as other gentlemen are that speak from memory at general Courts in Leadenhall Street. I therefore commit my name to the public and leave them to judge of the propriety of the subject, the time of publication and the necessity of its being now rightly understood that for the future such gross misapplication of the stockholders' money shall effectually be prevented. I shall therefore, without further preface, declare myself to be the author of the following Reflections.

I am, Ladies and Gentlemen,
Your most obedient servant,
RD. HOTHAM

The *Reflections* that followed consisted of a shrewd attack, quoting chapter and verse, on the Company's slovenly methods, such as poor usage of space in employing charter ships for India and China. His indignation rose in his final paragraph:

> The innumerable evils that want to be rooted out crowd so upon my mind while I am writing that I find much difficulty of stopping within the bounds I prescribed to myself.

Hotham's pamphlet was published on 18 March 1773 from his father's house in Fludyer Street, Westminster. As intended, it certainly made an effect, though perhaps not in the direction Hotham had expected. The East India Company rode the storm but it was Hotham and his shipping partners who now came under attack.

He bided his time. He waited a year, watching the varying trading fortunes of the East India Company, and then went into print again. His second missile was *A Candid State of Affairs relative to East India Shipping for the year 1773* and it was projected at the public from Merton Grove on 14 February 1774. He explained to the shareholders that the aim of this new pamphlet was to defend himself and his fellow shipowners against the attacks made on them since the publication of the *Reflections* in the previous year. No words were wasted and his blunt opening sentence had drama in it:

The Company's present distress originated with, and has been artfully upheld by, some of the leading members of their own body.

Again he gave documented instances of bad management in Indian and Chinese waters and the wanton waste of shipping space. He quoted many letters between himself and the Company and in conclusion acquitted himself with some vigorously nautical rhetoric:

My cables are made of plain truth and my anchors are tough, stout English honesty.

One would naturally like to know exactly what the directors of the East India Company thought of these northern blasts but, apart from one or two tactful decisions 'not to comply with Sir Richard Hotham's request', the tenor of their correspondence with him was discreet. They continued to charter his ships for freight-carrying and five surviving letters between 1782–85 refer only to business matters.

If those two pamphlets of 1773 and 1774 failed to split the East India Company asunder, they did not deter their author from ensuring that his side of the charter agreement was working efficiently. He was essentially a man of business and, as managing owner and husband of ships, he was the terror of his captains. One of them, Captain George Hayter, had already undertaken two voyages for him in command of the *York* and a third in a new ship of the same name. It was after a fourth voyage to Bencoolen, Sumatra, that Hotham expressed himself strongly on the subject of Hayter's worthlessness. He laid nine objections to the captain's conduct before the joint owners of the *York*. Time was money, and Hayter had apparently been dawdling across the oceans. He had, first of all, neglected the stowing of the ship's cargo at Gravesend when he sailed in 1773. Then he had lost time in a devious passage to St Helena in the South Atlantic. He had caused an anchor to be broken unnecessarily, found fault with the ship's supplies of bread and flour and finally disobeyed orders by attempting to call at Batavia on the outward voyage. This last offence must have led Hotham to believe that captain and crew had been drinking too heavily and had run out of liquor before they reached the end of the voyage. He had intended them to pick up supplies on the way home, for in his sailing orders to Hayter the 61st article of instructions had plainly stated: 'You will buy so much Arrack [an East Indian liquor distilled from rice and coconut juice] at Batavia for the use of your ship's company as you shall judge necessary for your homeward bound voyage'.

Hayter had wasted two months in the East Indies and did not arrive home till October 1775. When the case was brought against him, he blamed Hotham and his charter-party owner Nathaniel Tanner for creating impossible conditions by overloading the ship in the first place. Casting his mind back, he explained how Hotham and Tanner had gone down to Gravesend to superintend the loading of the ship two years before. 'It's as full as an egg', Hayter had protested; but Hotham, by way of reply, had knocked down partitions and put on another 300 tons. 'My ship's officers', said Hayter in defence, 'were obliged to crawl upon their hands and knees to get to their cabins, and the doors of the cabins were obliged to be cut in halves about three feet above the deck for them to creep in and to go to rest when it was not their watch on deck'.

However, Hayter was dismissed and Captain John Atkinson Blanchard took over command of the 755-ton *York*. Four years later, in 1779, Blanchard too was in trouble. The *York* was wrecked. This was an extraordinary wreck. The East India Company had chartered the ship from Hotham and she was on her way home with cargo from Bombay. On Friday, 1 January 1779, she reached Margate in a high gale and anchored for safety in the roads. At the height of the storm she slipped her cables, was driven over Margate sands and lifted right on to the jetty, where the crew got out and walked to land. Members of the East India Company arrived on the scene to salvage the cargo. Saltpetre and pepper, though damp, were unloaded, taken to London, processed and marketed. The ship was eventually refloated and arrived in London with the remainder of the cargo.

At this point, Hotham, Tanner and Blanchard brought a case against the East India Company. Hotham maintained with customary determination that his ship had duly arrived at the port of discharge and that he was entitled to be paid for the freight of all the goods, including those saved at Margate. The Company disagreed but, if that was his attitude, they said they would deduct an appropriate amount from the value of the goods and also claim the expenses of getting the cargo up from Margate. Hotham won the case, but he was ordered to pay a share of the expenses of transporting the salvaged goods.

No point escaped him in his long dealings with the Company and in 1787 they were fighting in court again. This time it was about his new ship *Royal Admiral*. The Company's Eastern agents, said Hotham, had short-loaded his ship. She could have carried at least 100 tons more. The ship had therefore been underloaded in direct contradiction to the charter agreements. This meant that he had lost freight money. There was no more to be said. Hotham won his case.

*   *   *

From all this turmoil of trade on the high seas, it is interesting to drop back into the peaceful Wimbledon countryside for a while to see how Hotham was faring against the rural background of local affairs. Life was by no means uneventful, for he had quickly discovered that the Wimbledon Vestry Committee had much in common with the East India Company. They, too, did not know how to manage things on the far boundaries of their parish. There was in Hotham's nature a constant desire to improve the state of things, and it was in South Wimbledon — or in Merton, as he preferred to regard his place of residence — that his future interest in planning and building began to assert itself. Running past his house from east to west was the turnpike road from Tooting to Morden. A little way up this road in the Tooting direction a track known as Iron Mill Lane turned off northwards, leading to the common lands called South Fields and thence into the parish of Wandsworth.

Hotham's own land extended eastwards as far as this lane and it seemed to him that the track could be developed into an important road to the Thames. Accordingly, he opened an attack on the Vestry Committee, sitting unsuspectingly up on the hill. By 23 November 1773, both sides were mustering. Hotham had prepared his indictment against the parish for the repair and maintenance of Iron Mill Lane, and the Committee had briefed an attorney to defend the case.

It was a long drawn-out battle and came to an end in 1777. Like other occupiers of the lane, Hotham had helped to keep it in order with new hedging and ditching at his own expense; and this gave him an advantage over the Vestry Committee who had done nothing at all. By the summer of 1776, the case had been heard and a King's Bench decision given. The lane was declared a public highway and the parishes of Wimbledon and Wandsworth were enjoined to keep it in repair. Of course, these repairs were not carried out speedily enough for Hotham. He continually harassed the Committee with letters and finally, on 7 September 1777, they wearily entered their admission of defeat in their minute book:

> Whereas, for compromising and putting an end to all further disputes between Sir Richard Hotham and this parish concerning the road leading from Wimbledon to Merton . . .

The compromise agreed to was that the parish highway surveyors should pay Hotham £100 in instalments for all the fencing, hedging and ditching he had done and for any ground used in widening the lane. Thus a new road grew between Wandsworth and Merton, which is still is use today.

After this, there was one obvious step left to the Vestry Committee and they sensibly took it. In 1778 they elected Hotham — now a widower — as Chairman and let him deal with the troubles of the parish in an official capacity. It is amusing to contrast his rumbustious and colourful life in the shipping world with the picture of him sitting in judgment in the Wimbledon schoolhouse on 28 December 1778 listening to Mrs. Haybull, matron of the poorhouse, laying complaints against 'Henry Potter and William Gumble for indecent and abusive behaviour to her and the women and children in the workhouse'. Doubtless, Hotham proposed some sensational fate for these two wastrels — especially as he was a contributor to the relief of Wimbledon's poor to the extent of £8 5s. 0d., the fourth highest assessment in the parish.

The dilapidated state of St Mary's church became one of his chief concerns. He set himself to speed up the repairs, once the Vestry had decided on 22 May 1786 that restoration was necessary, and a fund-raising committee was instituted by the vicar, Herbert Randolph. Hotham and his wealthy neighbours, William Wilberforce, Henry Dundas and Earl Spencer were both subscribers and committee members, and on 26 February 1787, at a meeting in the *Rose & Crown*, High Street, Hotham and George Chamberlain were empowered to negotiate with contractors for repairing and enlarging the church. It may have been Hotham's enthusiasm for architecture that caused the original restoration scheme to be abandoned and what was practically a new church to be erected instead. It cost some £2,000 and, in the fashion of the time, was Grecian in style and not particularly suited for country worship. (It was rebuilt in 1843.) On the opening day, 7 July 1788, a gallery collapsed, bringing 38 choristers and musicians unharmoniously down to the floor of the church. But, on that day, Hotham was busy down at Bognor.

During the period just described, he had received a far greater honour than his appointment to the local Vestry Committee. He had been elected a Member of Parliament for the Borough of Southwark, the constituency in which he lived. This was a considerable triumph, for he defeated Henry Thrale, the famous brewer, who had sat for the borough for 15 years. Most of Hotham's life so far had been spent acquiring a fortune and a certain social standing. Though he was a self-made man, outspoken and possibly a little too bluff for society's taste, he had won considerable esteem and had made many useful friends in the political world. Perhaps it was a suggestion from his influential Wimbledon neighbours; perhaps it was his own urging to right the wrongs of mankind; whatever it was, he set out boldly in the spring of 1780 to gain a seat in Parliament.

Just as he started to woo the 'sweet voices' of Southwark, Hotham's opponent Thrale suffered one of his apoplectic fits and a much more formidable adversary now confronted him. This was none other than Dr. Samuel Johnson, rallying to Thrale's aid and settling down to write his election address for him. Many of Thrale's other friends also helped and his wife canvassed for him, but nothing they did in the cause was quite as scarifying as Johnson's gibes at 'Hotham the Hatter'.

But Hotham was full of confidence. One of his first moves was to try and win the interest and possible co-operation of his fellow-candidate, Nathaniel Polhill. (The borough returned two members.) Polhill was a Sussex man from Burwash, who had married Elizabeth Coppard of Hastings in 1750 and now had a country seat at Howbury Park, Bedfordshire. He was a banker in the City and well-known in Southwark where he had a tobacco business. He also owned two snuff mills at Morden. Polhill, however, decided to fight on his own and Dr. Johnson sent a crumb of comfort to Mrs. Thrale in a note from Bolt Court, Fleet Street, on 9 May:

> '...Mr. Polhill, as I suppose you know, has refused to join with Mr. Hotham and is thought to be in more danger than Mr. Thrale'.

Hotham, meanwhile, was withstanding the Doctor's literary guns with some success. He had his own winning ways and, with his flair for advertising, resorted to a skilful line in 'bribery' when canvassing the poorer folk. With great courtesy, he would approach them and say: 'I wait upon you, sir, to request the favour of your vote and interest at the ensuing election. To bribery and corruption I — will — not — have — recourse, but, sir, if — Why, bless me, sir, what a shocking bad hat you've got! Really, you must allow me to send you a new one! — But, sir, as I was about to say, if you can conscientiously . . .'.

Thrale's chances were now regarded as uneven and his friends were worried. Even Fanny Burney, far away in Bath that June, became incensed enough to record in a letter to her father: 'Some infamous villain has put it in the papers here that Mr. Thrale is a Papist. This, I suppose, is a Hothamite report, to inflame his constituents'. In view of the feelings aroused at that time by the Gordon Riots, this would have been a devastating libel on Thrale's name.

As for Dr. Johnson, he could neither understand nor tolerate Hotham's rise in public favour and became immensely sarcastic in another note to Mrs. Thrale on 15 June: '. . . among the heroes of the Borough who twice a day perambulate, or perequitate, High St. and the Clink, rides that renowned and redoubted knight, Sir Richard Hotham. There is magnanimity, which defies every danger that is past, and public spirit that stands sentinel over property that he does not own. Tell me no more of self-devoted Decii, or of the leap of Curtius. Let fame talk henceforward with all her tongues of Hotham the Hatmaker'.

Johnson's classical allusions were eloquent of his deep contempt for Hotham; he classed him even above those Roman exhibitionists of the 3rd century B.C. who quite uselessly sacrificed themselves in a misguided display of bravery. Unfortunately for the Doctor, what was intended to be bitter sarcasm proved to be (for him) the bitter truth, for on 15 September 1780 the tongues of Southwark were indeed wagging in acclaim of Hotham the Hatmaker. He had come top of the poll with 1,177 votes! Mr Polhill was close behind with 1,025, while Mr. Thrale could only muster 769 supporters. Johnson, in a note to Boswell in October, put the whole defeat down to Thrale's loss of health.

Hotham entered Parliament in troubled times. The futile colonial war in America was soon to collapse with the surrender of Cornwallis at Yorktown, the naval conflict with France was at its height; Ireland was simmering; and in the House itself the cry for Reform was loud, ugly and persistent.

Peace and prosperity returned with the signing of the Treaty of Versailles in 1783. Pitt the Younger was now due on the scene, and Hotham and a number of fellow-M.P.s met at St Alban's *Tavern* in the winter of 1784 to promote a union of the two rival parties. Pitt was agreeable to the idea of a parley. That year, however, brought another general election and, when the count came in Southwark on 24 July, Hotham received the cold news that he had lost his seat and would therefore not be in Mr. Pitt's first Parliament. Characteristically he demanded a scrutiny of the votes, but the result was the same: his opponent Mr. Paul Le Mesurier was the victor by 11 votes and, to make the occasion even blacker, Mr. Le Mesurier happened to be a director of the East India Company.

Hotham had now reached the age of 62. His political career was behind him. He had not made any great speeches nor achieved much advance in social status. Neither had his colleague Polhill, for that matter, but Polhill was lucky enough to be returned unopposed. The only permanent memorial to Hotham's brief Parliamentary career were two bells, Nos. 8 and 9, which were hung in St John the Evangelist's at Horselydown, east of London Bridge, in 1783. On them was inscribed:

> The gift of Sr. Ricd. Hotham, Kt. and Nathal. Polhill Esqr., representatives in Parliament for this borough. Chapman & Mears fecerunt.

He returned to Merton Grove and it was then that he began to feel tired. The disappointments of the election, the strain of political life, the wear and tear of amassing wealth, induced in him the desire for a rest, perhaps even for retirement. Above all, however, the immediate need was for the restoration of his health and, in common with so many of the London social set, he turned his eyes towards the sea.

* * *

The seaside was the new attraction of the age. There had been a startling sea-change in people's minds and what had been regarded 25 years ago as a vast waste to voyage upon or to drown in was now the object of a cult that was soon to become a craze and later a national institution. To bathe in sea water was healthy, so the physicians had been saying for some time, and when in 1753 Benjamin Beale of Margate perfected a bathing machine, and the celebrated Dr. Richard Russell moved from Lewes to Brighton to continue his advocacy of the sea cure, the move towards the coast became intensified.

By the 1780s, the sea was the toast of the town. Doctors told you to drink it in pint doses. And in 1782 Royalty, by taking notice of its littoral territories, made the seaside fashionable. The Duke of Cumberland, youngest brother of George III, took a house on the cliff near the Steyne at Brighton. Dr. Johnson went down with Mrs. Thrale and her daughters in November, and Fanny Burney recorded the cold but pleasant experience of their first early morning dip. William Cowper caught the public mood in verse and described the 'rush into the sea'. In 1783 George, Prince of Wales, aged 21, joined the rush and stayed with his uncle at Brighton. He enjoyed the unfettered surroundings of the Sussex coast and returned there in the summer of 1784 to set up a house for himself and to become Brighton's never-to-be-forgotten patron.

Now it was to be Hotham's turn. Weary as he was, there may have come to him an inkling of a new adventure awaiting him on the coast.

He summoned his four-horse coach, took his friend Captain Blanchard with him and set off on the road outside his door. It led him south, through Epsom, Leatherhead and Dorking — and, by chance, to Bognor.

Fig. 2. Hotham's trade tokens.

Chapter II

THE BIRTH OF HOTHAMTON

WHAT CHANCE it was that led him through the farmlands to the sea edge at Bognor is something that remains an 18th-century secret. He would have crossed the Weald of Sussex by way of Billingshurst, Pulborough Common, Wiggonholt, Amberley, up Houghton Hill and over the wooded South Downs into Arundel. There before him lay the narrow coastal plain, hazy in the gold of harvest, and beyond it sparkled the sea.

He and Blanchard may have stayed the night in Arundel to discover the lie of the land, and it is not unlikely that someone in Arundel knew a farmer in Bognor willing to accommodate two gentlemen who wished to investigate the new phenomenon of the sea. So, following a meandering lane some nine miles across the plain, they entered the coastal parish of South Bersted and arrived one August day in a quiet hamlet of fishing huts and farm buildings. It was a place that had seldom appeared on a map and was usually called Bognor Rocks — not for itself but because of the character of its coast.

Here, staying in a farmhouse, they spent the rest of that summer of 1784. The blue sea, the cornfields and the peace of the little fishing hamlet worked their wonders. Hotham returned to Surrey with the approach of autumn, came back to Bognor the following summer and by 1786 was fully restored to health.

By now it had occurred to him that he should have a summer home of his own, somewhere in which to spend three months each year enjoying the sea air and the bathing. And where better than this tranquil part of Sussex that he had come to know so well? Before him was the sea; behind him, and on each side of him, was farmland dotted with rustic villages and threaded by lanes. The spire of Chichester Cathedral, pricking the north-western horizon six miles off, promised the amenities of a learned old city whenever he had need of them. Nobility was represented to the north of him by the powerful third Duke of Richmond, living in a mansion at Goodwood that he was soon to rebuild, close to a ridge of downland that he was soon to engineer into a racecourse. To the north-east was Charles Howard, 11th Duke of Norfolk, who was restoring Arundel Castle in medieval style. (The Duke's strange taste for old hats might provide Hotham's opening gambit if they happened to meet.) Six miles along the coast, to the east, the Arun flowed into the sea at Littlehampton and in this ancient port there was certainly something, apart from shipping, to arouse his interest. Here in 1775, Lecoq, the French owner of a London coffee house, had been quick to assess the profitable possibilities of transforming the village into a popular bathing resort. He had built the Beach Coffee House and Assembly Rooms on Little-hampton Common and had already won a good following, helped considerably by a useful 'puff' for the establishment in a London-published account of a holiday there in 1778.

Not only had Hotham weighed up the advantages of the district as a place to live in, but he had also noted that lime could be made from the outcrops of chalk on the beach and that the Bognor earth itself was suitable for brick-making: two assets that had either been of no interest to, or had remained undiscovered by, the local inhabitants. They, it is recorded, had gone as far away as Lymington in Hampshire for their bricks and to the Downs for their chalk.

It was fortunate that Hotham had the perspicacity to note all this, for otherwise his decision to convert the farmhouse into a seaside 'hermitage' would have proved expensive, in view of the cost of transporting materials. However, with the return of his health and his old pioneering spirit — and rather in the manner of that earlier 'foreigner', St Wilfrid, teaching Selsey folk how to fish — he taught the Bognor villagers to make bricks, and in time was able to boast of the superiority of his Bognor-made bricks over those of the Duke of Richmond.

During those annual visits, he had also made friends with the nearest clergyman, the Rev. Thomas Durnford, M.A., a son of Thomas Durnford, D.D., vicar of South Harting, and friend of the Rev. Gilbert White of Selborne. Durnford's stepmother was the younger sister of William Collins, the Chichester poet. In 1776, he had become vicar of South Bersted, was curate of Felpham and also rector of a little tumbledown church perilously near the seashore at nearby Middleton. After a decade of uneventful years, Mr. Durnford's life had brightened considerably at the prospect of a wealthy London merchant coming to live in the Bognor tithing of his parish. His people were poor and suddenly here was a prospective benefactor. With the vicar's assistance, Hotham began his new adventure.

It was on 1 December 1786 that he made his first purchase and became the owner of the acre of land containing the farmhouse in which he had spent the last three summers. The previous owner, George Moore, a riding officer in the Customs, had only bought it that same year, but he accepted £200 for it. No time was lost and less than two months later — on 18 January 1787 — with local labour and local materials, Hotham began the rebuilding of the farmhouse into a commodious mansion, an event of such outstanding importance for the hamlet that Mr. Durnford, in his large and orderly handwriting, entered a record of it in the parish register.

It was while his house was being built and while he was also busying himself with the restoration of St Mary's, Wimbledon, that Hotham conceived the bold idea of creating a seaside resort. But it would be a resort that was different, as unlike Brighton or Margate as possible, a select paradise by the sea where the nobility could disport themselves without being annoyed by the rowdyism that was already creeping into other resorts. It would be a garden town. There were already trees and fields extending to the water's edge. Here and there he would put houses and terraces, spaced far apart in the splendid isolation of their own grounds. It might even be likened to a Wimbledon-on-Sea. But he would not call it that. He had a better name; one by which he would be remembered. It would be called Hothamton.

The idea obsessed him — particularly as, 26 miles away to the east, the Prince of Wales was just completing the transformation of another farmhouse into what was later to become the Royal Pavilion. Fashion was flocking to Brighton, because a small town was already there to offer accommodation. What better than to divert the cream of Brighton's visitors westwards into a town that he would build specially for them?

By the following year, 1788, his house was finished and — a choice possibly inspired by the Prince's Brighton House — was named Bognor Lodge. Facing the sea across a quarter of a mile of grazing land, it stood by the side of the high road at the eastern end of the hamlet. In some of its details there were resemblances to Merton Grove; again a semi-hexagonal porch, ogee-arched windows on the first floor and round-headed windows below. Within, there was a pleasant hall and handsome staircase, a drawing-room, dining-room, breakfast room and five bedrooms. There were labyrinthine servants' quarters, together with wash-house, laundry, dairy and cellaring. Women servants slept in, the men had apartments over the double coach-house. At the back of the Lodge, Hotham retained the original farm buildings, including an octagonal barn and a granary on stone piers. A big walled vegetable and fruit garden was planted and, at the entrance to the drive, he erected a picturesque Gothick gatehouse.

*   *   *

The scene was now set for the realisation of his dream. He took up residence at Bognor Lodge, with Blanchard as companion, and drew up his building scheme for the new resort. He was a man about to change the face of this part of the coast as no other conqueror had done, but there was no tawdry element in his building, no suggestion of the brick warrens that were soon to spread across the industrialised green pastures of his native Yorkshire. He had absorbed, as had most privileged men of his age, a knowledge of ancient culture. He would have read translations of Greek and Roman authors, and he made himself conversant with the principles of classical architecture. He was aware of the value of quality in craftsmanship, appreciative of good design and sensible of the new trend towards elegance and simplicity. Refinement, introduced by the researches and skill of the Adam brothers, was the current key to architectural taste. It was the beginning of an era of orderly town planning. Though other men were to apply similar ideas to the development of such places as Eastbourne, St Leonards and Bournemouth, Hotham unknowingly was about to contribute to the history of his times by being the first man to plan a seaside town by himself.

A few hundred yards to the east of Bognor Lodge, a stream or *rife* flowed into the sea through a sluice. The low-lying brookland on each side of it, being always subject to flooding and the inundations of the sea, formed a natural barrier between the village of Felpham and the fishing hamlet of Bognor Rocks. Hotham therefore decided to project the new Bognor in the opposite direction, westward through the fields that ran to the edge of the beach and tumbled over the low brown cliffs of earth and clay. Benefiting from Mr. Durnford's local knowledge, he purchased land all along the seashore.

By April 1788 he had spent £6,225. From John and Mary Cosens and William and Catherine Blake he bought 88 acres for £2,725. This largely comprised all the fields around Bognor Lodge, including the land occupied today by Hotham Park and the houses on the adjacent Sudley Lodge estate. The Royal Norfolk Hotel stands on another of these 88 acres; and a further 25 of them, then named Charlwood (and now commemorated in Charlwood Street), covered the area north and south of the present-day Aldwick Road shops.

For £700 he bought a two-acre property, farther west in Aldwick, with a house called Micklams; and he paid £700 to Mrs. Ann Smith, a Chichester widow, for 35 acres immediately west of the Royal Norfolk Hotel and also the field close to Bognor Lodge on which he was to build the Chapel House. Another purchase of 55 acres gave him most of the land in the centre of Bognor's present sea front, between the Steyne and Clarence Road, and also the site to the north of Bognor Lodge on which he would build Hothamton Crescent.

And so with all this land in his possession — he was to acquire more later on — Hotham began to build his resort. Terraces were fashionable and his first move, after the completion of Bognor Lodge, was to build a pair some distance to the west. They were three storeys high, each with a garden in front and a common carriage drive giving access from the road that was to become the High Street. They were named Hothamton Place (seven houses) and East Row (six houses) and both had an uninterrupted view across the newly-named Hothamton Field, now Waterloo Square — ideal for the visitors whom they were specifically designed to accommodate. Neither terrace exists today.

Hotham's hotel came next, rising on the shore during 1789, just as Pitt's bubble of peace burst and the French Revolution began. Since it had as yet no rivals it was called simply the Hotel, though at first it was not so much a hotel as a converted public house, for Hotham purchased the dilapidated thatch-roofed *Fox Inn,* off the end of the present West Street, and started adding to it. Gradually, over the years, it assumed increasing grandeur until it was hard to discern the original smugglers' tavern among the three storeys of eight dining rooms, 17 bedrooms, coffee room, parlour, bar and taproom. Stabling for no less than 80 horses and 15 carriages was added. All this was too much for George Grinder, the proprietor of the *Fox,* to manage. He preferred the life of an innkeeper to that of a hotelier, so in 1792 he took over a tavern at Felpham. This was also owned by Hotham, who had in fact partly rebuilt it in 1790. It seems possible that Grinder renamed it the *Fox* after his original inn at Bognor, for his obituary in the *Brighton Herald* (1828) refers to him becoming the licensee of the tavern at Felpham 'now called the Fox'. Presumably, therefore, that had not always been its name.

To the west of his Hotel, Hotham laid out a garden in which he built a smaller building to serve as a social centre for the new resort. Upstairs was a spacious subscription room and lounge where newspapers and magazines were provided and entertainments took place. Downstairs was a small library, a milliner's shop, a toy shop and a warm sea bath.

One cannot help thinking that these developments at Bognor may have given Jane Austen the idea for her unfinished novel *Sanditon* on which she was engaged when she died in 1817. 'Sanditon' is the name of a newly-erected Sussex seaside resort, promoted by a Mr. Parker to whom 'Sanditon was a second wife and four children, hardly less dear and certainly more engrossing. He could talk of it forever . . . it was his hobby horse, his occupation, his hope and his futurity'. Miss Austen might have been describing Hotham himself. And when, in introducing her readers to the principal landmarks of Sanditon, she refers to 'the milliner's shop and the library; a little detached from it, the hotel and billiard room', who would not be tempted to believe that she herself must have visited Bognor and perhaps even stayed at the Hotel?

The Hotel was the western limit, so far, of the plan for Hothamton and, in Hotham's mind, was the less exclusive end of his town. The better-class district, as one might expect, was to be nearer his own residence on the eastern boundary; and here in the early 1790s he built extensively on the sides of the road (now Upper Bognor Road) which curved north-west towards South Bersted. Next to Bognor Lodge rose his own future home, the Chapel House, resplendent with an Italianate loggia and balcony. (It was to change its name twice in the course of the 19th century and once again in the 20th.) On the other side of the road he laid out his showpiece, Hothamton Crescent, which consisted of three large detached buildings. The centre one in pleasant red brick, with its array of elegant windows, noble front entrance and unexpected dome, was decorated with a plaque bearing the name 'Hothamton Crescent', Hotham's coat-of-arms and his motto *Deus Noster Resurgam*. The house was 123 feet long and contained about fifty rooms, with a tea room under the dome.

There was purpose in such splendour. Hotham hoped that it would be only a matter of time before George III, or at least the Prince of Wales, availed themselves of the amenities of Hothamton and made the Dome House their seaside residence. The mansion was designed so that it could be transformed into three separate dwellings — which soon happened — and, in similar fashion, the two flanking buildings were each divisible into two houses.

West of the Crescent he erected Spencer Terrace, a formal row of seven houses (one detached, two semi-detached) in the same red brick as the Dome House. Royal retinues could be suitably accommodated here. As in Hotham's other terraces, the interiors of the houses differed in plan and dimensions and the largest, No. 4, contained nine bedrooms, four dressing rooms, a drawing room, dining and breakfast parlours, kitchen, servants' hall, wash house and pantry. There was a mews at the back.

As Hotham was now a resident in the parish of South Bersted, he showed his appreciation of the vicar's help by giving £600 for a new pulpit, reading-pew, gallery and other improvements to the church. With each of his houses went a pew in the gallery, pew No. 1 being allocated to Chapel House and pew No. 2 to Bognor Lodge. (The gallery was removed in 1879.)

In addition to his land in Bognor, Hotham acquired an outer ring of property, some of which he farmed along modern lines; he was the owner of one of the only three threshing machines in Sussex. At Felpham he owned Dry Grounds Farm, the *Fox Inn* and the lime kilns at the sea end of Limmer Lane. He had some 16 acres in Flansham, additional land in Aldwick, 13 acres with cottages in South Bersted, property in Middleton and a coach house and stable in Chichester. His Bognor buildings dotted themselves along the coast for three-quarters of a mile through the meadows and trees, all linked by the lane that wandered up from the beach towards South Bersted and which later became West Street, High Street and Upper Bognor Road. Altogether, he was the owner of 1,600 acres in the parish. He also became Lord of the Manor of Aldwick in two strokes, purchasing half of it from Canon Combe Millar for 4,000 guineas on 5 June 1789, and the other half from Dr. William Heberden on 25 January 1798. No expense was spared. His 30 houses were well equipped with furniture and fittings. Everything was done in the grand manner, even to the extent of digging up gravel on Wimbledon Common and shipping it by barge from Wandsworth to make Bognor's new paths and roads.

There is no record of what the local fishermen and farmers thought of this expensive transformation of their peaceful hamlet, let alone of the attempted change of name to Hothamton. Certainly, a useful new market had now come into existence for them. Many of the farmers owned their own land and were proud of the wonderful yields of wheat, never less than four to five quarters an acre, from crops sometimes grown on the same ground for five successive years. From Chichester to Littlehampton, the fertile plain was known to agriculturists as 'the vale'. Average food prices included butter at 8¾d. per pound, pork at 7½d., cheese at 6d. and flour at 11¾d. per gallon. However, in 1789 the average country labourer in the vicinity of Bognor would have welcomed any employment offered by Hotham to supplement his usual wage of 8s. a week, which he spent in this way:

52	herrings & 42 halfpenny loaves (3 per day)	3s. 6d.
7	quarts of small beer	7d.
	cheese	6d.
3	candles, soap, starch, thread, etc.	6d.
	a bushel of coal and carriage.	1s. 2d.
	rent	1s. 0d.
	remaining for clothes, etc.	9d.
		8s. 0d.

Vegetables from his cottage garden also helped to maintain him; and he might poach for extra food, risking imprisonment or a £25 fine at Chichester, or earn a little extra money at harvest time. There was also the allurement of joining the flourishing industry of smuggling at 10s. 6d. per journey plus a 'dollop' (14 lbs.) of precious tea, with a horse and all expenses found by the organisers.

It was such countrymen and fisherfolk as these — together with the members of the cathedral chapter at Chichester, the nobility on their Downland estates, the rivals along the coast at Littlehampton and Worthing and the host of friends and scoffers in London — who watched with interest and curiosity the rising of the curtain on the new Bognor in the summer of 1791. That was the date of the official inauguration of 'Hothamton' as a watering-place.

It was purely by chance that the name which Hotham devised for his resort inevitably called to mind the names of towns with the Old English ending 'hampton', one of which was only a few miles to the east. The derivation of Hothamton was, of course, quite different, but it was all too easy to assume that there should be a 'p' in Bognor's new name, as in the case of Littlehampton, Southampton and the others. It therefore often appeared as Hothampton (even, when the time came, in Hotham's epitaph) though Hotham himself, needless to say, always stuck firmly to his own spelling.

*   *   *

Unofficially, Hotham's extraordinary activities down by the sea had been causing wide comment for some time. People had begun to find their way into the half-built resort before he was prepared for them, and one such party consisted of William Lock and his family. Lock was a wealthy amateur art collector who, with his wife Frederica, was popular in society. He lived in a mansion called Norbury which he had built in 1774 above the lovely Mickleham valley north of Dorking, and on 4 August 1789 he happened to be with his family on holiday near Chichester. They wanted to see the sea, and his wife described what happened:

> 'George and our girls were very eager to see the sea and their kind father was as desirous to indulge them. Bognor Rocks was the nearest and thither we were directed. Wretched accommodation, the Inn newly built. My poor Augusta got a bed that Puss had visited, but we made up in laughter for all that was wanting in convenience. The chairs and curtains were all damp and sticking to us. Sir Richard Hotham had built a house for himself near this Inn, which also belongs to him, and he very hospitably sent to offer us accommodation. I believe the new neighbouring houses are his. A bathing machine is kept here.'

If Mrs. Lock's candid comments had been published at the time, they might have caused a decline in the number of carriages and coaches that rolled down the highway into Bognor. But there was no ill wind blowing through the resort as Hotham awaited the first patrons of the season in 1791. The Hotel was ready, the houses were ready, the vicar was ready; and, as a sort of major-domo of the whole place, there was his agent, Mrs. Jane Cowan, ready to welcome the new arrivals, install them at the Hotel for the time being and then accommodate them in one of the elegant lodgings for five to ten guineas a week.

So passed his first short and successful season. Wimbledon still saw him between times and his chartered ships still sailed the seas, but he had not in any way deviated from his professed intention of making Bognor the resort of more select company than was to be found at other bathing-places. And his confidence seemed justified, for he was to discover that he had not yet made the place large enough to contain the august company anxious to stay there; in fact, what had been his hobby-horse was beginning to run away with him. From now on, he would be involved in adding new houses, spending more money and, above all, finding means of inducing the throng of visitors to become residents.

So, to ensure the future of Hothamton, he played genial host. Occasionally he issued general invitations to public breakfasts, not only to those staying at his houses but also to any of the Chichester gentry who cared to avail themselves of his hospitality — which included a band and free use of all the sailing boats which he had hired. By such means, and by the amount of money he was spending in Chichester, he became a popular local figure, so much so that at the 1790 election he had been persuaded by his new Sussex friends to offer himself as a Parliamentary candidate for Chichester. But he was in his 70th year and perhaps it was as well that he made no headway among the voters against the two established members, Thomas Steele and George White Thomas, and therefore declined the poll.

Bognor thus remained the centre of his ambitions; and, in any case, there was something else to claim his attention: the brand-new house to which he moved in 1792 and which was to be his home for the remainder of his life. This was the fine mansion which he built just to the north of his original residence, Bognor Lodge, and indeed still stands as his principal memorial. It took its name, the Chapel House, from the chapel which Hotham erected against its north wall, with the object of saving his more distinguished visitors the inconvenience of the half-mile journey to South Bersted church. Not without reason, the vicar was furious and his friendship with Hotham abruptly ceased.

On 12 August 1793 the villagers had their first taste of ceremony when the Duke of St Albans arrived to lay the foundation stone of the new chapel. The occasion was a gala day in more than a local sense, for Hotham, shrewdly angling for future Royal patronage, had arranged the ceremony to coincide with the Prince of Wales's birthday. The Duke, who was staying at Hothamton Place, set out with his family along the High Street in an open carriage, preceded by a band. In his wake followed an assembly of 'noble personages and ladies and gentlemen of the first respectability'. At the Chapel House, Hotham laid an inscribed sheet of lead recording the event, the Duke set the corner stone on top and the band — an amateur one, mainly recruited from Portsmouth — responded with *God Save The King*. The thudding of gunfire for the royal birthday, echoing gratuitously from Portsmouth, served to enhance the occasion and was, no doubt, regarded by the inhabitants as further proof of Hotham's amazing influence in higher circles.

The 120 invited guests included the Earl and Countess of Newburgh from Slindon, the Haslers of Bognor and Richard Barwell and his wife, who had recently bought Stansted Park, Chichester, for £102,500 and had had their grounds laid out by Lancelot 'Capability' Brown. After the ceremony, everyone crossed the road to the grounds of the Crescent for refreshment in marquees and at 3 o'clock they entered the grand salon of the Dome House, which was decorated with plumes of feathers, mirrors, branches of laurel and a portrait of the Prince. Here, Hotham provided them with a sumptuous collation of 'every dainty the season afforded'. That night must have been a risky one for the smugglers, for later he gathered all the elite for a ball at the hotel and then lit up the normally dark shore with a firework display.

There was another notable picture on view at the Dome House, apart from that of the Prince. Some time during that busy day a few of Hotham's distinguished friends must have joined him in the Chapel House and there they would have seen George Romney's portrait of the host. It had arrived from London in May. Negotiations for the painting of this portrait had been undertaken by one of Hotham's new circle of neighbours, the eccentric William Hayley. Six and a half miles due north of Bognor, Hayley spent his time presiding over house parties in his rural retreat at Eartham. Among the artistic coterie that gathered in this pretty Downland spot were Romney himself, William Cowper, Charlotte Smith, Flaxman, Gibbon, Anna Seward, Mrs. Unwin, Hurdis and the American poet Barlow, together with leaders of West Sussex society from Chichester and Petworth, such as Lord Sheffield, Lord Egremont and Mrs. Harriet Poole.

William Hayley, reckless, extravagant and generous, wrote mediocre verse till the day he died and is remembered best for his lengthy *Triumphs of Temper*. But he delighted in the company of his more talented friends and did everything possible as a patron to further their careers. It was during Hotham's first season, in 1791, that Hayley's usual indifferent health led him to buy a cottage at Felpham, a village he had known since he was a boy in Chichester and had gone bathing there with his mother. Now, aged 46, he resumed bathing again, riding down from Eartham on his white horse Hidalgo to spend two days a week at Felpham teaching his delicate son Tom to swim.

It did not take Hotham long to strike up a friendship with him. Both genial hosts, they had much in common; and when Hotham heard of Romney's annual visits to his new neighbour he became more than interested. In the following summer, 1792, he put a suggestion to Hayley. Instead of Romney spending the whole of his visit at Eartham, why not allow him to become Hotham's guest at Bognor, enjoying good food and sea-bathing, and at the same time earning a handsome fee by painting Hotham's portrait?

Hayley, ever willing to assist friends and rather liking the 'cheerful adventurous disposition of that commercial knight', wrote to Romney in London and asked if, during his next visit to Eartham, he would comply with this request. But Romney preferred not to mix business with the pleasures of staying with Hayley. 'I am pleased with your account of the Knight of Bognor', he replied on 16 July, 'but cannot engage to paint his portrait in the country. However, I am obliged to the Knight for his civility. Be so good as to thank him for his kindness'.

Hotham was not put out. The introduction had been made and he followed it up by sitting for Romney in London. It was a well-composed portrait, painted at the *York* Hotel, in Blackfriars, in January and February 1793. After the eighth sitting, it was judged ready and Hotham paid him in full: 130 guineas. However, two more sittings proved necessary (2 and 8 May) and in due course Romney dispatched the portrait to Bognor. Hayley was very impressed when he saw it. He regarded it as one of Romney's 'happiest performances in fidelity of resemblance and in the ease, spirit and harmony of the whole composition'.

The portrait, which shows Hotham seated and holding plans for his new resort, while a plan of Bognor Lodge lies on the table beside him, was bequeathed in his will to his godson, Richard William Turner.

It remained with the Turner family until 1919, when it was sold to Mr. James Fleming, whose son Lindsay presented it to the town in 1972. Unexpectedly it bears the name not of Romney but of Dudman, a little-known painter who worked closely with Romney and appears to have been entrusted by him with the task of completing or 'touching up' some of his portraits. This was presumably the case with the portrait of Hotham, which now hangs grandly and appropriately on the staircase wall of the Town Hall in Clarence Road.

Bognor Lodge Seat of Sir J. Harrington.

Fig. 3. *Bognor Lodge, from Dally's 1828 Guide.*

Chapter III

EARLY VISITORS

IT WAS NOW 1794 and the fourth season had come and gone. Money was pouring out of Britain to maintain the war against the French, but not enough money was coming into Bognor. In the winters, when the little brick village stood forlornly by the sea and the waves dashed up at the Hotel and swallowed pieces of the mile-long common, Hotham and his faithful agent Mrs. Cowan must sometimes have felt that 30 houses in fields swept by sou'-westers represented the last word in financial folly.

Recognition, however, though slow to arrive, was on its way and during that year Hotham achieved one of his great desires. Not only was his enterprise praised in a guidebook but the resort was alluded to, for the first time in print, as Hothamton. The author of the guide — who may have enjoyed Hotham's hospitality — was the Rev. Alexander Hay, formerly assistant curate at Selsey and now vicar of Wisborough Green, near Horsham. Early in 1794 the Chichester firm of Seagrave issued the second edition of *Hay's Guide to Chichester*, which was now given the sub-title 'and the fashionable and elegant Watering Place of Bognor'.

Mr. Hay was obviously determined to give the new resort a refined boost: 'About 7 miles south-east of Chichester is the retired and beautiful village of Bognor, now called Hothamton, situated within a quarter of a mile of the sea'. He praised the houses, 'most of which, for elegance, would not disgrace the squares of the metropolis', and mentioned that the place had been well patronised for the last two seasons. He added that Chichester and Bognor fishermen were now co-operating in a joint fishery at Bognor, with benefit to both communities.

*   *   *

The first real fruits of Hotham's gigantic outlay were borne during 1795, and one cause of the sudden stream of notabilities in his direction that year was detectable to the very circumstance that had originally prompted his creation of a genteel watering-place: the coarse pleasures and noisy dissipation of other resorts. Brighton was beginning to lose some of its fashionable company. They were being frightened away by the behaviour of Royalty. The Prince was trying to discard Lady Jersey, had parted from his wife Mrs. Fitzherbert and was now, that June, to be seen in Brighton enduring his enforced marriage — which he had contracted to relieve himself of debts — to his boisterous and slovenly first cousin, Princess Caroline of Brunswick. It was she who, as the rhymesters alleged later on, 'combed her hair with a leg of a chair'. In addition, the enormous military encampments, parades and reviews for defence purposes were driving the quieter nobility away. Guns blazing away in mock battles as Brighton (re-christened Dunkirk for the purpose) was 'captured' by eight regiments, to say nothing of 15,000 troops desporting themselves over the Downs and seashore, amounted to overmuch in the way of diversion.

So the carriages began to take unfamiliar roads into south-west Sussex, and Hothamton's list of visitors at last began to scintillate with distinguished names belonging to the class for which the resort was intended by its founder. The jewels were now in their setting and that summer they included the Duke of Devonshire, a subsequent holder of whose title was to improve Eastbourne, the Duchess of Rutland, who was the rival of the Duchess of Devonshire in beauty and was painted four times by Reynolds, Lord Spencer from Wimbledon, after whom Hotham had named a terrace, and the Earl and Countess of Pembroke from Wilton, near Salisbury. Lord Lucan, Lord Dunwar, Sir Edward Leslie and Lady Jane Halliday were others; and there was also Lady Uxbridge, whose husband in the years to come was to lead the famous Life Guards' charge at Waterloo and to lose his right leg and have it buried on the battlefield.

From her home at Putney had come Lady Grantham, a singularly plain daughter of Earl Hardwicke; her marriage to Lord Grantham, on his return from being British Ambassador at Madrid, had caused Horace Walpole to comment that he supposed Grantham 'had contracted some Spanish ideas, and minds blood more than beauty'.

Two other well-known visitors were the playwright Richard Brinsley Sheridan, who had brought his second wife down to recuperate, and George Tierney M.P., who regarded Hotham's seaside scheme with amused wonder. Hotham had once told him all about it and had rather given him the impression that one day Bognor would rival Portsmouth — a line of expansive talk that was quite in keeping with the other occasion when Hotham informed Tierney that he had been a member of a St Martin's Lane club that had produced three great men. One was Sir Eyre Coote, the second was Moore, Archbishop of Canterbury. 'And who was the third?' asked Tierney. 'That was I', replied Hotham.

Already a resident from the previous year was 20-year-old Tom Sheridan, son of Richard Sheridan by his first wife, the lovely Elizabeth Linley. Tom, who in later life was to become Colonial Treasurer to the Governor of the Cape, was supposed to be studying hard at the seaside with his tutor Mr. William Smyth (great-uncle of Dame Ethel Smyth, the composer), but he could not help wondering why he had not heard from his father for a long time. The reason for the silence was that the love-lorn Sheridan was busy convincing the Dean of Winchester that he would make a fit husband for the Dean's daughter, Esther Jane Ogle. The Dean thought it a bad match, but Sheridan set up a trust fund of £12,000 (by selling shares in his Drury Lane theatre) and, with £8,000 from the fund, bought Polesden Lacey, a Surrey estate which he settled on his wife-to-be. Then, as the wedding drew nearer, he decided that Tom ought to know of his plans and the long silence was broken by a letter which arrived at Bognor one breakfast-time:

My dear Tom,

Meet me at dinner, at six o'clock on Wednesday next, at Guildford: I forget the inn;
I want to see you.

Ever your affectionate father,

R.B.S.

What, thought Tom and his tutor, could this mean? Was it a proposed seat in
Parliament — a good marriage for Tom — anything to do with Drury Lane? The
boy rode off to Guildford on the Wednesday, leaving Smythe expecting him back
next day, but there was no news until Tom's letter arrived from Guildford the
following Monday:

My dear Mr. Smythe,

Here I am, have been and am likely to be; my father I have never seen and all that I
can hear of him is that, instead of dining with me on Wednesday last, he passed through
Guildford on his way to town with four horses and lamps, about 12. I have written him
letter after letter to beg he will send me his orders, and at all events some money, for I
have only a few shillings, having paid the turnpikes faithfully, and I am so bored and
wearied out with waiting here, and seeing neither father nor money, not anything but
the stable and the street, that I almost begin to wish myself with you and the books
again.

Your dutiful pupil,

T.S.

Two months went by. Smythe paced the sands. Then came Tom's second letter
with the real news:

My dear Mr. Smythe,

It is not I that am to be married, nor you. Set your heart at rest, it is my father himself; the lady, a Miss Ogle, who lives at Winchester; and that is the history of this
Guildford business. About my own age — better me to marry her, you will say. I am not
of that opinion. My father talked to me two hours last night, and made out to me it was
the most sensible thing he could do. Was not this very clever of him? Well, my dear Mr.
S., you should have been tutor to him, you see. I am incomparably the most rational of
the two, and now and ever,

Yours very truly and affectionately,

T.S.

Smythe, being one of Sheridan's close friends, was justifiably annoyed at this
lack of any communication from his employer since the advent of Miss Ogle.
Futhermore, he had not received any salary. He wrote a strong letter and, on
receiving no reply, left the coast for London. Sheridan, however, soon won him
round and the tutor apologised for sending such an angry note. 'Be good enough
to think no more of it', he urged. 'Oh, certainly not, my dear Smythe', replied
Sheridan, 'I shall never think of what you have said in it, be assured. Here it is.'
Smythe gladly took the letter and threw it in the fire — and, as he did so, he
was astonished to see it had never been opened. His dealings with Sheridan had, in
fact, always been of this perplexing nature, even from the time when Joseph

Richardson, Sheridan's associate in theatrical finance, arranged an interview at which he would introduce Smythe as a suitable tutor for Tom. On the day of the appointment, Sheridan forgot to arrive. Smythe wrote a memoir of these tutorial days when he later became a professor of Modern History at Cambridge.

*　　　*　　　*

It was indeed a select season at Bognor and, though the 1st Company of the Radnor Militia had arrived from Kent in June to defend the coast, Hotham had prevailed upon them to set up camp out of his range, on Aldwick Green a mile and a quarter westward. It is through the eyes of a woman visitor that we can enter right into the atmosphere of the season at Bognor in its early days and share the experiences of a holiday there during that warm thundery August of 1795. She was Lady Hester Newdigate, then about 55 and suffering from a knee complaint for which sea-water bathing had been recommended. Her husband was Sir Richard Newdigate, founder of the Newdigate Prize at Oxford. She said good-bye to him early in the month and journeyed south with her sister, Milly Barton, and her servants from her home at Arbury in Warwickshire.

She stayed first at Stansted Park, near Chichester, with Milly's great friends, the Barwells. Mrs. Catherine Barwell, a remarkably beautiful American, was a daughter of Admiral Sir Isaac Coffin, son of Nathaniel Coffin, cashier of the Customs at Boston. Her husband, Richard Barwell (1741–1804), was a haughty insolent nabob, who had returned from India with the usual colossal fortune and a reputation as a tyrant, gambler and trickster. He insulted the Mayor of Chichester by refusing to attend a welcoming dinner when he settled in the district and was subsequently hissed at by the local villagers. The little good said of him was that he had been a supporter of Warren Hastings in the development of India.

On Friday, 14 August, Mrs. Barwell took her guests to Bognor to show them the place suggested for Lady Hester's cure. They had a picnic on the beach and Lady Hester asked her manservant Bill to take the carriage ponies on to the sands, where they allowed the sea to wash over their hoofs without any sign of fear. Bognor made a favourable impression on her and she wrote home to her husband:

> 'We were quite delighted with the Place. Sir Richard Hotham to whom it belongs has built 30 or 40 neat convenient Houses of different sizes for ye reception of Company, all pleasantly situated and with full view of ye Sea. A convenient Hot Sea Bath is also just made, and the Great World has taste enough to prefer it to all others upon this Coast. Whilst we sat at dinner, there pass'd the Duchesses of Devonshire and Rutland, Lady E. Foster, Dowager Lady Sefton, etc., and we saw ye Names and Titles of at least 20 more of ye very supreme set.'

Though she felt that such superior company would be 'much too fine to notice us', she decided that their activities would be interesting to watch and the presence of such notabilities would certainly ensure a good supply of food in the town. She sent for Mrs. Cowan to see if there was a house to let:

'She at 1st said there was not one of any size vacant, but at last own'd that one very small one, 4 guineas per week, was just given up, but that a Lady had secured ye refusal of it. We went to see it and it is so perfect a Little Cabin that I am quite wild to have ye Lady's answer. How we shall all squeeze into it I can't tell, for ye whole consists of 2 little Parlours in one of which there is a bed; above a little Dining Room and Bed Chamber; over that 2 bed Chambers and below a Kitchen and Scullery. Bill must have a bed at ye Inn with his horses, and the 2 Men have ye Parlour, but how shall we do for house maid and Cook?' Bill was later accommodated in the parlour, 'so that he may not be led into Evil by sleeping at ye Inn.'

Mrs. Cowan soon sent word that Lady Hester could take the house, so on the following Friday, 21 August, they left Stansted and drove along the plain to Bognor, arriving at six in the evening in time to 'feast our eyes on a full Sea'. The servants had gone on ahead in the morning to get various articles at Chichester that might not be available at Bognor. Before she left Stansted after lunch, Lady Hester was given a telescope by her host and found time to write a note to her husband who had been puzzling over her reference to the rocks at Bognor:

'I don't wonder you could not find our Rocks; they are to be seen only when ye Tide is out and are just what ye Maps describe, black spots that run in a Line 2 miles out to sea, and are an effectual Guard against foreign invasion; for no vessel dare come near them.'

In high spirits and already feeling better, she settled in at Bognor with Milly. The novelty of a seaside holiday intrigued her and 13 letters of gossip and neat comment were sent to her husband before she returned home on 18 September. She omitted to say exactly where the house was, but it was probably in Hotham-ton Place or East Row, for her first letter, in the style of any holiday letter of today, says: 'I am writing at my Dining Room Window. Ye Moon and Jupiter are now just opposite to me and are most beautifully reflected in ye Sea'. Bognor that summer was brimming with people who were known to her, but the atmosphere remained a little formal:

'Mr. and Mrs. Sheridan and the Speaker and his family (besides some others who could not get houses and went back to Chichester) arrived yesterday, and ye only empty house in ye Place is I hear engaged for Lord and Lady Loughborough who come tomorrow; but nobody visits or associates with any but their own party, so you may imagine that we have time enough on our hands, but so far as I can judge from ye 2 Days I have been here the Life of Bognor will be a busy one.'

On her first Sunday she intended going to South Bersted church, but Mrs. Cowan let her down over seat reservations:

'I sent to her yesterday for information about Church and she sent word that ye Parish Church was so small that ye Company was forced to divide and part go to the Church at Felpham, but that we should get no places at all unless she first put us in a way. So we sat with our Cloaks on expecting the Old Lady and she never came at all. The reason was Company pour'd in so fast that she could not get to us till it was too late.'

Monday was a busy day:

'Milly goes into the warm bath at 8, after which we breakfast and then drive to Chichester to bespeak new springs for my Phaeton. We also must get materials for

Bathing Dresses. I must be back by 2 to take my Warm Bath and at 3 we dine upon roast Beef and good Potatoes and ye finest large Prawns or most excellent small Lobsters or Crabs that can be eaten. We feast upon them alternately and always wish that we could send you some in a letter. At 5 we sally forth to walk upon ye sands or beach according as ye tide serves. To-night it was ye latter, full tide, and 2 large Ships in view tacking against ye Winds ye whole afternoon. My Knee feels quite Well, but sleep does not come yet.'

On Tuesday she drove her carriage on the sands:

'We work ye Dear Poneys well, they were 2 hours upon ye Sands this morning and behaved Charmingly. We quited our Carriage where ye Sands were fine and walk'd. Oh! it was delightful!'

She had also been looking at the countryside:

'They are busy as possible in this Country getting in Barley, pease and Beans, most of the wheat is in and they say the Crops are in General pretty good.'

Then she met Mr. Prestridge:

'The Man who supplys us here with excellent Milk and Butter is a Warwickshire man — his name Prestridge; enquires most affectionately after you and remembers that you rode a fine spirited horse when you was Major of ye Warwickshire Militia. He is a fine Grey headed old man . . . he keeps Bathing Machines, but they stand at an inconvenient distance from us.'

Her Friday evening stroll brought two encounters:

'A Lady who was sitting on a bench by Lady Pembroke got up and spoke to me as I pass'd. It was Mrs. Robinson, Lord Malmesbury's sister, and at 10 just as we were moving towards bed a Message came from Lord and Lady Hood. They were to sleep at ye Hotel and depart at nine this morning. I mounted the Dear Grey at ½ past seven and as I came up from ye sands saw Lord Hood's long Nose and scorch'd face looking out of ye Window. I Turn'd my horse to speak to him when Lady Hood also appeared. We sat with them whilst they Breakfasted and then walked home to our own.'

Her fondness for her husband in far-off Warwickshire peeps out at the conclusion of this letter:

'I pleas'd myself with thinking that our Eyes met in ye Moon last night.'

On Sunday she was determined to get to South Bersted church this time:

'Church is in ye afternoon at ½ past 2, but we shall be there sooner to secure places as they say some Ladies sat by the Door last Sunday and some could not get in at all. It is ye smallest Church I ever saw. Sir R. Hotham has built a very spacious chapel joyning to his own house, but it is not quite finished and if they are as tedious about that as about ye Warm Bath there may be no Service in it till ye Place is out of fashion.'

Her second week at Bognor was one of glorious weather, renewed health, good food and social excitement. One day she sent the servants to get provisions from Chichester — or Teachester as they nicknamed it — and they had a feast of neck of mutton, lamb steaks, cold beef, lobsters, prawns and tart. Later, the great event occurred:

'As we were sitting quietly with our Book and Work yesterday, a Coach stop'd at our Door and the Dutchess of Devonshire was announced. She was quite shock'd to learn that we had been more than a Week in this Place. She did not know it till she saw us in Church on Sunday. She should have said "till I saw your pretty singular Equipage and enquired who it belong'd to" for I am sure she could not remember either Milly's face or mine. She told us that her Children and all ye young people ye Place affords were to meet at her Lodgings this Evening and to have a dance and she should take it as a particular favor if we would Look in upon them. I find everybody she visits intends to do so, therefore to avoid being particular we must do ye same. We shall see assembled all ye great World of Bognor Rocks. I have made my Lame Knee *that was* a bandage so Complete that I should not be afraid to dance a horn pipe with ye Duke of Devonshire if he should be very importunate.'

The Barwells came over from Stansted that week:

'We gave them a most excellent Dinner, dress'd by Betty [her cook] at a little fire about ye size of my Bed Chamber grate at Arbury — 2 courses, a remove and desert. They stayed with us till 7 and having a relay of horses at Chichester would be home before nine.' Sir Richard Newdigate also received a hint of what his dear wife's holiday was costing him: ' "Of all ye Places I ever was in this is ye Dearest, one week's bill for my 3 horses and standing of Carriages £3 4. 6., but you seem not to care how I ruin you, so God bless you".'

There was a thunderstorm on 6 September which 'made such a Combustion in the Air and Sea that the Latter was quite tremendous to behold all friday and yesterday and I thought ye Wind would have blown us in our Little Cabin to Chichester'. Two days later, she and Milly decided to visit Worthing:

'Tomorrow not being Bathing day, we mean to take a frisk and see Worthing, 20 miles, Charming Road, ye Poneys will do it in 3½ hours. We'll take our Night Caps as there is a good Hotel in case we should meet with any agreeable friend or for any reason wish to stay all night, but our plan is to set out at 8, arrive at ½ pass 11, dine and see ye Lyons [local attractions] by 3 and return before dark, for we are aware that we have no Moon.'

Lively impressions crowded upon her during her last week:

'Our Dutchess is still here, that is her Children and family, for she spends most of her time at Goodwood. Ye Dutchess of Rutland also and her two Beautiful Boys ride about and ornament ye Place. She has generally Arthur Paget by her side. I find he succeeds his brother in her good Graces; she seems quite proud of shewing that at 40 she has charms to attract a young man of 20. What a foolish Woman!'

On Tuesday, 15 September there was a touch of adventure:

'Here has been a 3 mast vessel, so near that with ye Telescope we could distinguish every Rope, hovering about us all morning. It is now about ½ mile off with all its Sails down. I suspect it to be a smuggler and hope now to succeed in getting you some India Handkerchiefs which hitherto I have try'd for in vain. So if you have any Commissions for me, send them directly. I can Smuggle almost as well at Stansted or Southampton as here, but don't publish this beyond your own circle. If you do I shall have Commissions to fill a Waggon.'

Finally, on 18 September, this amusing middle-aged woman and her entourage set off home. She stayed again at Stansted:

> 'I had a charming Bath before I set out from Bognor yesterday. It revived and Cooled me and enabled me to bear the very hottest and most dusty drive I ever had in my Life. We were glad to rest a little at Chichester and arrived ourselves at Stansted just at 4.'

The journey north was long and just as dusty:

> 'Weather and roads were delightful, but ye Dust insupportable and so deep ye sand and gravell from Farnham to Windsor that I did not think ye Poneys could have drawn us up ye Hills. I never in my Life had a better bed than last night at ye Bush at Farnham . . . we are drinking your health in tea.'

After another stop with relatives at Harefield, Middlesex, they took the road through St Albans to Warwickshire where she hoped 'to eat ye most relishing Michaelmas Goose that ever was roasted with you on Tuesday'.

Two years later, in 1797, Lady Hester was off again on another holiday. This time she went to Brighton, though at first Bognor had been selected. The reason for the change of plan would have infuriated Hotham, had he known. Milly's doctor, hearing that they were going to Bognor again, immediately deduced that the name indicated a bog and warned her that Bognor had by no means a good air and wondered that they were not annoyed by the stinking marshes when there. So the charming Lady Hester and Milly spent that summer at No. 15, Marine Parade, Brighton.

SEA BATHING.

BOGNOR-ROCKS, SUSSEX.

7 miles from Chicheſter,	22 miles from Shoreham,
9 miles from Goodwood,	29 miles from Brighthelmſton,
12 miles from Weſtdean,	25 miles from Portſmouth,
16 miles from Midhurſt,	15 miles from Stanſted,
18 miles from Petworth,	18 miles from Up-Park,
7 miles from Slindon,	11 miles from Weſt Stoke,
10 miles from Arundel,	40 miles from Southampton,
14 miles from Littlehampton,	63 miles from London.

TO BE LETT,

SEVEN HANDSOME HOUSES, built laſt Summer, on a moderate ſcale, on a plan of great convenience and comfort, the whole completely furniſhed, in a ſtyle of elegant neatneſs; with Gardens to each, laid out in walks and planted with ſhrubs.—The ſituation is truly deſirable, being within a quarter of a mile of the Sea, from which there is an extenſive and grand view of the Main Ocean, and the Iſle of Wight; the eye is at the ſame time preſented with pictureſque views of a rich and fertile inland country, commanding the Surrey and Suſſex Hills, with diſtinct views of Chicheſter, Stanſted, Goodwood, Slindon, and Arundel.

Fig. 4. Advertising the new resort in The Sussex Weekly Advertiser, *19 May 1792.*

Chapter IV

HOTHAMTON'S HEYDAY

IT WAS NOT until late in 1796 that Hotham at last achieved for his resort the full recognition that he had been seeking for so long. It had been a fairly interesting year so far, with the presence of such visitors as Sir John Webb, Lady E. Drummond, Lady A. Thorpe and the elderly Countess of Dunmore who, so they said, was taking to religion in her old age by way of expiating the sins of her gay youth. Another familiar face was that of the Dowager Countess of Albemarle who, after losing both her husband and her father in the same year, seems to have consoled herself by becoming one of Bognor's most faithful patrons each season.

But it was the long-hoped-for arrival of the Prince of Wales in September that gave Hotham real heart. He had begun to suspect that the creation of Hothamton had been an expensive gamble. Receipts from lodgings in 1795 were only £1,919 5s. 6d. and this year they were to drop to £1,803 9s. 6d. The presence of the Prince, provided he brought no riff-raff with him, would be an excellent stimulant to waning trade.

His Royal Highness's visit, however, was brief and he did not come especially to see Hotham. His chief interest lay in Lady Jersey, who was staying at the Dome House in the Crescent, and their Bognor reunion marked the close of an unsavoury episode.

The tranquil, rural surroundings of Hothamton in the late summer were indeed a haven for Frances Villiers, Countess of Jersey, in whose ears the hisses of Brighton still lingered. She had, that year, overplayed her hand and upset the intimacy of her relations with the Prince.

Her rival, Mrs. Fitzherbert, had retired abroad, a sad victim of her husband's decision to marry Princess Caroline in 1795. This mockery of a marriage was engineered in no small way by Lady Jersey, to whom it gave even greater access to the Prince's affections through her new appointment as the Princess's lady-in-waiting. Adept at mischief-making, she had then sought further to tighten her hold on him by lowering the Princess in public esteem. She intercepted some private letters from the unhappy Caroline to her mother in Brunswick, one letter containing reflections on Queen Charlotte, and brought them to the notice of the Queen. The Princess, however, discovered what had happened, and public opinion did the rest. The London press rejoiced in the scandal: 'Lady ____ is said to be one of the most adroit hands in England at opening a letter that is not addressed to herself' (*Morning Herald*, 26 May 1796). George III induced her to resign her position in the Princess's household and the people expressed their hostility by hissing her and her children when she went down to Brighton in July.

The Prince was disturbed, not for his 'damned Frau' but for his fascinating 43-year-old mistress. Though his relationship with Lady Jersey was, by now, becoming slightly tedious and he really hankered after a reconciliation with Mrs. Fitzherbert, he disliked Brighton for showing its noisy contempt. His annoyance flared up. He talked of leaving the town for good and giving the Pavilion to the troops for a barracks. And Lady Jersey, despite the fact that she had brazenly settled herself in Mrs. Fitzherbert's former Brighton house, now began to have qualms about her security. It would be better if the two of them sought some less conspicuous place for a renewal of their jeopardised alliance.

However, as she expressed it, 'the tide began to turn' and the incident faded. The Prince became himself again and, though he intended eventually to get rid of her, he was in no immediate hurry to do so. He made arrangements for their pleasure during the rest of the summer and autumn and, when Brighton asked him to stay, he administered a cutting rebuke by announcing that he was leaving for Bognor.

The Countess had already gone there in the first week of August and there was restrained excitement at that end of Sussex. 'Lady Jersey has been at Bognor some time; the place is filled with the most fashionable company. The Prince of Wales has been for some time past expected; it is said some of his Stud are arrived', stated *The County Mirror and Chichester Magazine* in its September issue. And on the evening of 1 September he arrived.

He was then 34, tall, good-looking and blue-eyed, a man of charm and graces, noted for his pleasant voice, good taste in clothes and amazing zest for the enjoyment of life, on and off duty. That Lady Jersey knew she had come near to losing her influence over him was apparent from her ecstatic reception of the Royal visitor. Describing her feelings in letters to Edward Jerningham, an intimate friend of both herself and the Prince, she wrote: 'When I have got over the agitation of seeing him again after three weeks' absence, I shall be more comfortable than I have been for some months. At present I feel giddy with something which I suppose is joy . . . He is in great beauty, spirits, and pour aimable il est toujours like himself, and not like any body else.'

They spent pleasant days in the quietude of the Dome House. 'I am very well, very happy and very gay', she wrote to Jerningham on 5 September. 'Our future plans you shall know when we meet. At present I can only tell you that the Primate [her discreet "cover" for the Prince] is delighted with the quiet life and with the place, and seems not to have any desire to change it'. When the Prince left Bognor on the 10th, she observed that he was 'very sorry indeed to go, having passed his time quite to his liking'.

Those 10 days in Bognor enabled her to re-establish herself, at least in her own estimation. Leech-like she clung to him, indifferent to hints, cajolery or snubs, and it was to be at least another seven years before she would admit to herself that their romance had finally cooled.

When he had gone and she was left to enjoy the more mundane company of her children and her husband, the Earl, she turned her attention to Hothamton. Edward Jerningham, who wrote bad poetry and plays and 'collected' people

like another Hayley, was told what the resort and its founder looked like in her
letter of 16 September:

> 'This place is delightful, in itself quiet, cheerful, clean. The air is delicious and the
> country around it beautiful. But it wants some of God's creatures. My house is delightful,
> much better than any lodging at Brighton; my eating- and drawing-room just the size and
> shape of my rooms at the Pavilion. Sir. R. Hotham, the King of the place, has taken me
> under his protection, sends me fruit, has put up a tent for me and the children under my
> windows, and appears to like me excessively. He is a clean old man, with white hair, white
> eyes and white hands; was a great merchant; and has laid out above £100,000 in making
> this place. He will die contented if any of the Royal Family inhabit one of his houses.
> Vous sentez bien qu'il est au pieds de Francisca.'

On 29 September Lady Jersey and her family left Bognor, having whiled away
the remainder of her time with riding, drawing, music and books and 'every sort
of comfort which gives me no sort of amusement'. She set off for London in a
restless frame of mind, for the Prince had not returned to Bognor as she thought
he might. There is no record of her visiting the town again and 15 years were
to pass before the Prince was seen again in the district. The Dome House, in spite
of all the hopes which Hotham had pinned on it, was not destined to become a
substitute for the Royal Pavilion.

Apart from Hotham's businesslike attentions while she was there, other visitors
called on Lady Jersey, among them the Duke of Richmond's sister-in-law, the
Hon. Mrs. Anne Seymour Damer (1748–1828), an astonishing woman who was
the pet of Horace Walpole, her second cousin: a much-travelled sculptress who
had executed Nelson's bust in Naples after the Battle of the Nile, yet who, along
with her fellow Whig, Charles James Fox, never ceased praising Napoleon.

Pretty Mrs. Damer was a pupil of Giuseppe Ceracchi who carved the statue of
her as the Muse of Sculpture which stands in the King's Library at the British
Museum. Illness dogged her, necessitating frequent trips abroad in search of health
and new interests. 'I always have some plague', was her own brief summary of her
ailments. The fact that she fell off the scaffolding while at work in her studio on
an eight-foot statue of George III in June 1791 did not improve her well-being;
and Fordyce, her doctor, recommended sea-bathing in July. To her dearest friend
Mary Berry, she announced the beginning of the rest-cure: 'I will endeavour to
find some *stupid* [dull] place where there is no company and where I can be
quiet.'

Felpham was the chosen spot, as she would be near her relatives at Goodwood.
But she missed the companionship of Mary, then in Florence, and wrote on
15 August 1791:

> 'I have been bathing, and then taking my solitary walk by the sea, and sitting, like King
> Canute, till the waves washed my feet, but, thank Heaven!, without his crown or his
> courtiers. I grow quite fond of this place. The day was so fine, the sun so bright and the
> sea so smooth and so divinely beautiful that I could not help wishing that some of those
> good spirits, many of which, I trust, hover round your sweet head, would gently transport
> you through the skies to me for one half hour.'

Bathing, modelling a head in wax for Mary and writing numerous letters filled
her time at Felpham. Her brother-in-law, the Duke, drove down from Goodwood

in a phaeton on Saturday, 20 August, and took her out, expounding his local knowledge, naming all the hills, pointing out Bognor Rocks and the lightship which was hardly in sight. When they walked on the beach, the Duke examined the groynes thoroughly and told her how they should have driven in the piles. He also cast an experienced eye at the drainage on the land. The following Friday she went up to Goodwood House for a few days, where she found life very informal. Guests who felt so disposed were at liberty to join in any of the Duke's hobbies. The latest was chemistry. A laboratory had been fitted up and the young secretary in charge of it decided to give the guests a course of lectures. Mrs. Damer was most interested, but Madame de Cambis, a beautiful French refugee, did not understand a thing. Further diversion was provided by the Duke's regimental band, made up of his militia men, who blazed away every evening in a room next to where everyone was sitting.

In October 1794 Mrs. Damer was summoned from her new London home at 9 Upper Brook Street, Mayfair, to Goodwood, where the Duchess had been suddenly taken ill. The house was very noisy as the Duke, who was Master-General of the Ordnance, was busy with the country's defences. 'This place is now anything but pleasant or comfortable,' she reported to Mary, ''tis the uncertainty of hours, and such a shoal of heterogeneous bodies — officers and the Lord knows who, reviews and long dinners at which we must assist.'

A year later, she was there again. The Duchess was on the wane and very irritable. The Duke had provided his usual doctor, John Hunter, but was willing to do anything to keep her content, 'for if she said but a word, any physician would be sent for the next moment, were it from Pekin'.

Finally, in July 1796, Mrs. Damer took lodgings in West Street, Bognor, to be on hand in case the Duchess needed her. The end came in November. With Mrs. Damer on this occasion was Mary Berry whom she had brought with her for a change of scene. Bognor, it was hoped, would repair Mary's broken heart, for she had lost a possible husband in the courtly General O'Hara who had become tired of a procrastinated courtship and had departed to become Governor of Gibraltar.

So, with a little sea air, a little visiting to people like Lady Jersey and some sketching — she drew the Hotel on 25 July and Pagham church on 18 and 19 August — Mary's heart was more or less healed. She recovered enough, at any rate, to write a remarkably forceful reply from Bognor on 30 August to O'Hara's friend, John Barnes, who had clumsily tried to justify the General's course of action:

> 'I do you the justice to believe that nothing but your earnest desire to make some sort apology for your friend, and to spare what you might suppose my wounded pride, could induce you to pay so bad a compliment to my understanding . . . You know it is no *unheard of thing* for people to change their minds on these occasions . . . and I am persuaded that, in spite of your admiration of your friend's conduct, you would have thought it much more worth of his character to have honestly owned the change in a very different manner instead of always putting *me* in the wrong . . . and *deceiving* me for months as to his real wishes.'

Another safety valve for her feelings was her correspondence with Horace Walpole, who enjoyed a tender and skittish friendship with both Mary and her sister from the age of 72 until he died at 80. He called the girls his 'twin-wives' and was disconsolate when they were away from him. When Mary wrote from Bognor, informing him that the local Rocks were big enough to prevent the French from capturing her, his reply was typical:

Strawberry Hill, Twickenham, July 26, 1796.

I received your letter from Bognor this morning and am mightly glad your rocks are not of a temper to receive vessels with open arms. It would not be pleasant to have one's betrothed turned into the Fiancée due Roi du Gallia.

Mary, in fact, never married. She went on, with her sister Agnes, to enliven the lives of others; and the famous gatherings at their *salon*, first at 26 North Audley Street and then at 8 Curzon Street, held the pick of the beauty and wit of London society till the sisters died in 1852.

And Mrs. Damer? She, too, went gaily on, inheriting Walpole's Twickenham villa, visiting and exchanging gifts with Napoleon, siding with Princess Caroline against the Prince and eventually losing touch with Mary and dying at the age of 79. She was buried at Sundridge church, Kent, with her working tools and the ashes of her dog. Romney's portrait of her is at Goodwood.

*   *   *

Hotham had now been running his resort for six seasons. Ten years had gone by since that January day when the excitement of creation gripped him and the building of Bognor Lodge began. His mile of seashore, green with grass, partly bowered with trees, backed by a scattering of houses and terraces, had now been visited by the curious, the wealthy and famous (even the heir to the throne), the pleasure-seekers and those who sought what it was his real purpose to offer, a select place for retirement combining an almost rural tranquillity with the health-giving sea air. Even refugees from the French Revolution, arriving unannounced on the beach having successfully evaded the menace of the Rocks, found ready hospitality among the inhabitants of this foreign shore. But as more winters passed and Hotham journeyed down from Wimbledon yet again to illuminate the season of 1797 with his cheerful personality, there were two spectres grinning over his shoulder. One was his weakening health; the other was the appalling fact that he was now losing his fortune.

The amount of this fortune, so Tierney told Lord Broughton in after years, was £120,000, all of which went into the building and maintenance of Bognor. Lady Jersey had mentioned over £100,000 being spent on the town up to 1796. The trouble lay in the constant drain on his capital, apart from the enormous initial outlay. He alone was responsible for the high-class reputation of Hotham-ton and it was he, as the owner of the visitors' accommodation, who had to pay the servants and other employees and cover the cost of breakages, waste and inattention to his houses. To his desk came the bills for repairs and renewals of furniture as the wear and tear of each season was accounted for. There were taxes to pay and, as a landowner in both Sussex and Surrey, he was subject to further expenses. On top of all, he was still managing his shipping business.

Yet who was to tell him that he would not eventually make a success of it? He was a man of very strong will and, though he may have deceived himself by illusory hopes because Hothamton was his favourite enterprise, he would not abandon it now, even though debtors or death might overtake him. He was resolutely bent on achieving the certainty of ultimate success.

That success, provided he could find more money to sustain the town till the income quickened, was not far from his grasp. He had met with great encouragement from the right class of visitor and, given a few more years, he would complete his building plan and supply what some of his patrons felt was still lacking: larger assembly rooms, a better library, some more shops and perhaps a theatre or some pleasantly designed centre for the town-to-be. All would be in dignified good taste — and, from what his celebrated visitors were saying, he had already created a place of certain distinction. London society recognised that there was some point in going to Hothamton, and he felt no competition yet from neighbouring resorts. Littlehampton was still insignificant, even though the Earl of Surrey had built a house there and was attracting company. Worthing had another year to go before the hopes of speculative builders would be raised by Princess Amelia's knee complaint, which caused the King's 15-year-old daughter to seek the sea cure there. Farther afield, Bournemouth was still but a chinkle of water running down a chine, and the anti-invasion troops had not yet brought custom and cacophony to the few houses and inns on the seashore south of the old village of East Bourne.

Therefore, in spite of failing health and financial worries, he did not feel completely despondent. He possessed one of those minds not easily overcome by disappointment, and this characteristic cheerfulness carried him through 1797. More money was procured from various sources. He leased some of his seaboard at Aldwick to the gentry for building and leased small pieces of land in Bognor to local carpenters. Between June and December, he easily persuaded a number of people to lend him money by offering them large portions of his undeveloped land as security and promising to redeem the debt with interest by the following year. Charles Jacques, a Chichester brewer, and Mrs. Wooldridge of nearby Rumboldswick lent him £1,000 on 37 acres. Edward Box, a Chichester watchmaker, obliged with £500. Another £1,000 was raised by mortgaging Bognor Lodge to James Brewer, a miller of East Meon; and the bonds of close friendship proved equal to the strain when Captain Blanchard handed over £3,600 that August and received as security 68 acres and Hothamton Mews at the back of Spencer Terrace.

As for his health, he sensed the shortening of his days and on 22 May he made his will. The complications of this will form the subject of the next chapter, but it is mentioned here because it touches on the subject of his family life. His wife Frances had died 20 years earlier, on 4 February 1777. There appear to have been no children and Hotham, who was known for his generous help to young men in their careers, regarded his great-nephew, William Knott, in the light of a son. William was now living at Bognor with him, and on that day in May when Hotham cast his thoughts forward towards his end, he decided that the undoubtedly distinguished future of Hothamton should lie in William's hands.

The sea war was still on, but in that summer of 1797 the bright little waves of the Channel afforded no anxiety and the whole subject of the war was being treated jocularly, especially by William Hayley who had started building a house at Felpham that April. 'I am not only building', he told his friend Rose, the attorney, 'but at the same time buying an estate! ay, verily buying an estate by the sea, which, considering the reports of invasion, is like the spirit of the old Roman, who bravely bought the very ground in Italy on which Hannibal was encamped.'

The visitors, more and more of them and still of the *haut ton*, continued to seek Hotham's sanctuary by the sea after the exhaustion of the London Season, and those who had been there the previous year found that, among other improvements, the resort was now graced at last with its own chapel. The rumblings of the feud between Hotham and the Rev. Thomas Durnford had now ceased. Though the chapel — which formed a northern extension of the Chapel House, Hotham's new residence — had been finished for some time, the vicar had opposed the whole project and the building remained unconsecrated. To be baulked by a country vicar was vexing enough, and all Hotham's experience, forged in the heat of the Wimbledon Vestry meetings, was put to the test. Astonishingly, he found Mr. Durnford quite immovable. A year had passed in cold warfare, with Hotham trying to bring pressure to bear from higher ecclesiastical quarters — so high that they probably involved the Archbishop of Canterbury, of whose province South Bersted happened to be a remote dependency by ancient gift. His perseverance prevailed. Difficulties were smoothed. On 13 August a distinguished congregation listened to the opening sermon of the first chaplain, the Rev. Archer Thompson, who diverted any thoughts of his auditors away from Napoleon and the Italian campaign with an oratorical blast on the subject of the profanation of the Sabbath.

The chapel, dedicated to St Alban, was admired for its 'chaste simplicity'. It was 60 feet long and 40 wide, with enclosed pews, a vestry, galleries, an organ loft, pulpit and reading desk. Over the altar were three paintings representing the Entombment of Christ, the Descent from the Cross and Our Saviour on the Mount of Transfiguration. A clock tower rose from the building and engraved on part of the clock mechanism was the information: 'Made by John Thwaites, Clerkenwell, London, 1794, for Sir Richard Hotham Kt.' (This clock still chimes the hours for Bognor, though the chapel itself has gone — pulled down by a subsequent owner, Mr. J. B. Fletcher, in 1859.)

As September came round, the most awe-inspiring figure in the place was that of the aged 'Tiger', the ex-Lord Chancellor, Edward Thurlow. He, too, was inspecting Hotham's watering-place and comparing it with his usual place of resort at Brighton. Thurlow's conversational thrusts had earned for him a feared reputation — so much so that, in years gone by, Dr. Johnson had confessed that 'when

I am to meet with him I should wish to know a day before'. Formidable and
forbidding, his high career at law and at court had been conducted in a welter
of profanity, hard drinking and impropriety. He feared neither God, man nor
the Devil — Gillray indeed on ːe caricatured him as Satan. Vigour of speech was
his to the last, and Samuel Rogers tells how, as his servants carried him upstairs
just before his death, they hit his gouty legs against the banisters, whereupon he
roared out the last words he ever spoke, which were some fearful imprecation on
all their souls. At Brighton, Thurlow and his bibulous acquaintance Charles,
Duke of Norfolk, were on the fringe of the Prince's colourful circle; and the Duke
used to tell an amusing anecdote. Among the collection of Virginian horned owls
in the keep at Arundel Castle was one named 'Lord Thurlow', owing to a certain
resemblance. One day, when the Duke was engrossed in electioneering business
with his solicitor, the owl-keeper came hurrying to the library and gravely
announced: 'I have great news to give your Grace. Lord Thurlow has laid an egg'.

His boyhood friendship with Cowper and his patronage of Romney displayed,
however, another side to Thurlow's character and one of the things that brightened his stay at Hothamton was the knowledge that Romney was nearby at
Eartham. The painter was going through another unhappy period. Health was
poor and his skill was declining. With his nerves on edge, he had come down for
his annual visit on 7 August and the Hayleys worked hard to enliven him. Young
Tom Hayley frequently drove him in his chaise to bathe at Felpham. Tom, aged
17, was the idol of Romney, as he was of the sculptor Flaxman, whose pupil he
was — and, of course, of his father. However inferior William Hayley's contributions to poetry, his letters to his son remain as truly moving evidence of a
wonderful devotion.

By the middle of September, Romney's spirits flickered to life again. He began
a portrait of Miss Le Clerc, the Duke of Richmond's natural daughter, using the
studio at Eartham that Hayley had made for him out of a covered riding-house.
Tom, too, cheered up Romney by finishing a bust of him; and the sudden appearance of Lord Thurlow lightened and, for a while, lifted the gloom entirely.
Thurlow had found Lady Donegal staying in Felpham and brought her along to
Eartham with him. She was an amateur artist, just then learning to paint on
glass, but what was more important was that her late husband had owed Romney
money. The visit resulted in a clearance of the debt. Thurlow, enjoying the effect
of his good deed, became the soul of good humour, so much so that he then
almost unnerved young Tom by deciding to let the boy practise his sculpting
on himself as well.

For several days, Thurlow's carriage clattered out of Hothamton, across the
farmlands and up into the hills at Eartham. There the household watched, hushed,
as the great man sat patiently while the 'little unpractised hand was employed in
modelling perhaps the most awful features that an artist so young ever aspired
to represent'. When the bust was finished, the sitter and his daughters and
Romney were quite kind about it; and Tom had the considerable satisfaction of
hearing later that the Princess of Wales had used a cast of it as a decoration at
one of her entertainments.

During that month, news of Lord Thurlow's sojourn at Hothamton spread to the ears of his intimate friend Joseph Richardson in London, who hankered to join him for a few days by the sea. Sheridan, who happened to be on his way down there again to see how his wife's health was progressing, invited Richardson to accompany him. What then happened is best left to Sheridan's own graphic account:

> 'My friend said "Nothing can be more delightful; what with my favourite diversion of sailing; my enjoyment of walking on the sands; the pleasure of arguing with Lord Thurlow and taking my snuff by the seaside, I shall be in my glory".
>
> 'Well, down he went, full of anticipated joys. The first day, in stepping into the boat for sailing, he tumbled down and sprained his ankle, and was obliged to be carried into his lodgings, which had no view of the sea; the following morning he sent for a barber to shave him, but there being no professional barber nearer than Chichester, he was forced to put up with a fisherman who volunteered to officiate and cut him severely just under the nose, which entirely prevented him taking snuff; and the same day at breakfast, eating prawns too hastily, he swallowed the head of one, horns and all, which stuck in his throat and produced such pain and inflammation that his medical advisers would not allow him to speak for three days. So thus ended, in four and twenty hours, his walking, his sailing, his snuff-taking and his arguments.'

After all this, one likes to feel that the unfortunate Richardson found some consolation in the new-found geniality of Lord Thurlow.

*   *   *

The high winds and waves of another winter swept over Bognor. The storms whirled about the Chapel House as Hotham dealt with the accounts of the past season. Business was improving and there was, in this coming year of 1798, the very heartening prospect of substantially replenishing his purse. That angry sea which he could hear pounding on his shore would be throwing up some gold in the form of prize money. One of his ships had sighted an enemy vessel and he had laid claim to its subsequent capture. The distribution of the prize money was to set everything in motion again; his plan for Hothamton would go forward to its completion. It was true that there were strong objections to his claim and that a legal fight was now in progress, but he felt confident he would win.

So as he sat at his desk in that wild February, looking out eastwards over the flooded brookland, watching Felpham's great white smockmill being battered and almost overturned in the gale, and listening to the tinkle of broken glass from his own property, he felt he was still king of the coast. Those who sought him found him still of good cheer. Hayley came puffing and limping in from inspecting storm damage to his nearly-completed Turret House close by the church at Felpham and together the two neighbours drank coffee. Benevolently, the white-haired old builder of 30 houses listened to the request of a poet who was happy with one. Would the obliging Knight of Bognor favour Mr. Hayley with a piece of his land at Felpham? His new marine villa with its conspicuous turret needed larger grounds for complete comfort. And because he was certainly in no position to refuse any deal in the off-season, the Knight obliged, which was a considerable change from his prevaricating tactics with Hayley over a similar request three years before in 1795. On that occasion, when Tom Hayley heard about it in London, he wrote back to his father: 'I wonder the old Knight of Bognor was not ashamed to look at you after having failed in so many fine promises. I suppose he is as young and active as ever?'

In the third week of July 1798, Tom who was now slowly dying of a spinal disease took possession of the curious house at Felpham, designed by his father and Samuel Bunce, the architect who had also been working on Romney's new home at Holly Bush Hill, Hampstead. (The Turret House was demolished a few years after the Second World War and was replaced by a not unpleasing block of flats which preserves the name.)

But as the year unfolded, as the tide of war turned with Nelson's victory at the Battle of the Nile, as the Prince sobered up at Brighton and Society began to look elsewhere for diversion, as the watery summer passed to an even more watery autumn, so the thin chain of Hotham's luck finally snapped.

He lost the lawsuit over the captured enemy vessel. The result was heart-breaking, for not only had he lost all participation in the prize money, but on to his already monumental pile of debts was added another: a large sum for legal costs.

The century was nearing its close. So, too, was Sir Richard Hotham. Few, perhaps, knew the real state of his affairs as he lay ill in the Chapel House, tended by William Knott and Mrs. Cowan. He had caught a cold through getting wet and he had neglected it. Meanwhile, all along the mile of grass common, past the lonely Hotel, the sea was hitting the beach in mountainous foam and the salt-drenched wind scoured the paintwork of the houses and brought down limbs from the village elms. The ailing Tom Hayley went down to the shore each day at high tide: 'I admire the grand yet desolate spectacle,' he told his father, 'and see the waves beat over the cliff. The whole shore in mist from spray and foam. Men and boys running backward and forward on the beach, to try what they can pick up. The wind blowing their hats off, and the sudden dash of a wave wetting them from top to toe.'

That has always been Bognor, even till today. The fury of winter was to return every year, Hotham or not. His life was now ebbing. Christmas passed and those clean white hands, which had been so favourably noticed by Lady Jersey, turned the pages of his will. Whatever happened to him, he had made provision for Hothamton to survive. The standards by which it had been governed were to continue. The place was to be an example for posterity.

On 18 February, he made a codicil to his will. One of his executors-to-be (the Rev. Amezia Empson of Scawby in Lincolnshire) had died and his great-nephew William Knott was elevated to the position. Hotham revoked a few legacies and added several more. Then, as he lay there, he carefully thought over every detail of his property's management. Suppose William, in his ignorance, sold all the furniture and tried to let the lodgings unfurnished? He added another codicil. No household furniture to be sold or disposed of but to remain in and go along with the houses as heirlooms.

Some more ready cash, also, was needed to launch the new season in proper fashion. It was a little harder to raise than previously, but by making over 20 acres of Bognor to two Chichester gentlemen, Thomas Gawne and James Champ, on 7 February hc persuaded them to couple the goodwill of their names with his in order to secure £1,600 by bond from a Mr. John Jenman.

He had also been pondering on something else that was to perpetuate his memory: his fine old Yorkshire name. That should live, even if he had no children. William Knott, already apprehensive of the burden of Hothamton that would lie upon his shoulders, was summoned to the bedside and told of his new estate in life. He was to become William Hotham, and by Royal sign manual on 25 February he assumed the name and the arms.

It was nearly spring again and Hotham was 76. But his disappointments, increasing cares and diminished fortune had exacted their price. He had come very near to the complete success of his project. In a few more years, his cultured village could have grown to a select town. He might have been able to nod to Queens and walk the sands with Kings. But he was not to know how the future would handle his cherished toy, for on Wednesday, 13 March, 1799, at the Chapel House the founder of Bognor died.

Fig. 5. Mary Berry's drawing of the Fox Hotel, Bognor, 25 July 1796.

Chapter V

THE AFTERMATH OF HOTHAM

ON THE THURSDAY of the following week, 21 March 1799, the Rev. Thomas Durnford stood at the gateway of South Bersted churchyard to receive the remains of his ex-adversary. The ceremony was a simple one. It was far too early in the year for any distinguished visitors to be present, so on that first day of spring there were gathered just a few relatives and friends, together with his tenants, tradesmen and servants, to bid him farewell. He was laid to rest and his executors, great-nephew William and Mrs. Cowan, returned home to mingle their grief with the more pressing problem of what to do with Bognor.

Before we say good-bye here to Hotham, something should be said about his actual burial-place. The site of the original grave in the churchyard is unknown. A writer in 1807 referred to his 'turf-built shrine' and mentioned a simple inscription in prose on the door of the vault, an inscription that he deemed better than most epitaphs. This inscription was, in all certainty, the work of Hayley, to whom death was always a subject for florid inspiration — so much so that he was regarded locally as an authority on epitaphs, either suggesting examples or contributing epitaphs of his own composition. His friend Flaxman, the sculptor, received the wording for Hotham's epitaph at his London workshop. It read:

In Memory
Of Sir Richard Hotham, Knight,
The Founder of this place.
Beginning life in a very humble line
Of Commerce,
He rose, by commercial virtues,
To considerable opulence:
After retiring, at the age of 70,
He embarked his ample Fortune again
In the Hazardous Adventure
Of Building Hothampton,
And lived to rejoice in its Success.
In the perplexity of many concerns,
He corrected the Failings of a man
By attending to the duties
Of a Christian:
He lived continually impressed
with a deep and lively sense
of manifold blessings
Bestowed on him by Providence
In a Long and Prosperous Life:

39

He died with exemplary sentiments
Of undiminished Gratitude
And of perfect resignation
To God.
By His Death
Society and Commerce
Have lost an active, cheerful, intelligent friend;
Infirmity and Indigence
a compassionate and charitable
Benefactor

Hotham had not been interred for more than a decade or so before he was removed elsewhere — to an unusual resting-place beneath an exterior flight of stone steps against the north wall of the church. These led up to the outside door of the gallery within. The space below the steps was bricked in to form a tomb, and a slab of black slate with a brief inscription was fixed to the wall above the gallery door. Here, beneath the footsteps of the faithful, he rested until 1879. The inscription on the slate had the wrong date of his death and meagrely announced:

Underneath are deposited the mortal remains of Sir Richard Hotham, Knight and Founder of Bognor. He died on the 14th day of March, 1799, in the 77th year of his age.

The rest of the tablet was left blank, rather suggesting that it had at first been intended to re-engrave the words of the original epitaph but that a shorter form of words had been chosen for reasons of economy.

*   *   *

Though William and Mrs. Cowan were soon to be struggling in the deep waters of debt, the passing of Bognor's Founder caused merely a ripple on the surface of the outside world. His death had been briefly noted in *The Times*; while the *Sussex Weekly Advertiser* referred to the 'singular diligence and unblemished integrity' with which he had raised his fortune and how he was led to 'create a colony for the accommodation of persons in elegant life who wished to pass their summers by the seaside and at the same time to avoid the follies of public dissipation. He had the satisfaction to see so adventurous a project completed with success and died rejoicing in the benevolent idea that the new scene which he had been tempted to form so late in life, by the uncommon activity of his nature, might prove a public benefit to his country'.

These well-meant sentiments were echoed by *The Gentleman's Magazine*, which stated that 'to the spirit and liberality of this gentleman the country is indebted for the establishment of the new and fashionable watering-place called Hothampton, better known by the name of Bognor Rocks.' Mention was made of his generosity and of the fact that, due to his patronage and persevering attention, many a young man had made good in the service of the East India Company. 'Bognor is a property,' asserted the magazine, 'that is of course rising in value every year, as a large extent of land belongs to his family, and the express condition of their retaining it is to increase the buildings for the purpose of letting them to the occasional frequenters of the place.'

It was precisely this express condition that was now of some concern to the three executors as they debated the terms of the will in those early spring days of 1799. The third executor was another Hotham, William Hotham of York, about whom family history is reticent, except that he may have been a nephew of Sir Richard and was probably the same William Hotham who was apprenticed to Thomas Yeates, a hatter of St Martin-in-the-Fields, from 1763 to 1774.

In the will, which was proved on 19 April, Hotham had laid down a firm understanding that the development of Bognor was to continue in the plan already begun. The money raised by the sale of his real estate and from the residue of his personal estate was to be devoted by the executors to 'completing the buildings at Bognor and in erecting new ones on the present plan as they shall think fit'.

At first sight, apart from this onerous building commitment, the rest of the will was simple enough. Everything he possessed in the way of land and buildings in Bognor and the surrounding villages went to a Trust consisting of Sir Beaumont Hotham and his heirs, William Hotham of York, the Rev. Amezia Empson of Scawby in Lincolnshire, and Mistress Jane Cowan. As previously mentioned, Mr. Empson had since died and William Hotham (previously Knott) of Bognor had been appointed an executor in his place. Sir Beaumont Hotham's family were to take possession of the estate at the expiration of 200 years, but meanwhile the income was to support great-nephew William and any family of his for the rest of his life. When William died, the beneficiaries after him were, in this order, his sons and daughters, Richard Empson (Hotham's godson) and Beaumont Hotham, son of Sir Beaumont. There were also three life annuities for William's relatives to be provided from the estate: £20 each to his sisters, Eleanor Pratt of Round Court in the Strand and Charlotte Little of Crutched Friars, London; and £40 to his mother, Sarah Knott, who lived at Donington near Boston, Lincolnshire.

The Wimbledon house was to be sold and the proceeds to become part of the residue of the Bognor estate. Having paid off all debts and funeral expenses, the money left over from the sale of his goods and chattels and from the sale of his real estate was to be put to the enlargement of Bognor. As an afterthought, Hotham stated that if insufficient money was raised to cover remaining debts or to pay legacies by the methods ordained, then he empowered the Trust to mortgage the whole or part of his Bognor property to meet these commitments. Finally, with superb optimism, he advised them to devote any spare cash to the purchase of further real estate.

To William, as chief executor, the most disturbing of all his difficulties was not so much the duty of building a bigger Bognor as having to fill it with rich visitors, small though it was. Trade had been poor over the last few years and receipts were low. A new season was now approaching and it was essential to forestall any wild rumours that might be calamitous for the summer revenue of 1799. The public must be advised that the resort was still a going concern.

William's first move, therefore, was to insert this advertisement in the *Sussex Weekly Advertiser* on 10 June:

EXCELLENT SEA BATHING
BOGNOR ROCKS NEAR CHICHESTER

The Executors, Executrix and Heirs at Law of Sir Richard Hotham deceased beg leave to inform the public that the houses at Bognor are in complete repair; the furniture modern, in good condition and well adapted to the premises which are now fit for immediate reception of the families of noblemen and gentlemen. There is a neat chapel in the centre of the estate in which the duty is performed by a very respectable clergyman. The houses may be taken, and every particular known, by applying personally or by letter to Mrs. Cowan, the Executrix, at Bognor Rocks.

The next step was to start raising money for the settlement of debts, as laid down in the conditions of the will. Consequently, at midday on 29 July, there was a considerable flutter of interest among the summer visitors when Messrs. Skinner, Dyke & Skinner of Aldersgate Street, London, set themselves up at the Hotel to start the series of auction sales of Hotham's property. First to be offered was the outlying ring of land that had been purchased some ten years before. It was parcelled into 11 lots and comprised the 146 acres and house of Dry Grounds Farm, Felpham; the two lime kilns, cottage and 30 acres at the end of Limmer Lane, Felpham, occupied by Thomas Stocker; Flansham Farm, which consisted of a barn, stable, sheepwash and pastures, rented by Henry Boniface; the *Fox Inn* at Felpham, of which George Grinder was landlord; fields and five cottages at South Bersted; and the 338 acres and house of Aldwick Manor Farm, let to George Parham.

By October the auctioneers were busy disposing of some of Hotham's personal possessions. They cleared his books and his household linen, his china and his glass. The contents of his cellar were what one might have expected: 120 dozen old Port, East India Madeira, Claret, Sherry, Champagne, Graves and 23 dozen Arrack. Some of the farm stock and equipment on the Chapel House estate were also sold, including six draught horses, 45 Somerset ewes, three stumps of hay, waggons, ploughs, carts, harrows, a pile engine, a two-wheel chaise and harness and a Yarmouth cart.

His house at Wimbledon, Merton Grove, was bought by Mr. Benjamin Hays. He sold it in 1806 to Sir James Allan Park, a Judge of the Court of Common Pleas, who lived there for 32 years and earned himself a mural tablet in St Mary's commemorating his good work in parish affairs. The rest of Hotham's Surrey estate was sold to a Mr. Greaves. This consisted of land to the east of Merton Grove and also just south of the Tooting highroad in Merton parish — where, though the evidence is slight, it may have been Hotham who had built a brick mansion called Merton Place. If so, it is possible that this was the origin of his building experiments; the house certainly had architectural details in common with the Dome House later erected at Bognor.

Merton Place, which had a small moat with a rustic bridge, was purchased from Mr. Greaves by none other than the hero of the day, Lord Nelson. Here Sir

William and Lady Hamilton joined him in 1801, and he spent a happy year or so till the summons came which took him to sea again. Merton Place, as well as Hotham's home, Merton Grove, has now gone.

To all outward appearances, apart from the diversion provided by the auction sales, the Bognor season of 1799 was much the same as usual. The carriages still bowled along the firm sand; the fishermen still brought catches of prawns and lobsters up to their thatched huts on the narrow common between the houses and the sea. Along at the Hotel, guests still waited while the sea-water baths were warmed up, and off-shore there was the occasional excitement of seeing a clash between the revenue officers and the brazen smugglers. In April 500 casks had been captured from a Cowes ship, the *Liberty*, off Felpham by Officers Ragless, Whitcomb and Lower, and some of the year's haul of contraband to date was being sold on 4 July at Arundel Custom House. There were 30 gallons of rum and 520 gallons of Geneva; and, if visitors felt so inclined, they could go over and taste some of these 'seized and legally condemned' goods before 11 o'clock on the morning of the sale.

As some small comfort to the worries of the executors, the nobility and gentry did not desert the place. Old patrons such as Mrs. Barwell and Lady Albemarle returned to Hotham's town; and, though perhaps they missed his courtly attentions, it was still pleasant to enjoy such sedate privacy in this quiet stretch of semi-country on the sea edge. Many distinguished newcomers also graced the season. Count Starhemberg, the former Austrian Ambassador, was there and two peppery personalities, Sir John Orde and the Marquis of Lansdowne. Sir John, that June, had been appointed Rear-Admiral of the Channel Fleet. He had seen service in the American war, commanding the *Zebra* at the reduction of Charlestown and the Delaware forts, and had capped his exploits by marrying a Charlestown girl, Margaret Stephens. He gained his knighthood by quelling native unrest while Governor of Dominica but was to cause considerable unrest on his own part, when back in European waters as third-in-command under Lord St Vincent, by writing to complain that he had been superseded by Nelson and Curtis. His complaint led to such hostility between himself and St Vincent that both parties were bound over in £5,000 to keep the peace. Nelson always said afterwards that Orde was a nuisance at sea and once commented curtly: 'I shall never enter into a paper war with him or anyone else.'

As for the Marquis of Lansdowne — who, as Lord Shelburne, had been Prime Minister in 1782–83 — he was one of the most unpopular statesmen of his time, due no doubt to his outspoken contempt for political parties. At Lansdowne House in Berkeley Square he was the shining patron of literature and fine art, but in political circles he was regarded as possessing the characteristics more of a cunning woman than of an able statesman. George III, probably because of his lordship's belief in religious equality and Catholic emancipation, dubbed him 'The Jesuit of Berkeley Square'. Others nicknamed him 'Malagrida' and cartoons depicted him as Guy Fawkes blowing up his comrades.

The parade of fashion that season included Lord Lansdowne's sister-in-law, the Duchess of Bolton (sister of Lord Lonsdale), Lady Clifford, Lady

Musgrave, Lady Nugent and Lady Dalling, wife of Lieut.-General Lord John Dalling of Barwood.

But, behind the scenes, the future for Hotham's great-nephew was as black as night. By now William had discovered the worst and, as the year came to an end and he surveyed the full extent of the financial liabilities facing him, he realised that there was only one remedy. Bognor itself would have to be sold.

The discovery that had alarmed him was the cold fact that the executors were responsible for finding nearly £50,000 for the settlement of claims on the estate. They had now done all they could to clear Hotham's debts by the means he had suggested in his will, but the claims were still mountainous. Hotham, it now appeared, had died heavily encumbered. Mortgage debts, debts by bond, debts under decree, simple contract debts: all these amounted to over £33,000. And, since his death, there were now law fees, debts undisclosed, demands in litigation, annuities and other divers claims. The legacies alone amounted to upwards of £10,000.

William had not his great-uncle's capacity for laughing it off. There were now too many persons involved. Apart from his own dismal financial outlook, he had his two co-executors to consider and also several other people, including the important Beaumont Hothams, who thought they were coming into money from the estate. It did not look at the moment as if anyone was going to receive a penny; and so, before the serious situation developed into disaster, William acted. He filed a bill in Chancery and hoped for the best.

The long sad tale was unfolded before the Law during the early months of 1800 and the Trustees' case called for some sympathy. They could not, they pleaded, raise sufficient money if they abided by the terms of the will, even if they had recourse to mortgaging. There was so little money to be made out of Bognor. The annual income from the 30 houses had been only £930 for the last three years. The value of the estate not yet sold was £2,183 and brought in only £700 a year in rents. This unsold property included the Hotel, the so-called West Shops (four fishermen's huts on a site now occupied by the western end of Marine Park Gardens), the Manor of Aldwick and various parcels of land and cattle-grazings in Bognor Brooks.

The charges for maintenance, superintendence, management, taxes and repairs to houses and furniture were constant and heavy; and, as the furniture was now liable to be seized by creditors, this meant that any income from letting the houses would be completely lost. Therefore, it was the considered opinion of William, Mrs. Cowan and William Hotham of York, backed by Sarah Empson, aunt of Richard Empson, and Philadelphia Hotham, mother of the infant Beaumont Hotham (her husband, Sir Beaumont, had died the previous August), that 'It is totally impracticable to continue the letting of the thirty houses to Company resorting to Bognor as a watering-place, as seems to have been the desire or will of the testator'.

It stood to reason that if the furniture were sold, thus preventing the letting of the houses, then William — though he was supposed to be the first to benefit — would actually be without any benefit whatsoever from the bounty of his great-uncle. Therefore, all parties concerned made this request: that the part of the will in question should be revoked so that, instead of trying to mortgage Bognor as Hotham suggested, they should be allowed to sell it. They mutually agreed that everything should be vested in the Trustees and sold on trust and the money put to paying off debts. If there was any residue, this could be devoted to settling the various claims of individuals mentioned in the will.

Their plea was accepted and on 30 June 1800 a private Act of Parliament was passed enabling them to dispose of Bognor at once. Its title was: *An Act for vesting part of the estates devised by the will of Sir Richard Hotham Kt., dec., in Trustees, to be sold for payment of incumbrances.* With debtors pressing on all sides, the Act had an inspired spirit of urgency about it and gave special powers to the Trustees to demolish buildings and sell the material if this was likely to prove a quicker way to raise money than by waiting for a sale. Buildings that were authorised to be razed if necessary included the Dome House, the chapel and the minister's little house attached, the farm buildings and workshops in the grounds of Bognor Lodge and the Prawn Buildings, which were in what is now Norfolk Street.

No time was lost and on 27, 28 and 29 August the freehold, leasehold and copyhold estates comprising the whole of 'that delightful and much-admired watering-place, Hothamton or Bognor Rocks' came under the hammer.

To Messrs. Skinner, Dyke & Skinner this was a far more illustrious occasion than merely trying to sell off odd scraps of surrounding property, as they had done the previous year. They now had something substantial to offer, described in their catalogue as 'Seven elegant and spacious mansion houses, forming the Crescent; two beautiful villas and 20 genteel dwelling houses comprising Hothamton Place, East Row and Spencer Terrace, also the Lawn and Garden Cottages, the excellent building known as the Hotel, now in full trade, with the Subscription Room, Library, Shops and hot bath, a mews with stabling for 44 horses and 12 coach houses, together with The Gardens, Lawns, Shrubbery Walks, fertile meadow, pasture and corn fields containing about 570 acres; also the Manor, or reputed Manor, of Aldwick.'

It is not to be wondered at that such an unusual sale caused considerable crowds to foregather in Bognor. Ironically, the selling-up of the resort attracted more people than had ever taken lodgings there in past seasons — though, from the late Founder's point of view, many of them were probably quite the wrong type of person. London speculators, old friends from Wimbledon and City acquaintances — and also, admittedly, a leavening of nobility — were among those who crowded each day into the salon of the Dome House in Hothamton Crescent where the sale was to be held.

As the nearby chapel clock struck midday and the line of waiting horses on the high-road stamped restlessly in the summer heat, Lot 1 — the Chapel House itself with its 39 acres — was put up for auction. It was the best house in the town, Hotham's own home, and whoever lived there would, as it were, ascend a throne. There was already an aura of regality about the Chapel House in the imagination of local people. The bidding closed at £3,650. The new owner was disclosed as Richard Scott of Kensington Square, London, a Colonel in the service of the Honourable East India Company.

Bidding and local excitement remained high that week. Half a mile away at Felpham some inkling of what was happening doubtless reached the ears of a dark, determined-looking stranger from London who had rented Rose Cottage from the landlord of the *Fox* for £20 a year. His name was William Blake, an engraver who in June had been invited by his friend Hayley to come and live near him at Felpham. The death of William Cowper in April had been followed only a week later by that of Hayley's son Tom, and the double blow had so depressed the occupant of the Turret House that his friends tried to coax him to life again by suggesting that he should write a biography of the poet. Blake was to engrave the illustrations to Hayley's text.

Bognor Lodge was also sold on the first day of the sale — to Mr. John Dudman of Deptford, Kent, for £3,500 — and the executors' unavoidable duty of raising money demanded a sad little sacrifice when Mrs. Cowan's home, Lawn Cottage, went to a Mr. Middleton for £500. Bit by bit, in 65 lots, Bognor disintegrated from being the compact vision of a single mind into a collection of isolated properties subject to the whims of different speculators. It was an undoing from which the town never recovered. Every scrap of land went, even down to the four pieces at Felpham (Penny Mead, Pease Croft, Dry Grounds and Ragless's Mead) which Hotham had marked down as the source of the annuities, totalling £80, for William's mother and sisters. Colonel Scott, with an apparently unlimited purse, paid highly as chief purchaser of Bognor. Including the Chapel House, he acquired over 120 acres of land and buildings at a cost of £16,684. A condition of purchase was that he redeemed all mortgage debts on the properties — so, among other settlements, William had the relief of seeing Hotham's loyal friend Captain Blanchard receive back his £3,600.

The Dome House was bought by Charles Edward Wilsonn of Wimbledon, who had served with Hotham on the Vestry Committee and was an M.P. and Receiver-General for Middlesex. Three properties originally advertised for auction were sold by private contract. These included two terraces: Hothamton Place, which went to Mr. Hurst for £4,400, and the adjacent East Lodge for £3,100 to Mr. Metcalf, who also made other purchases of land. He was a director of the East India Company; whether friend or foe is not clear. The disposal of the third building, the Hotel, involved the future of the landlord, Richard Pink, who was leasing it for £210 a year, and his sub-tenants in the annexe, James Binstead who kept the library and toyshop and the Misses Hope and England who had the milliner's.

On the following Monday, 1 September, the auctioneers disposed of the 'neat and genteel household furniture' in some of the houses of the Crescent and Spencer Terrace adjoining. The items included full drawing-room suites in fine calico, 74 bedsteads with calico and dimity hangings, goosefeather beds, looking-glasses, carpets, stoves, kitchen furniture and Staffordshire services.

That was the end of the sale and the end of Bognor's inaugural years as a seaside resort built and controlled by one man. The auctioneers had done their best to impart an air of dignity to their work by stating that the sale was held in a watering-place 'now in high esteem and resorted to by families of the first respectability'. As for William and Mrs. Cowan, they had striven honourably, if desperately, to clear Sir Richard's name of debt. As arranged, the proceeds were paid into the Bank of England in the name of the Accountant-General of the Court of Chancery. According to Richard Dally, a solicitor in Chichester whom we shall encounter again quite shortly, the sale realised £68,000 and the final total of the claims on the estate, apart from legacies, came to £56,000. But by the time the auctioneers had been paid, titles to property made out for the new owners, and the Chancery suit, the Parliamentary Act and various other expenses accounted for, the executors found themselves left with clear consciences, a little bit of property for themselves to live in and only £8,000 remaining in cash.

THE
P A R T I C U L A R S
OF
VALUABLE
FREEHOLD, COPYHOLD, & LEASEHOLD
ESTATES,
COMPRISING
THE WHOLE OF THAT DELIGHTFUL AND MUCH ADMIRED
Watering Place
HOTHAMTON OR BOGNOR ROCKS,
NOW IN HIGH ESTIMATION
AND RESORTED TO BY FAMILIES OF THE FIRST RESPECTABILITY;
SITUATE
CONTIGUOUS TO THE SEA
ON THE
SUSSEX COAST,
IN THE PARISHES OF SOUTH BERSTED, FELPHAM, AND PAGHAM,
Seven Miles from the City of CHICHESTER, Ten from ARUNDEL, Sixteen from PETWORTH, and Sixty-seven from LONDON;
LATE THE PROPERTY OF
Sir RICHARD HOTHAM,
DECEASED:

Fig. 6. Sale particulars of Hotham's Estate, August 1800.

Chapter VI

BOGNOR AGAINST NAPOLEON

IT WAS barely half built. Call it what one would, Bognor Rocks, Hothamton or Hothampton — or Great & Little Bognor as Thomas Gream titled it in his map of 1799 — it was still only a village. The new brick houses and terraces stood at very wide intervals along the highway, facing the sea across a quarter of a mile of meadows. Where the lane (which would become West Street) turned down to the shore, the fishing community still had their thatched huts, there were two or three other little houses and then the hotel and library standing alone on the small cliff above the sands. It was very pastoral and tranquil, green and wooded; and yet, with its suggestion of architectural pretension and urban elegance, it was a rather unusual place to come upon after the miles of untampered coast each side of it.

Following the sale in the summer of 1800, there was no outbreak of building activity on the part of the new landholders. No rows of houses shot up to fill the gaps in Hotham's plan. Colonel Scott and his fellow speculators did nothing with bricks and indeed were probably unable to do anything until the legal ramifications exhausted themselves. And this was to take six years.

But if no new houses were built, certainly none remained empty. Some of the larger estates changed hands, bringing a new set of important residents into the district and thus restoring any lustre that the villagers felt they had lost. The most prominent hero now in their midst was Admiral Sir Thomas Troubridge (1750–1807), back from the excitements of the Mediterranean and now First Sea Lord. He bought the Chapel House from Colonel Scott.

Troubridge was Nelson's devoted comrade-in-arms. As 18-year-old seamen they had joined the crew of the frigate *Seahorse* and gone to sea together in February 1786. In 1797 both had been in the triumphant action against the great Spanish fleet off Cape St Vincent. On that memorable St Valentine's Day, Nelson turned his blind eye and captured two enemy ships, using one as a stepping-stone on which to board the other. As the British sailed into the action, the commander, Sir John Jervis, was watching his leading ship, the *Culloden*. 'Look at Troubridge!' he exclaimed. 'He handles his ship as if the eyes of all England were upon him.'

Five months later, Nelson and Troubridge were trying to storm the impregnable Spanish fortress of Santa Cruz, a forlorn effort under a hail of fire which resulted in Nelson being wounded. Troubridge succeeded in leading 400 men right into the heart of the town before being compelled to listen to the sensible reasoning of the governor of the citadel. The governor then entertained him to dinner, gave his men food and lent them boats in which to return to their ships. Again, at

Nelson's tremendous Battle of the Nile against the French, Troubridge was there in command of the reserve fleet, but this time he ran on to a sandbank in the *Culloden* with the night battle raging before him. Though he may have thus unwittingly provided the fleet with a warning of the existence of shoals, his remorse was acute. Afterwards, when sending condolences to Captain Darby of the *Bellerophon* on his wounds and the number of his dead, he wrote that even if Darby's sufferings had been fifty times as great he would rather have been in his place than have undergone the anguish of running aground. He confessed that he had frequently wept and felt like shooting himself. In 1799 he was blockading Italian ports and was created a baronet on 30 November. The following summer, he turned for home and was appointed to the Channel Fleet in August. Nelson, on the other hand, was in Italy, caught in the snares of Lady Hamilton's charms and tending to lose the respect of his friends. It was thought that his career was over. Troubridge himself may have openly expressed his distaste for this association. At any rate, when a fresh turn of war brought Nelson back to duty in January 1801, it was as Commander of the Channel Fleet and Troubridge was moved away from his old comrade and given a shore appointment in Whitehall.

After thirty-odd years at sea, Troubridge found himself under his old chief, Sir John Jervis, now Lord St Vincent and First Lord of the Admiralty in Addington's government. As naval officers could also hold a seat in Parliament, he sat for Yarmouth, an Admiralty pocket borough. His wife had died in 1798, so his deaf and elderly sister Elizabeth acted as housekeeper, presiding over the Chapel House and their London home, Arlington House, on the west side of Turnham Green. (This house was pulled down in 1877. The site is now occupied by Walpole Gardens.) Troubridge's son Edward had followed in his father's career and at this time was a lieutenant.

Another person of equal importance in Bognor's new hierarchy was a bright little Irishman, Arthur Saunders, Viscount Sudley of Gore and later 3rd Earl of Arran, who bought the east house in Hothamton Crescent and named it Arran Lodge. Here, with his wife, he eventually settled down to take over Hotham's rôle as genial host to the neighbourhood.

Lord Arran (as he became in 1809) was born in 1761 and was M.P. for Baltimore, Co. Cork, in 1783-90 and for Co. Donegal, 1800-06. Though he owned a large Irish property, he was an absentee landlord and left the management of the estate to his brother, Colonel W. J. Gore. In 1787 he married into money by choosing for his wife Mary Tyrell, the heiress of Sir John Tyrell of Heron Hall, near Brentwood in Essex. Lady Arran was indeed a 'Lady Bountiful' and Bognor was to have good reason to mourn her death in 1832. Her acts of benevolence began in her younger days in Essex. The steward of her father's estate was John Pearson, noted for his magnificent wraps and gorgeous waistcoats, and his twin sons, John and Arthur, became her special charge. After they had been shepherded through University careers, they became clergymen and were given the two family livings. The Rev. Arthur received the living of Springfield, near Chelmsford, while the Rev. John was rector of East Horndon, near Brentwood, for 42 years, as well as acting as steward to the Bognor estate.

The generosity and far-reaching influence of the Arrans was to have a notable effect on the fortunes of the stranded resort for the next 30 years.

Three other large houses, newly occupied after the sale, were Bognor Lodge, which was acquired by Sir John Edward Harington, who had seen service with the East India Company, and the two other houses in the Crescent, the westerly one by the Haslers and the central Dome House, as stated in the last chapter, by the Wilsonns from Wimbledon.

Though only half built, and though rival resorts such as Worthing and Brighton were expanding daily while Bognor stood still, the aura of glamour that Hotham had managed to cast over his creation by the sea continued to linger in Society's mind. The rich were still intrigued. The place had an air — and it was now possible to buy a house and live there. There may have been nothing much to do at Bognor, but that very lack of activity seemed to exercise a certain attraction. By now, at long last, the important guide-book writers were catching up with fashion and including Bognor in their wordy volumes, although they appeared rather puzzled that people should want to go there at all. In fact, their attitude to these new bathing-places, which they were now being forced to 'cover' as well as the old-established inland spas, was generally patronising. They wrote superciliously and adopted a tone of amused surprise at this craze for 'dipping' which had been so much advertised by the resorts themselves. Two extracts from early guides show how the comparative lifelessness of Bognor was a revelation to writers who had heard that the place was a centre of fashion.

In 1800, the author of *A Companion to the Watering and Bathing Places of England* called it Bognar and wrote:

> 'The persons who visit this little village are, it should seem, fond of keeping their dignity entirely to themselves; the place being very little dipped into by the middling ranks of life. Indeed, the style of the buildings and the little intercourse of general society here are not calculated for those who emerge from the region of smoke to see a little of life and mix among "the gay licentious crowd"; although in its infancy, it has grown great and it seems as if it would hold up its head above the laughing crowd for several years to come.'

George Saville Carey was less optimistic. He was the author of *The Balnea; a history of all the popular watering-places in England* and was determined to be blunt about everything, warning the reader in his preface that, regarding watering-places,

> 'there are partial accounts, but they have been written by some hireling who, for the sake of his own interests, has been obliged to say something handsome, should the situation be ever so ugly, and give the qualities of each place the insipid sameness of perfection'.

In his 3rd edition (1801) he trounced Bognor:

> 'It is a desirable spot, and like a well-compiled newspaper, in lack of customers, is only wanting to be read; so Bognor is only wanting to be seen; there is a good hotel and small assembly room near the ocean, which presents itself to you with the same kind of aspect as when you are at Brighton. It appears at present merely calculated for the superior sort of society, and as there is often a peculiar shyness in them from pride, in respect to rank

and etiquette, they seldom associate, or are seen together; the want of which makes it appear desolate and throws a melancholy shade over the whole neighbourhood. Were there a few humbler habitations built for the middling race of his majesty's subjects, it might be a consideration worth attending to. It would add life to the scene by furnishing it with moving objects; whereas those which are there at present, whether it be from pride, or that they are ashamed at being looked at, sit brooding in their chambers the whole day, or if they venture abroad, they huddle and curtain themselves up invisibly in their carriages. The amusements of Bognor are few in number, and little varied, but if health is the object of pursuit, she may be found here as readily as in places of greater concourse.'

This aspect of Bognor was, of course, no new discovery. Lady Newdigate had commented on it six years ago, but in 1795 there was at least Hotham still at the helm to provoke the genteel whisper that Bognor was growing into the most dignified town on the south coast. Now, however, despite nobility in residence, there was some uncertainty about the future among the invisible inhabitants; and, despite the peace treaty with Napoleon that set the church bells clanging in October, there was no sign that anyone at all was going to 'create new buildings on the present plan as they shall think fit'.

So in 1801 the Bognor scene remained unchanged, and in the surrounding countryside everything was very much the same as when Hotham had first arrived. Duke Charles was still directing his Cumberland masons in the partial rebuilding of Arundel Castle; they were just starting on the north-east wing. Up at Goodwood the 3rd Duke of Richmond, with the architect James Wyatt, was now building his new house round the old one and had hired the poor of the district to collect tons of flint from the Downs for the purpose. That April, members of his Hunt and officers of the Sussex Militia had held a private race meeting on the Harroway, north of the house, and it had been so successful that the Duke was thinking of erecting a wooden stand with a thatched roof for a public meeting next year. At Felpham, Hayley was now finally settled at the Turret House, surrounded by exceptionally high walls, and was frenziedly busy accumulating Cowper's correspondence in order to write the poet's *Life*. Blake, too, was fairly happy in his cottage nearby, at the moment engraving pictures of animals for some nursery *Ballads* by Hayley. Occasionally he walked through the peaceful country behind Bognor — through the beautiful 'expanded meadows', as he called them — to visit Seagrave the printer at Chichester and to collect paper for the printing press he had installed at the cottage.

At South Bersted, whose villagers looked on to the backs of Hotham's houses between them and the sea, the Rev. Durnford was no longer to be seen. He had died on 4 December 1800, and had been succeeded as vicar by John Phillips, who for some reason did not officiate at an important wedding in his parish a few months later. This took place not at the church but at Hotham's chapel, still unconsecrated but licensed. The bridegroom was Henry Howard, younger brother of the next Duke of Norfolk and later M.P. for Arundel. Another clergyman, passing through Bognor in May, was the Rev. John Skinner of Camerton, near Bath, en route from Devon to Kent. 'I believe it would be difficult,' he wrote in his diary for 22 May, 'to find anywhere at a distance of a hundred miles from the metropolis such curious display of citizen-like habitations and ornaments, rendered still more conspicuous by being built of flaming brick. The hotel stands on the beach and here I took up my abode for the night. Although I have been sufficiently imposed upon along the coast, the last mentioned exceeds them all in charges.'

He departed abruptly next day: 'May 23. I left Bognor Rocks this morning with the same kind of regard that sailors feel for the spot where they have suffered shipwreck.'

*   *   *

While the lawyers were still sorting out the complicated tangle of new title deeds and the new owners of Bognor remained silent, peace with France came, not unexpectedly, to an end. In May 1803 Bonaparte seized all British citizens in France and made them prisoner, Portsmouth became a boiling pot of cheerful warring preparation and the renewed threat of invasion was the main topic in the coastal towns.

Bognor was fully prepared for war. The village already had a signal station, set up during the scare of 1795. It consisted of a mast and hut, equipped with a red flag, a blue pennant and four black balls made of canvas stretched on hoops, 3 feet 4 inches in diameter. The station was manned by the local branch of the Sea Fencibles, a coastal guard founded in 1798 and consisting of fishermen, boatmen and longshoremen serving of their own free will for 1s. a day. This arrangement rendered them inviolate from the Navy press gang, but they were never quite certain that the guarantee was sacred. Nelson, who was in charge of the Sea Fencibles for a time, said he felt they were 'always afraid of some trick', meaning that they were suspicious of setting foot on a Naval vessel in case they should be immediately impressed into foreign service. By October, the hundred fishermen who formed the Bognor Fencibles were thirsting for action and vainly scanning the Channel for the invaders. Fingers itched to let off their 'great-guns', in the use of which they were reported to have acquired 'incredible felicity'.

Bonaparte, not France, was the ogre now. Therefore, there must have been a great agitation of gossip behind those discreet curtains when an obscure resident of Felpham was brought to trial at Chichester in January 1804 for allegedly stating, among other seditions, that if Napoleon landed, every Englishman would have the choice of either joining the French or having his throat cut. William Blake — for it was against him that this trumped-up charge was brought by a drunken soldier — was acquitted, but the unpleasant experience remained in his mind. After he had left Felpham and had published his poem *Jerusalem*, most of which was written at Rose Cottage, he worked off personal grudges in subsequent writings by mingling the names of real people with mythical characters. The soldier Scofield is mentioned with fury and Blake also raves against three men, Kwantock, Peachey and Brereton, who may have been connected with the trial or offended him in some other episode. All three were well-known landowners and public figures in the district between Bognor and Chichester and they can be identified, I believe, as John Quantock of South Mundham, John Peachey, a Chichester J.P., and William Brereton who happened to acquire Aldwick Farm from Hotham's estate.

Bognor's rocks, which formed a great elongated black S curling out to sea, remained a comfort to the inhabitants throughout 1804, even though the rocks were only visible at low tide. They were thought to be a fairly effective defence against invasion, though in fact there was little chance of the enemy appearing so far down Channel. Napoleon that summer was at Boulogne, standing in the wide bow window of his pavilion on the cliffs and surveying Dover through his telescope. Optimism was high in France. Victory medals had already been struck with 'Made in London' inscribed on them. As many as 175,000 men, it was computed, were ready for the Emperor's signal. And the Emperor in his black hat and grey coat was looking into the sky for a favourable wind.

By 1805, tension had increased. On the windy hilltop of the Trundle at Goodwood one of a chain of invasion beacons had been prepared. Nearly 6,000 volunteers were being enrolled in Sussex to assist the military. Sunday after Sunday at South Bersted, the Rev. John Phillips and his churchwardens signed on the able-bodied parishioners between 15 and 60 years of age and collected the local returns of horses, cattle, waggons and food required by the County Lieutenant. Now the vicar was busy with evacuation plans. On the sound of the alarm, women and children in carts and the herds of cattle were to be moved inland by pre-arranged routes. Picked bands of volunteers would block the lanes and harass the enemy. Regiments were marching down to the coast, and, for the first time for years, a new building appeared in Bognor. This was a small barracks, erected within about six weeks and made of prefabricated timber walls on brick footings with slate roofs. It had accommodation for officers and men, with some stabling and a hospital. It stood in the fields near Bognor Lodge and was dramatically described as a little outpost of brave men round which 'their brethren in arms would soon plant their standards should the enemy venture to appear.' (The site is now occupied by the police station in London Road. Some cottages opposite were formerly known as Barrack Cottages.)

By mid-September, Nelson had left the wooded seclusion of Hotham's former estate in Merton and had sailed from Portsmouth in the *Victory* to annihilate the French fleet. Towards midday on 21 October, off the gates of the Mediterranean, his men received the famous signal. But though the result of the decisive victory of Trafalgar brought sudden rejoicing and the end of the threat of invasion, Britain's war had in fact hardly begun. With winter came the chill news that Napoleon was now master of all Western Europe and his legions were nearing the territories of the Tsar.

During all this time, a young English doctor of 26 was being detained at Napoleon's pleasure at Verdun. His name was John Bunnell Davis and he came from Clare in Suffolk. His father, a surgeon at Thetford, had had him educated at Guy's and St Thomas's Hospitals; and, with the diploma just received, the young man set off on his first and very pleasant appointment. It was as medical adviser to a family travelling in France during the brief peace. When war broke out again and he found himself arrested, interrogated and confined along with hundreds of his compatriots, he decided to make the best of his enforced leisure. At Montpelier he was allowed to study and there he took his degree. When he was moved to Verdun, he filled his days by writing a book with a singularly gloomy title, *Observations on Precipitate Burial and the Diagnosis of Death*. He arranged for its publication and sent a copy, together with a petition for his release, to the Emperor's personal doctor, Corvisart. Corvisart was sufficiently moved by fellow feeling to put in a plea for him. In May 1806 Dr. Davis was released. He came thankfully home and decided that the best tonic after those years of exile would be some sea air. He went straight to Bognor.

There very little had been happening in the way of new developments. Legal restrictions had been removed but only now, at long last, were Colonel Scott and the others beginning to advertise the fact that they were prepared to lease or sell their precious land. There were now, as Hotham had hoped there would be, many permanent residents — in fact, most of the terraces and lodging houses had been divided or converted into family homes — and these newcomers had been disgruntled to see Worthing growing fast while the enterprise of local builders was baulked by the stonewall tactics of the Colonel from Kensington. Furthermore, visitors were on the increase every year and there was insufficient room for them. The Hotel was packed in the season and newly-arrived holidaymakers had to trudge across the field paths to Bersted or Felpham to see what the cottagers there had to offer in the way of expensive rooms. Prices in these villages had indeed bounded, as was disclosed by Mr. Grinder, landlord of the *Fox* at Felpham, to a writer on a walking tour in 1802. To the enquiry as to whether Felpham was benefiting from the rise of Bognor, he replied: 'Why, here are several cottages that might have been let heretofore for four or five pounds a year, that being now furbished up and whitewashed, with a little furniture and staircase carpets put into them, the Londoners and others that comes down in the summer now gives a guinea and a half or two guineas a week for one of them.' Mrs. Cowan, still in the town, must have been distressed at this collapse of her well-organised booking arrangements in the Hotham era.

Only about seven or eight houses had been built since Hotham's death, mostly in the area near the Hotel. In the road from the beach, George Field in 1804 had opened the first butcher's shop (now Swansea Lodge, West Street); and, a hundred yards west of the Hotel, Daniel Wonham — who later on, with his son, William Kimber Wonham, became the town's busiest builder — had erected three small houses facing the sea which were to grow into a modest crescent of popular lodging-houses called The Rock Gardens. Down on the beach, below the slight promontory on which stood the Hotel and the neighbouring library, the sea had never ceased its scouring, so a length of sea wall had been engineered: a curved defence as high as the little cliff and made of blocks of stone from the Bognor Rocks. Farther west along the beach there were signs that the hamlet of Aldwick was now more mindful of Hotham's ideals than Bognor itself, for a few pleasant retreats in their own grounds had sprung up on land purchased at the sale. The Earl of Newburgh, from Slindon, had built an Italianate villa called The Pavilion;

a certain Alderman Newnham had named his house Barn Rocks, after a smaller line of rocks that ran south-east from Aldwick shore; and Sir Thomas Brooke Pechell had succumbed to the current craze for the picturesque by erecting a pretty *cottage ornée* with an immense thatched roof and a rustic verandah inter-twined with honeysuckle and jasmine.

To Dr. John Davis, as he settled in, examined the seawater, enjoyed the lob-sters, tested the air, discussed local problems and rode round the neighbourhood on his horse, Bognor seemed the ideal rural bathing-resort in which a right-minded physician should spend his summers. It surprised him that it was still so small and, though he felt that Hotham had been right in not copying Brighton and Ramsgate and keeping the place retired and select, he felt that the time had surely come to introduce its charms to a wider audience. He set to work and in the following year, 1807, the sneers of George Carey were erased by the publication of the first serious book devoted wholly to Bognor. This was Dr. Davis's *Origin and Description of Bognor, or Hothamton; and an account of some adjacent villages*, published at 5s. by Samuel Tipper, Leadenhall Street, London. It was a neat 4 inch by 6 inch volume with 124 pages and a view showing the Hotel, the beach, three bathing-machines, 27 people and a dog.

Those who read the book gathered that Bognor was a quiet and healthy village, shunned by the gay and licentious because it was not immoral, and excellent for convalescence, retirement and sea-bathing. It was an inexpensive place in which to live and apparently somewhat altered in tone from Hotham's day, for 'there is no inducement whatever to be extravagant in dress, or to make inconvenient sacrifices for the purpose of keeping up an appearance of style'. For the visitors, rents were reasonable. You could take three rooms for two or three guineas a week, but generally the inhabitants preferred to rent you an entire house for four months for five or six guineas. Thus, families stayed on till late in the year and many ladies braved the whole winter at Bognor because of the agreeable society and inexpensive long-term accommodation.

The chief diversion was bathing, which was mixed and took place east of the Hotel. You took your dip at any time, for the bathing-machines, in which you changed and were drawn out into the sea by a horse, were ready from six o'clock in the morning. A bathing woman looked after the ladies. Immediately the tide went out, everyone went on to the smooth, firm sands to indulge in deep breath-ing, to walk with friends, to gallop for miles on horseback or to bowl along in a carriage. If you felt like having a warm sea-water bath for 3s. 6d., there were still the two baths attached to the library where Lady Newdigate had treated her knee. The water had to be pumped up into a cistern and then heated; and, as there was no rush of customers, you always had to warn the proprietor to light the fire in advance. While you waited, you sat in the hotel garden or went upstairs to the reading-room above the library and enjoyed the wide view of Selsey Bill or the Downs. By paying 10s. 6d. for the season, you were entitled to read the two daily papers, the Court Calendar, Army and Navy lists, directories and magazines. The library below did not offer much variety. Dr. Davis had seen little more than a carefully-guarded copy of Hay's new

History of Chichester and a few novels, so he advised you to take your books with you when you set off for your holiday.

Food was plentiful. Butcher's meat was sweet and good because of the fine grazing. Countrywomen came in regularly to visit all the houses with their poultry, butter, fruit and vegetables, whether you had asked them to do so or not. The Bognor lobsters, prawns and oysters were highly prized and any surplus was supplied to London markets.

It was the tranquillity of the resort that Dr. Davis particularly stressed. Bognor was 'an asylum remote from tumult and dissipation'; a place of simple pleasures, where there were a few dances at the Hotel, where you could walk to old Bersted and read the 'village poetry' on the tombstones, or look at Hayley's turret at Felpham or roam along the shore collecting shells and gaze wonderingly at Middleton's crumbling church. If you liked sailing, you could visit the Owers lightship nine miles out at sea or take a voyage round Selsey Bill to see the Fleet at Spithead. The only possible annoyance was the commotion at the annual fair on 6 July, which the countryfolk held rather thoughtlessly on the common near the Hotel.

Altogether, in Dr. Davis's opinion, there was no better spot on the coast of England for the twofold purpose of sea-bathing and retirement. But he did not overstate his case, despite his obvious affection for the village. Bognor had suffered from its founder's death and, for all the money he spent on it, it was still only mediocre in resources compared with similar small resorts. There was, indeed, a distinct doubt that it would ever rise in public estimation if the lethargy of the landowners persisted. But if more houses were built, then Bognor could 'rest assured of having an annual influx of visitors of the highest respectability, and of being able to vie with her contemporaries in splendor and renown'.

*   *   *

The doctor's little book was to have some effect. In fact, it was to start a trend with which Bognor was to be closely associated: the British family holiday. Bognor gradually became famous as the perfect holiday place for generations of children — and the two persons chiefly responsible for this happy change of fortune were young Dr. Davis himself and, appropriately enough, a jolly, boisterous little girl of eleven.

The care of children was to become increasingly important in Dr. Davis's career, so much so that it grew into a campaign. In the middle of what was nothing more than a simple guide to a tiny resort, he had suddenly spoken his mind on this subject. His message was: Send your delicate children to Bognor; set up a school for them by the sea where they will be invigorated. 'I beg leave to state,' he wrote, 'that disease is seldom seen amongst the persons who reside upon the seashore. The children, to my own knowledge, have the aspect of health, are blooming and vigorous.'

In July of the same year (1807) that the guidebook with this piece of authoritative advice was set in circulation, the other party mentioned, the child of 11, was staying at Warwick House in Worthing. She had been met at Findon, 4½ miles outside the town, by a troop of mounted Yeomanry who escorted her into the gaily decorated resort, with the carriages of cheering gentry and visitors joining the procession. Illuminations blazed at night, a salute was fired from Lord Craven's yacht offshore; and at the newly opened Theatre Royal the comedian Oxberry wished long life to the 'royal sweet blossom' in their midst. For the little girl was Princess Charlotte, only child of the Prince of Wales and Caroline of Brunswick. She was in the direct line of succession to the Throne.

Rock Buildings. Bognor

Fig. 7.   The Rock Buildings, a 19th-century engraving.

Chapter VII

THE LITTLE PRINCESS

CHARLOTTE had been born on 7 January 1796, and within a few months her parents had separated because, as the Prince put it, 'Nature has not made us suitable to each other'. He could not abide his wife's hoydenish personality. Caroline moved to Blackheath and was allowed to see her daughter at frequent intervals. Charlotte's early life, watched over by three governesses, a bishop and chaplain, was mostly spent either in a house adjacent to her father's luxurious palace, Carlton House in Pall Mall, or in the stiff atmosphere of Windsor.

Public opinion always remained in favour of Charlotte and her mother and considerably against the Prince, and for the whole of her life the young princess was the nation's idol, the 'daughter of the Isles'. The Prince purposely kept her away as much as possible from what he considered to be the undesirable influence of her mother, who had sided with his political enemies, and he left the responsibility of her upbringing largely to the Queen. He seemed jealous of his daughter's popularity as she grew older, was often harsh in his dealings with her — and, naturally, was regarded as a monster by the general public.

Princess Charlotte was a tomboy, a quick, vivacious, plump child with fluffy fair hair and big round eyes. She could never keep still and was always thirsting for rough amusement and practical jokes, delighting in giving her governesses the slip and even indulging in the pastime of ringing doorbells for fun. She chattered away on all sorts of topics and had an easy friendly way with grown-ups. Anybody interested her, whatever their rank or station, and she enjoyed associating herself with the people; but at the same time she could rapidly assume fire and dignity as a person of royal blood. Her hilarity and ebullient spirits, her awkward way of flopping about, all seemed far too modern for the Queen; but her small circle of friends, though often startled by her forthright behaviour, loved her for her good nature and perhaps admired the dutiful resignation she showed in the face of her dreary, cloistered life.

She first went in the sea at Southend when she was five and the decision as to which new seaside bathing-place she should now visit was, no doubt, influenced by the King and Queen who remembered how their own daughter Amelia had enjoyed her stay at Worthing. So, in July 1807, Charlotte saw the English Channel for the first time and won the gratitude of Worthing's traders for attracting such crowds. Her father entertained her at Brighton on his birthday on 12 August, taking her with him — he in a diamond-studded uniform, she in a white muslin frock and straw hat — to review a mile of troops on the Downs. Afterwards she met her beaming collection of royal uncles in the Royal Pavilion, where they had refreshments; and, after dancing on the lawn with one of them, the Duke of Clarence, she went back happily to Worthing at six o'clock with her chief governess, Lady de Clifford.

It is extremely unlikely that anyone in Worthing ever mentioned an inferior place like Bognor to the Princess. Therefore one can only assume either that, with her usual curiosity, she inveigled her governess into permitting an exploratory excursion along the coast that summer and discovered Bognor for herself — or that Dr. Davis's book, with its praise of the new resort, had reached Court circles. But whatever it was that prompted Charlotte to take her first brief look at Bognor, she obviously liked what she saw. For she personally decided in favour of it for the summer of 1808 and, finding that she preferred it to other resorts, she spent the next three seasons there. She and her governess stayed with Mrs. Wilsonn at the Dome House.

Freed from the restrictive atmosphere of the Court and the despairing glances of her grandmother, Charlotte reigned most happily over her tiny holiday kingdom. Here were no brassy bands and cavalry, only a few sick soldiers with eye-trouble back from the new campaign in Portugal and being treated at the barracks. Here, besides Mrs. Wilsonn, were friendly people, such as Lord Sudley (shortly to succeed to the earldom of Arran) who became her close friend; Mr. Binstead at the library, who found her what books he could; and, of course, Dr. Davis. Here at Bognor the 12-year-old who might one day be Queen could enjoy herself with the business of being just a child.

Her days at the Dome House were organised by Lady de Clifford into mornings and afternoons of exercise or visitings, with the evenings devoted to light studies. If tea was taken at home, she had the adventure of climbing up the little stairway into Hotham's rooftop dome, which became the royal tearoom, with a wonderful view over her rural domain. Sometimes she went out to tea. Lord Sudley and his wife took her across to Felpham on 26 August to see William Hayley. Tea at the Turret House was very convivial and Hayley inevitably commemorated the occasion in verse and was 'highly pleased by the graceful manners of his young extraordinary guest'.

As part of her education, it was then arranged that she should visit William Mason, Hayley's printer in East Street, Chichester. More verse was immediately supplied by Hayley, the idea being that Mason should circulate the district with these four lines on a tastefully embellished card:

> *Princess! who deign'st a Printer's task to view!*
> *This card of duty at your feet would fall*
> *Imprest with all the Blessings breathed on you.*
> *Vain wish! No volume could comprise them all.*

Regrettably, in the excitement of the royal visit, the typesetter made the mistake of substituting 'thy feet' for 'your feet' — and then failed to make good his blunder by neglecting to replace 'on you' by 'on thee' in the following line (which would have wrecked the rhyme, of course).

The botched verse was duly presented to the Princess as well as to the loyal citizens and Hayley felt that his reputation as a poet was at stake. But he realised that it was his own grammatical error that was largely to blame, for 'deign'st' should rightly have been followed by 'thy'; so he changed the first line to:

Princess! so kind a Printer's task to view!

and had all the cards reprinted. Lady Arran was asked to ensure that one of the corrected cards was included among the Princess's local souvenirs. Hayley's two letters to Mason in September 1808 regarding this bloomer were seriously comic:

> 'Why did you fail to inform me by post yesterday how the interesting scene of a royal visit to your press succeeded? Did you discover a mistake you made in printing the card by changing *your* into *thy*? — an unlucky mistake, as *you* follows so soon. Perhaps I led you into this little impropriety by the expression "who deign'st" — an expression that would, on that account, be better avoided as it seems to require *thy* to follow it. You had better reprint the card thus corrected, and if it is not too late I will request my friend Lady Sudley to exchange with the princess the second card for the first. Your feathers formed a proper and pleasing decoration.

The second letter came a few days later:

> 'I was glad to see your corrected card. My good friends, Lord and Lady Sudley, called here on Wednesday and assured me they were all highly satisfied by the visit to your press. I took the opportunity of requesting Lady S. to assist us in correcting our little inaccuracy by exchanging the first cards for corrected copies, which she kindly promised to do. I would advise you to call in every copy of the first impression that you delivered in Chichester, that none may appear to reproach us for our inaccuracy.'

The Princess bathed three or four times a week. She walked on the sands — looked 'very cool and stately' reported the *Morning Advertiser* — and was often accompanied by a young man who was spending his childhood at Felpham. He was eight-year-old Lord William Pitt Lennox, fourth son of the fourth and new Duke of Richmond, who in later life remembered his royal playmate's 'affability of manner, extreme beauty, cultivated mind and energetic spirit'. He witnessed an example of this energy when

> 'on one occasion a man-of-war anchored off Bognor, and nothing would satisfy Her Royal Highness but paying a visit to it. The captain's gig took the princess on board and, as she was approaching the vessel, a chair was about to be lowered into the boat on which she was to be hoisted on deck. Scorning, however, this mode of transit, she, to the delight of the sailors, though evidently to the surprise of the captain, scrambled up the side steps with an agility and grace that delighted all. A salute was fired and instead of stopping up her ears to deaden the noise, or exclaiming that she was awfully frightened as many a young lady of that period would have done, she stood on the quarter-deck braving the noise "of battle and the breeze", for the wind was blowing fresh from the west-south-west. I had, in company with my tutor, been taken off in a shore-boat and, when within hail, the captain asked me to come on board, the good-natured heir to the throne having expressed a wish to that effect.'

Those high spirits never left her and she made her governess suffer in the cause of good health by forcing her to clamber all along the shore in wild autumn winds, ostensibly to collect the hard black berries from the seaweed to thread into necklaces. In a particularly bumpy meadow belonging to Sir Edward

Troubridge (probably the area east of the Chapel House) she turned charioteer, driving her pony cart at full tilt, with Lady de Clifford shrieking at every jolt and the Princess artfully exclaiming: 'Nothing like exercise, my lady, nothing like exercise.'

In simple undistinguished clothes, usually a green coat and little straw hat, she explored the neighbourhood, apparently bursting to help people and entering into anyone's cottage to enquire after the occupant's welfare. It is easy to catch her personality from a memory of her 'often stepping forward to open the gate of a Bognor cottage to persons on horseback who knew not the rank of their smiling attendant'. Richardson, the baker, who had his premises on the corner of Mead Lane to the west of the Dome House, would hear her tripping along to him about the time when she knew his buns were ready. She would sit there in the shop, eating a bun and talking seriously with him about his business as if she were a partner in the firm.

Her impetuosity broke out occasionally. An officer stationed at Bognor got into debt, was arrested and, having no friends to go bail for him, was on the point of being taken to prison at Arundel. Charlotte erupted when she heard this. 'I'll be his bail!' she announced; and then, with her governess doubtless reminding her who she was, she quietened down, asked the amount and said almost regally: 'Take this to him. It is hard that he who has exposed his life in the field of battle should ever experience the rigours of a prison.'

There was one episode during her stay that showed her the fickle way of the world. She had managed to persuade the matronly Lady de Clifford to walk about two miles along the beach to Middleton. Suddenly they found something most exciting – pieces of fossil wood thickly encrusted with what looked like bright gold. This was actually the highly crystalline iron pyrites, spectacular to look at and often found on this part of the coast. Probing about, she found another embedded mass and two labourers were fetched to dig it out. The colourful treasure was taken home and Charlotte gave a manservant two guineas to pay the labourers for their trouble. Some unkind gossip then began to spread. When three weeks later the wife of one of the labourers was expecting a baby and Charlotte sent a messenger with a supply of linen for her, the woman took the royal gift and declared: 'Now let people say what they will. I'll maintain she is a princess and God bless her for ever!' 'What reason,' asked the surprised messenger, 'have the people to say that Her Royal Highness is not a princess?' The reply was revealing. 'They're saying,' said the woman, 'that it was mean and scandalous in her, when my husband and Tom Farlingham digged those queer things for her out of the bank by the seaside, that she did not give them as much as a sup of beer although they sweated manfully for her.' Charlotte was hurt, and a quick investigation soon nailed the guilty manservant who had kept the two guineas for himself. He was dismissed from her service.

In the season of 1809, the cheerful princess came back to Bognor. When she arrived on 26 July, it was clear that her health had improved. 'Looks better than I have ever seen her . . . and [has] more penetration than generally belongs to her age. This I know from having seen much of her last summer here,' wrote the

new Earl of Arran next day to Lord Liverpool. She now began to devote her time
to co-operating with Dr. Davis in looking after local children. She was doing, at
13, exactly what her mother had done at her age in Brunswick long ago — attending to the needs of cottagers' children. The grey ponies, given her by her father,
took her in the market cart along the lanes round Bognor. A page, dressed in
red, sat behind her. Every sick person was enquired after and, with great concern,
she took ailing children in charge and delivered them to the doctor.

Her hostess, Mrs. Wilsonn, had become very interested in this work and between
the three of them an idea grew which soon developed into the fulfilment of the
doctor's dream: a little school by the sea. By the autumn of 1810 the plan was
complete and on 25 October, to celebrate King George III's Jubilee, Mrs.
Wilsonn's Jubilee School for the education of poor children was established.
Naturally, Charlotte was the royal patroness and the day was a merry one. Even
Colonel Scott participated in the Jubilee celebrations, thought not in connection
with the children. He had been jerked into activity by the rude sea which was
eating up his expensive land. To save the meadows on which more of Bognor was
to be built, he had supervised the construction of 1,200 yards of wooden sea wall
which was named the Duke of Kent's Bulwark. The completion of the wall and
the King's Jubilee were jointly celebrated by the builders, known as the Bognor
Groiners, with a feast of roast mutton and local ale from Turner & Hardwick's
new brewery which had risen round a remarkably good well in Mead Lane. In
the evening the feast concluded with 'that decent hilarity which characterises
the labouring order of men in Bognor'.

With the end of Charlotte's régime by the sea, she said goodbye to her happy
childhood days. By 1811, she had become a figure of greater importance, for her
grandfather had become permanently insane and her father was now Regent. Her
last Bognor holiday began that year on 28 July 'after a very long and tiresome
journey, being 7 and a half hours in the carriage'. Writing to her closest friend
Mercer Elphinstone, the 23-year-old daughter of Lord Keith, she described how
she had done some of the packing herself: 'Figure to yourself my quizzical figure
puffing over a trunk this hot weather and called off almost the moment I am
knelt down and begun again. I must own it is *not a little* trying to my temper
and I *have got* as *far* as "Deuce take it!"' During that summer, the Regent paid
her a flying visit from Brighton and on his return spoke affectionately of her and
said he had been very happy at Bognor. At the beginning of September, she went
to spend a day with Mercer's family at Purbrook Park, on the north slope of
Portsdown Hill at the back of Portsmouth. That very day her much-hated sub-
governess, the bad-tempered Mrs. Udney, actually passed through the neighbourhood en route for Bognor, thinking the Princess would be there to receive her.
The atmosphere was frigid when Charlotte eventually returned in the evening to
find Mrs. Udney waiting and angry on the threshold of the Dome House. 'She is
now gone out to walk,' wrote the unabashed Charlotte on 6 September in a letter
of thanks to Mercer. 'Inhaling the pure air of the sea will, I hope, refresh her and
blow away some of the clowdes that are flying about her noddle.' By October
she was back in London. 'You have grown very fat and very much sunburnt,'

said her ramshackle old maternal grandmother, the Duchess of Brunswick, in an unintentional testimony to the benefits of a Bognor holiday.

As Charlotte advanced boldly into her 'teens, the Regent tried to bottle up her spirits and finally to marry her off to the Prince of Orange. The breaking of this engagement, her flight to her mother and her eventual sentence to a state of exile at Cranborne Lodge, Windsor Park, is an exciting tale of father versus daughter. Unknown to the Regent, she had already experienced the thrills of secret romance and was now deeply in love with Prince Augustus of Prussia. But this alliance was not to be, and her excursions in search of a husband brought both the pangs of a broken heart and misgivings about her previous love letters to others. Resilient as she was, her nerves wore thin and physicians fretted round her. Weymouth was her summer resort now, and life might have deteriorated completely had she not confessed her innocent 'past' to her father and found fresh hope in the person of an earlier admirer, a dark, prim, shrewd young soldier, Prince Leopold of Saxe-Coburg. The Regent approved, was reconciled to her and the romance finally flowered at a family gathering at Brighton, to which Leopold was invited in February 1815. The marriage took place the following year on 2 May at Carlton House. Britain rejoiced and wishfully looked ahead to an end to the Georges and their beloved Charlotte on the throne. At Bognor, where the villagers and visitors had been keeping the Jubilee School going by subscriptions, the children in white dresses sat down to a big dinner, the fishermen in alcoholic fervour fired guns all day and the inhabitants staggered to bed muttering 'God bless Princess Charlotte!'.

Inspired anew by their patroness's wedding, Mrs. Wilsonn and her supporters decided to build a new schoolhouse. The plans were submitted to Charlotte, now living in supreme contentment with her adored husband at Claremont, a mansion built by Lord Clive on the edge of Esher Common. Back came her approval, together with a handsome sum towards the building costs and an express command that her dear friend, the Earl of Arran, should lay the foundation stone for her. Doubtless everyone missed the presence of the Princess at the ceremony and just now she was especially close to their hearts because she was soon to have her first child. But his lordship carried the day well and gave a public breakfast afterwards. The site for the new Jubilee School was at the western end of the main street, in a meadow next door to Hotham's first terraces, and it filled up one more gap in the village. The inhabitants watched the Earl as he carefully placed a lead box under the foundation stone. In it were two 1817 shillings resting on a lead plaque, on which was inscribed 'On the 2nd of September 1817 the Rt. Honble. Earl of Arran laid the first Foundation-Stone of this Building, erected for the Jubilee School, for the Education and employment of 50 poor Girls, and instituted at Bognor the 25th October 1809 being the 50th anniversary of His Majesty George the Third's Accession to the Throne'. [The carver should, of course, have inscribed the year '1810'.]

With that done, Bognor and the rest of Britain waited. Charlotte, still full of fun, was being taken for little outings in a pony chaise round the gardens and grounds of Claremont with the attentive Leopold walking beside her. October

came and then November. At nine o'clock in the evening of 5 November, the
child, a boy, was born dead. And at 2.30 a.m. that night the tragedy completed
itself, for in restless agony Charlotte died.

The whole nation was crushed with shock and grief. In Bognor, where the
walls of the new school were rising by the highway, they could hardly realise
that the building would now be a memorial to the last public act in which their
princess had been involved. From Aldingbourne House, outside Bognor, the
Henry Howard who had been married in Hotham's chapel in 1801 left for London
to supervise the funeral and order the general mourning. He was deputising as
Earl Marshal for his Catholic brother, the 12th Duke of Norfolk. Late in the
evening of 19 November, escorted by Royal Horse Guards (one of whom was her
childhood friend, Lord William Pitt Lennox), Charlotte and her infant son were
buried at Windsor. The aftermath of the catastrophe gradually broke over the
people. Where, now, was there an heir who would bring to the throne the bloom
and promise of youth? Later on we shall find her, another little girl followed
Charlotte's royal footsteps to Bognor.

*   *   *

Having come thus far through the years, we must return to earlier days at the
seaside to meet new people; but before we go, it is interesting to see what
happened to Dr. Davis.

As well as those summer visits to Bognor, he had been busy graduating at
Edinburgh, gaining admission to the London College of Physicians and, in 1809,
attending the fever-ridden soldiers returning from the disastrous Walcheren
expedition. He settled in practice as senior physician to the London Dispensary,
but at the back of his mind he had another scheme to benefit children. He proposed the setting up of a separate dispensary where sick children could be taken
in and where the knowledge won from a special study of their illnesses could be
circulated with a view to reducing infant mortality. Influential support was
needed; but although Dr. Jenner and Sir Walter Farquhar promised help when he
had done the groundwork, they would not be the founders. Davis did not give
up. He gathered friends, such as Mr. Abernethy and Dr. Saunders, and appointed
himself as attendant physician. On 21 June 1816, the Universal Dispensary for
Sick Indigent Children opened at 5 St Andrew's Hill, Holborn. It was the first
of its kind and within a year there were 1,021 patients.

The object of the Dispensary was to give prompt medical aid to poor children
up to the age of twelve; and in they came, not only from adjacent London
parishes, but from Hampstead and Stepney and villages all round the capital.
One famous patron of the Dispensary was the Duke of Kent, father of Queen
Victoria; another, his brother, was that most progressive and liberal-minded of all
George III's sons, the Duke of Sussex, who always delightedly took up sides with
his niece Charlotte against her father.

Dr. Davis seems never to have rested from work. Books and papers continued
to flow under his name. By 1817, he had already conducted a *Cursory Inquiry*

into the Principal Causes of Mortality among Children. After the Dispensary had been running five years, he published some pieces of advice on looking after children. They are home truths nowadays. 'Ever bear in mind,' he wrote, 'that it is generally right to be sparing in the quantity of food. Overclothing, and clothing improperly, make a child tender and subject to cold.' Nor did he ever forget the seaside: 'Frequent bathing is conducive to cleanliness, it imparts vigour to the muscles and nerves and promotes alacrity and cheerfulness of mind.' He himself must have possessed all these assets, but he died young, aged 44, in 1824.

BOGNOR.

Fig. 8.   Peter de Wint's view of Bognor in 1820.

Chapter VIII

POST-WAR PERSONALITIES

THE EFFECT of Princess Charlotte's visits was to be gradual rather than immediate. In 1809, in contrast to the ebb and flow of battle that was taking place not too favourably in Portugal, at Bognor there was still little progress in the way of development.

One cannot say whether this was due to a particular canniness on the part of Colonel Scott in waiting until times grew better or whether (unlike Hotham) he was simply cautious. The resort, therefore, remained rural. When it was summer and you came in from a day's fishing, you still saw no town. Beaching your boat on the sand between the breakwaters, you looked up at nothing but fishing gear: prawn pots, lobster pots, herring nets drying in the sun and, above them on the low cliff, the line of huts built of elm slabbing and thatch, with thigh boots hanging on pegs, wooden buckets, bundles of withies, the skin of some big fish nailed up, coils of rope, ships' anchors, grapnels and a fine smell of tar on the breeze.

When you came up on to the cliff, there was the Hotel along to the left and the few new houses and shops spreading up the lane — the future West Street. More fishermen's huts dotted the shore westward towards Nyewood Lane and Aldwick. In the long meadows before you, the cows grazed or stood beneath the trees spreading down towards the sea. There was, of course, no promenade; just earth and clay crumbling down to the pebble beach below. Beyond the meadows, the two terraces and the few houses of the High Street-to-be faced towards the sea, all in a long line, with Hotham's larger mansions and the clock tower of the Chapel House clustered in the trees over to the north-east. Farther inland, across the fields, you could see South Bersted church and then the pastoral landscape rising gently to the line of the Downs. Everywhere windmills broke the landscape; the white smock mill on Felpham's shore was nearest. Halfway along the main street they had started building a few houses up a lane that ran north through cornfields towards Bersted. In years to come, this would be busy London Road, but first they were to call it Dorset Gardens. From the sea edge, where Clarence Road is now, a footpath went straight across the meadows to Bersted; it was the path the fishermen trod to church.

But in winter there would be those tempestuous seas, battering the sea wall by the Hotel, driving spray into Mr. Binstead's library, flattening the meadow grass, rocking the bare trees, flooding the brookland for miles and keeping the inhabitants as much out of sight as when they retreated from the visitors in summertime.

Amid all the uncertainties of this scattered village, only one thing was certain in 1809 for old Mrs. Jane Cowan. She made her will on 10 September and died four days later. Once more, a piece of Bognor went up for sale, but this time there was no commotion. The land, which had come to her after her employer's death, was barren from a speculator's point of view. It had a covenant, forbidding the erection of any further building on it under a penalty of £5,000 per acre. The covenant preserved the unbroken view of the sea from Hotham's two early terraces and was one of his lasting pieces of good planning, for the land was to become Waterloo Square, today an attractive public open space in the centre of the sea front. The sale by auction was arranged by Mrs. Cowan's executor, Richard Dally, at the Hotel on 31 October; and Hothampton Field, as it was then known, was sold to William Youatt for £650. For some undisclosed reason, Dally then persuaded the buyer to accept other land in lieu of the covenanted field, which he then re-sold for the same sum to Miss Dorothy Bringloe.

Dally, whose round and robust signature was to appear on every other Bognor deed and document for the next 30 years, came from Chichester and was a solicitor who, it may be recalled, numbered Hayley among his clients. An ancestor had been Mayor of Chichester in 1690 and Thomas Dally, presumably Richard's father, now ran a draper's shop in East Street. In 1794 he had issued a halfpenny tradesman's token which had Queen Elizabeth's face on one side, the Market Cross on the other and 'Payable at Dally's, Chichester' round the edge. He also issued a silver shilling and a sixpence in 1811.

When Richard Dally was in his twenties, he combined poetry with the law and became a contributor to *The County Mirror & Chichester Magazine*, published by Seagrave. Each month's issue contained something from his pen. During March and April 1796 he had roamed the range of mankind's progress in five sonnets: To Adversity, To Pity, To Resignation, To Sensibility, To Prosperity. Originally he practised in North Street and after 1804 his firm was listed as Fowler & Dally, Attornies. Then his practice spread to Bognor, together with his ambitions, and he became Lord of the Manor of Aldwick in 1810 and had his office in East Row. From there, his next steps took him to the powerful position of Clerk to Bognor's first Board of Town Commissioners in 1822 and to the Secretaryship of the first local Board of Health in 1831. He was, with his literary leanings, his interest in local antiquities, local eminence in law and his bankruptcy in 1826, just the right type of man to be in at the beginnings of Bognor's latest chapter.

For there were indications now that better times might be on the way. From the depths of gloom in 1810, when the Peninsular War seemed doomed, the spirit of the country began to rise with the glimmerings of victory in 1811. Though the King's insanity had thrust the Prince of Wales into an unpredictable rôle as Regent, the country could accept this domestic disaster if Wellington did not fail them abroad. Nor did he, and news began to spread from Portsmouth of distant successes in places with sinister-sounding Spanish names.

The old threat of coastal invasion was now past and Europe was beginning to ease itself very slowly from Napoleon's grip. Those reformers in Britain who had favoured parleying and surrendering to Napoleon now found themselves in a difficult situation. On one celebrated old radical, however, who stopped in

Bognor in August 1811 the seaside air seemed to have a mellowing effect. He was William Godwin, the 'philosophical representative of English radicalism', whose fame rests on his great work *Political Justice* (1793). Because when first issued it was a three-guinea book, the Government imagined it would do little harm, but it was to have quite a profound effect on the young thinkers of the time. Though poor, Godwin found himself accepted in Society and applauded by Wordsworth, Coleridge and other radicals who were enjoying the French Revolution from the security of England. His wife was Mary Wolstencroft, authoress of *Frankenstein*; and in 1816 Shelley married their daughter Mary.

Godwin that August was staying at Chichester and walked over to investigate Hayley. It was a hot day, and Hayley — who had been re-married two years before at the age of 64 to a girl of 28 — rushed him round the house at midday, up the ladder to the turret and through his library of treasures. He then dismissed his caller without a meal, saying that he never invited anybody to dinner. 'Damn him,' was Godwin's comment in a letter to his wife on 31 August, but he went on to recount how his happiness began when he left Hayley and walked across to Bognor:

> 'I inhaled the life-giving breezes of the sea, which I think, were I expiring with the imbecility of old age, would make me young again. Bognor is a sweet place. Why is it so? Merely because it is on the open beach of the sea and is scattered over with neat little houses for the opulent, built for the purposes of health and recreation.
>
> 'Sarah Pink, the generous landlady of the hotel, gave me that dinner which the frozen-hearted Hayley refused. She completed all her other kindnesses by refusing me a chaise to bring me back to Chichester last night, so that I was compelled to spend till eleven at night — the beautiful, serene, moonlight evening of one of the most beautiful days I ever saw — on the open shore, and only quitted the beach to repair to my bed.'

By the winter of 1812, the news of the grim white death of Napoleon's army in Russia was reaching England. In 1813, after a brief armistice, the Emperor found Europe rising against him and Wellington driving up from the south. When, in April 1814, Napoleon abdicated the crowns of France and Italy, people could hardly believe that the war was over after 21 years and that Louis XVIII, exiled in Buckinghamshire, was about to return to his throne. It was with almost equal disbelief that they learnt the following March that Napoleon was in Paris again, having escaped from Elba. But by the end of June, the battle of Waterloo had been fought, Napoleon had obliged with a second abdication and, as a visible prisoner on board H.M.S. *Bellerophon*, was on 24 July providing the biggest attraction off Torquay that an English watering-place had ever known.

During these last few years, Bognor had relied for its more detailed war news on the stories brought back by the soldiers being treated at the barracks, which had become an Invalid Depôt about 1806. Ophthalmia contracted in the Peninsular fighting was still the chief ailment and it was the possible risk of contagion that had alarmed the Royal doctors when Princess Charlotte took up residence a few hundred yards away in 1808.

Meanwhile, there were no additions to speak of in the aristocratic north-east quarter where the nobility lived, save for Lord Arran laying out a huge walled fruit garden and erecting a fashionable mock 'ruined castle', and the new owners of the Chapel House diverting the highway slightly to the east so that it did not run so close to their front door. These newcomers were the Rev. and Mrs. Thomas Smith who had purchased the estate from Troubridge's son.

The fate of Sir Thomas Troubridge was a tragic end to a worthy career. In 1805 he received a new appointment as Commander-in-Chief of the East Indies and sailed there in H.M.S. *Blenheim* with his son Edward aboard as lieutenant. But he found that his duties were to be shared with another commander, thereby dividing responsibility for the area. This seemed to him unwise in the event of war, so it was arranged that he should take command at the Cape instead. He left Madras for Cape Town on 12 January 1807, and was never seen again. The *Blenheim* went down in a cyclone off Madagascar.

Edward, who had distinguished himself in the East Indies by capturing enemy vessels, was now captain of the brig *Greyhound* and had the melancholy task of searching the ocean after the disappearance of his father's ship. He returned home to find himself a baronet at the age of about 20, owning a fine house at Bognor (occupied by his old aunt) and with some prize money in his pocket as a result of the enemy captures. And at Bognor he might have remained, had he not married a Scots girl in 1810 who pined to live nearer Edinburgh. He therefore put the Chapel House and its 40 acres up for auction on 30 July 1812, and the sale particulars informed potential buyers that:

> 'the views combine every feature of beauty that Land and Sea can present: the adjoining and distant hamlets, bounded by hills of vast extent and richness, a charming Champaign Country, waving to the Ocean's edge . . . a short distance from the Duke of Richmond's fox hounds.'

However, Edward's wife had to contain her impatience for another three years, for he was suddenly removed a considerable distance from the foxhounds by the outbreak of war with the United States. The Americans were objecting to the European blockade and he went back to sea to forget all about the Chapel House in the excitements of storming the Capitol. Somehow he survived the British defeat at New Orleans on 8 January 1815, distinguishing himself, like his father, with the land forces who lost 2,500 men killed, captured and wounded. Back home again, his second attempt to sell the estate was successful and, 11 days after the Battle of Waterloo, at a London auction on 29 June 1815, the property passed to the Smiths. In view of the national mood of jubilation, he probably got a very good price for it. Old Miss Troubridge, his aunt, stayed on by the sea, ending her days in a little house called The Cottage.

The few new buildings erected in recent years had not altered the local landscape to any great extent. Bognor, compared with the furious bricklaying at Worthing and Brighton, was still but a cluster of prim houses and shops standing in and entirely surrounded by fields, with the sea coming a little nearer with every winter storm. Dr. Davis had complained that 'not even the common exertions are made to bring Bognor into higher estimation or general notoriety' (presumably referring to the lack of exertions to obtain publicity for the resort) — and the Ordnance

Survey, which had published its first inch-to-the-mile map of West Sussex in 1813, was not much help, either. Though the map showed the cluster of Bognor Rocks offshore and the track leading inland from the coast to South Bersted (with 'Hotel' marked at its seaward end), the village itself was unnamed. Perhaps no one could decide whether to call it Bognor or Hothamton. Yet neighbouring villages like Pagham, Felpham, Middleton and even tiny Flansham were clearly indicated, while Chichester, Arundel and Worthing were accorded the dignity of capital letters.

In the meantime, Bognor — or Hothampton, as Pigot's *London and Provincial Directory* still termed it — was as ready as ever for the patronage of the health-seeking gentry. Those summer visits of Princess Charlotte had sustained the prestige of Hotham's town; and Dr. Davis's modest guide was edited and reprinted in 1814 with a far more magnificent title: *A New and Complete Guide to Bognor or Hothampton in the County of Sussex comprising an account of that beautiful watering place and its Neighbourhood with every particular necessary for the information of the stranger and traveller.* Binstead, who published it, was able to describe himself on the title page as 'Librarian to Her Royal Highness the Princess Charlotte of Wales'. The *Guide* was printed by Mason of Chichester, from whose East Street premises was issued Bognor's first town map for visitors on 17 September 1817, engraved by Thomas King on a single sheet, 11 inches by 9 inches, and sold for 6d.

It was not so much the leaders of Society who were now coming to Bognor, as in Hotham's time. It was, rather, a select clientèle of regulars, as well as friends or relatives of such residents as the Earl of Arran, Sir John Harington, the Smiths, the Wilsonns and Sir Thomas Brooke Pechell at Aldwick, who joined the Bognor house parties in summertime. Felpham, which had been a bathing-place long before Hotham created Bognor, also had its old and new friends, many of whom were discovering Bognor next door. From inland seats such as Goodwood, Arundel, Petworth and Cowdray, guests would come down to see Bognor for a diversion. And in circles such as the Law and the Church, the little resort's reputation for health and quiet was beginning to take effect. The Revivalists summed up Bognor perfectly in their *Evangelical Magazine* for June 1816:

> 'To the friends of religion who leave London in the summer months to enjoy the advantages of a country retreat, Bognor presents many attractions. To the most pleasant rural scenery, it unites the finest opportunities of sea-bathing and, while sufficiently frequented to afford ample society, it avoids the dissipations of places more generally resorted to.'

There was certainly no dissipation. As Dr. Davis had so firmly remarked: 'None but the votaries of pleasure, or the dissolute, would fear an abode like this . . . all those disgusting scenes, which are a just cause of complaint in bathing places where there are harbours for shipping, are never seen here'. But a little more provision of amiable amusement would have been preferred by at least one of the more discerning visitors who arrived for a six-week health cure in August 1816.

His name was John Campbell — 'plain John Campbell', as they called him in the courts — and he was to become Lord Chief Justice and Lord Chancellor. He came from Cupar in Fife and never achieved great distinction either as orator or writer, but he had an immense and driving faith in himself. Knowledgeable in mercantile law, he rose from struggling barrister to the heights of his profession and left his name on the many 'Campbell Acts' which he drafted, such as the Libel Act (1843) and the Obscene Publications Act (1857). With unsparing toil and amazing speed he wrote the still famous *Lives of the Lord Chancellors of England*. He died, aged 82, in 1861.

For a man of prodigious activity, it must have been galling to be slowed by ill health at the age of 37, and even more irksome to have to while away some dreary weeks at No. 4 Dorset Gardens. The chart of his convalescence is apparent in his letters from Bognor, commencing on 30 August:

> 'Dear Father,
>   . . . I have followed your advice by taking up my quarters by the seaside . . . The place is extremely quiet and secluded and for that reason I have preferred it . . . We are here without any public amusements, and in all respects very dull . . . Upon the whole, I like the solitude in which I have placed myself, but sometimes it is a little too much for me . . . The weather here is now delightful and I believe there is a prospect of an abundant harvest . . . '

On 15 September: 'I live here very quietly and very stupidly. The length of my stay is uncertain . . .' and on 23 September:

> 'Have you found out Bognor on the map? I am going to ride today to Selsey Bill, a promontory you will observe a little way south-east from Chichester. This is perhaps the finest climate in England, having the mildness of the western and the dryness of the east coast. We have a profusion of fine timber trees growing down to the water's edge. Were it not for the laziness of the people, the harvest might have been well over, but they go on as they usually do when the reaping begins in early August and there is no danger of bad weather. You seldom see above 3 reapers at work together in the same field and these are the ordinary servants of the farmer. The corn will not all be housed for a fortnight or 3 weeks. To do them justice, however, they begin to make stacks in the farmyard and some of them who have visited the Northern country have even reached the refinement of stathes. But I do not believe there are 3 threshing machines in Sussex and the process of winnowing is generally performed by the stream of air between 2 farm doors. We had 10 days of dry and sultry weather. At present it is again rather unsettled . . . '

On 27 September, his brother George received a cry of despair:

> 'This is the stupidest place on the face of the earth and affords no topic whatever for correspondence . . . Once more I look to the Woolsack!'

And when Campbell returned to his chambers in the Temple on 8 October, he sent George a summary of the holiday:

> 'Last night I returned from Bognor . . . I continue quite well — no return whatever of my complaint. The last fortnight I was at Bognor I bathed in the sea every morning without inconvenience. This seems to show there could be no harm in the chest . . . I never devoted myself to anything more completely than the acquisition of health during the six weeks I was at Bognor . . . I was in the open air by myself about 5 hours a day, and all the rest of the time I was in my solitary lodgings over a book.'

Dull though it was, Campbell's stay was enlivened for him by the occasional visitor, such as his family cousin, the Duke of Richmond, and by meetings with a fellow holidaymaker, the renowned Dr. Matthew Baillie (1761–1823). The doctor was a staunch advocate of the seaside, particularly as he knew the good effects it had on his own not very robust constitution. He had been physician to St George's Hospital, London, for 12 years, during which time he had published the illuminating results of his anatomical researches into the brain and the abdomen. Then, from his position as Physician Extraordinary to George III, he took charge, with two colleagues, of the health of Princess Charlotte. No doubt he headed the commission which pronounced Bognor suitable for her in 1808 and he might have sent her back to Sussex in 1814 had not Weymouth been chosen by the Regent. At the time of his own holiday at Bognor, he was in attendance on the Princess at Claremont and may well have taken back to her an eye-witness account of the Earl of Arran laying the foundation stone of her new Jubilee School in High Street.

Few doctors would have envied his lot the following year during those tragic hours of the Princess's confinement. Forbidden to attend the birth by the *accoucheur*, Sir Richard Croft, he remained on hand in another room, wondering and worrying about his young charge, and he was only summoned by the alarmed Croft when her agonies began after the baby's death. It was Baillie who saw the seriousness of her condition and realised the sadness of what was soon to happen. He sent warning to the Privy Council. Croft committed suicide three months later. Dr. Baillie is commemorated by a bust in Westminster Abbey; and Bognor, to which he returned again and again, used his name as a recommendation in town advertisements for at least twenty years after he was dead.

John Campbell did not say whether he met a fellow judge, Mr. Justice Abbott, who was also there in the summer of 1816, likewise suffering from ill health, and was to become a resident. Like Campbell, Charles Abbott shone at mercantile law, but he, too, was an indifferent speaker though respected for his good sense. He had just been appointed to the King's Bench and in 1818 became one of Campbell's predecessors as Lord Chief Justice. Bognor suited him, as it did Admiral Sir John Orde and other previous visitors who had decided to settle there, and his name as a donor of guineas began to appear yearly on the subscription list to the Bersted & Bognor National School which had been built next to South Bersted church. In 1827 Abbott rose to the peerage and the villagers were able to boast that Lord Tenterden was one of their patrons.

The private entertaining that went on in Bognor in these first few post-war years helped to maintain the tone of the place. Local government, such as it was, remained the responsibility of the South Bersted Vestry Committee, but to Lord Arran and the Smiths the resort owed the unexpected wonder of suddenly encountering a duke on the sands or a distinguished hero in the library. Both Mrs. Smith and his lordship had friendly connections with the Court, and one of the attractions of Bognor for Royalty and the high-born was that staying there was less like being in a town than residing on a private seaside estate with a few shops and houses scattered outside the gate.

Lord William Pitt Lennox, now 18, was one of the homecomers from the war. Goodwood House had been empty for a long time, as many of the Lennox family had been in Belgium. It was William's mother who gave the famous Brussels Ball on the eve of the battle of Waterloo and young Lennox used the same room afterwards to organise his own celebrations in the form of amateur theatricals. His father, the Duke, had ridden out on the morning of 18 June 1815 to shake hands with Wellington, the family's great friend. Two of William's brothers were serving soldiers: the eldest, the Earl of March, as aide-de-camp to the Hereditary Prince of Holland, and Lord George Lennox on Wellington's staff. William himself was one of Wellington's attachés and saw some of the battle, though an accident with a horse prevented him taking an active part. And now he was back again, staying with his eldest brother Charles, Earl of March, at Molecomb, the dower house built by the 3rd Duke of Richmond in a valley of Goodwood Park.

Both William and Charles were adventurous spirits. Their boyhood among the hunting fraternity at Goodwood had been somewhat lively, and one person who disapproved of their behaviour was a tall, thin, morose huntswoman, Henrietta Le Clerc, a natural daughter of the 3rd Duke by his housekeeper. She later became the wife of Major-General John Smith-Dorrien. Once she reported the boys for a prank and their tutor stopped them from going out riding. A suitable revenge was arrange. They poured coloured inks into each of her riding boots outside her bedroom door and the result was an enraged woman rushing about the house screaming and flourishing a red and a black stocking.

Charles, in April 1816, had married one of the loveliest girls of the age, Lady Caroline Paget, daughter of his comrade-in-arms, Lord Uxbridge; and when they became Duke and Duchess of Richmond a few years later, she sat for Lawrence's finest portrait, which can be seen today in the Blue Hall at Goodwood. On succeeding to the title, Charles's life as 5th Duke was largely occupied with the excitements of racing and the development of the Goodwood stud and race-course. William, on the other hand, sought the bright attractions of the social world and it was in search of the latest news and gossip that he rode down across the farmlands to Bognor one summer afternoon in 1817. He stabled his horse and strolled into Binstead's Library. There he found Miss Charlotte Binstead, who was then 'as pretty a girl as you would wish to meet on a summer's day'.

'Happy to see you, my lord,' said Miss Charlotte with the bewitching smile of the perfect saleswoman, and immediately set to work to relieve Lennox of 7s. 6d. for raffle tickets: a half-crown ticket for a lady's work-box and a five-shilling one for a book of pressed seaweed. In addition, she felt that he really ought to take home with him certain new delightful 'Trifles from Bognor'; and while William was unprotestingly purchasing nutmet-graters, pin-cushions and pen-wipers, she divulged what a gay week the resort was having:

'I hope you are coming to stay. We're quite full. We have His Royal Highness the Duke of Clarence, the FitzClarences' beautiful young ladies, Lord and Lady Ashbrook, Captains Samuel and George Pechell and others who are on a visit to Mrs. Smith. Then Lord Arran's house is full, and yesterday it was so fine that we might really call it a Bond Street day.'

While she chatted away, there was a loud, hearty laugh and someone entered the library with a party of friends just as William was paying for his pin-cushions and Miss Caroline was saying: 'Thank you, my lord. I hope Lord and Lady March are well.'

It was Mrs. Smith's distinguished party from the Chapel House (now renamed Bersted Lodge) who had arrived. They caught the word March as they entered, and Mrs. Smith and George Pechell, who had known Lennox when a boy, recognised him and came up to shake hands. As they did so, the bright, breezy, red and round-faced Duke of Clarence peered at the youngster. 'Who is it? I didn't catch the name.' 'Lord William Lennox.' 'Oh, I know,' said the sailor prince. 'Lately come home from Cambrai. On the Duke's staff. Present him to me.'

Lennox, probably dropping pen-wipers in confusion, was propelled forward and stood his ground well as the cheerful brother of the Prince Regent roared out a battery of questions: 'Where are you staying? Molecomb, en? How are Lord and Lady March? Handsome woman! Does he suffer from his wound? Good soldier! Have you joined your regiment — the Blues, I think? They used to be the poor King's delight. How's old Athorpe [Colonel Athorpe of the Blues]? Jolly as ever?'

The audience over, William was about to make his exit from the library when Mrs. Smith, after a word with the Duke, invited him to join her house party for a week at Bersted Lodge. 'I fear,' she said, 'that the only room I have vacant is a rather noisy one, near the clock.' His Royal Highness was still all ears. 'What's that? The Clock Room?' he boomed. 'His lordship will be sure to be called on time, which is not very usual with the young men of the present day. We shall see you at dinner? If you get under weigh at once, you will be able to get to Molecomb and back. We don't dine till seven.'

As it was then nearly 4 o'clock, Lennox obeyed this command like a battle order. He rode at top speed to Chichester, ordered a post-chaise to follow him up to Goodwood, galloped on ahead and was ready, dressed and with his things packed for the journey back to Bognor, before the chaise had even reached the door. The driver then set a cracking pace down to the sea and Lennox took his place among the waiting guests just before the Duke entered the drawing-room.

William, Duke of Clarence, later to succeed his brother as William IV, was, like most of the royal dukes, financially embarrassed. He lived at Bushey Park with his 10 FitzClarence children — the result of his 20 years' harmonious alliance with the actress Mrs. Jordan, who also helped to support him. When in 1811 he began to realise that there were only three people between him and the throne — the Regent, Princess Charlotte and the Duke of York — he dutifully discarded Mrs. Jordan and sought a wife, a search which landed him on his knees before a succession of heiresses in Ramsgate and Brighton with little success. But very soon after his return to Bushey Park from Bognor, the startling news of Charlotte's death was to jerk him once more out of retirement and into the frigid arms of Princess Adelaide of Saxe-Coburg-Meiningen, who had been selected for him by his mother. To this royal manoeuvre, by which he was expected to give Britain an heir, the Duke proved quite agreeable, provided the Government paid him

well; and in due course the salty-tongued, odd-mannered old sailor found himself
King — though without an heir apparent.

Mrs. Smith's houseparty went on for two weeks and William Lennox looked
back on it as one of the most delightful fortnights of his long life. Among the
pleasant diversions were Channel trips in a small cutter, organised by George
Pechell who probably steered the guests past Aldwick to show them his father's
mighty new sea defences, consisting of Bognor rock boulders piled up in front
of his cottage. George was to become M.P. for Brighton for 25 years and equerry
to Queen Adelaide, and to have a rare fossil mollusc, *pholas pechelle,* named
after him by his friend Dr. Dixon, the Sussex geologist.

Land excursions took the party to Goodwood, Arundel Castle, Slindon and
Chichester; and in the evenings they were musically entertained by Lady
Ashbrook, who lived at Beaumont Lodge (later Beaumont College), Old Windsor,
and was one of the most accomplished harpists of the day. All day long, the
Duke of Clarence remained the very soul of the party with his good-natured
affability, but it was when the ladies retired that he really came into his own.
That fruity maritime vocabulary, dreaded by the Royal Family on more formal
occasions, was given full rein as the candles burned low in Bersted Lodge and the
sandwiches and port circulated. 'Not one of the party could tell a better quarterdeck, gun-room or cockpit story,' said Lennox. 'The Duke recounted his adventures at sea, told us anecdotes of those he had served under, laughed, jested and
kept the company in a state of delight until the clock in the tower reminded His
Royal Highness that it was time to seek his "hammock", as he nautically
termed it.'

Hotham's clock was usually striking two when Lennox got to bed and he
himself had done a considerable amount of the talking, answering the Duke's
continual questions about Wellington and what had happened in Paris and
Brussels and at the Congress of Vienna. And when Mrs. Smith finally said good-
bye to her jovial royal guest, there was Lennox in the carriage with him. For the
Duke was taking him off to Lord Egremont's great house at Petworth, so that
Egremont, another personal friend of Wellington, could also hear all this interesting information at first hand.

During this period, one of the things to do when visiting Bognor was to elicit
an introduction to William Hayley, who was gradually abandoning his air of
secrecy at Felpham. He was becoming more mellow. His second wife had now left
him and the task of writing the *Lives* of Cowper and Romney was long over. His
one success, *The Triumphs of Temper,* was to be found in every dutiful girl's
library and it ran into 14 editions. So, in these last years of his life, he had grown
into an amiable invalid, suffering from kidney trouble, given to religious contemplation and, in between compiling his *Memoirs,* writing verse for his friends
and, of course, epitaphs for them as they departed.

Though no churchgoer, Hayley held his own services with servants and friends
in the Turret House. Sussex clergy, nevertheless, knew him well and they sang
his hymns, several of which were set to music by his friend Thomas Bennett,
organist of Chichester Cathedral, and published in the hymnal *Sacred Melodies.*

He also enjoyed writing simple hymns for children and wrote a special one for the children of Petworth school. Every now and then, he bestowed a benevolent glance at Felpham's Amicable Club, and in 1817 wrote a patriotic song for its members. Just as Blake had referred to the village's 'soft Female charms', so Hayley also praised his neighbours in this song. One verse ran:

> *Ye daughters of Britain! this island for you*
> *Was form'd, as a paradise, sweet to the view;*
> *And your charms, when display'd in their own native worth,*
> *Are the darlings of nature, the pride of the earth!*

Hayley's literary fame, together with the strange combination of an aura of sanctity and various ogre-like legends concerning his morals and treatment of his wives, naturally made him a figure of utter fascination for visitors; and so many people sought introductions that he blandly commented to his house-guest, the novelist Mrs. Opie: 'I think, my dear, you had better show me at a shilling a head'.

Soon after their arrival at Bersted Lodge in 1815, the Smiths, with the co-operation of Mrs. Opie, secured freedom of entry to the Turret and established very friendly relations with the ex-Hermit. With them on their visits to Felpham they brought members of their family, in particular the Earl and Countess of Mayo who had come to live with them at the Lodge. John Bourke, 4th Earl of Mayo, had been M.P. for Naas in County Kildare and had married Arabella Praed in 1792.

Others ushered into Hayley's rather commanding presence were Viscount Galway and his wife Cathleen Handfield, the Earl and Countess Paulett and the distinguished administrator and diplomat Sir John Malcolm. As a negotiator and fighter in the conquest of the East and the author of *The Political History of India*, Sir John made more impression than most callers and Hayley was 'greatly pleased and equally delighted with his gallantry as a soldier and his talents as a literary man'. Old and dear friends, too, came along to Felpham when visiting the Sussex coast. One of them in 1818 was the Rev. Henry Francis Cary, the skilled translator of Dante, who had been staying at Littlehampton and no doubt brought an account of his unexpected meeting with the poet Coleridge on the beach there.

Local concern increased as Hayley's health declined. One royal friend and visitor, the artistic Princess Elizabeth, a daughter of George III, did not forget him when she went to Germany in 1818 as wife of the Prince of Hesse-Homburg and sent over a recipe that she thought might be beneficial. His first apoplectic fit in September 1819 brought Mrs. Opie hurriedly back to Bognor and Mrs. Harriet Poole over from Lavant. So many people enquired at Binstead's Library after his health that a bulletin was sent there every morning.

It would be uncharitable, perhaps, to suggest that such expressions of concern were merely in accordance with what was regarded as the correct thing to do in polite society, and in any case the sudden appearance of the Prince Regent in Felpham at the end of August did seem to indicate that the health of the occupant of Turret House must be a matter of national concern. However, it turned out that it was not Hayley but another declining invalid who had drawn the Regent temporarily away from the Oriental splendours of his nearly-completed Brighton Pavilion. This was the Prince's boyhood tutor, Dr. Cyril Jackson, who had retired in 1809 to a house within a few yards of the Turret. Jackson's eminence as a scholar and his 26 years as a renowned Dean of Christ Church, Oxford, had led Hayley to seek the acquaintance of his new neighbour, but the Dean is popularly supposed to have remarked: 'Our books, Mr. Hayley, may frequently visit each other; ourselves never'. Another and kinder version of this exchange infers that the Dean was wise in the ways of village life and that his reply was 'I hope we shall be what is called good neighbours; that is, see as little of each other as possible'.

The Regent, in the 23 years since he had first been seen locally, was now a much steadier man and was at last nearing the end of his worst period of unpopularity. In five months' time he would be George IV. He reached his venerable tutor's bedside almost too late, and Richard Dally in sombre prose described the scene:

> 'The prince, taking him by the hand, affectionately addressed him. The latter, then almost in the arms of death, turned his eye on his Sovereign, but knew him not; the lamp of life was rapidly waning and soon afterwards went out. The prince turned aside and wept; and recalling to his mind the scenes and impressions of days gone by, he silently left the chamber of death, deeply regretting that his interview with the Mentor of his youth had been procrastinated to so late a period.'

It is said that respect for one's schoolmaster lasts all one's life. This, then, must be a memorable example, considering that Jackson, a stern disciplinarian, used to strike his royal pupils so forcibly on the forehead with a silver pencil that blood would flow.

Dr. Jackson died on 31 August 1819. Hayley rallied, recovered, subsided and finally expired from a stone in the bladder the following year. His friend the Rev. Robert Hardy, vicar of Yapton three miles away, came over to give him the Sacrament. Felpham's best-known resident died on 12 November 1820, asking God to 'forsake him not'. He was buried in Felpham church.

Visitors and residents missed him. And Hayley himself, no longer scanning the western landscape from his turret, missed the eruption of some more little houses, shops and chapels that disturbed the surface of Bognor's fields in the 1820s. Speculation had really begun.

Fig. 9. Dr. Jackson's Retreat, the Old Rectory at Felpham.

Chapter IX

THE BEGINNINGS OF
LOCAL GOVERNMENT

THE SHAPE of Bognor has often been described as 'irregular', meaning that it has no common centre on which principal streets converge, such as the Steyne at Brighton or the Old Town Hall (now demolished) at Worthing. This makes no difference to the mass of holidaymakers who, for some reason, tend to congregate east of the pier in whatever seaside resort they frequent; but on the inhabitants of Bognor the absence of a central stamping-ground, graced perhaps by a statue of Hotham, had, in the course of time, the effect of producing more local apathy than is customary in English towns.

When Hotham died in 1799 and ceased, as a chronicler put it, 'either to exercise or to be the object of worldly anxieties', the plan for the ultimate shape of Bognor ceased with him. Those who came after him forever tried to link his scattered creation together. In the 1820s, there was the highway (no more than a dusty lane) running parallel with the sea and separated from it by meadows. At the eastern end of this lane lay the aristocratic quarter and at the other end, three-quarters of a mile away where the lane turned down to the beach, were the original fishing huts with the Hotel by the sea and Hotham's first terraces a little way inland. Between the two colonies, there had long been a blank. Here Hotham might have laid out his *piazza* and fused the peerage with the fishermen in one lively concourse. However, he was now in what Dally called 'a better and happier world', and in the subsequent 20 years there was no strong mind to decide which way Bognor was to grow. Consequently, and quite naturally, the original fishing settlement began to spread in haphazard fashion up the path from the shore and then along the lane eastwards towards the bosky stronghold of the aristocracy.

That it was to grow and had a future remained unquestioned. Though life was changing in Britain, though commerce was being strangled by prohibitive duties, with taxation crushing the spirit of enterprise, ex-soldiers seeking any work anywhere and the fluctuating price of corn resulting either in dearer bread or a rush of imported corn to cause farming slumps, none of this was to stop visitors relaxing by the sea. The grim mutterings of social unrest, and the Government bobbing steadily along through troubled waters towards the cataracts of the Reform Bills, meant little when the sun shone on Bognor. Probably the visitors' nearest contact with high politics was the occasional sight of Hayley's early protegé, William Huskisson of the Board of Trade, who now lived in Hayley's old home at Eartham and was fighting to free Britain's ports to the commerce of the world.

There was no reason to doubt that people would ever tire of the sea, now that they had discovered it. It still had its mystery and its magic, despite the perplexity of George Carey who had witnessed the overwhelming popularity of the Sussex coast and remarked: 'There must be some other more prevailing inducements, arising from amenity of situation and salubrity of air, else we should not find every town and village along the coast more or less peopled during the summer with *dabblers* in salt water.' There were certainly other contributory inducements. The recuperative benefits of the seaside were still being lauded by the medical profession, both for holidaymakers in summer and for convalescents all the year round. And, above all, it was becoming more common for the growing middle classes to follow the steps of Royalty and the social set to their favourite watering-places.

Apart from Hotham's original grandiose buildings, Bognor now possessed many humbler dwellings, all the work of local men. Eight tracks, if not yet proper roads, now ran south across the meadows from the highway to the beach, and it was alongside them that the occasional small shop, house, cottage or mews took shape.

Joseph Pipson, for instance, who was the ostler and tapster at the Hotel, had built a pleasant bow-fronted house (now Portland House) in West Street in 1816. Colonel Scott had come to terms with James Tomsett, a South Bersted builder, and William Collins, a Bognor cordwainer, whereby they could develop West Street, the Steyne and the western end of High Street. The high-sounding name of The Steyne was borrowed from Brighton by both Worthing and Bognor, and in Bognor's case this approach to the sea, with a lawn down the middle, was intended from the beginning to be as dignified as any of Hotham's work. Mr. Collins in 1818 gave James Gardner permission to build Nos. 1 and 2 in the Steyne (at the south-east corner) and covenanted with him that he should build the houses in 'a neat and handsome manner with stucco front or rough cast and cover all roofs with slates and not permit the business of a butcher or blacksmith, or any noisome or offensive business, to be carried on thereon'.

William and James Smith of Bognor, painters and glaziers, already had their place in local affairs and when, on 30 March 1823, Colonel Scott sold them a site on the west side of the Steyne, they proved they had foresight. William sold part of the site to James in 1824 and by the following year James had built Bath House. He connected the premises by pipe to the sea and then launched into a long career as proprietor of several boarding-houses, with Bath House as the only public establishment in the town where one could get a cheap hot bath. James died in 1870.

The Wonhams were increasingly active and had filled up the west side of Waterloo Square with a row of smart, bow-fronted lodgings with canopies and balconies all trellised in the fashionable Chinese design. Daniel Wonham's Rock Crescent, by far the largest building on the shore, was proving a good proposition and he had issued his trade card, giving the prices of each of the 11 houses throughout the season. No. 9, for example, had 11 bedrooms, two parlours and a drawing room and could be rented weekly for four guineas in April, five in May,

£7 17s. 6d. in June, 11 guineas in July, August and September, £8 18s. 6d. in October, four guineas in November and £2 12s. 6d. from December to March.

Brickfields were being carved out of the meadows to the west, and up the slipway off West Street the fishermen brought their loads of limestone taken from the Rocks. So much of this stone was used for the early building material that Symons, who had erected many of the Martello towers in East Sussex during the war, said one day when he saw a boatload arrive: 'You may depend upon it, Neptune will fetch it back again'.

His words were proved. As buildings went up, the ever restless sea took others away. One devastating storm broke upon the town on 30 October 1820. Mr. Binstead, long reconciled to clouds of spray, found his whole library awash. The coach-houses behind the Hotel fell to the ground and the row of fishermen's huts by Waterloo Square was blown to pieces. Quarter-ton pieces of the rock barrier protecting the houses along Aldwick's shore were hurled into the air by the waves. Between Bognor and Felpham, the sea made its dreaded way over the beach and flooded the Brookland. Isaac Sadler, who lived in a house by the bridge over the rife, just managed to get his children out as the water reached his chin. Luckily, Lord Arran's house nearby remained dry and here the distressed families were received, fed and comforted.

That storm provided one more warning of possible disaster, and by the winter of 1822 Mr. Binstead had had enough. As a result of the encroaching sea, the Library was now on the edge of the cliff and it was hazardous to change your book there. With the materials of a sea-battered house that had been removed from Aldwick, Binstead had built his own private residence a little distance back from the sea, between the Hotel and Waterloo Square. This was called the Manor House. Thither in 1823 he removed the Library and resumed business with a much improved collection of romances, novels, travels and memoirs. The fancy articles presided over by the Misses Binstead included jewellery, colours, music, prints and Tunbridge ware. Next door, he built a billiard room and on the neat enclosed lawn before the house was a flagstaff and two small cannons, which delighted visitors as being truly marine and almost gave the impression that it was a government house or fort. Here, with only occasional spray to distract him, the proprietor enjoyed tending the intellectual needs of Bognor and entertaining visitors with reminiscences of his royal patrons, particularly the beloved and lamented Charlotte. (Part of the Royal Hotel now occupies the site of Binstead's second library.)

Before James Smith started opening up the Steyne, Daniel Wonham had already foreseen that this field could gain importance in view of the way in which present development was tending; and here in 1821 he built a large box-like chapel — it would be a chapel-of-ease in the South Bersted parish — with an interior gallery and sittings for 784 people. This venture was less speculative than it might seem, for in December of that year he sold the building for £1,650 to a trust which included the Rev. John Phillips, vicar of South Bersted, the Earl of Arran and Sir William Dick, Bt., of South Bersted. The site had cost him £100, but he presented the land as a gift. On 25 January 1822, Bognor welcomed the

Archbishop of Canterbury, Dr. Manners Sutton, to consecrate the chapel, which was dedicated to St John, and a month later the Rev. Frederick Gauntlett of Wadham College, Oxford, took charge as the first chaplain or perpetual curate.

The village was now becoming large enough to consider taking itself seriously. There had been hints that the gentry would like to establish some official administration, such as Worthing had been enjoying for the past 20 years. But to many of the native inhabitants, who had seen Hotham come and go and new faces scanning the lucrative possibilities of their quiet neighbourhood, the thought of officialdom was resented. Nevertheless on 15 May 1822, officialdom came into being, created by Act of Parliament. Sixteen of the gentry succeeded in being granted powers for the improvement of Bognor (which was a 'tithing' of South Bersted parish) and, as newly-appointed Commissioners, they met at the Hotel on the second Monday after the passing of the Act and thus began their reign as Improvers of what Hotham had begun.

*   *   *

Here we will leave them for a while and turn to the native inhabitants just mentioned. Since a seaside resort was being thrust upon them, it is as well to know what sort of people they were. To find out, we must turn to the Vestry Committee of South Bersted which was responsible for the 2,684 acres of the parish.

The Vestry, with its officers, resembled a parochial parliament representing the inhabitants. The little republic of South Bersted parish (which, of course, included Bognor) was administered by the Vicar, his two churchwardens, the Guardian of the Poor, the Overseer and the Assistant Overseer, the Parish Constable and deputies, and the two Waywardens or surveyors of the highway. Monthly meetings, attended by a dozen or so Committee members, took place either at the church or at the *White Horse* at South Bersted to discuss the work of the parish officers and the welfare of the inhabitants. The making of bye-laws, the regulation of common property, the upkeep of roads, drains and bridges, the levying and collecting of rates and the appointment and bonding of officers were among the Committee's many duties. In the slow course of time, the functions of the Vestry were to be taken over gradually by the Board of Commissioners which was itself to swell and grow into an Urban District Council. Meanwhile, however, the parish was still very far from being an urban district.

Though the Vicar was chairman of the Vestry Committee, it was the Guardian of the Poor who figured most prominently in the administration of the parish. William Woodroffe Phillips was the local Guardian for over 30 years, at a yearly salary which started at £30 in 1823, rose to £40 and by 1854 had dropped to £25 with the lessening of his duties. The post of Overseer was put out to tender. His duties included the collecting of rates for the church, the poor and the highway. The salary was £20 a year and the Overseer had to be bonded in surety of £300. The Parish Constable received £10 a year. All the officers were allowed expenses.

In 1822, there were 1,851 inhabitants of South Bersted parish, 93 of whom were 'on the parish' and regularly receiving poor relief. Mr. Phillips kept his accounts carefully and placed the poor into neat categories: Men receiving pay for children (35), Widows (17), Young Women infirm or afflicted (4), Old Men married and unable to work (4), Widowers (7), Widows with children (5), Legitimate Children (1), Women whose husbands are absent (5), Bastards (15).

He made changes in these categories as the years passed. In 1830 his list comprised: Men receiving pay for children, Old Widows, Young Widows with children, Orphans, Old Men, Women whose husbands are absent and Women receiving pay for bastards. In the hungry days of 1836, the first category was changed to 'Men receiving relief in bread'.

Monetary relief was adjusted from time to time by resolutions of the Committee. In the memorable 'mobbing winter' of 1830 when unemployed southern farmworkers were wrecking the new agricultural machines which, so they said, were depriving them of employment, the Committee fixed the scale of weekly relief at 2s. 6d. for boys from 10–13 years, 3s. 6d. from 13 to 16 years, 6s. for boys over 16, 8s. for an able-bodied man and wife, 9s. 6d. if he had a child and an extra 11d. for two children. Though rioting and fire-raising took place in nearby villages such as Walberton, Westhampnett and Bosham, the mob of labourers who gathered on 15 November 1830 were quite orderly and dispersed after a sympathetic hearing and promise of better wages.

Able-bodied unemployed were found work on the roads by the Overseer. A second form of relief was in kind, namely the provision of food, drink, fuel and clothing, as well as certain necessary services such as medical attention, hair-cutting and shaving. Temporary accommodation was found for the poor in the parish cottages at South Bersted and the destitute were taken in the carrier's cart over the Downs to the poorhouse at Sutton, near Petworth. South Bersted was one of a union of 13 West Sussex parishes which maintained this particular poorhouse and the parish was rated for its upkeep.

Those who received relief in kind were given a ticket which they presented to one of the tradesmen who had been fortunate enough to secure a contract with the Vestry to supply the local poor or the paupers in the workhouse. The Guardian entered into a firm contract with such tradesmen, as in this agreement which the baker had to sign on 5 January 1837:

> 'I, Joseph Bigwood Junr., do agree to supply the poor of this parish, having the Guardian's order, with the best wheaten flour at one shilling and twopence halfpenny per gallon. Bread in four-pound loaves of the quality of the best wheaten household at seven shillings and three pence per dozen loaves, for the term of one month to commence January 9th, 1837.'

The bills for supplying the poor came to the Guardian in a never-ending stream, mostly on small scraps of paper from traders who had not yet achieved the dignity of an engraved bill-head. Here are examples of these accounts. Henry Charlett, Bognor butcher, in July and August 1817 charged 4s. 8d. for 7¾ lbs. of mutton and 1s. 5d. for 2 lbs. of beef. Drink supplied on medical grounds resulted in such items from T. Bicknell's account as:

			£	s.	d.
1841.	Dec. 22 to	1 pint of Porter per day for 64 days for William Jelly		16	
	Feb. 20				
		½ pint of Porter for Sally English for 63 days		7	10½

Richard Roe, cobbler in Bognor High Street, repaired many poor children's shoes:

			£	s.	d.
1834.	Jan. 4	Master Panels gals shoes sold & mended		2	0
	Feb. 14	Harris boys New Half Boots		10	6
	,, ,,	Broadbridges gals new shoes		5	6

Richard Wonham, linen draper at Waterloo House in Waterloo Square, supplied clothes and materials:

			£	s.	d.
1829.	April 20	Round frock		6	0
	June 8	41 yds. Blue Print @ 10½d.	1	15	10½
	,, 25	Pr. Trousers		3	0
	July 11	27 yds. Calico @ 8d.		18	0
	,, ,,	1 doz. Girls slate worsted hose		14	11

and the girls of the Jubilee School in the High Street made and supplied other articles:

			£	s.	d.
1830.	March 1	Making the parish pall		4	0
		Making 1 gown for E. Hart		1	00
		,, 2 chemises			8
		,, 2 petticoats			6
		,, 2 aprons			2
		,, 1 handkerchief			½
		,, 1 pinafore			2
		,, 1 gown		1	0
		Cotton			1½
				7	8

Medical officers served the poor on a half-year arrangement. Their annual salary was £36 15s. 0d. and their cases often involved minor accidents peculiar to coastal villages, such as Surgeon George Peskett's fee of 7s. 6d. for

> Removing a Large Fish Hook from the Large joint of Thumb. Applications and Cure.
> Master Watkins.   Sept. 20, 1838

Vaccination came into their work to defeat the cholera and smallpox. Between 5 November 1840 and 20 January 1841 Mr. Peskett vaccinated 186 children in the parish at 2s. each. To the doctors also fell the work of certifying the insane poor and, with an order for committal to an asylum given by the Justices, the sick in mind were taken by the Guardian to the hospitals at Camberwell or Bethnal Green. A parishioner would go with them in case help was required on the journey and the expense of this assistance would appear grimly in his account book:

			s.	d.
1846.	Nov. 7	Mrs. Wheatland attending Emily Green and going with her to the asylum	10	0
		For washing strait waistcoat		4

The whole sad picture of one such journey in 1837 can be visualised from the Guardian's bill to the parish:

	£	s.	d.
Conveying Mrs. Stowe, a lunatic, to Bethlem Hospital			
Mrs. Swan [stable owner] . Fly to Chichester, and Man.		8	6
Coach hire to London. 3 persons	3	6	0
Belle Sauvage Inn, and servants	1	14	7
Coach & Turnpike gate to the Hospital		2	9
Dinner		1	10
Breakfast		1	8
Expenses on the road to and from London		3	3
Gave Mrs. Stowe to buy tea		3	0
Paid Mrs. Herman for her time		10	0
Coach hire Mrs. Herman from London		15	0
Coach hire myself	1	3	0
Time myself	1	0	0
	£9	9	7

The Guardian and his overseers, in administering the poor laws, had to bear certain points in mind: the expenses must be kept down, mercy and fair dealing should not be forgotten entirely and the undeserving should not take sly advantage of any benefits available.

Application for relief was constant and, as the depression grew between 1820 and 1830, so did the demand for assistance. Whereas in 1823, during the week commencing 29 November, there were only three men out of work, requiring 13s. assistance in all, in the same week in 1830, 56 men were unemployed, which cost the parish £18 5s. 11½d. The problem of providing work and preventing idleness and distress was very real and the Vestry minutes were always bristling with short and pointed resolutions to this end:

1827.	Oct. 8	That the potatoes at the parish cottages be given away to the poor who have no gardens.
1828.	Jan. 14	That William Raines be employed in working for the parish to the amount of the money lent him.
	April 7	That in future the men employed by the parish shall work from Lady Day to Michaelmas from half past six in the morning until five in the evening, and for the rest of the year from half past seven to half past four.
	Dec. 8	That Ricd. Blunden be allowed a pair of half boots when he is in constant work.
1829.	July 16	That Stephen Sparshott be sent to the poorhouse if not satisfied with his present allowance.
1830.	April 29	That no women are to be employed in weeding as long as there are any men out of employ.

continued on next page

continued from preceding page –

| 1832. | Sep. 27 | That if any persons receiving parochial relief are found drinking in Beerhouses after nine o'clock at night or during divine service their pay shall be stopped. |
| | May 30 | That paupers who keep dogs shall not be allowed relief. |

One means of preventing poverty, so that the person should not become a parish liability later on, was to apprentice poor children – preferably outside the parish, where after 40 days' residence they could gain a legal settlement in another parish. Girls would be apprenticed in the 'art and mystery of huswifery', which meant that they acted as servants. Local parishioners boarded girls as servants at 6d. a week. Boys were apprenticed to tradesmen or farmers and an agreement between the Guardian and the master would be drawn up, as in this instance of a local shoemaker's apprentice:

> The said Henry Bircher of the Parish of South Bersted does hereby agree to teach and instruct or cause to be taught and instructed the said John Herman in the art of a cord-wainer which he useth. And the said John Herman does hereby agree faithfully to serve in all lawful Business according to his Power, Wit and Ability, and honestly, orderly and obediently in all things demean himself towards the said Henry Bircher his master and all his. The term of this agreement to commence on 19th November, 1835, and to end on 31st December, 1837.

The boy was to receive one shilling a week for his final year.

Sometimes all did not go well with the boarding-out arrangements. In 1826 a mentally backward child named Ann Combe Richards, whose only relative was her grandmother, was taken in by Miss Sibley of Bognor who kept and clothed her for 3s. a week, provided by the parish. Later that year, Ann left the parish in the care of a Mrs. Parsons who entered into the usual agreement with the Guardian to look after her at 3s. a week. The child was taken first to Bath, where Mrs. Parsons had a home of her own, and then to Shalford in Surrey where the lady had employment at the *Sea Horse* inn. In August 1828 the Committee decided to stop its payments for Ann's upkeep. The child was now 12 and the Guardian apparently thought that she was either legally settled in Shalford or else she should go to an asylum. Mrs. Parsons, outraged at this treatment, wrote to Mr. Phillips:

> 'In what way can the child have gained a settlement here when she is not a Hired Servant? Therefore it is a thing impossible that she can belong to any Parish but Bersted ... It is not possible that a child so young can be free from a parish, at least in any way capable of getting her livelihood, whatever she may be at 14. I consider I have up to the present time done my duty by her in every respect and if they think proper to stop the allowances they must take her to their own care, which if they do they will I have no doubt find her much improved.'

Though Mrs. Parsons wrote again, thinking that if no money was forthcoming the Vestry would arrange for Ann to go to an asylum, she heard nothing for a year. On 5 September 1829 she wrote refusing to keep the child any longer unless the parish paid up. Furthermore, Ann wanted to go home 'and indeed she is so very anxious to come to Bognor that it is quite troublesome to persuade her to stop at all. Therefore I think it will be much the better way to let her come and no doubt but amongst her friends they may find her a little Service as she have done a part of my Household work for sum time and promises to make a good Sirvant and would be much better in a private House now than a Publick one till she have past a few more years. Therefore you will lett me know in the course of next week and I will convey her safe to Chichester, carriage free to you.'

And, as far as we know, Ann came back home to her parish.

The limited opportunities for work in the parish made it very necessary for the Guardian to assist men to obtain employment elsewhere. Those who wished to enter the Merchant Service were allowed £1 for clothes. Single men who joined the Navy were given money to get them to Portsmouth and £2 for clothes. The continual expense of supporting a poor child over the years sometimes resulted in a lump sum being found to put him into the Navy and out of the parish accounts for good. Young John Ballard, for example, had been a liability to the parish from 1827, when the parish first provided his clothes and Mrs. Halstead was allowed 1s. a week for boarding him. But by 1832 he was in the Navy and the parish paid the Portsmouth outfitter £6 9s. 11½d. to equip him for his new life, which required among other items that he should have 22 pearl buttons on his jacket at a cost of 1s. 6d. Many boys were taken by carrier to Chichester and then to Portsmouth by coach, there to be equipped by Mr. John Wheeler at 67 Broad Street, who in due course would send a receipt for such payments as 'the sume of Two Pounds, Eleven Shillings on the part of the Parish of Bersted for goods furnished to a Lad entered on Board H.M.S. Victory, 23rd. Jan. 1839.'

The desire of poor people to emigrate during the agricultural distress of the 1830s naturally found favour with the Vestry, except for the fact that large sums had to be provided for their journey expenses. Sometimes a benefactor appeared from among the gentry and contributed towards this expenditure. When on 23 May 1831 the Vestry voted a loan of £27 to George Grinder and Thomas Greenwood to take them out to America, it was a local landowner, Richard Hasler, who contributed £20 of it, leaving the Vestry to cover such other outlay as Mr. Wheeler's bill of £6 13s. 5d. for new clothes.

In the following year, on 16 March 1832, three families – James Goldring, wife and eight children: Henry Goldring, wife and five children; and Thomas Joyce, wife and seven children – applied for assistance to get to Canada. The Guardian put it to the Committee that, as these three families were anyway costing the parish an average of £80 a year, it would be worthwhile finding the necessary £250 required for their emigration. The Committee saw the sense of this and voted £80 assistance if the other £170 was contributed by the ratepayers. Mr. Charles Tipper, the Assistant Overseer, was requested to make the rounds of local property owners to see if they would be willing to contribute in equal proportions according to their Poor Rate assessment. This took 10 days; and on 26 March he reported to the Vestry that the ratepayers had agreed unanimously. A sub-committee of seven was appointed to facilitate the departure of the families, who were to meet them to discuss the first details at 11 o'clock the following morning. Meanwhile, Mr. Tipper was to go round the parish again and collect the £170.

Three days later, the Vestry paid £78 into the bank at Montreal so that the 26 emigrants could collect £3 each on arrival. During that week, Charles Briant, successor to Mr. Wonham as outfitter in Waterloo Square, was ordered to provide new clothes for the three families at £2 per family, but the clothing was to remain in the custody of the Guardian until the embarkation.

Another parishioner, Thomas Ewens, left for North America that August, receiving £2 10s. 0d. towards his expenses. Neighbouring parishes, such as Aldingbourne, were also sending families across the Atlantic. The Southertons, Bridgers and Whites went that year to New York. Two years later, in 1834, members of these families remaining in the district applied to South Bersted for assistance to enable them to follow their relatives overseas, but the Guardian refused to oblige 'foreigners' from across the parish boundary.

In 1835, with the reforms of the new Poor Law Act of 1834 in force, the Vestry held one or two meetings to consider 'the expediency of promoting emigration of certain paupers' to Canada, but as the Guardian had received only one application recently, and as many ratepayers now declined to contribute, the matter was dropped for the moment. In 1838, Henry Mitchell and his family received £20 6s. 6d. to help them on their way to Australia. Within a short time, however, the Vestry was relieved of the organising burden of this work by making use of the Petworth Emigration Committee under the leadership of the Rev. Thomas Sockett.

Thomas Sockett (1777–1859) is nowadays commemorated by a plaque in the sanctuary of Petworth church, of which he was rector. He was the son of a book-seller and stationer living at Weston Underwood in Buckinghamshire; and when William Hayley was visiting Cowper there in 1792, he met young Thomas, who assisted him in giving some of the famous electrical treatment to Cowper's ailing friend, Mrs. Unwin. Thomas asked Hayley for advice on getting a job as a clerk, whereupon he became yet another of Hayley's protegés and was taken back to Eartham to teach Tom Hayley arithmetic. Later, George Wyndham, eldest natural son of the Earl of Egremont, joined them for tutelage. Sockett's subsequent rise to fame took him first to Lord Sheffield's at Fletching, near Lewes, to help transcribe Gibbon's memoirs, then to Petworth as tutor to Egremont's children and finally in 1806 to Oxford, where he was ordained while still studying for his degree. By 1816 he had become rector of three livings, at North Scarle in Lincoln-shire, Duncton and Petworth, which gave him an income of £1,755.

He progressed as only a boy could who had once spent his pocket money on buying a Latin grammar and was noted for his love of the classics and quiet humanitarianism. As official Visitor to the Sutton poorhouse (with Richard Hasler of Bognor as his deputy), Thomas Sockett had more than a working knowledge of the Poor Law and eventually inaugurated his scheme for promoting emigration to Canada, first for Lord Egremont's tenants and then for others. 'It affords me great pleasure,' he wrote to Mr. Phillips, 'to be of any service either to ratepayers or paupers.'

Of the many similar emigration committees then formed to relieve over-population and the increasing poor rate, this one was the most successful. Poor

people of good character in Petworth parish, almost all of which was the property
of Lord Egremont, were first offered the chance to settle in Canada in 1832,
entirely at his lordship's expense. The offer also applied to other parishes where
he owned property. Posters were put up in the district, stating that 500 lbs. of
baggage would be allowed each emigrant on the ships *Lord Melville*, *England* and
Eveline. A list of suggested clothing and necessities was included and it was
stressed that they should take, 'if they have the happiness to possess one', a
witnessed testimonial to their worthiness as prospective settlers. Those three
ships carried 777 Sussex emigrants and landed them at York (now Toronto)
after a seven-week voyage.

In April 1845 Mr. Sockett arranged for three South Bersted parishioners to
go to Montreal — George Goldring, Thomas Luff and Charlotte Attrill. They were
fitted out by Petworth tradesmen down to razors, stationery, blankets and
counterpane, Bible, prayer-book and a marriage licence for Charlotte. They were
taken to Woking, then by train to London and in a van to the ship. Each passage
cost £4 5s. 0d., including emigrant tax, and the total cost to the parish was
£33 13s. 7½d.

*   *   *

The problems and expenses of dealing with vagrants were fortunately not heavy,
as Bognor was well south of the main coastal highway. As long as the wanderers
did not linger and the Parish Constable saw them off at the boundary, the
Guardian did not object to the occasional item in the Overseer's or Constable's
accounts, such as 'Gave a man 6d'. Innkeepers, also, were reimbursed for their
help, as in the case of the Irishman and his family who wandered into the *White
Horse* at South Bersted on 2 August 1832. His wife was pregnant. The parish
would not support them, so the man and his two children were sent on their way,
having been given 6s., and the wife was left behind at the inn for two months
to receive provisions and board during her lying-in, at the cost of £2 6s. 6d.
The odd wanderer usually found charity: 'George the traveller, bread and cheese
and beer, 6d.'; 'Italian boy ill at Witham's, 3s.'; 'Sailer man, 7 nights lodgings,
3s. 6d.' Now and then a little tragedy unfolds itself, as in the items of this
account presented to the Vestry by a parishioner, John Burrough:

		s.	d.
Sept. 13, 1832	Tea and Greuel for sick man		
	Firing and use of room	4	0
	Tea for the two wimmen [to nurse him]	1	4
	3 pints of beer for ditto		9
	2 gallons of beer for funeral	4	0
		10	1

If a person entered the parish, obtained work and then fell on bad times and
sought relief, the money-wasting complications of the Law of Settlement and

Removal came into play. If he was legally settled in another parish — either by
having once rented a £10 house or paid poor rate, served in office, been apprenticed, etc. — the Guardian tried to get him removed back to his own parish, once
the facts of his settlement elsewhere had been proved by a legal examination.
Occasionally the other parish refused to admit responsibility and contested the
case. Usually, however, the Justices gave the Order for Removal and the person
was taken by the Constable on a specified route to his own parish, at that parish's
expense. Similarly, any roving South Bersted parishioner who became a burden on
another parish would be examined and Mr. Phillips notified that he was to be
charged with the relief. The pauper would then be returned to him.

Whenever possible, legal expenses were avoided by exchange of letters and Mr.
Phillips would receive a polite note from the other parish, such as this one from
Mr. Cochrane, Assistant Overseer of the London parishes of St Giles and Blooms-
bury, on 5 March 1832:

> 'I beg to inform you that a person named Thomas Algar with his wife and two children
> have become chargeable to these parishes. The man states he lived in your parish as
> servant for 12 months with Mr. Ewins, that he received £9 per ann. and has left there 16
> years and has never been in service or gained any legal settlement since. He also states
> that his father was a parishioner of yours previous to his death and that he received relief
> from your parish. I trust under these Circumstances you will not put us to the unneces-
> sary expense of Removing them home.'

In the face of that evidence, it is possible that Mr. Phillips decided to admit
parish responsibility for the Algars. He kept records, however, and was not
inclined to swallow every tale of woe from afar. There was, for instance, the
case of Thomas Pannell, a South Bersted man living at 17 Nottingham Street,
Brighton, in 1826. He could not pay for his wife's funeral expenses and applied to
the vicar of St Nicholas' church for assistance. The Rev. H. M. Wagner was quite
prepared to waive his own fees for the burial service, but there were certain other
expenses that he thought South Bersted should pay. Mr. Phillips was firm in his
reply to the vicar:

> 'I am not aware that he belongs to this parish and if he did I should not relieve him till
> compelled by law because he has a house and cottage at Bognor which he lets, I believe,
> for something considerable. I hope you will not suffer yourself to be imposed on.'

Rather more dramatic was a request for reimbursement from Mr. Leney, Vestry
Clerk of Wrotham, Kent, for relief paid to a Bognor man in December 1829. This
man, James Ware, said he was a paperhanger. He had been found on the evening
of 19 December, between seven and eight o'clock, lying in the road half a mile
from Wrotham. His hands were tied behind him, and wire, such as poachers use,
was bound tightly round his neck. He told his rescuers that he was travelling
from Stowmarket, Suffolk, to Bognor where he had a child living with its
grandmother. Two men had set on him, robbed him of nearly £7 and a bundle
of clothes and left him as he was found. A collection was made for him at
Wrotham and he went on his way. But when Wrotham's parish officers applied
to Stowmarket, word came back that no such man was known there. Consequently

on 27 December, Wrotham enquired if Bognor had any knowledge of him. Mr. Phillips's reply revealed an intimate knowledge of his parishioners:

'Sir: The person mentioned in yours of the 27th instant is not known to me, and I think it very likely he is an impostor. There is a widow woman living at Bognor whose name is Ware, but the only son she has is in the Army and before he enlisted was a labourer. Her daughter about two years ago had an illegitimate child which is living with the grandmother. Perhaps the story has been framed from these circumstances. About the latter end of November a fellow absconded from here against whom a warrant was issued for felony. He was a great poacher and competent to practice such a deception. He is a tall, stout made man of swarthy complexion, dark hair and eyes, used to wear very large whiskers, his manner of walking deliberately and very heavy, by trade a Blacksmith, two fingers on his left hand grow together.'

Why husbands leave home is still an interesting subject today, but to the Guardian of the Poor it usually meant another drain on the parish purse, because the family immediately sought relief. A warrant for desertion would be issued in such cases. An example of the cost to the parish is provided by the case of Thomas Boniface. A warrant signed by William Blake's old Chichester enemy, John Peachey J.P., for the apprehension of Boniface 'who hath run away and deserted his wife and children' was issued on 27 October 1820. He had vanished on 23 July and by 3 December the expense of maintaining the family amounted to £14 12s. 4d.

Illegitimate children were a further parish burden. A bastardy warrant would be issued for the arrest of the father and sometimes the constable caught him at once, as in the case of William Wingate, a Pagham labourer, in 1817. The warrant was issued on 4 October. On 6 October the Constable thankfully scribbled on the document: 'Takin up and married'. If there was no wedding after the serving of the warrant, an affiliation order was made for 2s. 6d. a week, to be followed by another warrant if the father did not pay. Edward Pratt, a Brighton baker, was ordered to pay 2s. 6d. a week in 1829 for Charlotte Goldring's child and by 1833 the Constable was after him for £20 in arrears. Letters calculated to melt the Guardian's heart were often sent by fathers in arrears. Mary Richards had a son by James Groves Oldfield of Cosham, Hampshire, in 1819 and correspondence was still going on about the child in 1832. Oldfield, then in Portsea, owed £3, on payment of which he would be clear of all obligation, but he wrote that, being hounded by creditors, he would be forced to sell his watch first. If South Bersted would not believe his distress, he begged to refer the Committee to

'others of my creditors at this place to whom my real circumstances are most likely better known than to yourselves and who would no doubt sue me if they thought there was a prospect of obtaining anything from me. The principal of them are Mr. G. Baker, cheesemonger, Queen St., Portsea, and Mrs. Daubney, grocer, also of Queen St.'

War took husbands away from the parish and brought soldiers into it, and the consequences are illustrated in two bastardy warrants. One, on 12 July 1817, was for a South Bersted labourer, William Mitchell, regarding his child born to Mrs. Catharine Stevens, wife of Private John Stevens of the 52nd Foot Regiment, 'who has been abroad with such regiment in France for 2 years'. The other, on 7 February 1818, was for the apprehension of Private James Lacey of the 10th Regiment of Dragoons, whose child was born to Mary Ann Rayner of South Bersted. To serve this warrant, William Swan, the Constable, had to journey to Middlesex and have the warrant re-authorised by a Middlesex magistrate on 27 February. By 3 March, the Guardian was able to add a final note: 'Committed to Prison'.

If an illegitimate child belonged to a parishioner living elsewhere, naturally the Guardian of that parish sought payment from the home parish for its relief. Harriet Morrant of South Bersted had a daughter Eliza by Lieut. Bersteed of the 57th Foot in 1812. She went to live with Eliza in Whitchurch, Hampshire, and in 1817 the South Bersted Guardian was ordered by the Hampshire justices to appear at Overton to give any reason why Eliza should not be supported by South Bersted. There was no good reason, so Eliza was maintained by South Bersted for two years until she was seven. The payments were then stopped and, apparently with no husband, Harriet could not find enough for her daughter's keep. Two years later, on 23 November 1821, she wrote this pathetic letter from 15 Castle Street, Long Acre, London:

> 'I endeavoured to support her myself which I have done for more than two years, but now find it impossible to do so any longer without some assistance. I came up to town thinking to get a little support but cannot keep a hard place [permanent job] so must entreat you to take her under your care for a little time. I am desirous of giving as little trouble as possible and am exceedingly sorry to have thus to appeal for your relief, but necessity obliges me.'

Seldom did the gentry of the parish figure publicly in such matters as love-children, but when they did the Vestry took it as a matter of course and the upkeep of the child went into the account books in the usual way. Admiral Sir John Orde, referred to previously and now a Bognor resident, was maintaining Miss Mary Ann Stewart's boy at 5s. a week, which was collected from him in instalments by Mr. W. Hardwicke, the Overseer, at intervals varying from three months to six months. The boy was named John Stewart. On 19 February 1824 Sir John died in Bognor after a long illness, but he had made provision through his executors for the payments to continue. In 1825, Mary Stewart married and became Mrs. Alder, and the boy was sent away from Bognor to the care of her brother Charles Stewart, living at Bristol. For another five years the Guardian forwarded the half-yearly instalments to Bristol. Then, with John growing up and ready for the world, the question arose of what next to do with him. The parish solicitor, Mr. William Butt, was sent to London in October 1830 to discuss the matter with one of the executors, Sir Francis Ommanney, brother of Admiral Sir John Ommanney and M.P. for Barnstaple. A further meeting took place that week in Chichester between Sir Francis and the Overseer. It was decided that the boy should remain where he was until something could be done for him.

At one time, Sir John Orde had been M.P. for Yarmouth, Isle of Wight, so the following February the solicitor went to the island in the hope of finding some old friend who might take the boy as an apprentice. He drew blank and returned to Portsmouth to interview a Mr. Keet, who suggested that his brother at Newport might help. But the solicitor had no intention of spending another 4s. on the fare back to the island and wrote to Newport instead. The last instalment of the weekly five shillings went to Bristol in September 1831 and the ultimate fate of young John, like that of so many other parishioners, is unknown.

*   *   *

Here is a final case of Settlement and Removal, showing how the expenses regarding one bad Bognor woman ran through the Guardian's books for a period of 14 years.

In 1826 Lucy Parsons of Bognor, wife of Thomas Parsons, was receiving 2s. a week from the parish for her illegitimate child. By November 1829 the allowance had been reduced to 1s. 6d. and Parsons had disappeared and was a 'wanted' man. Two hundred notices for his arrest had been printed by Phillips of Petworth and both the Guardian and a Constable had been searching the Midhurst district for him, hiring a horse and gig at 12s. for the purpose. In March 1830 they caught him in Worthing and delivered him to the Chichester magistrates at a cost of 30s. Then they turned their attention to Lucy. Her rightful place of settlement was Sidlesham, four miles away. An Order was obtained and on 1 May she was carted off to Sidlesham for 1s. 6d.

A year later she was back in Bognor and pregnant. Thomas, meanwhile, was under sentence of transportation. Lucy was summonsed. The parish was not going to keep another of her illegitimate children. This was a matter for Mr. Rusbridger, Overseer of Sidlesham, so the Vestry voted that she be removed again to her own parish or else committed to prison, whichever the magistrates decided. Legal verification of Thomas being a convict was required and on 23 May the Guardian and Constable went to Portsmouth to obtain a certificate of his confinement aboard the *York* hulk. This journey cost £1 16s. 9d., which included one shilling for the boat to row them out to the dreaded hulks in the harbour containing the convicts.

Lucy seems to have stayed in Bognor, receiving 3s. 3d. relief for her first child who was occasionally boarded out. An appeal for shoes for the child was dismissed in May 1832, and on 5 April 1834 there was a warrant out for Lucy and an order for committal to the prison at Petworth. Mrs. Boiling, a parishioner, received 2s. for escorting her to prison. But by May Lucy was out again and inevitably returned to Bognor. Elizabeth Harris, who had been looking after the child, took her back to Sidlesham once more on another Order.

There Lucy presumably stayed for the time being, but in January 1839 she was back in Bognor receiving relief in the form of 2s. cash and 1s. 4½d. in bread. Once again the magistrates examined her but seem to have regarded her as beyond hope, for she was allowed to remain in Bognor and the last we hear of her is that Sidlesham is sending £1 4s. 0d. for her relief in 1840.

*   *   *

Violent crime did not often disturb the parish. The Constables upheld the law with the aid of their brightly-painted staves (price 5s.; painting 1s. 1d.) and the threat of detention in the stocks for misdemeanours. The stocks stood outside South Bersted church (today they can be seen in the vestry) and were occasionally repaired by order of the Head Constable. On 5 December 1836, 1½ days' work on them included the fitting of new ironwork, an oak plank, three padlocks and painting, at a cost of £1 5s. 3d. Typical offences were: 1829, Mr. Tipper, the schoolmaster, assaulted, reward offered; 1833, Messrs. Ragless, Firminer, Jay and Tomsett arrested for damage to Mr. Parson's house; 1832, Richard Allen summonsed for stealing grapes from the Overseer's garden. And, in the same way that many unfortunates today find the police a friend in need, so did a pauper girl of 17 in 1846. She received 8d. in relief from Constable Henry Puddick at 11 o'clock one Saturday night in April.

The Waywardens or Parish Surveyors had the chief responsibility for keeping the roads and bridges in repair. It was a thankless and unpaid office. Some of the labour was supposedly supplied by the parishioners, who had an obligatory duty to put in four days' maintenance a year on their local roads. The main source of labour, however, was the able-bodied unemployed, provided they did not object to hard work. The parish found the men their baskets for carrying stones and their pickaxes which were re-sharpened regularly at 4d. each by Charles Hammond, the South Bersted smith.

Being a seaside parish, the materials for making up the roads lay on the beach ready for the taking and the only expense was in the loading and cartage. Cartage was by yearly tender; Reuben Marner's renewed bid for 1837–8 was still the lowest out of seven tenders and he undertook to carry the pebbles at 6d. a ton for half a mile, 8½d. for one mile and 1s. 7d. for three miles. The loading of the material averaged 6d. a ton. The customary spot on the beach for loading was called The Lows, or Lowlands, at the east end of Bognor, where a lane ran down to the sea (today Gloucester Road). Vast quantities of shingle were taken from the shore and deposited where the surveyor needed it. In 1837, between 11 January and 7 March, Marner shifted 249 tons. Individuals who collected baskets of flints or boulders from the fields or shore were paid 1d. per basket. Sometimes they did this in teams, which was less fatiguing and more rewarding – as when Messrs. Ragless and Etherton received 11s. 8d. from the Overseer for 140 basketsful in January 1851.

The diversity of items and duties paid for by the parish officers either for the poor or for general maintenance is too wide to give in detail, but here are some miscellaneous examples. Sparrows, regarded as destructive vermin, were captured in nets by the parishioners and the heads produced as evidence. In 1826–7, churchwarden John Reed paid out for 6,372 sparrow heads at 3d. a dozen. One guinea was paid to W. Whittington at Easter 1842 for 'attendance in the gallery of the church to keep order for a year'. The census of 1841 cost £16 5s. 0d., made up of the fees to the Superintendent Registrar at Chichester, the local Registrar (Dr. George Peskett) and the enumerators of six parish districts, as well as the price of the registration bills. On 2 April 1835 the Vestry voted that

'George Parsons do have another leg'. The casual expenses of Osmond Heath, Assistant Overseer, on 7 May 1842 included: 'For burying human bones found on shore, 1s.' Not ungenerously, on 20 February 1836, the Vestry advanced £2 to 'John Hopkins to pay for boat'.

Lastly, a few particulars on rating. In the 1820–40 period just described, the Poor Rate was 1s. in the £, the Highway Rate 10d., with an occasional 6d. rate for the upkeep of the church. The chief items of expenditure under the Poor Rate in South Bersted parish were: payments to the poor on the permanent list, payments to the sick and other forms of relief and incidental expenses, payments to men out of work, the workhouse bill at Sutton, surgeon's salary and bills, salaries of the Guardian and Overseer, apprenticeship premiums for girls and boys, clothes for girls and boys in service, tradesmen's bills and emigration expenses.

For 1831, the Poor Rate expenditure reached a peak of £2,174 9s. 9½d. This was one of those bad years, as the amount brought in by the rate collectors was £2,390 15s. 1d. and left very little in hand. The men out of work had been paid £460 7s. 8d. for their labour on the roads. Emigration had cost £28 6s. 9d., the permanent poor £759 13s. 9d., the sick and other relief £431 15s. 4½d.; and the tradesmen's bills amounted to £154 11s. 1½d. Distress among poorer ratepayers had led to the magistrates allowing them their rates, so the parish that year also lost £112 of its income. Expenditure then declined to £1,019 in 1838, dropping to as little as £983 in 1848 and rising slowly to £1,282 in 1859–60.

This chapter has been, of necessity, full of small pence and poor people. The object has been not to give a full account of parochial government but to sketch the administrative background against which the prophecies and promises of a new seaside town were now to be tested.

Fig. 10.   Waterloo Square in the 1840s.

Chapter X

'DEAR LITTLE BOGNOR'

WHILE IN 1822 the newly-crowned George IV was engaged in a triumphal tour of his kingdom, many of Bognor's inhabitants were simmering with resentment against its 16 new rulers in whose hands — under the Act of 1822 appointing a Board of Commissioners for the Improvement of the Town of Bognor — the town's future now officially lay. They were the indispensable Earl of Arran; Sir John Harington; Charles Wilsonn of the Dome House; Richard Hasler: Richard Clark, a new speculator; Daniel Wonham, the lodging-house keeper; Richard Wonham, the draper; William Hardwicke, the brewer; Thomas Rusbridger, the coal merchant; John Price Gruggan, the banker; Dr. James Woodman; and Messrs. Thomas White, Frederick Temple, Charles Walkden, John Dennett — and, needless to say, Richard Dally, who was appointed Clerk to the Commissioners at £12 a year.

All Commissioners had to reside in Bognor or within eight miles of it and should either have an estate worth £1,500, occupy lands worth £80 a year or be in receipt of rents worth £60 a year. The Board was to meet every month either at the Hotel or the *New Inn*, and at least three members had to be present. Under the Act they were given authority to establish a market for the sale of meat, fish, vegetables and household articles, to improve and repair certain roads, to levy tolls on coal, culm and coke coming into the town by sea, to stop carts and carriages obstructing the roadways, to prevent nuisances on the footways, to provide a pound for straying cattle, to prevent undressing on the beach except from a bathing-machine and to lay down rules for issuing distress warrants.

The chief cause of resentment among local traders was the first item, the official establishment of the market. It was felt that the selling of cheaper goods there would be unfavourable to the few shops already established.

The market building itself was already there, having been erected in 1821 by Richard Clark on a site in the Steyne immediately alongside the almost-completed St John's Chapel. The building was open on all sides, with a slate roof supported by 12 classical stone columns. Angry bills of protest were printed and circulated; but there were also those in favour of the market, such as the public letter from Chichester, dated 21 September 1821 and addressed to 'the Inhabitants Bognor'. It was signed simply 'Visitor'. Very probably the writer was Richard Dally, angling for the town's legal business, for 'Visitor' informed the inhabitants that not only did he approve the lately abandoned scheme for a promenade — which would have 'put your Town on a level with other fashionable places of resort' — but he also thought so highly of the public value of a market that he had recommended to the proprietor that he should procure an Act of Parliament to regulate it. If the town agreed with him, then the writer of the letter urged them to persevere:

'Do not let any temporary wrath deter you. Your Town depends chiefly on casual Visitors, rich and respectable as your permanent inhabitants may be; and if you do not afford *them* facilities — if you do not administer to *their* comforts — if when they come to breathe your salubrious air they must pay a dearer price for the provisions of life than then can obtain them at other places; and if they cannot have a Promenade to while away their time, they will forsake you — they will come once, and only once, and you must then depend upon those who are settled amongst you for support.'

Such a warning may have helped to swing the battle in favour of the pro-market party. In any case, the 1822 Act gave the Commissioners authority to establish a market and their aim was eventually to buy it from Mr. Clark. In the meantime, the Commissioners were in charge of it. This meant renting out the stalls at 2s. a week, fixing a table of tolls on the goods sold there and applying some of this revenue to the provision of proper weights and other equipment, as well as keeping the building in repair and prohibiting hawkers in the streets of town. Joseph Harfield was appointed as Toll Collector at 3s. a week and Richard Dally agreed to be Receiver of the money, which ensured him a further annual salary of £7 16s. 0d.

The optimism of the Act was never borne out in practice. Dally's salary seems to have removed any possibility of profit or even of Mr. Clark ever receiving an instalment of the purchase money. In 1827 the Board decided to lease the tolls and rents to Charles Drover for £40, with William Peachey standing as security. But Peachey failed in trade and only the first quarter's instalment was paid; so for 1827–29 the auditors presented a statement which read: Receipts, £16 11s. 0½d., Expenses £16 2s. 5d. The following year was worse. Receipts were £4 10s. 1½d. and expenses £6 13s. 2½d. Some of the expense was incurred by the unwelcome appearance of Mr. Charles Tipper calling round for a contribution of £1 from the market for the Poor Rate and also the demand from Mr. Phillips for 3s. 6½d. highway tax. It was not until 1875 that the Board was finally able to purchase the premises for £500.

But in 1822 the question of buying the market had to take a minor place. The Commissioners' first problem was that the costs of the Parliamentary Act had to be covered before anything else, and they also had to find some money for the proposed roads. For these purposes, powers were given them to levy a duty of 1s. on every ton of coal, coke or culm brought to Bognor by sea. (Culm was poor-quality coal for lime-burning.) If the duty was not paid within a day, a fine of 20s. a ton would be imposed, and after three days the coal would be sold by auction. Duty had to be refunded on coal that was merely unloaded and taken out of the town to another district. If the Commissioners failed to refund, they themselves were fined £5 over and above the amount of the duty.

The levying of duty on coal was common practice along the Sussex coast. Collier brigs from Newcastle, Sunderland or Seaham, with flat bottoms which enabled them to run aground on the beach at low water, brought the cargo to Bognor. The coal was whisked out of the hold by baskets on ropes and discharged down a chute into carts. Strong light horses took the load up the beach, where it was dumped on a piece of ground which Thomas Rusbridger termed his 'coal wharf' — at the bottom of what is now Lennox Street, just east of the pier. The business was conducted at full speed from the moment the collier ceased to heave-to offshore and came in on low tide. There was just enough time allowed for the crew and local men to unload, refill with a ballast of sand, shingle or locally-gathered iron pyrites and then haul off into deep water with the help of an anchor laid out astern. Otherwise, there was always the danger of a storm springing up and damaging the ship while she lay aground. In the early days when the village was smaller, coal had come by cart from the quay at Chichester and was apparently just tipped into the road outside one's door. Hayley, writing from Felpham to his Chichester printer on 6 October 1809, asked for this message to be conveyed to his coal merchant: 'Our coal does not arrive as desired. Pray tell Mr. Trew I shall be much obliged to him if he will send them in sacks because in being dropt at our door they collect many stones that have a dangerous effect in the Fire.'

As in the case of Mr. Clark's market house, there was an over-optimistic estimate of the revenue to be expected from the coal trade. The Commissioners raised £508 on the credit of the estimated duty on incoming coal in order to start paying off the charges of the 1822 Act which had put them in office. However, no part of this borrowed money could be used for town improvements until the whole cost of the Act had been cleared. By 1825 the amount of coal duty was still so small that the Commissioners realised it was going to take years to pay for the Act, let alone improve the face of Bognor.

Consequently, they applied to the Government for permission to increase the coal duty to 2s. a ton. This was granted on 10 June 1825 in the form of 'An Act to amend an Act passed in 1822 and for making a road along the sea coast and for otherwise improving the said town or tything.' They were also permitted to use some of the coal duty to assist the town's general revenue as well as paying off old charges and were empowered to levy a new duty on sea-borne ashes, cinders and timber. So, with a duty now of 2s. on coal, 1s. on ashes and cinders and 1s. 6d. on every load or 50 cubic feet of timber, the depression temporarily lifted and the Commissioners voted themselves 5s. each for refreshments at their sittings. (These dues were repealed in 1917.) One obligation under the 1825 Act was that the town had to provide a mooring chain so that a ship would ride more safely at anchor. This expense was offset by charging the captain a mooring fee of 10s. a day. (It is said that an old mooring chain still lies under the sand and is exposed after a rough sea.) Over the next 30 years, the annual coal duty revenue increased slowly. In 1835, the tonnage landed was 1,686 and the duty was £168 12s. 0d.; in 1857, tonnage was 2,594 and the duty amounted to £259 8s. 6d.

*   *   *

The procuring of Acts of Parliament did not in any way sever the 'tything' of Bognor from the rest of the parish. It remained, in all its little straggling glory of houses, hotels and chapels, still part of South Bersted and subject to all the Vestry's demands for rates, tithes and taxes. Dally, also, had certain rights that Bognor had to respect, for Colonel Scott had sold him the Manor of Aldwick in 1810 and, as a minor landowner, he had ensured that the Acts did not infringe on any of his privileges as Lord of the Manor.

But the Acts did give a certain status to Bognor. It could now begin to organise itself. The Commissioners could elect their own Constable and appoint night-watchmen if necessary to guard the town. They could also engage their own dustman, or scavenger, with the words 'Scavenger's Cart' plainly painted in Roman lettering on the side of the cart. They could give permission for anybody to take away sand, shingle and chalk from the beach and, if the money was available, they now had the authority to make a road along the line of the coast from Felpham to Aldwick.

If dignity was to be judged by the possession of one's own Scavenger and Constable, then Bognor now had it. In fact, the time was ripe for development. By 1825, within three years of the original Act, the number of Commissioners had jumped from 16 to 33. Something was afoot. Mouth-watering plans of spectacular grandeur were brewing. The visitors, so long neglected from the point of view of accommodation and entertainment, were now to have all they required.

The topic which had set speculative minds alight was the railway. Though it was to be another 40 years before Bognor saw a train in the town, it seemed in those early days of the 1820s as if the line was almost there. James Rennie had been appointed Engineer to a new enterprise — the Surrey, Sussex and Hampshire Railroad Company — which with a capital of £750,000 had been launched to promote a railway linking London, Lewes, Brighton, Shoreham and Portsmouth. The final sentence of the Company's announcement fired Bognor's imagination. It referred to 'lateral branches therefrom to several Maritime Towns'.

The railroad, it was prophesied, would bring a multitude of visitors compared to the number at present transported by stage coach. Visitors at present arrived either by the *Comet* coach at the *New Inn* after a 10-hour journey from the *Ship Tavern* at Charing Cross or by a local carrier who collected them off the London coach at Chichester. But once they had arrived, the problems arising from the lack of accommodation still had to be solved.

So in January 1825, intoxicated by the mirage of a railway and golden hordes of visitors, and buoyed up by the substantial fact that half Bognor still consisted of empty fields waiting to be built on, the speculators floated the first of what was to prove a succession of over-ambitious development schemes. It was entitled The Bognor New Town Company, with an anticipated capital of £300,000 in £100 shares. The chairman was the Rt. Hon. John Calcraft, M.P. The directors numbered 12, among whom were Sir W. Champion de Crespigny, Bt., M.P., and Mr. George Isaac Call, head of a Bognor and Arundel banking firm which had a small office in the High Street. The architect was Mr. Samuel Beazley Jnr. and the solicitors were Messrs. Fox & Prideaux of Austin Friars.

It is quite likely that some impetus to the creation of this company was given by Lord William Pitt Lennox who, until his death in 1881, always seems to have regarded himself as a genial, if usually moneyless, promoter of Bognor. Since his last visit he had been overseas as aide-de-camp to his father who was Governor-General of Canada in 1818–19. While trying to separate a pet fox and a dog, his father was bitten and died o˝ hydrophobia near Montreal, and now William's brother Charles was the 5th Duke of Richmond. William himself had been a page at the Coronation in 1821 and was enjoying himself to the full in social and sporting circles, keeping up with his amateur theatricals, going to race-meetings and indulging in amiable eccentricities, such as competing in a 100-yards race at midnight in Hill Street, Mayfair. He was to have three wives and to turn to literature in the form of writing poor novels, but in the 1820s he was a carefree man-about-town. Among his particular friends was John Calcraft who kept open house in Hanover Square with talented daughters to entertain the famous — such as Lord Brougham — who gathered round his table. Doubtless, therefore, it was in Hanover Square that the Bognor New Town Company was first mooted, discussed and launched.

In order to·attract shareholders, the Directors in their prospectus decided to adopt an air of faint bewilderment that no one had hithero realised what a gold mine there was in the mere building of houses at Bognor. Omitting any mention of Hotham's original enterprise over 30 years earlier, they stressed the perfect bathing beach and the beauty of the inland walks and rides, 'unusual in the vicinity of the ocean'. Given such attractions,

> 'it has long been a subject of regret that Bognor possesses so little accommodation for anything beyond a mere temporary residence and of surprise that it has never been made an object of Building Speculation. The total inadequacy of the present Town was shown daily, and during the last and preceding seasons (1823 and 1824), in the disappointment of families who sought unsuccessfully for permanent accommodation.'

Their stated objects were to build houses for residents and visitors and to offer building sites, even advancing money to would-be builders on security of the finished houses. Architectural beauty was not to be ignored and the proposed houses would be unconnected except by light colonnades. Trees and shrubs suitable to the situation would be planted. By this foresight — and here Hotham would have agreed with them — they intended to avoid a closely-packed con-glomeration of dwellings that 'has taken from Brighton the chief benefit of a Marine Residence'. Thus the rural appearance of the town and neighbourhood, the *rus in urbe* which was Hotham's ideal, would be preserved.

There was no stampede to buy shares and, when a further public announcement was made on 24 April 1825, it was apparent that some reorganisation had quickly taken place. The company had appointed a new chairman, Vice-Admiral Sir Jahleel Brenton, Bt., who lived at Aldwick and was one of Bognor's new Com-missioners, and the enterprise was renamed The Bognor and Aldwick Improve-ment Company. The required capital was still £300,000, but the price of a share had dropped by half to £50. The main objects of the undertaking remained more or less the same, but the boldly confident approach was missing. One gathered that the idea now was to buy a large tract of land at Bognor from the chief proprietors — who were apparently agreeable to taking two-thirds of their price in company shares and required only a portion of the remainder to be paid down. The greater part of the land would be let on lease to various builders and it was also intended to erect private houses, lay out plantations and advance money on mortgage to builders as before.

Sir Jahleel, a new arrival in the neighbourhood, was another of those middle-aged naval heroes for whom a trim white residence on the shores of the Channel held a natural attraction and to whom the assumption of the rôle of a local Commissioner and improver was second nature. He had just returned from the post of Commissioner at the Cape of Good Hope, was married to his cousin Henrietta Brenton and was at the moment in command of the Royal Yacht. His family had emigrated to America early in the 17th century. He was born at Rhode Island, N.Y., on 22 August 1770, the son of a rear-admiral, and was sent to Britain for naval training when the War of Independence began. He was wounded in an action off Naples in 1810, at which his gallantry was rewarded by a knight-hood. In 1831 he was to become Lieut.-Governor of Greenwich Hospital and he died in 1844.

His main occupation was attending to the business side of his brother Edward's charitable and religious activities, which included an organisation for the relief of shipwrecked sailors, the Children's Friendly Society and the promotion of temperance. Edward Brenton was a Navy captain who retired on half-pay in 1813 and was now writing books about the Service. His latest, published in five volumes in 1823, was *A Naval History of Great Britain from 1783–1822*. His next, in 1828, was *The Life of John, Earl of St Vincent*. An account of the Children's Friendly Society came out in 1827 under the title of *The Bible and The Spade*.

Edward, also, was one of Bognor's Commissioners in 1825 and another was the gentleman with whom the Brenton brothers were residing at the Pavilion on the shore at Aldwick (later Craigweil House, destined a century later to play a signifi-cant rôle in the history of Bognor). This was the Rev. Henry Raikes (1782–1854), nephew of Robert Raikes, the well-known promoter of Sunday schools. Henry Raikes, a distinguished scholar and antiquarian, had explored the newly excavated temples in Greece in 1806 and was curate at Burnham, Buckingham-shire, before coming to Bognor in a similar capacity. He was the author of a very popular series of original sermons and in 1846 edited a ponderous *Life* of his old friend Sir Jahleel. He left Aldwick in 1828 to become examining chaplain to the Bishop of Chester and later chancellor of the diocese and an honorary canon of the cathedral. He maintained his antiquarian interests by arousing Chester to the merits of its past as President of the local archaeological society.

To be able to claim as new Commissioners three men of the calibre of Sir Jahleel and Edward Brenton and Henry Raikes showed that the Board was at least gaining a diversity of brain-power that might be usefully employed in assisting the great speculative ventures along the best possible channels when the time came. Lord Arran and Sir John Harington were still on the Board, so were the Wonhams and the Haslers. Sir Thomas Pechell and Sir Simon Clarke, both of Aldwick, had joined and so had the Rev. Edward Eedle, chairman of the South Bersted Vestry Committee.

All was ready. In London the Bognor and Aldwick Improvement Company waited for money, and continued to wait. Public interest was still lacking and on 26 June 1826 the resort's modest supply of accommodation for visitors was rendered even more inadequate by the sudden and complete destruction of the Hotel by fire. A General Election was pending at that time, one of the candidates for the two Chichester seats being Sir Geoffrey Webster. A party of Sir Geoffrey's supporters arranged to have lunch at the Hotel before going on to Chichester for a meeting. They arrived at Bognor by boat, but the lunch did not take place. In preparation for this important function the kitchen fire at the Hotel had received a special stoking-up, with the result that the chimney caught alight while the food was cooking.

The flames spread through the building, which was soon a total loss, and set light to 16 nearby cottages. They also threatened the Rock Buildings to the west (though it would be over a century and a half before they, too, disappeared from the scene) and the smoke could be seen as far away as Chichester, where someone on horseback rode to summon the firemen. Eventually, with the help of the Chichester fire engine coming at the gallop across seven miles of farmland, the fire was brought under control.

Thus perished Hotham's shrewdest piece of enterprise after a career of 37 years; and the Guardian of the Poor found himself with several homeless families on his hands. Their fellow-inhabitants had to rally to their relief with subscriptions.

The disaster did, however, act as a much-needed spur. The provision of accommodation for visitors was now no longer merely a dream for speculators but a matter that demanded immediate action. For the sake of Bognor's future prosperity, a new hotel had become an urgent necessity and within two years a small square inn had been built 300 yards up West Street from the ruins of the Hotel. Named the Claremont after the last home of Bognor's beloved Princess Charlotte, it was managed by Mrs. Mary Hewlins, 'whose assiduity and attention to those who honour this establishment with their company, combined with the arrangements of the establishment, justifiably entitle it to the appellation of *comfortable*, a term peculiarly English and always duly appreciated by the inhabitants of our favoured isle.' (*The Watering Places of Great Britain and Fashionable Directory*, 1831). Unfortunately, Bognor's visitors were destined to be deprived of the comforts of the Claremont when the hotel closed down in 1887 and the building, which still stands, became a shop.

Meanwhile, the inactivity of the Improvement Company had caused a group of businessmen to proceed with an independent scheme. They included Richard Clark, the Market owner; the banker George Call who, as we have noted, was one of the Improvement Company's directors; and a newcomer, Andrew Sarel from Enfield, who joined them when their plans for a development farther to the east along the sea front were already well advanced.

It is probable that Clark and Call were the only men who, in the early 1820s, could cast their hungry eyes along the salty grasslands by the sea and visualise, in practical detail, a promenade and hotels. In September 1823 they had commissioned Edward Fuller of East Street, Chichester, who did the surveying for everybody in the district, to draw them a plan of Bognor. Clark was the owner of one of the fields that ran to the water's edge, so he would have benefited by the schemes of the Improvement Company. With the Company still left at the post, he saw his opportunity vanishing. But now, with Sarel and Call to back him and with the Company's architect Samuel Beazley to design for him, the work on the New Crescent began.

The early print of Bognor most commonly seen nowadays shows Beazley's New Crescent, with boatloads of visitors being bumped about in a choppy sea in the foreground. It was a shallow crescent of four large and very commanding buildings, three storeys high, with parapets above which rose massive roofs peppered with dormer windows of attic bedrooms. The only decorative touch on the cement façades of these French-looking buildings consisted of three shallow recessed arches. The eastward block, which was an hotel, had extra grandeur in the form of a large central bow window extending to the second storey, with a balcony on top. At first it was simply named the Hotel, in imitation of Hotham's original, but later it assumed the title of the Royal Clarence in honour of the royal Duke who was now heir to the throne and had graced Bognor by his jovial presence.

The Crescent stood alone in the fields, facing the sea at the east end of the beach. Dally was immensely impressed by it. He had been compiling a *Guide* to Bognor, which was published in 1828, and he informed his readers that 'This costly and superb structure, and the Baths adjoining, have been lately erected at great expense for the accommodation of the public and are almost unequalled on the coast'.

It was Lord William Lennox again who had introduced his friend Beazley to the original Improvement Company; and if only the whole plan had been carried out on the lines of Beazley's crescent, Bognor might have become a coherent town with Hotham's gaps magnificently filled. For Beazley believed in the grand manner, though with less space around the houses than Hotham would have wished.

It was in 1817, when Lennox was 18, that they first met. Lennox became infatuated with the architect's friend Mrs. Robinson, who was a Drury Lane actress, and sent her a love letter and flowers, to which Beazley strongly and understandably objected. He called on his rival and violently demanded an apology, but was pacified by the young lord and the two became lasting friends.

Beazley was an explosively comic character and he has an important place in Bognor's story, being one of the two known architects from outside who contributed to the progress of the resort. So it is perhaps worth giving some details of his career. He was born in Parliament Street, Westminster, in 1786 and in the course of a whirlwind life managed to blend his two loves, playwriting and architecture, so successfully that his plays were often performed in theatres which he himself had designed. He wrote his first play when he was a 12-year-old schoolboy at Acton.

Beazley served as a volunteer in the Peninsular War and had his sense of humour severely tested when he woke up one day and found he was in the death-house at Lisbon, laid out for burial. As a theatre architect, little of his work survives, but in his time he rebuilt London's Royal Lyceum in 1816 and again in 1831 after a fire. In 1822 he remodelled Drury Lane Theatre, adding its long colonnade in 1831, and earlier he had rebuilt the Birmingham Royal, retaining the 18th-century façade. Other theatre work included designing Dublin's Theatre Royal in 1821, the Soho Theatre in 1834, St James's Theatre in 1836–37, the façade of the Adelphi in 1841 and theatres in Belgium and Brazil. He also made additions to the University of Bonn and was responsible for castles in Inverness-shire and Warwickshire, the *Lord Warden* Hotel and Pilot House at Dover and the New Town at Ashford, Kent. The most important work of his final years was for the South-Eastern Railway Company for whom he built London Bridge Station and stations on the North Kent line.

Amid this welter of turrets, station platforms and dress circles, he conducted his other life as a dramatist, turning out over a hundred comedies and light operas and making his biggest hit with his first piece to be staged, an operatic farce called *Five Hours at Brighton*, music by Horn, which was produced at the Lyceum on 26 August 1811. Harley, the Drury Lane comedian, included it in his summer seasons at the Worthing theatre in 1816 and 1820. How far Beazley's inspiration as a comic dramatist took him may be judged from the critic of *The Gentleman's Magazine* who reviewed one of his first nights at the Adelphi on 3 December 1829:

> 'An exhibit of great novelty was introduced. A new piece written by Mr. Beazley under the title of *The Elephant of Siam, or The Fire Fiend*, was brought forward for the purpose of introducing the sagacious female elephant from Siam. The principal aim of the spectacle, as the name signifies, is to show off to great advantage the tricks which the elephant can perform. At the conclusion of the piece, a cry was raised for "The Elephant" who made her obeisance to the audience in a very grateful manner.'

Another popular piece was his one-act opera *Is He Jealous?* with music by T. Welsh and produced at the English Opera House on 2 July 1816. Other productions included his comedies *Jealous on All Sides* (1818), *The Lottery Ticket*, *My Uncle*, *The Oxonians*, *The Roué* (1828), *The Divorce* and *Hints for Husbands* (1835). The source of one of his comic operas, *Philandering*, presented at Drury Lane in January 1824, was a picturesque French festival: the crowning with roses of the most virtuous girl of the most virtuous family in the Picardy village of Salency. The village elders choose the queen from three nominated girls on 8 June each year and she is led to church on the arm of the squire and crowned at the shrine of St Medard, who originated the pretty ceremony in the 5th century.

Little jokes and puns added to Sam Beazley's colourful reputation. Whenever he was confronted with anything new a pun sped forth as comment, and it would be interesting to know what he said when he first saw Bognor. Once when a lady told him she could not hear herself speak because of the rookery near her house, he observed: 'Madam, they have caws for conversation'.

A great joker is often an oddly serious person and Beazley displayed this side of his character when Lennox decided to put him into one of his novels, *Percy Hamilton* (1851), almost drawing him to life. 'You are as welcome,' he wrote to Lennox, 'as the flowers in May to all the jokes I have ever perpetrated, and I therefore confer on your Lordship the perpetual copyright of them. But pray never print my name, for somehow or other I have a most inveterate aversion to seeing my name in print, and my greatest living wish is that I may be forgotten the instant I am dead.'

It was not the first time he had been used as a character in a book. The light, airy, graceful Sam, with his easily-worn refinement, was a 'natural' for the witty pen of his close friend, the novelist Theodore Hook (1788-1841). Beazley is 'Daly' in Hook's *Gilbert Gurney*, which was the best of his stories and was, in effect, an autobiographical account of the racy London life of himself and his associates. In it he pictures Beazley: 'His conversation was full of droll conceits, mixed with a considerable degree of superior talent and the strongest evidence of general acquirements and accomplishments'. Hook was a notorious practical joker and, as 'Gilbert Gurney' in his book, he describes an episode when innumerable letters were sent inviting a huge collection of people to the home of the wealthy Mrs. Tottenham at 54 Berners Street — beginning with a dozen chimneysweeps at dawn and including jewellers, coalmen, drapers and doctors. The street was packed until midnight with people and carriages, while 'Gurney' and a friend enjoyed the chaos from a window opposite. Beazley could take credit for the entertainment for in the story 'Daly' is made to say: 'I am the man, I did it; for originality of thought and design, I *do* think that was perfect.'

The rush and tear of Beazley's life resulted in a heart complaint. 'He was always in a hurry,' said Lennox. 'A more active, energetic man was never known. If you met him in Regent Street, he would declare he was just come up from Hastings, was off to Theobald's — seat of Sir Henry Meux — but should be back for dinner. If you met him in Brighton, he would say he had just arrived and that he should have to proceed immediately to Bognor.'

The knowledge of his bad heart caused him to be prepared at any moment to fall down dead. Hook had even jotted down an epitaph for him:

> *Here lies Sam Beazley*
> *Who lived hard, and died easily.*

Beazley always carried a piece of paper on him, bearing his Soho Square address and a request that his body should be taken there. Apoplexy claimed him in the end — not in the street but, suitably enough, at a castle in Kent — on 12 October 1851, and he was buried near his London Bridge Station in the churchyard of Bermondsey old church.

*   *   *

At some later date the New Crescent, with the Clarence Hotel, became known as Colebrook Terrace and it would be pleasant if one could proceed with an account of Richard Clark going from success to success. Unfortunately, his name figures more prominently in the Constable's accounts under 'Summonses' than as an hotelier.

In engaging Beazley, opening up a brickfield and erecting the Crescent where it was, Clark had run contrary to the wishes of those who were visualising a much

in one small spot'. In other words, the horrors of creating another 'London-on-Sea' like Brighton were fully appreciated and a delayed tribute was being paid to the foresight of Hotham in scattering his early houses so far apart.

So while Clark and Beazley were busy down by the beach, his lordship in 1827 engaged the services of John Shaw the Younger to develop the area slightly to the north of them. Shaw, aged 25, was the pupil of his father, whom he had succeeded as architect and surveyor to Christ's Hospital in London. It was while he held this post that he undertook the work for Arran, one of his earliest commissions. He held very independent views on architecture. As he grew older, and every other building in England sprouted pinnacles in imitation of the popular Gothic style, he spurned fashion and chose to revive the style of Wren. In 1838 he built Holy Trinity church off Fetter Lane with round Italianate arches instead of pointed medieval ones. The same forgotten classical mannerisms were introduced into the Royal Naval School, New Cross, which he built in 1844. But his fine audacity in the face of the all-prevailing Gothic was best displayed when his chance came in 1856-59 to design Wellington College in Berkshire. An interesting comment on this work was made by the architect H. S. Goodhart-Rendel:

> 'I can think of no other British architect then alive who would have dared to plan a great public school as a symmetrical whole and to dress it in architectural clothes no older than the late 17th century. John Shaw did both and produced his masterpiece.' (*R.I.B.A. Journal*, 1949).

Shaw was an early member of the Royal Institute of British Architects, and from 1844-55 was one of the official referees of London building — duties now carried out by the Ministry of the Environment. He died on 9 July 1870, and was buried at Kensal Green.

The plan that he devised for Lord Arran at Bognor had considerable grace. It embodied a large oval lawn stretching north from the highway, with a 30-foot-wide private road running all round it and back into the highway through lodge gates. Round this green were to be built 13 handsome houses in large grounds. There was also to be a private entrance to the estate from the north. The idea was that Shaw should design and supervise the building of houses for any private persons wishing to lease a site on the estate and that he was to remain the referee on any matters concerning the appearance of the estate, such as the cutting down or trimming of trees.

So often does one have to record 'Now gone' after mentioning a period building in Bognor that it is quite a relief to be able to state that John Shaw's first excellent house of 1827, Sudley Lodge, is still standing. Taking its name from Arran's secondary title, it was marked No. 1 on his plan: a two-storey mansion of 17 rooms, with a bowed front, a low-pitched slate roof and deep eaves casting shadows over the plain white stucco. It stands well back from the High Street with a drive up to the door, a drive which also serves the other houses which have been built on the estate in recent years. Sudley Lodge has a simple refined air and it was to house, first of all, Richard Groom (Arran's solicitor from Henrietta Street, London) and subsequently such distinguished occupants as

Sir George Sitwell, Bt., great-grandfather to that brilliant literary trio, Sir Osbert, Edith and Sir Sacheverell; the second Viscount Bridport, a descendant of Nelson; and Mrs. Emily Ward, who founded the Norland Nursing Institution.

Mansion No. 2 on the plan, Sudley Cottage, was designed by Shaw for a Canadian lady, Mrs. Eliza Esdaile, who had been acquainted with the Duke of Kent when he was serving in Canada and whose little Gothic villa at the approach to Aldwick had succumbed to the sea. Sudley Cottage also had a touch of Gothic, in the pointed french windows along the ground floor, mingled with the characteristic stucco and bow front of the Regency style. Floors of oak, marble mantelpieces and an imposing oak staircase with fine balusters were features of the house, which stood in more spacious grounds than Sudley Lodge next door. After Mrs. Esdaile's death in 1831, the Cottage became the residence of General Isaac Gascoigne, who had just retired from Parliament after 40 years and was remembered for his strong support of all measures that might benefit the Army. Coleridge was generally supposed to be alluding to him in *The Devil's Thoughts* when he spoke of 'General . . .'s burning face'. In 1835, when the General decided to sell the Cottage, it had the distinction of being featured on the front page of *The Literary Times*, complete with a large illustration. After a few words about 'the pretty unique little villa', the article continues in praise of 'Bognor, or Hothampton, a very beautiful watering-place . . . projected by its enterprising proprietor, the late Sir Richard Hotham'. Hothamton Crescent is described as 'a princely habitation crowned by a handsome dome', from which — Bognor readers would have been surprised to learn — 'the Isle of Thanet is seen majestically rising from the ocean'.

That same year the property was bought by Christopher Teesdale; and from 1863 its most illustrious owner was Claude Bowes-Lyon, Earl of Strathmore and grandfather of Queen Elizabeth the Queen Mother. It was he who re-named the house 'The (Lyon's) Den', a joke nowadays perpetuated in Den Avenue which cuts into the former grounds.

These were the only two houses built. The rest of Arran's estate remained as fields, except for a spacious mews and a cottage which Shaw designed for Richard Groom and the Rev. John Pearson, Arran's steward. Sudley Mews, which was large enough to satisfy the constant grumbling from visitors about lack of stabling in watering-places (it accommodated a dozen coaches, 34 horses and the coachmen), was intended originally for the needs of the estate. Instead, it became a general stables for the use of the town.

*   *   *

To the list of doomed local enterprises in the 1820s one more should be added. This was conceived by a Bognor Commissioner — and, at this distance of time, it seems the wildest of them all. It was Nicholas Wilcox Cundy who in the autumn of 1824 fired the enthusiasm of his fellow Commissioners with his scheme for a Grand Imperial Ship Canal from Portsmouth to London. There was already a barge canal in the fields to the north of Bognor, running along the plain for 12 miles and connecting Chichester Harbour with the river Arun. It had been dug between 1818 and 1823. But Cundy's spectacular scheme – and he was an engineer of some standing – was for another canal 30 feet deep to take battle-ships and merchantmen from Spithead past Chichester to Arundel, up the Arun Valley to Pulborough and thence to Dorking, Leatherhead, Wandsworth, Kennington and into the Thames at Rotherhithe.

It was in the national interest, stated Cundy in his first report, that such a canal should be built. It would avoid the current navigational hazards between the Isle of Wight and the mouth of the Thames, whereby 110 ships were being lost annually. It would save our vessels from being captured in war, as in the case of the £3 million worth of ships lost to the French in the last conflict – and, Cundy added, 'what must we expect in the next French war from their Steam Privateers waiting off their coast?' Safety in war and a boon to trade were the advantages he stressed, giving this vivid pen-picture in his second report:

'When we contemplate the dangers and uncertainty (after making a twelve months' voyage to the Indies, laden with treasure) that we shall reach the port of London, this will relieve the merchant and the mariner's wife from thousands of fears and restless nights when they hear the raging gales, or think of the dangers of war. Their minds will be relieved by receiving their treasure into their warehouses and the mariners' safe return into the bosom of their families.'

Cundy estimated that the Ship Canal would cost £4 million and the annual revenue would be £500,000. A point in the report that appealed to his fellow-Commissioners at Bognor was that the effect of 'opening up a safe and easy communication by vessels to Bognor and other places of pleasurable resort on the Southern Coast would be highly beneficial'. Three of his colleagues – Sir Jahleel, Captain Brenton and Colonel John Camac – joined the provisional committee whose duty was to arouse interest among financiers and politicians; and Lord Arran put himself down as a member of the Board of the Canal when it came into operation.

Needless to say, the huge cost of the scheme did not stir the Government to show any interest at all and by 1828 Cundy was losing heart, especially as the sons of James Rennie stated that his plan was impracticable and a rival engineer accused him publicly of filching the whole idea in the first place. However, by the early 1830s he was again as busy as ever, revising the old canal plans and turning them into a survey for something equally adventurous: the proposed railway route from London to Brighton. But, even then, the Rennie brothers beat him to the coast.

* * *

The Claremont Hotel, the New Crescent and Shaw's two mansions and mews were not the sum total of the little speculative spurt of the late 1820s. The Steyne, West Street and High Street received some attention, but it was still possible to stand anywhere along the pebble-strewn tracks in the village and look between the scattered buildings to the open countryside beyond. However, the new decade brought an important piece of development when Andrew Sarel, who had assisted Clark and Beazley with the New Crescent, decided to erect his own hotel in Barn Field at the side of West Street. It was named the *Norfolk* in honour of Bognor's nearest duke and was later to be further dignified by the appellation 'Royal'. Heeding the warning of the noisy sea, which even now was washing the burnt-out ruins of Hotham's hotel close by, Sarel sited the building well back in the field with an intervening stretch of grassland as a protective buffer against the waves. This precaution had the effect, in later years, of providing the *Royal Norfolk*'s patrons with a spacious garden all to themselves in front of the hotel.

Another library appeared on the scene to give visitors and residents fresh hope and interest. Whether Robert Knapton, the owner, persuaded John Shaw to design it for him while the latter was in Bognor is not known, but the classic lines of the building have a completeness about them that suggests a trained hand. The library and bazaar, with its four Ionic pilasters and bow windows on the façade, was built on the opposite side of the High Street to Hotham's early terrace, East Row, and the architect did his best to match it in feeling and dignity. Though now serving other purposes, it survives today as one of the town's better examples of the Regency style.

Among the new library's first customers was Princess Augusta Sophia, one of the late King George III's 15 children. She was now a spinster of 61, and during the winter of 1829–30 was staying at Worthing, to which place she had been welcomed by the town band. Her appearance in Bognor was informal (her main object was to visit her close friend Lady Arran), but it was an indication that, however small the resort remained and however devoid of diversions, Royalty still held some regard for this spot on the coast where, according to the *Sussex Weekly Advertiser* (1 January 1828), 'the Ocean green tempts Rank and Taste to dwell'. Access to it from the coastal towns to the east was easier now that a new road had been made from Littlehampton to Felpham; and the crossing of the Arun at Littlehampton by the new ferry was a novelty that the lively Princess Augusta would certainly have enjoyed. A section of gravel road, wide enough to take a carriage and four, was laid on a barge. Ropes from each shore were connected to a windlass on the barge and two ferrymen wound the apparatus, transporting excited passengers and coaches across the river, a tranquil voyage of three to five minutes.

Princess Augusta was the favourite sister of George IV, whereas the member of the family whom he disliked most was his brother Prince Augustus, Duke of Sussex, who had created a certain commotion in Bognor in January 1823. We have met the Duke before as one of Dr. Davis's patrons and as the champion of Princess Charlotte against her father, a cause which accelerated the brothers' mutual antagonism. But it was his extreme Whiggish activities that upset both the Tories and the King. Not only did he attend meetings in support of Queen Caroline, but he travelled the country as a self-appointed link between the Royal Family and the common man — a triumphant progress made to the accompaniment of almost revolutionary cheering from the populace as they acclaimed 'Sussex, the friend of the people!'

The Duke, a massive man who enjoyed singing, married twice in contravention of the Royal Marriage Act and developed a morbid interest in his health, to the extent of protecting his head from draughts by wearing a black velvet skull-cap. It was this concern over his health that had led him to stay with Lord Arran at Bognor. Unfortunately recuperation by the sea was hindered by his poor eyesight, which once caused him to pour down his throat a powerful embrocation intended for rubbing on his asthmatical chest. 'A quantity of warm water relieved him from the perilous dose, the mistake being immediately discovered', reported the London *Observer* in announcing the near-disaster to the nation.

His health was not the only reason that brought the Duke to the seaside. There was also Lord Arran's half-sister, Cecilia, in whom he was more than usually interested. He had separated from his first wife, Lady Augusta Murray, in 1801 and now his devotion was centred on Lady Cecilia, whose late husband, Sir George Buggin, had been a power in the City. As his first wife was still alive, the Duke had to bow to convention and wait until her death in 1830 before thrusting his vast corpulent charms on Lady Cecilia. Under the Royal Marriage Act both his marriages were regarded as invalid, but in 1840 his union with Lady Cecilia was officially recognised and she was created Duchess of Inverness.

But of all the Royal personages who were to be seen strolling on the sands, watching the fishing boats or visiting the few shops of the growing Bognor in this decade, the most fascinating to the inhabitants was once again a small girl. It seemed to them almost as if their beloved Princess Charlotte was enchanting them all over again. The good looks, the high spirits, the juvenile air of authority, even the straw bonnet; all were there once more. The illusion was curiously complete in everything but name, for that of the newcomer was Alexandrina Victoria.

Possibly the strangest thing about her, as she roamed the quiet shore as Charlotte had done some fifteen years before, was that she was only in existence because Charlotte was dead. That calamity in 1817 not only removed the future heir to the throne but completely altered the lives of the royal princes. A new future heir had to be provided by one or other of them, as their natural children were unacceptable. Happy domestic liaisons were broken up as the princes sought suitable royal brides. Prince Edward, Duke of Kent, hurriedly bade farewell to his French-born mistress Julie St Laurent in 1818 and married Mary Louisa, the 32-year-old sister of Prince Leopold of Saxe-Coburg. The following year he found himself stranded penniless on the Continent with his pregnant bride. Despite desperate pleas to his royal relations for money to allow the child to be born on British soil, he was refused help. The Regent regarded this rush of his brothers into matrimony as most unseemly. It was the Duke's trustee, William Allen, the Quaker philanthropist and co-founder of the firm of Allen & Hanbury, who came to his assistance. Funds arrived at Frankfurt and the Duke hired a coach and drove it himself to the Channel port to ensure every care to his wife. On 24 May 1819 Princess Victoria was born at Kensington Palace.

She came into the world as a poor relation. Debts followed her father to his end, which occurred in a villa at Sidmouth in 1820. But she had a mother fierce in the knowledge of her child's great destiny and determined to preserve her from

the contamination of the Court. Furthermore, in Prince Leopold she had a
devoted uncle who could advise, even as he had advised his own Charlotte, on the
duties of monarchy.

In contrast, her British uncle, George IV, took little notice of her; but when
she was about six there came the famous first visit to Windsor. Victoria herself
described in later life how the large and gouty King took her hand, saying 'Give
me your little paw', and how he drove her in a phaeton round Virginia Water,
having said 'Pop her in', whereupon she had been lifted up into the carriage
and placed between him and his sister Mary, the Duchess of Gloucester.

Aunt Mary was one of the many relatives who gradually became fond of the
child. It was probably she who suggested Bognor as a suitable place for the
summer, for she had often stayed there with her friend Mrs. Smith at Bersted
Lodge (the Chapel House) and could personally recommend the little resort.
In the summer of 1821 the widowed Duchess of Kent took her two-year-old
daughter for a three-month stay at Bognor Lodge, and in subsequent years
Victoria made further acquaintance with the sea at Sidmouth, Brighton and
Ramsgate. In 1826 she enjoyed a pleasant holiday at Tunbridge Wells — pleasant,
that is, for a child whose parents had little money, whose life was severely simple
and strict and whose governess came with her to the sea in summertime and gave
her lessons in her bedroom.

It seems that Victoria returned to Bognor not once but 'for several summers',
which would have been between 1825 and 1830. Lord Arran, naturally, was the
host, and the Duchess of Kent and her daughter — and, no doubt, Baroness
Lehzen, the governess — stayed again at Bognor Lodge, opposite which was Mr.
Munday's cobbler's shop at the top of Gloucester Road (named after Aunt
Mary). Here Victoria is said to have bought her first pair of boots. It is possible
that Prince Leopold accompanied them, as he had done at Ramsgate, for not
long afterwards the Claremont Hotel proudly displayed the arms of the House of
Saxe-Coburg, doubtless in memory of his visits.

They were happy days; and when Victoria looked back over her long and great
life as Queen she always recalled them with pleasure. 'Dear little Bognor', she
said to her aide-de-camp, General Teesdale of South Bersted, when he conveyed
to her the town's heartfelt good wishes for her Golden Jubilee in 1887.

Fig. 11. Nineteenth-century view of Bognor.

Chapter XI

LURING THE SPECULATORS

ROYAL, RURAL and respectable were the values set upon Bognor by some; dead, dull and dreary were aspects discovered by others. It depended on what you had expected to find on the flat shore of a still comparatively unknown part of Sussex. It depended on whether you rode through it angrily on horseback like William Cobbett in 1832, muttering about 'a land of tax-eaters' [idlers], or just came there to join the circle of polite society and passed the season visiting friends and eating lobsters.

A sufficient number of years had now elapsed for people elsewhere to have some knowledge of the growing resort. The alternative name of Hotham(p)ton had largely dropped away in the 1820s, and on the stage-coaches the signboard no longer indicated 'Bognor Rocks' but simply 'Bognor'. Beyond the very occasional advertisement in a journal, however, there was no regular method of introducing the place to a wider public, and it was the cumulative effect of odd chances that succeeded in doing this. Artists played their part in the process.

One of the earliest was William Hodges R.A., who had been round the world with Captain Cook and, after staying with Hayley at Eartham in the spring of 1793, had gone down to the shore to draw some views of Hothamton for its founder. Three years previously, in June 1790, S. H. Grimm completed four line-and-wash drawings of Hotham's houses and the rebuilt *Fox Inn* (the Hotel) as part of the topographical record of Sussex that he was making for Sir Walter Burrell of West Grinstead.

Six pretty little sketches of the fishermen's huts and the church at South Bersted were the result of George Shepheard's visit in July 1805. He had studied at the Royal Academy schools and from 1811 to 1830 he used to exhibit the landscapes painted during his excursions through Surrey and Sussex. In another medium, Bognor Lodge, 'seat of Sir John Harington', had itself been depicted in tones of brown as one of a set of Sussex views reproduced on Spode plates in 1810.

The picture that did more than anything at the time to establish the resort in the public mind was William Daniell's aquatint of the beach and hotel published in 1823. This was one of over 300 views of Britain, all so original and so extremely truthful with their cool greys, greens and blues and patches of sunlight that no better picture book of this island's fringe has since been conceived.

Daniell was one of a famous family of artists. With his uncle Thomas he had visited India in 1785–94 and it was their colour-plates of the exotic architecture of the East that influenced the various designers who worked on the Royal Pavilion at Brighton. From 1813 to 1825, Daniell was engaged in publishing his *Voyage Round Great Britain*, which involved undertaking a sketching tour right round the kingdom, starting at Land's End, with the results being published at intervals in eight volumes. A writer, Richard Ayton, shared the work, but fell out halfway and the artist wrote the rest of the text himself. On reaching the mouth of the Arun in August 1822, Daniell detoured inland to Arundel, thereby producing what is regarded as his finest Sussex plate, the view south to the Channel from the top of Arundel Park. Having inspected mansions at Slindon and Madehurst, he returned to the coast and resumed the survey at Bognor. What he wrote about it was liberally quoted by guidebook writers throughout the 19th century:

> 'An elegant little bathing place known only as a fishing village and resort of smugglers . . . the sands are firm and good, the site of the village is secluded and the grounds in its vicinity, unlike those which are found near the greater number of watering-places, are clothed with a superabundance of wood.'

His Bognor aquatint was of a similar view to that in Dr. Davis's guide of 1807, with the beach even more sparsely populated – there were 26 people in sight, one fewer than in 1807 – but with a fine show of lobster and prawn pots on the little clay cliff and a carriage-and-pair bowling along the 'firm and good sands'.

From Daniell's narrative. Bognor seemed to meet almost all the exacting standards demanded of a resort by the late Dr. Richard Russell, the leading promoter of the sea-water cure in the previous century. For Russell's ideal resort was clean and neat, away from the mouth of a river so that the salt water was unmixed with fresh water, and had a sandy flat shore, with downs and cliffs nearby along which the refreshed bather could gallop on horseback.

But this was a strictly medical view and it contrasts greatly with John Stuart Mill's impression of Bognor on 20 and 21 July 1827. This brilliant young man was to devote his future political life to propagating principles which he regarded as essential to human happiness. It must have been the gloom he experienced in Bognor that started this train of thought. He was just 21 and a junior clerk in the India Office. With two friends he took a coach to Chichester and in the early evening walked to Bognor, arriving

> 'just in time to perceive its extreme ugliness both in what pertains to nature and to art. We put up at the Claremont hotel, preferring the name as well as the look of the building to a new house of much larger dimensions under the pompous title of *The Hotel*. [This would be Mr. Clark's establishment in the New Crescent.] In the morning before break-fast we walked out and looked at the town, which in situation possesses as few advantages as a place on the seaside can have, and in appearance, though an insignificant village, is full of abortive attempts to rival Brighton. We walked westward a little way on the beach, which we found still duller and more monotonous than the seashore usually is. It is not indeed wholly destitute of trees, but there are none of any great height and both trees and hedges uniformly grow away from the sea, so that the side of a hedge which is next the sea is as bare as if all the leaves had been picked off, or as if it were winter on one side of the hedge and summer on the other.'

Curiously enough, 93 years later, Mill's MS account of his walking tour found its way to Bognor and into the possession of Mr. W. H. B. Fletcher, who spent much of his life planting a woodland of fine specimen trees which beautify what is now Hotham Park, his former estate.

Two quite unexpected factors in the growing fame of Bognor as a resort were the gentry's interest in antiquities and the trend of early 19th-century taste towards romanticism: a love of moonlit ruins, crags and mossy medievalism, mainly engendered by the writings of Sir Walter Scott and which developed into what is known as the second Gothic Revival.

For both of these fashionable tastes, Bognor itself had nothing to offer. Nevertheless people arrived full of expectations, drawn thither either by the wonderful accounts of a newly-discovered Roman Villa or by the magic lure of the old name Bognor Rocks, which had a Tintagelesque appeal to innocent ears. It was the guidebook and gazetteer writers who led visitors astray in regard to the Roman remains, confusing Bognor with Bignor, a remote hamlet 10 miles inland where the finds were made. When, for instance, in 1833 Mr. J. D. Parry published his authoritative-sounding *Historical and Descriptive Account of the Coast of Sussex*, dedicated to King William and Queen Adelaide, no one in Bognor was going to deny the undoubted publicity value of such a statement as 'Near Bognor were discovered, in 1811, the spacious tesselated pavements of a magnificent Roman palace'.

As for the Rocks, they continually caused open-mouthed astonishment among the new arrivals — not for their awe-inspiring qualities but because they were such a disappointment. Dr. Davis had foreseen this and had done his best to soften the blow:

> 'When a stranger arrives at Bognor, he naturally enough looks out for the rocks; but in order to save him unnecessary trouble and disappointment, I shall inform him that the few stony masses that are only visible here at low water scarcely merit the appellation of rocks. Such persons as have been accustomed to contemplate the rocky coast of Wales, or the stupendous precipices of stone and rock in Switzerland, could not at least refrain from smiling at the application of such a term to a ridge of stones upon the coast of Sussex.'

One of the most amusing accounts of being thus misled was written by a stationer of Newgate Street, London, who, with a bookseller's apprentice, had made a walking tour through Hampshire and Sussex in 1802. Their pen-names were 'Peregrine Project' and 'Timothy Type' and on 14 September they arrived at Bognor and surveyed the sea. Mr. Project then narrates:

> ' "Pray," says I to a fisherman we saw standing by the seaside, "where are the tremendous rocks we hear of, that threaten destruction to the vessels of the unwary mariner? I protest I have seen nothing like a rock as yet". "Aye," says the man, "that's the case with all you Londoners, you hears of Bognor-rocks and comes here expecting to see large ones like those at the end of the Isle of Wight, and them sort of ones; but all we have here are those you seen upon the sands there to the right, running out for half a mile towards the sea, and they are quite hid at high-water." "What, those black stones," quoth I, "lying upon the sands there? Why, then they might as well be hid now, for any notice I should have taken of them, if you had not pointed them out".'

They resumed their walk, going through Felpham and Yapton towards Arundel, and on the way:

> 'Type observed that he could not help thinking of his disappointment in respect to the rocks at Bognor, as from the words Bognor-rocks he had seen blazoned upon the

stage-coaches and in large hand-bills posted up in London, he thought they must have been in themselves of sufficient consequence to excite the notice of travellers; whereas, it appeared that nobody but sailors, fishermen and smugglers could have any concern in such paltry stones. "Very true, Tim," said I, "but yet the word rocks being blazoned out, as you mention, may answer the end intended, as mankind are perpetually prejudiced or deceived by names, and none more so than we poor cockneys, who, having heard of the rock of Gibraltar, the rocks of Scilly, etc., etc., are led to imagine all rocks to be of that bold and formidable kind".'

However, Mr. Project allowed that Bognor was attractive enough, putting the Rocks out of the question, and when they stopped for the night at *The Royal Oak* at Avisford (which still stands beside the Arundel–Chichester road) he made notes for his book:

'"But what," said I, "shall I call Bognor? It is not a town, because it has no market; neither is it a village, having no parish church." "Call it a *place*, then," says Tim. "That's a comprehensive term to be sure," replied I, "but how will that distinguish it from London, Chichester, Salisbury, etc.?" "A bathing-place, however, you may certainly call it." "Well, then, let it stand thus — Bognor, a hamlet in the parish of South Bersted, a fashionable bathing-place in Sussex, seven miles from Chichester and about sixty-five from London; having commodious lodging-houses and famed for its alternatively visible and invisible rocks; which, I confess, I was also rather disappointed in, though not from the same cause as you, having hoped to have been able to eke out a page or two, and at the same time display a little learning, in describing the different *strata* of which they might have been composed. No matter whether right or wrong, as nobody would probably have examined them after us, for nothing exhibits an author in a more sagacious point of view than talking about strata, quartz, basaltes, argillaceous slate and siliceous grit."'

The Rocks were now even funny enough to appear in fiction, and in one of Theodore Hook's novels, *Maxwell*, published in 1834, a honeymoon couple, choosing a resort, were warned against 'Bognor, with its pebble-stone rocks, dullness beyond misery'.

But there were also serious writers to whom such things as Bognor's various rocks, Felpham's fossil forest on the beach and the local coastal erosion were a means of introducing people to the wonders of Nature. One such writer was the sincere and gentle Quaker, Maria Hack (1777–1844), who lived at Chichester and was the elder sister of Bernard Barton, the friend of Charles Lamb. Her brother was devoted to her and said of her that she was 'almost the first human being I remember to have loved fondly, or being fondly loved by'.

Mrs. Hack (who was the wife of John Hack, founder of the Chichester Bank), wrote some thirty books of instruction combined with amusement especially for children, maintaining that purely fictional stories weakened the intellects of the young. She combined theology directly with Nature in her stories and used the Bognor area for some illustrations of geological study. By inventing a boy with an enquiring mind called Harry Beaufoy, she was able to hold her young readers' interest as she led the lad along through the pages of *Geological Sketches and Glimpses of the Ancient Earth*, written at Chichester in 1831. Harry took everything in his stride — coal, fossils, chalk, salt, volcanoes, granite, earthquakes — and remained always keen and polite. When told, for example, that some French alps were formed of conglomerated pebbles, he would answer:

'When we go to Bognor again, and walk on the shingles, I shall think of those Alpine mountains of pebbles. How curious, how very wonderful is the structure of the earth! Wherever we go, surprising facts seem to claim our notice and give us something to think about.'

To which Mrs. Beaufoy, his mother, would reply:

'It is so, Harry. These cheap innocent pleasures are always ready for the enjoyment of those who will make use of their eyes. And how naturally they lead our thoughts to the great Architect who framed the world of wonders and *is* framing it — for we have ample proof that the work is still going on. Do you not remember how often we have noticed at Bognor what you used to call young rocks, masses of conglomerated shells and pebbles between which the clayey cement had not hardened? Can you not magnify such masses in imagination and suppose vast strata formed in this way?'

Of all the various impressions of Bognor at this period, the best, naturally, was given by Dally in his *Bognor, Arundel and Littlehampton Guide*, printed and published by Mason in 1828. Despite all his efforts to make money from local legal work, Dally had gone bankrupt on 26 November 1826, the petitioner being James Tomsett who had built a manor house for him and was owed £100. As his publisher, being appointed an assignee of his estate, now had a very close interest in the fortunes of Dally's *Guide*, the book was well produced and contained five plates and 251 pages. Not only were Bognor, Felpham, Aldwick and South Bersted fully dealt with, but all the surrounding villages and mansions; and the whole work bristled with the erudition of the author's own researches and the latest histories. Samples of his verse were sprinkled here and there:

Bognor, I love, when summer heats prevail,
Around the coast to wander; and inhale
The breeze, that blustering from the briny main,
Gives health and vigor to the rural swain . . .

and the reader was led to believe that this part of Sussex was paradise. Invalids would find their appetites increasing; beautiful trees and shrubs, such as the 'elegant Tamarisk', grew by the water's edge — unlike the treeless Brighton 'exposed to the impetuous blasts of the ocean' — and children could 'perambulate the smooth and elastic sands with perfect safety'. If you drove your carriage through the cultivated country, with no expensive tolls to pay, you passed 'pleasant villages where squalid poverty, or roofless or decayed cottages, are seldom seen'. It was indeed a helpful publication, containing impressive Latin footnotes and thoughtful warnings for ramblers, such as the fact that the number of foot-stiles on a walk between Bognor and Felpham 'are a great impediment to its enjoyment by the ladies'. But Dr. Davis would have been surprised by this new *Guide*. There was no reference whatever to sea-bathing.

*   *   *

The question of how Bognor now stood in the estimation of the public was of considerable importance, for Britain was changing in mood as quickly as April. The world of Hotham, though only 30 years gone, was already remote and the lid was finally shut down on it when George IV died on 26 June 1830. The King had been suitably prepared for his end. An old friend, Robert Carr, whose eloquent sermons and good conversation when vicar of Brighton had earned the royal notice and respect, was sent for. He was now Bishop of Chichester. Kneeling by the bedside, he read the prayer for recovery which was to be said in the churches of the land. 'It is in very good taste', commented the King. A few weeks later he was gone and the nation seemed to regard the affable eccentricities of the Sailor King, William IV, as a satisfactory exchange.

But throughout 1830 and 1831 the public mind was rather more concerned with the alarming spread of cholera and the battle for Parliamentary reform. Both were to affect Bognor and it was the possibility of cholera breaking out in what was now a reputable health resort that disturbed the Commissioners most of all. In London, the menace of the disease itself did not frighten an old warrior like Wellington. What he feared was the general panic that might arise if three or four hundred notable people left London to escape it — for then, he said, 'they would be followed by three or four hundred thousand and this country would be plunged into greater confusion than had been known for hundreds of years'.

Cleanliness and good drainage, noticeably lacking in most towns and villages, were the preventatives, and for approximately a month in the autumn of 1831 Bognor had its own Board of Health, acting unofficially and without real powers to carry out its recommendations. The receipt on 21 November of two circulars from the Privy Council on 'Removal of Nuisances' and 'Medical Returns' was construed — rightly or wrongly — as sufficient authority to set up a local Board of Health and no time was lost. On 24 November, the vicar as chairman and Dally as secretary, 15 local worthies, summoned by town crier, met in the school-room attached to St John's Chapel in the Steyne and passed resolutions for cleaning up the parish. These included the inspection of all houses, ditches and drains for any sign of filth and advising the poorer people to whitewash their dwellings, to keep their rooms ventilated and to apply for warm clothes or medicine if needed. Routes of inspection were arranged, a subscription fund was opened and handbills were printed by Mason, who was also doing similar work for Chichester's Board of Health.

In the meantime, Dally had been having misgivings as to the legality of the whole procedure. He had written twice to the Secretary of State to enquire if the two Privy Council orders could, in fact, be interpreted by the inhabitants of Bognor as authority to do what they were doing.

> 'In a place like this,' he wrote to Lord Melbourne, 'where vessels frequently come from Newcastle, or perhaps Sunderland, and where there are many poor residing in small confined dwellings, and nuisances existing, it is of great importance that there should be a Board of Health. If, therefore, the Board already established has been prematurely so, and should have had, for their sanction and authority, an Order of Council specifically constituting them such, I am anxious to impress upon your Lordship the immediate necessity of forwarding such order to me.'

He also wrote to the magistrates' clerk at Chichester to find out if that city's Board of Health was on a sound footing.

During December, Dally and his fellows proceeded in the dark. As secretary of the Board, he wrote letters to himself in his other capacity as Clerk to the Commissioners, complaining of noisome nuisances that the Commissioners must remove. At a meeting of the Board on Boxing Day, it was learnt that no one was co-operating in the hygienic purge, least of all the Commissioners, and by 2 January 1832 the Board of Health's brief life was over. Word had come from the Duke of Richmond at Chichester that it was not the habit of the Privy Council to allow local medical boards to be set up with full powers, unless the case was urgent.

Why then, deliberated the Board, had the Privy Council sent them two health orders in the first place, when there was no proper medical board at Bognor to deal with such matters? It was, apparently, a Civil Service mistake. So the Board's well-intentioned labours came to an end, Dally was thanked for his services and the balance of the subscription money, 11 guineas, was handed to the vicar to benefit the poor.

Thus the burden of coping with the parish sick fell back on the Vestry Committee. Bognor's little attempt to outstrip government routine had failed. Once more, the shillings and pence of the Poor Rate, aided by those welcome 11 guineas, flowed out through the Guardian's books and in the early days of 1832 he was making a note of:

Feb. 11	Relief to Jane Varion for looking after Page ill of the small pox	3/-
Mar. 3	Mrs. Knight for laying out Page	2/6
	For bread and cheese at the funeral of Page	5/2½
	Four men for carrying him to the church	5/-

But the zealous month's work of the short-lived Board had proved a beginning which led, in three years, to the town's third Act of Parliament on 31 August 1835. This Act placed the administration of Bognor on a more substantial basis, granting to the Commissioners those much-needed powers to water, pave, light and cleanse the resort, and to prevent the nuisances. It meant that Bognor was now, at long last, reaching away from its village status to become a well-run watering-place — provided it found the money to set its new authority in motion. Rates at 2s. in the £ were introduced for this purpose, and notices of all rates and public meetings had to be posted on the door of St John's Chapel.

The Commissioners were now 54 in number. Many familiar names were still there: Lord Arran, the Wonhams, the Haslers, Binstead and even Richard Clark. Dally and Lord Arran's solicitor, Richard Groom, were named in the Act. Sarel, who had built the new *Norfolk Hotel*; Turner and Hardwicke, the brewers; Colonel Teesdale, the magistrate; James Smith, owner of the Steyne Baths and the handsome *York House Hotel* in High Street; Gruggan, the Chichester banker; Knapton, owner of the new High Street library, and the doctors, Peskett and Thompson — all had been appointed Commissioners. Two newcomers to the town had also been chosen for office: Sir John Chetwode and Patrick Perse Fitzpatrick, a retired Commissioner of Excise from Dublin. Among the various powers given to the Commissioners by the new Act was the right to build their own office for meetings, provided the cost of land and building did not exceed £500. They could also have a fire engine. Annual licence fees could be extracted from the enraged fishermen to the extent of 5s. for a boat and 2s. 6d. for a bathing-machine. As for the beach, from which everyone had been taking materials where and when they liked, this was now to be more carefully controlled. Sand, rock and shingle were precious to the defence of Bognor, a point which had been apt to be overlooked by eager builders. Further powers on the beach included the construction of additional groynes and sea walls.

Since ready money was as important to the Commissioners as it had been to Hotham in building and conducting a town, it is interesting to inspect their statement of expenditure and receipts for this particular year of 1835.

They spent £1,142 19s. 3½d. and received £2,279 18s. 4½d. Their sources of income did not yet include the new town rate, so they were still limited mainly to the coal dues and the mooring fees. The latter produced £8 5s. 0d. During the year, 1,686 tons of coal arrived for local use, bringing £168 12s. 0d. in dues. A little revenue, amounting to £2 3s. 6d., had accumulated from penalties for straying animals put in the pound. Borrowed money constituted the largest item under 'Receipts'. This sum of £2,100 was needed for the purposes of the new Act and had been borrowed on mortgage: £600 from Mr. Knapton and £1,500 from a Mr. Leasley.

The largest item under 'Expenditure' was also concerned with the new Act, the expenses of which amounted to £913 12s. 8d. Mr. Knapton had been paid £10 interest on his loan, as well as £2 9s. 0d. for inserting advertisements for the resort in London papers. Mr. John Holden, the Town Constable or Beadle, was provided with a new coat at £2 18s. 0d., as well as his annual £20 salary. Hand-cuffs cost £1 7s. 8d.; sea defences, £2 8s. 9d.; promenade expenses, £5. Mrs. Gordon, for cleaning the Commissioners' meeting-room, £1; the town dustman, £6 10s. 0d.; Dally's salary, £12. Mr. Hardwicke, the brewer, received £2 10s. 0d. as half-year interest on a previous loan on £100; and £50 odd had been refunded in dues for coal taken out of Bognor. Whether the balance in hand of £1,136 19s. 1d. was going to see the Commissioners comfortably through 1836 was doubtful, as it would be spent largely on their new commitments. However, it looked more favourable on paper than the previous year's balance. This had amounted to 17s. 10½d.

Fresh hope swept through the building speculators with the passing of the Act. Surely, they felt, investors *must* stir themselves now, even though they had not shown the faintest interest in the Bognor & Aldwick Improvement Company of 10 years before. Apart from Mr. Clark's New Crescent, standing up with the starkness of a Stonehenge, there was still not another building on the sweep of green fields along the eastward shore. Any reasonable financier could not fail to see but a little way into the future, when hotels and apartment houses would be making fortunes for those who had had the foresight to build them in such a wonderful situation.

So once again, and for the third time, a prospectus was circulated. The 1835 venture was called The Bognor Improvement Company, for which a capital of

£200,000 was required in £25 shares. Missing from the board was the slightly reckless figure of Lord William Pitt Lennox. Sam Beazley had been replaced by another architect, James Pennethorne of Duke Street, Westminster. In fact, none of the old hopefuls was among the directors but, as before, the new board included men who were Bognor Commissioners with London interests. One of them, Thomas Brown, wrote the prospectus; others on the boards of both the town and the Improvement Company were William Banbury of Lombard Street, David Hickinbotham of Berkeley Square and Francis Graham' Moon of Threadneedle Street. Another director was John Humphrey who, like Hotham before him, was M.P. for Southwark and perhaps was blind to the difficulties encountered by his speculative predecessor.

Once more, the local *Lorelei* sought to lure the City financiers towards Bognor Rocks with the familiar phrases: 'Beautiful rural scenery . . . abundant foliage in the immediate neighbourhood of the town . . . excellent facilities for bathing . . . pure sea breezes.' The proposition this time was to develop what is now called an estate but was then referred to as 'erecting a new town, to supply the accommodation so much wanted in Bognor, with residences of a superior class upon a symmetrical plan, the absence of which is so conspicuous in the generality of watering-places'. Sites on freehold land were offered on lease to builders. There was an abundance of brick earth at hand. An 'inviting promenade' would probably be constructed all along the sea frontage. Then, indulging in the language of an inspired visionary, the prospectus announced that the Company intended to build a handsome pier, 'affording a safe landing not only from the Dieppe, Havre, Guernsey and Jersey steamers, but for passengers from all parts of the world passing up the English Channel'. This was not all, for the railways which were then being planned — first from Brighton to the port of Shoreham and then from London to Brighton — were duly woven into the scheme for the new Bognor, whereby 'A Communication will also be attempted and doubtless effected with the projected Shoreham Railroad, firstly by means of steam vessels plying regularly between Bognor and Shoreham and ultimately by a direct railroad communication, when the projected plans of the Shoreham Railroad Company, embracing a line to Southampton, shall be matured.' In due course, a London businessman would be able, in about four hours, to reach a resort which would offer him 'the facility of pure sea air, morning and night, with the opportunity of an interim visit to the Metropolis'.

Should anyone cast doubts on the Company's ambitious scheme, the triumph of Messrs. James and Decimus Burton's experiment in East Sussex in 1828 was given as an example of intelligent speculation:

> 'The success which has attended the new town at St Leonards, notwithstanding the very immediate neighbourhood of its rival Hastings, may be adduced in favour of a similar undertaking. The new town at Bognor may be confidently expected to attract an increase of visitors from the adjoining counties and the Metropolis, as well as from the redundant population of Brighton.'

Mr. Pennethorne's design for the 'new town' was quite in keeping with the lavish prose of the prospectus. The stretch of empty meadows, a quarter-mile in width, between High Street and the beach was to be laid out on the lines of a miniature spa, with a grand boulevard in the middle leading towards the sea (approximately where Clarence Road now is) and emerging on the shore between Clark's hotel and a projected replica of that building. The boulevard would terminate in promenade gardens, with a circular building in the centre designated as a library and observatory. Side roads off the main stem were packed with mansions, lawns, terraces, stabling and an Assembly Room.

It is perhaps unnecessary to add that no such 'new town' was built. The Improvement Company died at birth like its forerunners and the grazing meadows continued to lend a rural charm to Bognor's seashore for at least another 45 years.

*   *   *

It would have been hard in those days to convince the speculators, with their extravagant visions of Brighton's 'redundant population' being housed in Bognor, that this little town would never, in fact, grow into a great roaring resort, eating up its valuable capital of countryside and coast as it spread for miles over the plain. Bognor was destined for many years to remain small, peaceful and comparatively remote. Its very position of splendid isolation decided that. It had not the easy communication with the Metropolis that was to make Brighton into what Thackeray summed up as 'London plus prawns for breakfast and the sea air'. It lacked money and fashionable attractions and, like many other resorts, such as Worthing, it had reached stagnation. The fishermen out on the restless sea and the farmers in the whispering corn must have looked at the collection of houses on the shore and felt thankful they had stuck to their native Sussex trades while others lost fortunes in brick.

Bognor was beginning to droop and in any case its king-pin was soon to be knocked out by the death of the premier resident, the Earl of Arran. He had been deeply affected, as had the whole neighbourhood, by the death of his wife Mary on 31 August 1832. Locally she had gained something of the reputation of a saint and there were sad scenes at Felpham church on 11 September. Charles Gore, his lordship's nephew, described the day:

'The funeral took place yesterday and all went off very well. Lord A., Edward, I and Mr. Pearson in the first coach and the rest in the three other mourning coaches — and Lord A.'s two carriages bringing up the rear. Lord A., Edward and I were the chief mourners. He was much affected and shook like an aspen leaf on getting out of the carriage at the church door. He was hardly able to stand and when the coffin was put in the vault he cried excessively. The whole was well arranged and very respectable. The will was read on our return by Mr. Groom. It was a very long one and to me quite unintelligible, so full of technicalities! However, Mr. Groom has since explained it to me and it amounts to this — she has left everything to Lord Arran by deed of gift . . . Lord Arran is much broken, I think, and her loss, I am quite convinced, he will feel most deeply.'

Less than five years later, on 22 January 1837 at the age of 76, Arran himself died. For nearly three decades he had been at the helm of Bognor, the only man who had really appreciated the unfulfilled intentions of Hotham. He joined his wife in an elaborate tomb, rich with moulded coronets, in Felpham churchyard; and on the walls of the chancel, each side of the altar, there are black commemorative tablets, decorated with urn, crest and coat-of-arms. The inscribed epitaph to Lady Arran was written by Mr. W. Hutt, a college friend of the Rev. Arthur Pearson, brother of the Rev. John, the Arrans' steward. It refers to her charity and benevolence, which earned the gratitude of the poor and 'her sovereign's smile'. His lordship's epitaph is the same as that on Dr. Jackson's grave in the churchyard:

'Enter not into judgment with thy servant,
O Lord, for in thy sight can no man living
be justified.'

The Arran title and Irish estates went to his nephew Philip. The Bognor property was bequeathed to the Rev. John Pearson, who settled in Bognor Lodge for a few years. He was buried at Kensal Green and his widow Eliza married a Mr. Richard Robinson. Bognor Lodge passed to Pearson's son, Arthur Arran Pearson, who married Mary Tindal of Aylesbury, became a cotton broker and then took Holy Orders. He died in 1886 and his grandson was Sir Arthur Pearson, of St Dunstan's fame.

Who was now to take Lord Arran's pre-eminent place in local society? Charles, Duke of Richmond, certainly owned several acres in the parish, but he remained remote in the magnificence of Goodwood and was much more concerned with controlling the political colour of Chichester than with the waning fortunes of Bognor. Eyes, therefore, turned to Bersted Lodge (the Chapel House) and, though the occupants had not the fabled riches attributed to the Arrans, they were good patrons to the town and had those friendly ties with the Royal Family that seemed now a part and parcel of Bognor life.

There were three of them and we met them earlier on – Mrs. Smith, widow of the Rev. Thomas Smith (died about 1825), and her relatives, the 4th Earl and Countess of Mayo. On Mrs. Smith had now fallen the main burden of charitable works which had been shared in the past with Mrs. Wilsonn and Lady Arran. Charity, according to Dally, had not blossomed too freely in Bognor until the arrival of Mrs. Wilsonn and her help with the Jubilee School, now flourishing in High Street. In 1818, on the completion of the school building, the resuscitation of Charity at her hands was described by Dally in 30 lines, of which these five are probably enough:

The waves of the weltering ocean had drown'd it,
Its beauties were soiled with a stain;
The overgrown sea-weed was gathering around it,
When Wilsonn, protectress of Charity, found it,
And her touch soon revived it again.

Early in the 1820s, Mrs. Smith had founded her own charity school and, apart from all her numerous donations and attentions to the poor, she continued to run this small private institution at her own expense until she died in 1856. It was housed in the little brick and slate-roofed Laurel Cottage in the grounds of Bersted Lodge, and here 20 poor girls were clothed and educated in sewing, reading and general housekeeping under the tuition of a mistress.

Lady Mayo (1766–1843) was a forthright and humorous woman, though a remarkably plain one. On one occasion, her direct enquiry to Lady Glengall: 'I understand you said I was the ugliest woman in the world?' brought the equally straightforward reply: 'Well, I must say, Lady Mayo, I think you are the most frightful woman I ever saw in my life.'

In 1830 Lady Mayo had been appointed one of the six Ladies of the Bed-chamber to the new Queen Adelaide, and Bognor felt more closely linked to the Court than ever. The devout and agreeable wife of William IV enjoyed the Countess's company. The Royal circle was a pleasant and homely one, full of family visitings and the giving of presents, and Princess Victoria on her 14th birthday in 1833 received both a visit and present from the two ladies: a gold and turquoise brooch from the Queen and a glass bottle from Lady Mayo. In like manner, the King responded to the Mayos' company. He had not forgotten his Bognor visits — and neither had Bognor, where Clark's hotel, as already mentioned, was now called *The Royal Clarence* — and the atmosphere of Mrs. Smith's jolly house-party days at Bersted Lodge was continued at the Brighton Pavilion where the King took up residence for the winter of 1831 and invited his Bognor friends. While Lady Mayo and the others sat with the Queen, William IV enticed her husband to sing Irish songs for him — not that the Earl had any notion of tune.

Lord Mayo's character was summed up very aptly in verse by his nephew, Winthrop Praed:

> *A courtier of the noblest sort*
> *A Christian of the purer school*
> *Tory when Whigs are great at court,*
> *And Protestant when Papists rule.*

Whether young Praed, a barrister and a gifted writer of topical verse, ever came to stay with his aunt and uncle at Bognor is not recorded. He died so early, at the age of 37 in 1839, that people could only guess at what he might have become. But in those few years, his brilliant and precocious exploits at Eton and Cambridge, his parliamentary career and his political satires and leaders for *The Morning Post* had made him a much-loved and admired man of the moment, full of exciting promise.

Fig. 12. *Rock Buildings from the Beach, a sketch of 1842.*

Chapter XII

DIVERSIONS AND EXCURSIONS

THE EDITOR of *The Chichester Magazine* in 1838 made an apology to his readers, regretting the absence of Mr. Dally's usual popular contributions owing to his illness. The illness was severe and it carried Dally away from the Bognor scene at the age of 72 on 12 December 1839, though not before he had given the neighbourhood a final salute with his revised *Bognor Guide* of 1838. That 'the spirit of improvement manifested throughout Bognor, and the patronage it experienced, naturally extended itself to the adjoining districts' was one of his long-standing convictions. Whether Chichester or Arundel endorsed this assessment of the influence of a mere watering-place is doubtful, but in the town itself Improvement was indeed the watchword. Any visitors now seeking sea air in Bognor, and reading the latest guide, found a long list of newly-founded charitable institutions to which they were expected to contribute a donation – or, as Dally cleverly phrased it, 'in return for health restored, to leave a blessing behind them'.

Out of the gardens and Georgian buildings of Hotham's pleasance by the sea had grown a village, and now out of the village had spread a small town which was, in the words of the local jest, 'being built on coal'. For the coal duties were its lifeblood. The sparkle of the sea was matched by the white stucco of the neat villas and the new shops. The cattle and sheep still browsed near the beach, but the diminutive skyline round them was changing as the improvements took place. The Commissioners had now obtained the use of a Town Hall for their monthly meetings, a dignified rectangular block which Mr. W. K. Wonham had erected in Sudley Road, off High Street, in 1837. Its main function was to serve as Assembly Rooms for town gatherings, with two main rooms holding 200 and 250 people respectively. To the westward, in the Steyne, the tower added to St John's Chapel in 1833 was already a familiar landmark at sea. Mr. Wonham had been influenced by Pugin's campaign for more 'Christian-looking' churches and therefore the new tower was as near Gothic as funds allowed, with castellated parapet and pointed-arch windows. In the tower was a clock and a 4 cwt. bell named 'Mary Ann', presented by the Rev. Charles and Miss Baumparten of Aldwick. Still farther to the west, near the shore at the foot of Nyewood Lane, was another comparatively new sight, a windmill with canvas sails, built by Henry Martin in the late 1820s for the purpose of grinding the local 'kidney-rock' into cement for the use of the building speculators.

There had been no neglect of education and a little crop of schools had appeared, apart from the old 'National' or parish schools: the one for boys at South Bersted, with Thomas Wisdom in charge, and the girls' Jubilee School

under Miss Mary Scovell. There were now Sunday schools for children, an evening
school for adults, an infants' school in Dorset Gardens and three private academies
— Miss Beeding's, Mr. Bailey's and Mr. Sibley's — as well as Mrs. Smith's tiny
charity school at Laurel Cottage under the direction of Mrs. Sarah Heslop.

There had been valiant efforts to encourage the poor of the parish to help
themselves. A branch of the Chichester Savings Bank had opened, a free lending
library was set up in each of the National schools and a Clothing Fund was
instituted to 'encourage the industrious by small weekly deposits to furnish
themselves with Clothing at the end of the year'. A Female Friendly & Mutual
Assistance Society was in being to give help to its contributors in sickness and
old age. It had been founded on 25 June 1832, at a meeting in the Jubilee School,
with Lord Arran as president. At the 1836 General Meeting it was decided to
admit men to the benefits. The Society was then re-named The Bognor & Bersted
Friendly Society and the area of its usefulness extended to neighbouring parishes.

The poor were also being systematically dealt with by a District Visiting
Society, whose members distributed Bibles and prayer-books and vouchers for
coal, soup and bread to the deserving. Another good cause was the Lying-in
Charity, which provided the necessities in money and kind for confinements.
The honest working man was also granted an allotment at a low rent in the Field
Gardens in the centre of Bognor. Young allotment holders under 19 had to under-
take to attend evening school in the winter.

The visitor arriving for the bathing season in, say, 1839 would no longer have
to go to Chichester to buy materials for a bathing dress. The small shops had been
creeping up West Street and into Waterloo Square, the Steyne and the High
Street. Some had double bow-windows with small square panes, others had long
metal awnings supported by cast-iron pillars along the frontage to keep out the
glare of the southern sun. There were six tailors, five grocers and five bakers.
There were two each of the following trades: draper, straw-hat maker, stable
owner, saddle and harness-maker, hairdresser, pebble-polisher, coal merchant,
furniture-maker, greengrocer, chemist and bookseller; four each of milliner and
butcher; three each of painter–plumber, brewer and wine merchant. The largest
body was of bootmakers — eight of them, led by Mr. Francis Morris, the cobbler-
poet of Bognor, who had left the theatrical world for this totally different craft
and whose latest book of poems, dedicated in 1834 to the Duke of Richmond,
was entitled *Elva's Revenge*.

Other trades had only one representative, such as Thomas Kinchett, fishmonger;
William Puddick, corn-dealer; Thomas Shipton, ironmonger and auctioneer;
James Tomsett, brickmaker and carpenter; William Stringer, leather seller, William
Hammond, blacksmith; and George Munday, cowkeeper (or dairyman). The
letting of houses was in the hands of men who had helped to build them, such as
William Wonham, James Tomsett, Edward Curtiss and James Smith.

Visitors arrived on foot or on horseback, by private carriage, hired carriage or
coach. Any moneyed Londoners who decided to visit the resort in the early years
of Queen Victoria's reign would probably have sent their heavy luggage on ahead
by James Keywood's carrier van, which called at addresses in London on

Thursdays and Saturdays. If they travelled by coach, they could choose the old-established *Comet*, operated by Cross & Co., which could be boarded at Charing Cross, or the *Royal Sussex*, which had a convenient stage-point at the Gloucester Coffee House in Piccadilly. The journey took about eight hours, the *Comet* going through Dorking and Arundel, and its competitor via Guildford, Petworth and Chichester. On either route, passengers would have to get out and walk up hills; but, having toiled up the escarpment of the Sussex Downs, they were immediately revived by what seemed to be the tang of the sea — though in actual fact it was the smell of drying seaweed, carted inland by farmers for fertilising the soil.

Visitors arrived just before five o'clock and either settled in at one of the four hotels or rented lodgings or a house from one of the agents. Next day, if the tide was in, they would see neither the famous sands nor the fabled Rocks, but a bathe was possible at any time. A little crowd of health-seekers would be gathered round the sturdy neatly-painted bathing machines, paying over their shilling fee to the attendants. Then the horses would be harnessed and the occupants, disrobing within, would suddenly be jerked off their feet as the high-wheeled huts began their creaking progress out to the right depth. When the horse was unhitched and the bright water flicked and flapped beneath the floor, the bather opened the cabin door and gazed out upon an unusual view of the ocean, so shut in to the east and west by the curves of the coast that it had once been described as looking like 'a private lake belonging solely to the inhabitants of the vicinity'. Then, with apprehensive toe, down the steps into the sea went the visitor, naked if a gentleman, clothed from neck to ankle in a dark blue flannel gown if a lady — though, of course, the sexes were well segregated and mixed bathing was for the far distant and decadent future. Once in the water, there was plenty of splashing and squealing from mothers and children, and forcible ducking if one had sought the services of the tough old bathing woman, Mrs. Pipson. But swimming was rare. It was not yet a seaside sport.

Entertainment in the town itself was still frugal and was more or less limited to the occasional dance at the new Assembly Rooms in Sudley Road, a bout of billiards in the annexe to Binstead's Library and the purple passages in the sermons of the Rev. Edward Miller, the new curate at St John's. Lack of a common centre where one might stroll and meet people was still a serious drawback to social life, but a small stretch of promenade had appeared again on top of the clay cliff. It had previously vanished, almost as soon as built, in an April storm in 1831 and, in fact, would disappear regularly into the maw of the mountainous seas which were to provide future photographers with memorable pictures and generations of guidebook writers with the reason for their perpetually recurring remark about Bognor's sea wall and promenade — namely, that these had been 'recently repaired'.

One of the diversions of the day was watching the arrival and departure of the coaches. The stones and dust of High Street were scattered as one of the *Royal Sussex* vehicles rumbled in from Chichester every morning at 9.45 and paused at the *New Inn* on its way to Brighton. In the still of the afternoon would come the echoing notes from a 'yard of tin' as the *Era* and its posthorn from Brighton came over Felpham Bridge and down High Street to the *Norfolk Hotel*, en route for Portsmouth. And two or three hours later, in came one or other of the London coaches, which had enlivened its last lap by racing with Henry Charlett's horse omnibus bringing passengers and goods back from the daily trip to Chichester.

For the visitor, of course, the sea and the beach provided the strongest appeal. The sea, apart from its now famed health-giving properties, had still not lost its mystery and the beach was a place of curious discoveries and strange occupations. Scattered over the beach and lying in the hollows of the great tract of blue London clay exposed near low-water mark were nodules or 'thunderbolts' of iron pyrites, such as had excited Princess Charlotte in the years gone by. The sea was continually washing the pyrites out of its clay bed and in former times the local poor collected it and sold it for 3d. per bushel to a tanner near Chichester. But now it had a wider market as a source of sulphuric acid. When fishing conditions were bad, the foreshore was busy with searching figures accumulating their piles of mineral (or 'mine') to be sold at 1s. 6d. a cwt. to the coal merchant. When the next coal boat arrived, instead of filling up with a ballast of sand and shingle for the return voyage, a cargo of sometimes 25 tons of pyrites was loaded, which meant nearly £40 to Bognor's 'miners'. Like most trades, it had its hazards. The town still remembered those terrible cries from the sea on the night of 9 May 1834. Dick and Tom Allen had been helping to load a ship with 'mine', but somehow the tide had claimed them and the darkness hampered would-be rescuers.

Other workers to be seen on the shore were the cement men, digging up from beneath the clay and sand the peculiar septaria, or kidney-rock, which was then crushed in Henry Martin's black windmill. Either the sea scoured out pieces of the stone or else the men probed the sand for it with wire rods until they hit a protecting cover of rock which hid the clay-ironstone nodules beneath. Septaria is a finely grained greyish rock, laced with a network of translucent yellow veins or partings (*septa*, a parting) composed of calcite crystals. After being ground, the material was burnt with flintgrit in two nearby kilns and the result was the brown 'Roman' cement used throughout the parish for building and facing. It was hard and waterproof, so much so that nowadays a modern drill will wear out if used on the exterior of an old Bognor building, and paint will adhere only for a short period even though a sticky surface be applied beforehand.

If the visitor was fortunate enough to arrive on the right day in the short Bognor season, there was always the chance of seeing the sands or sea transformed by the liveliness of the July sports or the August regatta. In 1843, Bognor Rural Sports took place on the sands on Monday, 24 July, and the jocular wording of the bills informed competitors that 'As the Tides are not under the command of the Stewards the Sports must commence punctually at 2 o'clock'.

There were 12 events, one of them providing almost a Roman spectacle as horses and waggons careered along the sands in a half-mile chariot race for a £2 prize. Hurdle races, with horses leaping obstacles over a three-quarter mile course for £5, and pony, donkey, hack and galloway races completed the equine events; and then came the humans, crawling on all fours in a Quadruped Race, running with legs shackled by 14-inch straps, jumping along for 50 yards in sacks, and creating hilarity with a wheelbarrow race in which the participants were blindfolded and turned round three times before starting. Bobbing, with hands tied, for bread rolls swimming in treacle was one sticky way of winning 5s., or else energy could be withheld until the final event, also for 5s. — a Grand Contest for Hasty Pudding, the prize being awarded to 'the fastest eater and the cleanest finisher'. The day wound up with a 3s. supper at the *Berkeley Arms* in West Street.

The Deputy Constable sworn in for that year's Rural Sports was Henry Hammond, who worked as a blacksmith with his brother William in Chapel Street. He received 2s. 6d. for his services and there was only one arrest, which earned him another 1s. for 'assisting to take a man to the Caige'. The 'Caige', one of the new improvements, was in effect a police station for the temporary housing of troublemakers before they were roped to the back of a cart and taken to Chichester. It consisted of the Beadle's cottage, coach house and lock-up, all under one roof in the corner of a yard in Bedford Street, a lane off High Street. The lock-up itself was a solidly built room in the cottage, with a domed roof, iron rings low down in one wall and a heavy iron-studded door with a massive Chubb lock. The South Bersted Vestry Committee had assisted in making it more escape-proof by passing a resolution on 6 February 1834 that '£17 be allowed towards making the present lock-up house at Bognor more convenient and secure, upon condition that the Commissioners of Bognor do allow the whole parish the use of it as occasion may require'.

Heading the Sports Committee for the day was a new and distinguished resident, Lord George Lennox, a brother of the Duke of Richmond. Lord George had been through the Peninsular campaign and Waterloo. When the war was over, he married Louisa, daughter of the Hon. John Rodney, and set up house at Molecomb on the Goodwood estate. He had been M.P. for Chichester from 1819 to 1830. When in 1837 Lord Arran died, Lennox moved down to the coast and took Arran Lodge, renaming it Lennox Lodge. Bognor was delighted to have a sprig of Goodwood glory in its midst and Lady George Lennox soon found herself stepping into the benevolent rôle hitherto played by Lady Arran. On those occasions, for instance, when the high spring tides backed by a south-west gale burst over the low-lying Brookland on the east of the town, turning it into a lake, there was Lady George helping to rescue cottagers by boat and plunging about up to her waist saving pets, birds and poultry. Included in their household was Lennox's affable nephew, the Duke's third son, Lord Henry Lennox. He was then at Christ Church, Oxford, and was soon to begin a notable career in politics, which included representing Chichester for 39 years (1846–85). He was to be the last M.P. for that city before seats were redistributed and Chichester was merged with one of the new parliamentary divisions of Sussex.

*   *   *

Beyond the diversions mentioned, visitors would have found little else to hold their interest unless they made a few excursions. As the fashion was for the romantic and antique, the most popular expedition was along the sands eastwards to see whether there was anything still left of old Middleton church. Long, long ago, in 1724, the church was 60 feet from the high tides, but, when the sea encroached on the churchyard, subsequent neglect by the parish led to the collapse of the tower and south wall. By 1784, the crumbling stonework, thick ivy and general air of melancholy had given inspiration to the Sussex poetess, Charlotte Smith. Her sonnet written in the churchyard added considerably to the morbid reputation of the ruin, for she described the sea which:

> *Tears from their grassy tombs the village dead*
> *And breaks the silent Sabbath of the grave!*

During the 1820s, under a new Lord of the Manor, the church had been patched up and, though now almost on the brink of the cliff, was still in use in 1835. The painter John Constable had read Mrs. Smith's sonnets. During the last years of his life he formed a friendship with an Arundel man, George Constable, who was no relation but an amateur artist and admirer of Constable's work. In the summer of 1835, Constable and two of his children were staying with his namesake and he roamed the neighbourhood with his sketchbook. On 10 July, he found the subject of the sonnet and sketched it three times — two 'tries' and one finished in water-colours — with the church in the foreground and the coastline in the haze beyond. On the back of the sketch he wrote: 'Middleton Church. See Charlotte Smith's sonnet.' Then he went down on to the beach and investigated the face of the cliff, which was now the sliced-off side of the graveyard. Here the sonnet's 'village dead' were still on view, and his next sketch — showing layers of turf, cliff and shingle, with a dark streak in the cliff — was captioned: 'Form of a skeleton in the bank of the churchyard'. Among other sketches done during these happy few weeks on holiday 'amid most heavenly scenery', he drew the castle and watermill at Arundel and left this particular sketch with George Constable. Later in the year, George's son John wanted a larger picture made of it, so the sketch was brought to London and it was on this new picture that Constable was working when he died. Incidentally, his watercolour of Middleton church had been done just in time; a few more storms that year saw the beginning of the end, and by 1840 there was only a section of the north wall and roof standing by the shore. The beach was littered with masonry, and the urchins of the day — and for some years to come — indulged in macabre games with bones on the sand and used skulls for footballs. In 1847–48, a new church, using some of the old material, was built a safe quarter of a mile inland.

Where next might the visitors wander to relieve the tedium of the health cure? Perhaps westwards along the shore from Bognor, admiring the half-dozen hand-some houses of Aldwick's gentry, until after another two miles they reached the lonely-bird-haunted wastes of Pagham Harbour. This was a large natural harbour created by inroads of the sea, from which the tide ebbed through a 170-yard-wide channel in the shingle beach, leaving marsh, mudflats and small streams. If the tide was high, one might see a cargo vessel working a careful passage through the difficult channel, taking coal up to Sidlesham on the north-west shore of the harbour or bringing out a load of flour from the big tidemill in the village. In those years, one might have come across the recumbent but alert form of the Rev. A. E. Knox, who used to stay at West Cottage, Aldwick, while accumulating the experiences that he set down in his *Ornithological Rambles in Sussex*. Of lying on the barrier of beach that divides the harbour from the sea, and watching the birds, he wrote:

> 'Here, in the dead, long, summer days, when not a breath of air has been stirring, have I frequently remained for hours, stretched on the hot shingle and gazing at the osprey as he soared aloft, or watched the little islands of mud at the turn of the tide, as each gradually rose from the receding waters and was successively taken possession of by flocks of sandpipers and ring-dotterels.'

But the main attraction that drew the visitor was the Hushing, or Hissing, Pool. Just within the mouth of the harbour was a bar called the Dobbin, a dialect word for sea gravel mixed with sand. When the tide came in and flowed over this spot to the depth of five feet, the bubbling of a huge cauldron seemed to erupt on the surface. With a great hissing noise, giant bubbles shot up from the harbour bed and floated on the waves, creating a simmering, effervescent spectacle 30 feet wide and 130 feet long. The higher the tide, the noisier the bubbling. The only explanation for the phenomenon was a cavity below the gravel from which air was expelled at pressure when the tide rushed in.

Sea fishing might not appeal to all visitors, so the even quieter pursuit of freshwater angling could be followed, either for perch, roach and eels in the stream flowing through the Brookland between Bognor and Felpham or for tench, roach and perch in the Chichester-Arun Canal, two miles inland. Mr. Cundy's elaborate canal scheme, as we know, had not progressed any farther than his drawing board, so there were no men o'war from Portsmouth sailing through the farmlands, only the sight of an occasional barge sail lifting above the corn. Originally surveyed by the elder Rennie, and three years in the making at the cost of £160,000, the Chichester-Arun Canal was the last part of the navigation linking London with the coast. Eight barges had formed the opening procession on 20 May 1823, led by the vigorous old Earl of Egremont, then 71, followed by the Duke of Norfolk and a band in the second vessel. Several companies now had barge fleets, with their local agents accepting business along the route. At Arundel and Chichester, Mr. Thomas Bonamy took the money — and it had to be ready money — for the dispatch of goods by Messrs. Howell and Randell's barges. At the London end, cargoes sailed from the company's wharf at Queenhithe on Wednesdays and Saturdays and the long voyage through the thick woods of Surrey and Sussex was not without a touch of excitement; the company refused to be responsible for losses from river piracy.

Once a visitor got as far as the canal, he would see Arundel the irresistible and make haste towards this monument to Duke Charles's flight into Gothicism. For the Duke was now dead, victim of a cold caught while sleeping in a tent in his courtyard after reeling away from the junketing that had accompanied the opening of his new Barons' Hall in 1815. Now, for a while, the extensive remodelling of the castle was halted. It was an architectural fantasy and the buildings on three sides of a quadrangle were a gorgeous medley of styles, early Norman and 14th-century predominating, with a profusion of elaborate friezes, tracery, pinnacled buttresses, canopied niches, oriel and triple-arched windows and turrets. As you entered the courtyard, an enormous bas-relief, manufactured in Coade's Artificial Stone, faced you from its spectacular position under the machiolation of the east wall. It represented King Alfred instituting Trial by Jury on Salisbury Plain. The Barons' Hall on the west side had come straight out of a Gothic novel and boasted a roof of Spanish chestnut and 10 stained-glass windows depicting early ancestors. According to John Constable who looked at them in horror, they resembled 'drunken bargemen dressed up as Crusaders'.

The public saw none of the interior, being only admitted to the ancient ivied Keep from which they looked down through wire netting at the owls still breeding within. The glories of the private apartments remained a mystery safe from desecration; as a local guidebook put it, 'it is characteristic of an Englishman that he cannot be content with gratifying his sight, but must lay hands, if possible, on what he views'.

The Duke of Richmond, on the other hand, welcomed visitors to Goodwood when he was not in residence. Tickets could be obtained from his steward for a tour of the mansion or for a popular picnic excursion to Carné's Seat, a beautiful little gazebo of two rooms overlooking the plain and the sea. It was the splendour of Goodwood's art treasures and the grandeur of its life that drew the people, for the house had no particular antiquity. The neighbourhood was still talking of the wonders of the coming-of-age celebrations of the Duke's eldest son, Charles, Earl of March, on 27 February 1839. That was the day that began with a stag hunt and finished with a ball and supper and a beacon blazing on Trundle Hill. Nearly 700 of the county's nobility and gentry, including 33 of Bognor's élite, were guests for the evening and the Duke's house-party was enlivened by the presence of such famous figures as the Marquis of Anglesey, hero of Waterloo and maternal grandfather to the young Earl. Therefore, to enter such an establishment, to admire the collection of paintings, tapestries and china, to gaze upon the death-mask of Pitt, Napoleon's chair and Charles I's shirt, was an experience that few Bognor visitors missed. After which there were always the attractions of the park, with its strange cork oaks and cedars and unexpected conceits such as a shell grotto, Gothic temple, orangery, catacombs and mock ruins.

After the round of sightseeing excursions, the rest of one's sojourn by the sea might be occupied with recreation, such as archery or cricket, or in furthering one's acquaintance with marine life. There was a variety of shells, fossils and seaweeds to be collected or purchased. Dried seaweed, artistically glued into a pink and green spray round an engraving or the Steyne or the Rock Buildings, was a perfect souvenir to take back home; or one might choose a paperweight carved out of kidney-rock, or an agate pebble, split and polished, which could be set as a brooch. For real Nautical adventure, there was always a sailing-boat to be hired for a voyage to Littlehampton or Selsey Bill; and, once in the company of sturdy, quick-eyed fisherfolk like the Raglesses, Allens, Crees or Ides, the possibility of learning the whereabouts of some contraband goods was never remote.

*   *   *

Despite armed coastguards on shore and revenue cutters afloat, the illicit trade with France was still vastly profitable to anybody who cared to take the risk. In Bognor, the old military barracks had been taken over as one of the Kent and Sussex coastal blockade stations under a Navy lieutenant, but in 1831 this system of guarding the coast against smuggling was abandoned and an improved coastguard service came into being, backed by a mounted force which patrolled inland. At first this met with some success, with the result that some of those who were living on parish funds applied for more relief, as their secret income from smuggling had dropped considerably. But soon, having learnt the methods of 'the enemy', the trade reorganised its own methods and out from Cherbourg came the French luggers, towing tub-boats made of rough planking. On reaching the appointed spot, perhaps after having mingled with an English fishing fleet in the dusk to escape notice, the tub-boats were unhitched, rowed ashore and the cargo either hidden or run inland, while the cheap tub-boats were broken up to divert suspicion. Alternatively, kegs were lashed to a hawser like a string of beads and, having been weighted, were dropped overboard at a chosen spot, to be hauled up later on by lobster-men apparently engaged on their normal innocent occupation.

The strategical planning·of a smuggling run was worthy of a general. The miller at Littlehampton harbour would set his sails at a certain angle, indicating whether the revenue boat was active or not, and this code signal would be passed from windmill to windmill along the coast to Selsey. Decoy boats might also set off in one direction to distract the coastguard, while the brandy arrived elsewhere and was quickly worked inland to caves near Goodwood or Halnaker. Or it might be temporarily *cached* in the tombs of Middleton churchyard, in Becket's Barn at Pagham, under the pulpit in Yapton church or in one of the other innumerable 'hides', such as the double ceiling in the *Berkeley Arms* in West Street. Like lightning, the hidden 'tub-carriers' would spring for the beach as the cargo arrived early in the night and in a few minutes they were on their way, ready to duck into a ditch or culvert or even sling their precious load down a well if a coastguard showed up.

Five shillings a night was the carrier's reward, and 10 shillings if he succeeded in saving the illicit cargo in the event of a skirmish. Some gangs had armed protectors who earned £1, and often there was a turmoil in the surf and blood on the sand. One Saturday night in March 1835 a Bognor coastguard heard a keel grate on the beach and leapt aboard before the gang laid hands on the tubs. In the fight that followed, one of his bullets caught Jesse Whittington in the knee and the wounded man and three others were dragged into the coastguard station as prisoners. Next morning, Jesse's leg was amputated but he died, leaving a wife and three children. His fellow townsmen, as jury, returned an inquest verdict of 'justifiable homicide'.

Though in the coastal parishes smuggling was regarded as a natural if dangerous game, the strengthening of the Government's guards called for greater secrecy in organisation. The spreading of ghost stories and other terrors was a means of keeping the inquisitive indoors at night and informers were liable to meet a sudden end, one of them being burnt alive on the Yapton–Barnham road. But informing was not common despite the rewards offered, and it was more usual for a man to suffer a sentence than betray his comrades. This happened in Bognor on an occasion when a coastguard was nearly drowned. A gang had roped him to a breakwater and the tide reached his neck before the biased inhabitants troubled to rescue him. A suspected member of the gang who lived in Chapel Street was brought before the magistrates and told he would be freed on giving the names of his accomplices. His response was a dramatic gesture and a cry of 'You can slit me from here to here, but I won't tell!' Such reticence became an honourable tradition and parents impressed on their children the necessity of acting dumb when questioned by any revenue officers. It is said today that, as a result, many children in the Bognor area are unable to give you a straight answer.

But coastguards and customs men used their own ears and eyes to outwit this public conspiracy. They knew that innkeepers bought illegal spirits and that the kegs had to be delivered somehow. One day outside the *Beach Inn* — which had been built at the side of Waterloo Square — Tom Kent drew up with a loaded hay cart. A group chatting by the shore watched him. One said: 'I bet old Tom's got one hidden in there.' The next moment an apparent idler detached himself from the fringe of the group, walked over and challenged Tom. The idler was, unfortunately, a revenue officer.

*   *   *

When the summer visitors had gone, the calm of deep sleep descended over the small watering-place. The gulls dipped and cried over the long, silent sands in autumn. The carrier cart trundled off to the Chichester tallow factory with a load of butcher's fat for making candles, or 'dips', for the coming winter. When winter came and the fishermen in their huts sat among piles of withies making new crab and lobster pots, and the bitter gales and seas removed a few more yards of Bognor, the Commissioners gazed eastwards and thought hungrily of Brighton and its railway.

Brighton had finally been linked to London by rail on the foggy morning of 21 September 1841. Railway travel, a dusty choking frightening experience in uncomfortable open trucks and cramped carriages, now provided the opportunity for the new middle-class masses to get to the sea. Stage-coach travel, for those who could afford it, was on the decline, one reason being that the threat of railway competition had caused the coach proprietors to increase their speed on the road, so that a journey became more exhausting than ever. Cobbett said it was like being 'hurried along by force in a box with an air-hole in it'. Whether the railways were bringing the right sort of people to the sea was a much-discussed subject. Certainly Queen Victoria had found them 'indiscreet and troublesome' and left the Brighton Pavilion for good in 1845. But to some resorts still courting the iron road it was the quantity not the quality of clientèle that seemed so appetising, so desirable and so essential in the saving of speculatory hopes from extinction.

So in Bognor various interested parties watched and waited for the proposed extension of the line westward from Shoreham, and the resort kept its advertising up-to-date by announcing – in May 1845 – that one was now able to travel to London in five and a half hours. This miracle was achieved by boarding the *Railway Times* coach at the *Norfolk Hotel* any morning, except Sundays, at 8 and catching the London train from Shoreham. On the return journey, the train arrived at Shoreham at 2 p.m. and the coach was back in Bognor by 4.30 p.m. Both trains had the advantage of have 'Second Class *enclosed* Carriages' attached.

That year, 1845, the line reached Worthing and in December the Vestry Committee received a communication that excited some and appalled those to whom railways seemed a mixed blessing. Mr. Phillips, Surveyor of the Highways, issued a notice calling the parish to a meeting; and, as it was the most important local announcement for years, it is worth quoting in full:

Parish of South Bersted

Notice is hereby given that a Meeting will be held in the Vestry Room at the Parish Church on Friday next at ten o'clock in the Forenoon to take into consideration a Notice served on the Surveyor of the Highways by the Solicitors of the Directors of the Brighton Railway, which Notice states that it is intended to form a Branch Railway to Bognor from and out of the Brighton and Chichester Railway, and that such Branch Railway will cross the Public Highway in the parish aforesaid leading from Bognor to Felpham, and also another Public Highway maintained and repaired by the parish aforesaid called Gloucester Road, and the said Meeting will determine whether the Surveyor shall signify his consent thereto or not.

December 28th, 1845.

In plainer words, it was proposed to bring a branch to Bognor from the main lines now creeping along the coastal plain and this branch would cross the low-lying Brookland between Bognor and Felpham and then curve into the town from the east. The terminus, therefore, would be in those valuable empty fields right on the sea edge.

It must have been a heated meeting. No doubt the Highway Surveyor struggled with his conscience and finally blurted out that anybody who built a railway in such a position would find it completely submerged at regular intervals. Doubtless, too, local landowners raised objections to any alternative routes and even to the proposed one. The outcome was that the scheme faded away and the line went straight along from Worthing to Chichester in 1846, leaving Bognor stranded to the south. Out of all the shattered dreams and hopes came a morsel of solace from the railway company, a modicum of balm for wounded local pride, in the shape of a small wayside halt of brick and flint in the fields 3½ miles north of the town. It was opened on 8 June 1846, and was named 'Bognor Station'.

At this point of time, at this moment of disappointment, it almost seemed that one could have written Finis to the chequered progress of Hotham's town. This is not to say that Bognor looked like gradually dying out, becoming perhaps a scattered ghost-haunted ruin visited by the curious from Littlehampton and eventually succumbing to the sea in the manner of the original settlement. Families were still faithful to the little resort. The memory of Princess Charlotte still acted as a Pied Piper, calling children to the sands. But it now required something stronger than child visitors and a handful of well-connected residents to revive the impoverished purses and spirits of an unfinished town that defied speculators to lay another brick. Fortunately, just before it was too late, Bognor found its saviour. It was the horse.

*   *   *

Like Bognor itself, the annual Goodwood Race Meeting had been through troubled times. At the first public meeting on 28, 29 and 30 April 1802, the prize money was £1,001 but, as the years went on and the date of the meeting was advanced through May into June, the stakes dwindled (£262 in 1810). The meeting had become mainly a social gathering of friends and amateur jockeys, ending with mild celebrations at Chichester — such as, in 1809, a 10s. 6d. supper at the *Swan* and two entertainments, *The Bride of Hexham* and *The Lake of Lausanne* at the theatre in South Street. However, when Charles Lennox became the 5th Duke in 1819 he began to develop both the estate and his sporting instincts. A former Army comrade, Viscount Dunwich, advised him on the necessity of running a small stable and he also introduced him to a good trainer, John Kent.

Thus the seeds of the future glory of Goodwood were quietly sown and around him the young Duke accumulated a fraternity of bloods and 'Turf' men who enjoyed the training and racing of horses as a sport. By 1825 the meeting, coupled with the gaiety of the Duke's house party, was becoming more than a local event. That year the prize money beat the original stakes for the first time and reached £1,057, of which £50 was the reward for winning the first Bognor Plate Handicap. The Duke himself kept only seven horses but the admirable advantages of Goodwood for breeding and training were freely offered to his friends, so that in time John Kent had nearly thirty horses in his charge.

Then into the ducal circle entered a man who was to become known as the Napoleon of the Turf, Lord George Cavendish Bentinck. The stables he was using at this time were at Danebury in Hampshire, where John Barham Day was trainer. 'Honest John' Day read sermons to his jockeys on Sunday evenings till they fell asleep. In later life, he lived at Bentinck House, Felpham, and is buried in the churchyard. His grandson, Alfred Day, established Fontwell Racecourse, five miles north of Bognor. Lord George, being impressed by the superior prowess of Goodwood-trained horses over his own, began by sharing three or four horses with the Duke and also suggested improvements to the course. Another half-mile was added to it and George Draper of Chichester was engaged to design a new

Grecian-style brick grandstand, which was first used at the 1830 meeting. Sportsmen, perched 50 feet up on the top of it that year, had a splendid view of Fleur-de-Lys winning the Gold Cup. This was a fine Royal start to the improved meeting, for the horse belonged to the new King, even though William IV hardly knew one end of a horse from the other 'Take the whole fleet – I suppose some of them will win!' had been his characteristically nautical order to his trainer when asked which horses to enter.

By 1837, the prize money had reached £11,145 and Goodwood was the place to go to in late July. Rooms in cottages and farmhouses were fetching high prices. Vehicles thronged the highways leading into West Sussex. The brothers Moon, who kept inns at Kingston and Godalming in Surrey, had over 100 pairs of post-horses ready for the demands of racegoers toiling south in private carriages and coaches. When they finally reached the airy summit of the Downs, the beauty of the view and the charm of the course atoned for all previous discomforts. And already the familiar eccentric figures of the racing world were lending authentic atmosphere to the scene, in particular the freckled pale-faced Jerry, witty, impudent, half-crazed, all dressed up in cast-offs, including cocked hat and eyeglass, promenading barefoot among the carriages, ogling the ladies, selling race lists and exchanging non-stop comments with his noblemen 'friends' who delighted in his patronising banter.

In the autumn of 1841, Lord George Bentinck was permitted to bring his entire stable to Goodwood and soon, with sometimes 120 horses in training, new gallops and other improvements were needed. To all this, the Duke cheerfully acquiesced, fired by his friend's enthusiasm, but he was never quite swept away. His own stud remained small, because racing to him was still a sport, whereas Lord George was a dedicated prince of gamblers. Considering the Duke's dislike of betting and that he was concerned both with revising the Jockey Club rules and speeding Parliamentary action to regulate the conduct of horse-racing, it is remarkable that the two men, so opposed in views, remained such close friends.

Thus, in the 1840s, Goodwood became the perfectly administered race meeting, the model for all others and the one where the going was never upset by the weather, as a result of Lord George spreading tons of tan over the course to give it extra springiness. A weighing-room, an enclosure round the stand and a betting ring were other improvements; and at the back of the weighing-room one even found Hayley's godson, William Hayley Mason, printing off the race lists. 'With magnificent scenery,' wrote an eyewitness in 1845, 'first-rate racing and the cream of England's best society to inspirit and gratify him, a stranger would indeed be fastidious who did not consider the Goodwood course the perfection and paradise of racegrounds.'

Fastidious, too, would be anyone who did not follow up this verdict with the realisation that Bognor was perfectly placed for a stay during the meeting. It was an agreeable surprise for racegoers to discover that there was a little resort so conveniently to hand. Though many hardly knew its name – Bigner, Bagnar, Bugnor? – it offered sea breezes, beds and food in the hottest week of the year. Therefore the coaches rolled into the town, the stables were packed, Royalty trod the sands again and the town burst at the seams.

It was to be only once a year, but it was worth waiting for. It gave the place new purpose. Goodwood Week was to become Christmas in July for Bognor. To the inhabitants, particularly those with spare rooms to let, the horse was indeed a noble animal.

B O G N O R
SEPTEMBER 17ᵀᴴ 1853

Fig. 13.   Bognor Races, 17 September 1853.

Chapter XIII

MID-VICTORIAN PROGRESS

FROM THE TOP of the keep at Arundel Castle, the prominent landmarks discernible by visitors on a clear day were Highdown Hill to the east and Chichester Cathedral spire and the Isle of Wight to the west. To this fair prospect was now added a further wonder, the sight of a railway train cutting along through the fields, and the authors of Arundel's guidebooks made haste to include this new marvel amid their catalogue of ducal attractions. From observing ancient devices for pouring molten lead on besiegers, the attention of the visitor was next directed to 'the line of the South Coast Railway which may be traced for some distance, with the white smoke of the engine curling about in its rapid progress'.

This topographical observation, made in 1851, was in keeping with the times, for the railway's sudden and complete conquest of Britain was affecting everyone's life to some degree and it was impossible to ignore it. The young Queen's eventual approval of this revolutionary means of travel had removed many doubts, and soon the population in various districts was shifting, increasing and even falling, according to the incentives and ambitions kindled by the proximity of a railway station.

It was too early yet to notice any real effect that the nearby railway might be having on Bognor. Local soothsayers, who could now look back in old age to the boom days of Hotham, would have recalled the rash hopes of subsequent speculators and prophesied that the railway would not make much difference, either. They would have been right. Bognor was still a village at heart and liked its compact life within two main streets. Since the madcap days of the mercurial Beazley and the aspirations of Lord Arran, the population of the town had increased by only 500 in 20 years — from 1,399 in 1831 to 1,913 in 1851. In the coming 30 years the increase would be under 1,400 (1881: pop. 3,290), but this very smallness was, in the long run, to prove an unsuspected asset.

Some visitors must at first have thought the place even smaller than it was, when their train stopped in the thick of cornfields and the noticeboard proclaimed: 'Bognor Station'; but in 1852 this false impression was corrected by renaming the halt 'Woodgate for Bognor'. Outside in the lane there were sometimes two vehicles to transport passengers and luggage to the coast for 1s. One was Edwin Newman's horse-omnibus; the other was the official carrier and parcel agent's cart, owned and driven by Jeremiah William Swan. 'Is there any other way of getting to Bognor other than using Swan?' a visitor once enquired, having doubtfully eyed this rough conveyance. 'There is,' replied Swan. 'Walk!'

Going down to the sea by Swan was a very leisurely progress. His horse either trotted or walked, according as it felt inclined; and the visitor was lulled by the peace of it all as the cart slowly mounted the hump of the canal bridge at Lidsey and then came past Shripney where the meadows were dotted white with Farmer Hobgen's famous flock of Southdown sheep, founded in 1810. Eventually, the squat heavily-buttressed tower of South Bersted church came in sight and, after a twist and turn along the leafy highway, past the mansions of the gentry, the visitor suddenly saw the glittering sea and the cluster of prim clean buildings built in the cause of peace, respectability and health.

This cause was a lost one as far as the latest guidebooks were concerned. In comparison with the ever-increasing whirl of amusements at other resorts, Bognor was already being written off by the more humorous writers as a back number. The effort to find something interesting to say about it was too much even for a prolific journalist like E. L. Blanchard (no relation to the Captain) when compiling his 1851 *Guide to the Watering Places of England*. He diverted his readers' attention instead to a tour of surrounding antiquities and then, with witty despair, made the following concluding remarks:

> 'We throw out these hints as likely to prove of service to those who may feel otherwise at a loss to conceive how a month at Bognor or Littlehampton can be reasonably got through, without being driven to Zimmerman on "Solitude" as a preliminary course of study, or to the necessity of taking lessons on seclusion from a philosophically matriculated hermit.'

Such disparagement was a little unjustified, for there was no good reason, just because more people were coming to the seaside, for small resorts to court possible failure by aping the way of life of larger places. Supply and demand were as much a part of coastal economics as elsewhere and it so happened that Bognor's type of visitor was not very demanding and the town not always in the financial position to supply. Consequently there was an absence of what Blanchard and his fellow writers deemed as the essential exhilarating clutter of the popular watering-place. There was no pier, there were no weighing-machines, no telescopes through which to look at the lady bathers, no organ-grinders, itinerant fiddlers or military bands; no crackle of fireworks or gentlemen ascending in balloons, no lecturers or missionaries, no evening excitements such as raffles and concerts in the libraries and fancy bazaars, no awe-inspiring wonders like Hastings' castle and waterfalls or the chalk tunnels of Margate.

Dead, indeed, was Bognor if it were to be measured for attractions by this yardstick. Yet, such is the unpredictability of fashion, it was for the despised quality of solitude that the town found itself being taken quietly into the bosom of the Victorian family on holiday and carried gently forward to a modest fame and moderate prosperity, with Goodwood Week as a magnificent annual pick-me-up. In other words, peace and quiet had become the aim of the better type of middle-class holiday-maker as the mid-century was reached. Bognor could offer peace and quiet in abundance, even though few visiting families realised that the resort had been purposely created by its founder to provide these assets.

1. Sir Richard Hotham (1722-1799). Portrait by George Romney, finished and signed by Dudman. The original was painted in ten sittings at Blackfriars in 1793.

2. Merton Grove, Sir Richard Hotham's house at Wimbledon. (He is also said to have owned Merton Place, later the home of Lord Nelson.) (*From the collections of Merton Library Service*)

3. Sir Richard Hotham and his wife—miniatures by 'P.B.'. They were married at Chelsea Hospital in 1743; Lady Hotham died in 1777.

4. Bersted church, 2 June 1790, from the drawing by S. H. Grimm in the British Museum. Hotham paid for improvements to this church.

5. The birth of Bognor as a seaside resort, recorded in South Bersted parish register by the Rev. Thomas Durnford.

1787.

January 18th 1787 – The first Foundation Stone of a Public Bathing Place at Bognor in the Parish of Berstead was laid by Sir Richard Hotham Knt. at the House called by the Name of the Lodge.

6. Hothamton Crescent, showpiece of the new resort: the North Wing, later named 'Mordington'.

7. Hothamton Crescent: Dome House, the centrepiece, built to attract George III.

8. Hothamton Crescent: the South Wing, later known as Arran Lodge, and renamed St Michael's.

In Memory of
Sir RICHARD HOTHAM KNIGHT
FOUNDER OF BOGNOR
WHO DIED MARCH 13TH 1799
IN HIS 17TH YEAR

HIS MORTAL REMAINS WERE INTERRED IN
SOUTH BERSTED CHURCH, BUT, ON ITS RESTORATION
IN 1895, WERE REINTERRED IN THIS VAULT.

SUSANNA

BOGNOR ROCKS.

Mr WALKDEN proprietor of the extensive FAMILY HOTEL at the above elegant WATERING PLACE has the honor of announcing to the Nobility & Fashionables the completion of the expensive repairs & improvements his House & Baths have undergone & assures them, nothing has been omitted that could possibly conduce to the accommodation & convenience of Visitors: and he trusts that his selection of Wines of the finest quality & his assiduity in every branch of the Business will not fail to afford universal satisfaction.

Among the improvements a stud of most excellent Horses has been provided. the Subscription Room will be furnished with a liberal supply of Newspapers, & periodical publications, & every comfort will be found by Ladies & Gentlemen, who honor the Hotel with their company.

10. (*left*) An early trade card advertising improvements to the hotel built by Hotham and destroyed in the Great Fire of Bognor in 1826.

11. (*below*) Trade card advertising the Rock Buildings.

(*opposite*) Hotham's last resting
lace in South Bersted churchyard;
s remains were removed from the
hurch during restoration in 1879.

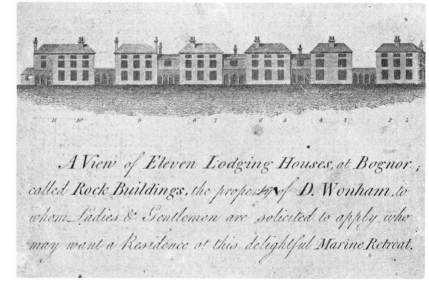

A View of Eleven Lodging Houses, at Bognor; called Rock Buildings, the property of D. Wonham, to whom Ladies & Gentlemen are solicited to apply who may want a Residence at this delightful Marine Retreat.

2. Rock Buildings (later called Rock
ardens) was Bognor's first seafront
rrace. It was built about 1804 by
aniel Wonham, and comprised 11
uses. Rock House (to the left of
e crescent) was No. 12.

13. (*above*) William
Blake's cottage at Felp-
ham. This was the home
of the poet and artist
from 1800 to 1803.

14. (*right*) The *Fox Inn*
at Felpham, before the
fire of 1946, had connec-
tions with the old *Fox Inn*
at Bognor (p. 13). Scofield,
the soldier who brought a
charge of treason against
William Blake (p. 52), was
quartered here.

The Fox Inn, Felpham

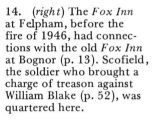

15. Turret House, Felpham, where Hotham's
eccentric neighbour, the poet William Hayley
lived. It was demolished in February 1961.

16. Princess Charlotte (1796-1817), from an engraving by Henry Meyer, after A. E. Chalon. Bognor was her summer playground from 1808 to 1811.

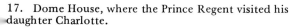

17. Dome House, where the Prince Regent visited his daughter Charlotte.

18. The Jubilee School, High Street was built in 1817 under Princess Charlotte's patronage. It was altered for council offices in 1880, and replaced by the bus station in the 1930s.

Particulars and Conditions of Sale

OF A DELIGHTFUL

MARINE RESIDENCE,

SUITABLE FOR

A FAMILY OF THE FIRST RESPECTABILITY;

WITH

GARDENS, PLEASURE GROUNDS, AND LAWN,

IN ALL

Forty Acres of Excellent Land;

THE PROPERTY OF

Sir THOMAS TROUBRIDGE, Bart.

SITUATE

AT BOGNOR, SUSSEX.

WHICH

Will be Sold by Auction,

BY MR. DORE,

At Garraway's Coffee House,

On THURSDAY, the 29th Day of JUNE, 1815,

AT ONE O'CLOCK,

(Unless an acceptable Offer is previously made by Private Contract.)

May be Viewed 'till the Day of Sale, and Particulars had on the Premises; at the LIBRARIES at *Brighton*, *Worthing*, and *Bognor*; at Garraway's, and of Mr. DORE, 2, *Little Brook Street, Hanover Square.*

Smith & Davy, Printers, 7, Queen Street, Seven Dials

THE LITERARY TIMES;

A Journal of Literature, Science, & the Fine Arts.

SATURDAY, NOVEMBER 14, 1835.

VIEW OF SUDLEY VILLA, BOGNOR.

AND VILLAS.

e little villa, which forms the
nt engraving, is no otherwise
being the residence of the
Gascoigne, of Parliamentary
Coleridge was supposed to
the Devil's Walk, when he
—'s burning face." It is
how long the gallant officer
present abode, as SUDLEY
der the hammer of the auc-
the sea, and in other respects
ty, with the little town of
d which we shall proceed
notice.

mpton, county Sussex, is a
ng place, situated on a dry,
able for the purity of its air,
assemblage of brick and
house are regular plan, pro-

Adhelm. It was subsequently held by various
members of the blood-royal, and other potent
barons, until it passed into the possession of the
Fitzalans, Earls of Arundel, from whom it was
conveyed by marriage into that of the Howards,
Dukes of Norfolk, with whom the paramount
influence still remains. The primitive castle was
deemed impregnable in the feudal times, and, in
consequence, is greatly celebrated in the civil
brouls by which they are so much distinguished.
It also underwent two sieges during the civil
wars of the seventeenth century, from which
period it continued little better than a mass of
ruins, till the late Duke of Norfolk undertook to
restore it to its ancient magnificence. It stands
on a knoll, partly formed by nature, and partly
by art, on the north-east side of the town of
Arundel, and commands a fine view over the sea
as far as the Isle of Wight; it is embosomed in a
luxuriant grove, and presents a singularly beautiful, imposing and majestic appearance. The
building is in the gothic style of free stone, that

mayor and twelve burgesses, with other officers,
the former of whom is annually chosen at a
court-leet of the lord of the manor. He has the
authority of a justice of the peace, and no writ
can be executed in the borough without his in-
dorsement. Great quantities of timber for ship-
building are annually shipped; the harbour,
which was formerly capable of containing vessels
of one hundred tons burthen, has of late years
been much damaged by the sea. The church,
dedicated to the Holy Trinity, and formerly col-
legiate, is an ancient gothic structure, with
transepts, from the centre of which rises a low
square tower, surmounted by a small wooden
spire. In it are beautiful monuments to several
of the Earls of Arundel, of the Fitzalan family,
and others to various members of the Howards.

REVIEWS OF BOOKS.

*Liverpool, its History, Topography, Society, and
Inhabitants.* 2 vols. 4to., illustrated. Liverpool and London, 1835. (Unpublished.)

We consider that we have been fortunate in
obtaining before our contemporaries copies of

without thinking of the ca
been employed upon this
rious and gloriously printed
believe that any other city
don, could have produced t
presses, and we must now
tract as we can from their p
for their praise.

If you want a congregated
and fashion of the town of
in the porch of the Lyceum Ne
and for three hours every day
talking, almost all of either se
see or to be seen. This is the l
Contrary, however, to the u
brated metropolitan namesake
here is greater than men, and t
by the latter, they escort one a
fashion; and the ladies meet
laxation, it would appear, ra
the intellect than the exhibitu
are generally to be seen wit
knowledge in their arms, name
the Lyceum library.

Bold-street is at present
structures and excavations
on at the same time als
is a pretty place for a p
not when the weather

19. (*opposite*) Sale particulars of Chapel House in 1815—the year of Waterloo. The house was bought by the Rev. Thomas Smith, who re-named it 'Bersted Lodge'.

20. (*above*) Sudley Cottage, known as 'the Den', from *The Literary Times* of 1835.

21. The *White Horse* inn at South Bersted was the meeting place of the South Bersted Vestry Committee.
22. The *Sussex Hotel*, High Street was formerly the *New Inn*, and stopping place for the London stage-coach. It was also the meeting place of the Board of Commissioners appointed in 1822.

23. Waterloo Square had houses on the west side built by William Kimber Wonham in the 1820s.

24. Steyne Place, West Street, overlooking the Steyne. This scene is typical of many Bognor buildings erected in the post-Hotham era. The Regency awnings have since been removed.

25. (*opposite above*) Bognor from the sea, in 1857. This is an engraving from the *Illustrated London News*, showing the *Norfolk Hotel* on the left, and Hothamton Place to the right.

26. (*opposite below*) The ketch *Annie*, unloading coal from Sunderland at Bognor. (*Photo: W.P.Marsh*)

27. The Library and Bazaar, High Street (now the Coffee House) was built in the early 1820s by Robert Knapton and visited by royalty. The *Bognor Observer* was founded here in 1872.

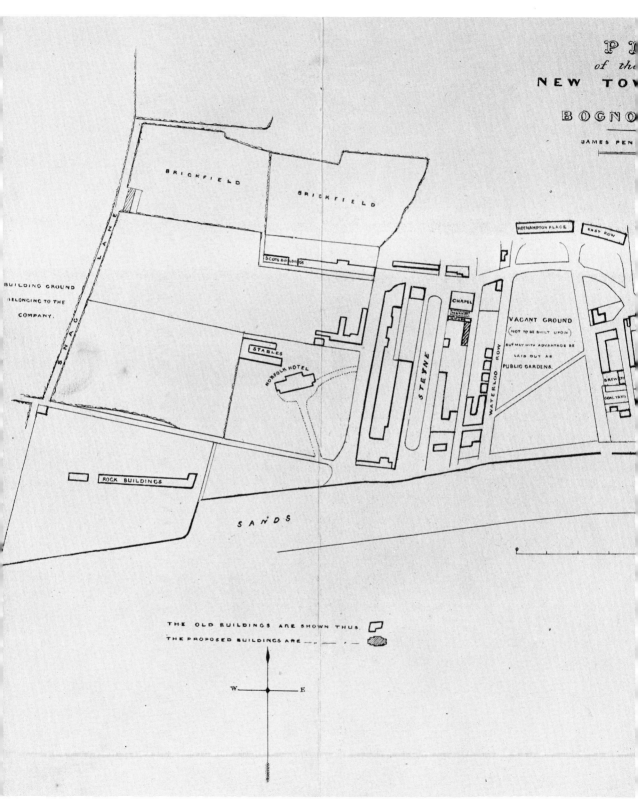

28. The Bognor Improvement Company's plan of 1835, for developing the fields west of Lennox Street and south of High Street (here shown as 'the London Road'). It envisaged a Winter Gardens, and a pier at the foot of York Road.

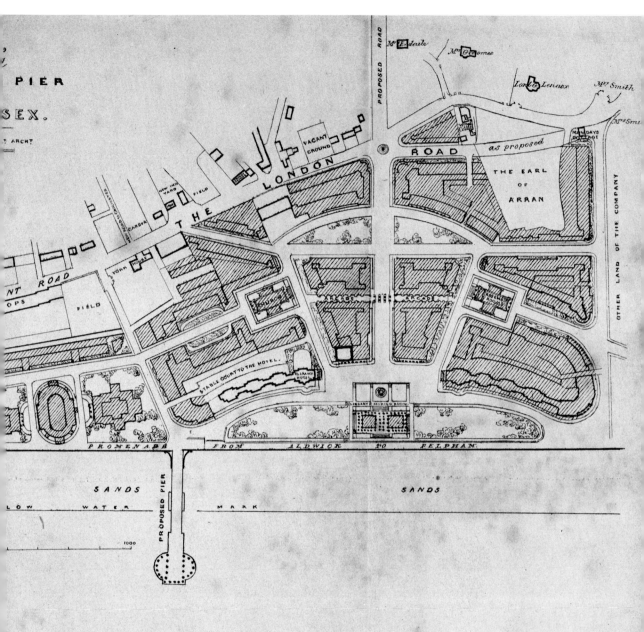

PIER

SEX.

ARCH^T

PROPOSED ROAD

Mr Easdaile

Mr C. Gomes

Lord G. Lennox

Mrs Smith

Mrs Smi

as proposed

MANDAYS HOUSE

THE EARL OF ARRAN

THE LONDON ROAD

OTHER LAND OF THE COMPANY

VACANT GROUND

NEW INN YARD

FIELD

BOWLING GREEN GARDEN

YORK HOUSE

NT ROAD

OPS

FIELD

CHURCH

STABLE COURT TO THE HOTEL.

NORFOLK HOTEL

LIBRARY READING ROOM

PROMENADE FROM ALDWICK TO FELPHAM.

SANDS

SANDS

LOW WATER MARK

PROPOSED PIER

1000

H E S E A

29.   Arthur Smith's view of his proposed Victoria Park Estate in the 1870s. Elizabeth Court (centre foreground) was one of the few features which did materialise.

30.   Robert Knapton's view of Bognor in 1823. West Street is on the left, and in the centre, where the *Royal Hotel* stands today, is James Binstead's Library.

History was repeating itself. Just as long ago, certain of the nobility had fled from the whirligig of the Prince's Brighton and found shelter under the wing of Hotham, so the changes in seaside life at other resorts were driving the more sensitive people to seek their holidays elsewhere. The level of public manners was dropping and the erstwhile courtly social life of the older-established seaside resorts had disintegrated. Day trips by rail now deposited vast new crowds of noisy pleasure-seekers on the esplanades, ousting the health-seeker from his dignified perambulation and jostling the delicate invalid in her wheeled chair. First-class hotels, accustomed to serving only the fashionable, now found office workers lolling like lords on the best sofas.

From the din of these over-populated seafronts, teeming with trippers engaged in hearty holiday riots, the middle classes recoiled and gradually the social stratification of the resorts came into being. Thus, in the south, for Cockney gaiety one sought Gravesend, Ramsgate or Margate, and for an extension of London life there was Brighton. The brand-new resort of Bournemouth was becoming the exclusive property of those seeking convalescence in comfort. Places like Worthing, St Leonards and Broadstairs offered peace without a hint of vulgarity, and for those who preferred something of the old aristocratic standard of manners there was to be found at Eastbourne, Folkestone, and Bognor a perfect background for gentility.

It had never occurred to the Commissioners of Bognor that its apparent dullness would be a saving grace and that the genteel, old-fashioned air of the resort had a definite appeal. Those familiar elements of the Bognor scene, the trees and meadows, the rural atmosphere, the garden parties on Mrs. Smith's lawn, the private carriages of the gentry in Hothamton Place, the servants in livery and the occasional sight of Mr. Fitzpatrick driving out of Fitzleet House (the former East Row) attended by his coachman and footmen with old-style powdered hair — all these were taken for granted by the inhabitants as part of an existence to which the town was long accustomed.

It was an unconscious detachment from the rest of the world that characterised Bognor. Yet, if you looked around, there were quiet echoes of the tumult of the expanding country and empire. Was not one of the very Conquerors of Scinde commemorated by a new tablet in South Bersted church? Sir Charles Napier himself had written the inscription to his memory: young Captain Edmund Brown of Bognor, Secretary to the Scinde Government, who had died in Bombay in 1848. Was not the fiercest political battle of recent years concerned with the repeal of the Corn Laws, with the Premier, Sir Robert Peel, facing the crisis of his great ministry — famine in Ireland, bad harvest in England and powerful agitation for free trade and the importation of foreign corn? Peel had the courage to back free trade and the Corn Laws were repealed. Corn could come into the country almost duty-free after years of fluctuating prices for the home product. Not that prices fell immediately after the passing of the Act in 1846, but the deed was done and Peel was out of office, a 'traitor' to his party. And after the storm there was no better place for a tired giant than somewhere quiet, somewhere by the sea, and he found it — in apartments at No. 6 The Steyne, Bognor.

And what of the other great national figure in this battle for cheaper bread and the happiness of man? He, too, was in Bognor a few years later, enjoying seaside simplicity with his wife and six children and working on his next pamphlet, *How Wars are got up in India*. Richard Cobden (1804–65), a West Sussex farmer's son, was a brilliant orator and agitator in the case of peace and non-intervention, and throughout his strenuous life of business travel — he was a manufacturer of printed calicos and muslins — he propagated his principles with immense persuasion. That the economics of wealth should never be divorced from the bodily health of mankind was one of his strongest doctrines and led to the formation of the powerful Anti-Corn Law League, with himself as its ablest speaker. When this particular victory was finally won, it was found that he had spent so much of his life freely labouring for world betterment that his own business had suffered. A sum of £70,000 was voluntarily raised by subscription so that he could settle with his creditors.

With part of the remaining money, he achieved an ambition and bought his birthplace, an old farmhouse at Dunford, south of Midhurst. This he rebuilt, retaining his mother's bedroom, and in the late summer of 1853 Bognor saw him — this man who had been described as 'an honour to England' passing his time between two houses, superintending the building of one and peaceably enjoying family life by the seaside in the other. Catherine, his wife, would drive him out of Bognor as far as Goodwood. From there he would set off on foot, through the Duke's park, up over the broad Downs, down into the Weald at Heyshott and through the woods to his old home.

*   *   *

Cobden's new house at Dunford was a plain, sturdy building with a square tower, which made it resemble an Italianate waterworks. But in its severe way, it was preferable to the new craze for elaborately picturesque Gothic mansions, tawdry with Tudorisms and bad jokes in Jacobean.

So far, this ostentation was not apparent in Bognor's new houses of the 1850s, mainly because there had been no one to employ a fashion-conscious architect. The sin of the future, the grotesque, bizarre medley of English seaside architecture, that curious coastal corruption of good taste that seemed inseparable from maritime development, had not yet set in along this part of the Sussex shore and was, fortunately, never to gain a great hold there. Far from spreading out miles to the east and west, obliterating the individuality of Felpham and Aldwick, Bognor was to remain dapper, almost as if it had heeded the advice of Dr. A. B. Granville, author of *The Spas of England*.

The doctor, whose opinions on health, climate and medicinal waters were held in wide respect, had informed the people of Bournemouth in 1841 exactly how to make their small colony into a resort for the better classes of society.

'You must not commit,' he warned, 'the many blunders that have been perpetrated in other watering-places, especially on these coasts and farther eastwards. You must not let in strangers and brick-and-mortar contractors to build up whole streets of lodging houses, or parades, and terraces interminable, in straight lines facing the sea, the roaring sea, and the severe gales that make the frames of an invalid's bedroom casement rattle five days in the week at least, and shake his own frame in bed also.'

Some such brick-and-mortar fate had occasionally threatened Bognor and had regrettably only been avoided not by the exercise of good judgment but by an absence of cash. Consequently, all that was being done at the moment was the slow local process of dotting the meadows with the solitary house or lonely terrace; and there was still time for someone, preferably like Dr. Granville, to be 'let into' the town to explain how it should grow up gracefully. Unfortunately, the doctor ignored Bognor's very existence.

The High Street was now the first complete street, with shops, houses and terraces on both sides. Any additions to the town naturally rose gaunt and box-like above the flat landscape, so that the need for careful treatment of the skyline was sadly brought home to those who viewed it from afar. A cry of agony broke from the biographer, Alexander Gilchrist, when he sighted Bognor from the rural seclusion of Felpham in the late 1850s. For some reason he had decided to write the first *Life of William Blake,* who was now almost completely forgotten. Charmed to find Rose Cottage and the village itself practically the same as they had been 50 years previously, the spell was shattered for him when he looked westwards across the Brookland as Blake had done. Something hideous had happened in the intervening years and when the *Life of William Blake* was published in 1863 one learnt that:

> 'Bognor was not then ugly and repulsive as a great part of it is now. At all events, there were none of those ghastly blocks of untenanted, unfinished houses, dreary monuments of building infatuation, which lower upon the traveller and put him out of heart as he approaches from Felpham, looking like so many builders' nightmares; erections that bespeak an almost brutish absence of natural instincts for the beautiful or expressive in construction.'

Bognor did not regard itself like this at all. It saw itself as 'a delightful watering-place, with a resident population of nearly 3,000 inhabitants; is a market and post town situated on the coast between Brighton and Selsea Bill: distant from London 63 miles (by South Coast Railway two hours)'.

These formed the opening remarks in the town's guidebook for 1852 and were still sound enough to remain unchanged when the book was reprinted in 1859. (The population figure refers to the parish of South Bersted.) A steady, dignified calm prevailed over the town. Hot, brutish speculative hopes had cooled and Bognor was quietly finding its place, after the uncertainties of its 50 formative years. Its early aristocratic training held good, imparting that faint air of propriety which had become such a joke to some and an undoubted attraction to others.

Though possibly not conscious that it was adding to the resort's reputation for well-bred inertia, the contents of the new guide-book displayed refined Victorian literary mannerisms wedded rather oddly to the antique phrases of Dr. Davis. None of Dally's learned work of 1828 was used, and this new publication of the High Street library, handsomely bound in scarlet cloth with gold title and fore-edge, merely reprinted part of Davis's original description of Bognor's assets in 1807, without mentioning when it was written. Consequently, even a mid-Victorian holidaymaker must have wondered why other resorts had bathing but only Bognor offered the advantage of 'an immersion in the invigorating fluid'.

In its more up-to-date passages, the guidebook drew attention to the reasonable rents of houses and lodgings, the excellence of the local beef, mutton, pork and veal and the plentiful supplies of fish:

> 'Bognor is celebrated for prawns, lobsters, oysters and silver mullet, and great quantities are sent to the London Market. The visitor is advised to order fish a day beforehand, or send to market early in the morning, when there is not much doubt of obtaining it; the fish-salesman cannot risk many hours when he has a certain market in London or Brighton.'

The first trace of an official awareness of the town's increasing respectability was perceptible in the use of consciously urbane language. Whereas in 1828 Dally had simply mentioned 'good lodging-houses', the author of the 1852 guide referred to 'exceedingly comfortable and genteel abodes' and to the fact that 'Manor House, York House and Bath House, being detached, have received the best attention of their proprietor, Mr. J. Smith, in order to render them marine retreats for families of distinction'. There was, also, the first reference to social differences between parts of the town, a distinction being drawn between Hotham's noble cluster and the rest of the neighbourhood:

> 'Bognor is nominally divided into upper and lower. The former consisting of several elegant marine residences and villas, standing in grounds tastefully laid out and surrounded by luxuriant foliage, enhanced by the beauties of Flora. Honourable mention may be made of Bersted Lodge, Bognor Lodge, Sudley Lodge, the Crescent, Spencer Terrace, the Lawn Villa and the Parsonage. Lower Bognor comprising the town with its numerous genteel residences, lodging houses, libraries, hotels and baths'.

Everything, in fact, about Bognor was 'elegant', 'genteel', 'nice' and 'delightful', and, in a limited way, progressive. Looking through the Commissioners' balance sheet for 1857, it is heartening to find that the improvements authorised by the Acts of over 20 years before were being carried out. The strip of land between Mr. Clark's New Crescent and the beach, which he had presented to the town in 1832, was at last being made into a promenade at a cost of £106 14s. 8d., of which £90 was contributed by the nine householders of the Crescent. Some street paving and drainage, assisted by proportional payments from the adjacent landowners, were also in progress. As always, the sea defence works were an expensive item. An extra £500 had been borrowed, with ratepayers' approval, for this special purpose, apart from the sum of £104 6s. 0d. which had already been spent in the normal yearly fight against the devouring tides. The lighting of the town and repairing of lamps had cost £211 14s. 5d.; and there was an indication of some unwelcome dissipation, causing perhaps a slight lifting of eyebrows when these accounts were being passed, in one item referring to the receipt of 6s. 6d. from 'some four-in-hand Gentlemen, for damages to a lamp post, driven against by them'.

The blink of gas lamps as the evenings drew in was now a well-established sign of progress and was due to the enterprise of John Hammond in 1840, who had set up in business in Dorset Gardens (now London Road). Ironmongery was his main trade, and the neatly engraved picture on his bill-heading showed three busy workers hammering away at sheet metal, with the results of their industry — coal-scuttle, containers, watering-can and fender — decorating the foreground. But apart from ironmongery he was a 'Brazier, Tin & Iron Plate Worker, Gas Fitter & Manufacturer of Register Stoves & the Self Acting Range, Bell Hanger & c.' At his works, he set up a plant to supply naphtha gas to parts of the town, and by 1852 this had led to the erection of a proper gasworks in a field to the westward, with Soloman Sayers as manager and W. F. I. Morris as secretary.

Hammond and his associates bought their gas coal at 14s. a ton, but every ton landed on the beach carried a 2s. duty. This burden was irksome enough for these pioneers, but when the parish levied a heavy rate on the gasworks, Hammond jibbed and hired a solicitor to send a politely veiled threat to the Vestry Committee. The letter, dated 3 July 1852, stated that

'after maturely considering the question of the rating of the gasworks, the proprietors have come to a deliberate opinion that they are rated at a much higher amount than can be sustained. It is obviously the interest of the proprietors, as undoubtedly it is their desire, to be on the best terms not only with the inhabitants generally of Bognor, but with the authorities of the parish of South Bersted. The estimate of the rateable value of the gasworks made by the proprietors differs, however, so widely from that made by the Vestry Overseers of South Bersted that they fear it will be impossible for them to adjust the matter except by an Appeal against the rate. Of course, they have no desire to appeal, but it appears to the proprietors that the parish authorities have arrived at what appears to them to be so extravagant an idea of the profits of the undertaking that no satisfactory result can be obtained without resorting to the tribunal to which such questions are referable. The proprietors will not act precipitately, but they feel they would not be acting justly to themselves were they to abandon their conviction that a great mistake has been made to their prejudice.'

The letter seems to have had an effect, for the lamps continued burning in Bognor and the proprietors eventually formed a £3,000 Bognor Gas Company in 1856, with all shares held by 16 residents and Mr. Hammond laying the first mains.

A sum of £30 10s. 3d. in the Commissioners' 1857 accounts had been spent on pumps and watering the roads, another refinement of living which reduced in summertime the amount of dust from the rough beds of shingle and flint which still formed the streets. Wells had been sunk here and there, about 25 feet deep, to supply the watercarts. The wells along the promenade were allowed to fill up with sea water at each tide, one pump and well being specially sited near the ships' landing place to mitigate the annoyance of coal dust.

Altogether, in this year of the Indian Mutiny, the accounts presented a favourable picture, with the coal and mooring dues and ratepayers' contributions all helping to bring the total of receipts to £1,448 8s. 4d., with expenditure at £1,402 15s. 10d. Even the market place which was let to Henry Digance, a greengrocer, was bringing in £10 annually.

Of the various tradespeople in the town, since we last looked at them in 1839, the greatest increase in the mid-1850s, as might be expected, was in the number of lodging-house keepers. There were now 10 of them apart from the six important house agents who each owned several houses for letting to families. Another increase, due to the passing of the Beer Act in 1830, was in beer shops. There were now eight ports-of-call, in addition to the five older-established inns — *The Wheatsheaf, Berkeley Arms* and *Claremont* in West Street, *The York* in High Street and *The Beach* on the promenade. There were no new trades, though two men combined unusual occupations: Thomas Walls of Manor Place advertised himself as both hairdresser and bird preserver, while William Henry Richardson of High Street was a 'Tobacconist & Bricklayer'. Thomas Tate's furniture-making business now had competition from two others in that line, Peachey and Richards; and four new dressmakers pointed to the expanding scope for fashion. Miss Augusta Binstead, getting on in years now, was still running the family library, which had moved out of the Manor House and round the corner into Waterloo Square; the bathing-machines were controlled by another veteran, Mrs. Martha Mills; and the cement mill was still turning, under the management of John Edward Standen.

One of the few uniforms to be seen locally adorned the person of Lieut. Thomas Lavington, R.N. He was in charge of the eight men of the Coastguard Station, which was a row of cottages on the cliff by the mill. Behind the mill was the cricket and sports field, where an occasional horse-race meeting had been promoted. Another uniform on view was the frock coat and top hat worn by Sergeant Edward Milham, the representative of the Law, a kindly man patrolling the town and parish outskirts with a large stick in his hand. The Solicitor and Town Clerk was Charles Constable, conducting local affairs from his office in Hotham's first terrace, Hothamton Place; and the chairman of the Board of Commissioners was James Smith, whose baths in the Steyne were still such an asset. A pump house at the rear of Bath House drew in sea water, which was piped to three bathing-rooms on the ground floor, providing warm or cold showers at 2s. and 1s. 6d. and warm or cold baths at 3s. and 2s. A course of eight warm baths could be enjoyed for a guinea. Mr. Smith's son Arthur, born in 1839, was training as an architect and was soon to return to his hometown with more elaborate plans for its aggrandisement than any other member of the family.

In spite of its vaunted 'gentility', the thing most noticeable about the resort in these 1850s was the absence of high society. The Royal Family now had its own holiday retreats at Osborne and Balmoral; and gradually, with the new allurements of Continental travel, the leaders of the fashionable world had deserted the seaside and Bognor particularly missed them. True, there were always distinguished people to be found gazing vainly in search of the Rocks, or buying some locally-made Tunbridge ware in the libraries, but the presence of admirals, generals and clergy did not quite kindle the same flutter and fluster of the old days. Many of those who had once graced the town were, of course, dead. The Duke of Sussex was laid to rest in Kensal Green in 1843; the beautiful Mrs. Barwell had died in 1847 and was buried at Westbourne, near Chichester; Mary

Berry died in 1852, Sam Beazley in 1851, Sir Jahleel Brenton in 1944, Princess Augusta in 1840. Others were now mere shadows in history: Sheridan, the Duchess of Devonshire, Lady Jersey, Romney, Lord Thurlow and Admiral Lord Hood.

There was an indication of the changing times in the conversion to other uses of some of the houses in Upper Bognor. In Hothamton Crescent the fine Dome House was still a residence; and one of the local aristocrats, Miss Martha Hasler, 'the best-dressed lady in Bognor', was living in the west wing. But Spencer Terrace nearby now contained a school, the Hope House Academy, conducted by Charles Hay Bevan, with two dozen pupils. Similarly, to the east of the Dome House, Lord George Lennox had left Lennox (previously Arran) Lodge, and the building now echoed to the tinkle of disciplinary bells and the sibilance of well-bred schoolgirls. For Lennox Lodge, in 1856, had become St Michael's, one of Canon Woodard's schools, with Lady Caroline Elliot as Warden of 50 girls.

The last link with the grand days broke when Mrs. Smith died in 1856. For 40 years she had been queen of Bersted Lodge, years of sedate splendour and of courtly entertaining, a régime of royal visitings and humours and happy house-parties. Quietly, her old world had faded and her companions had passed on; both the Mayos died there, the Countess in 1843 and the Earl in 1849. Now she herself had gone and the ticking of Hotham's great tower clock was the only sound in the multitude of rooms: bedrooms with private staircases, embellished with grained rosewood, where the Duke of Clarence had sought his 'hammock'; gold and pink drawing-rooms where the Duchess of Gloucester had retailed the latest news of the Court; the lofty dining-room where on so many nights the candles had lit up the jovial scene, illuminating the gilt mouldings of the ceiling, the ormulu enrichments of the black marble mantelpiece and the magnificent flock wallpaper of gold and crimson.

Such a house seemed destined as a setting for régimes. The next was to be more than twice as long, a span of 84 years in one family. On 18 May 1857 John Ballett Fletcher bought the property for £8,500. He lived only another five years, during which time he demolished the chapel, leaving only the tower. His son William, who inherited the estate, died in 1941.

Bognor, then, was on the threshold of another age, the age of the middle-class family seaside holiday. It was to rediscover itself, even to become 'select' again, though mostly to a different type of patron. There was to be a touch of pride, or snobbery if you like, in the associations of its past. When in 1857 the *Norfolk Hotel* changed hands and John Naldrett respectfully announced that he offered an uninterrupted view of the sea and every comfort for 'families and Gentlemen', there appeared at the top of his advertisement the Royal Arms. By whose permission it was there was not stated, but it had a finality that was impressive to the potential visitor.

For those visitors not swayed by such attempts to establish pedigree, there was a revival of the pseudo-scientific approach, the old call of the seaside as the cure-all of ills. The spirit, or languor, of the times was fully understood by Henry James, chemist of No. 1 York Place, High Street, in 1858. He called the attention of 'invalids and others visiting this delightful retreat' to the pure medicines available at his distinctive dispensary situated not at Bognor but at 'Bognor-on-the-Sea'. This was a new, explanatory and more inviting title for a town which, for too long, had suffered from being on the Rocks.

*   *   *

Any local residents who had been listening to the tales of what railways could do to towns were soon to watch the familiar sequence of events for themselves. When it all came, it came quickly. Within the 10 years from 1862 to 1872, Bognor acquired at last its own railway station, pier, newspaper and a rash of new buildings.

The railway was a single track which branched away from the main line at Barnham and curved down towards Bognor, entering the town from the north — not the east, as had been proposed in 1845. At the top of Dorset Gardens, which ran north from High Street, a wooden shanty-style station was built. The Bognor Railway Company, with £30,000 capital, had its offices at 41 Parliament Street, Westminster, and there on 28 May 1861 it held its first meeting, with Joseph Cary of 49 Pall Mall, in the chair. He had three fellow directors: Henry Hawes Fox, William Edward Knobel and Captain Robert O'Brien Jameson.

The Company had no difficulty in obtaining the landowners' agreement to a branch line crossing their fields and Parliamentary assent to the undertaking was given on 11 July. Negotiations then followed with the Brighton Railway Company who agreed to buy the branch line, when completed, for £24,500. The Brighton Company also undertook to build the station on land purchased by the Bognor Company and to supply materials for the permanent way. With the future thus safely assured, the first sod was turned at Bognor on 18 April 1863, and the Directors recorded in their minute book that 'the proceedings gave universal satisfaction'. The surveying for the line was done by Fuller of Chichester, the engineer was Robert Jacomb Hood — who became a director of the London, Brighton & South Coast Railway in 1883 — and the contractors, who were paid £22,500, were Jackson & Bissett.

The grand opening of the line took place on 1 June 1864. Flags flew from the windows of High Street and Dorset Gardens. The militia and band paraded the streets in a procession led by a gaily decorated farm waggon full of cheering people. The triumphal first train was seen off by the band and took a load of exhilarated company directors and gentry to Barnham Junction, where all of them gazed around with wonder at this foreign land — 3½ miles north of Bognor — to which they had been transported in a matter of minutes. Then the train returned to Bognor and the directors gave a luncheon at the Assembly Rooms in Sudley Road, while the rest of the town enjoyed free rides to Barnham and back for the remainder of the day. The Rev. Miller's sermon on this outstanding occasion was printed and a framed copy hung up in Barnham station.

The opening of the Bognor branch meant the end of the wayside station at Woodgate ('for Bognor'), which was closed that year, and the only remaining inconvenience to visitors was the change-over to the Bognor train at Barnham. For two months the line was operated by the private company and then, on 29 July, the control of the branch passed to the London, Brighton & South Coast Railway, who paid the final instalment of the purchase price on 11 January 1871. The 3rd-class fare to the three London stations, Kensington, Victoria and London Bridge, was 5s. 6d. single and 8s. 3d return. Ten years after the opening day, in July 1874, the first through train was inaugurated, leaving Victoria at 12.35 p.m., reaching Bognor at 2.50 p.m., and returning at 3.15 p.m.

*   *   *

Meanwhile, down on the sands immediately in front of Waterloo Square, the long-awaited pier was materialising foot by foot. The projection of a pier had become a sign of adult status in watering-places and the 'sixties saw a rush of iron into the sea. Brighton, as always, had been the early leader with its chain pier in 1823. Bournemouth built its first pier in 1861, followed by Worthing in 1862, Eastbourne and Bognor in 1865, Brighton again in 1866 (West Pier) and Hastings in 1872.

Some piers were built on piles driven into the sea bed. In Bognor's case, the engineers (Sir Charles Fox and J. W. Wilson) decided to use iron columns that were screwed in, the large flat flanges preventing any further sinking of the columns into the sand and clay. J. E. Dowson, the London contractor, used local labour, including fishermen, and by 5 May 1865 the job was done, several hundred flags were brought out again and the pier was officially opened. A slightly Oriental paybox stood at the shore end, with a turnstile on one side and a gate for the passage of bath-chairs on the other. The admission fee charged by the owners (the Bognor Promenade Company Ltd.) was 1d. Altogether, the Pier had cost £5,000 and was nothing more than an 18-foot-wide jetty extending for 1,000 feet, but its completion called for another gala day and in no time there were engravings on sale at the libraries, showing crinolined ladies swanning down the planked deck before making a slow turn to view the new prospect of 'Bognor From The Pier'.

The value of the Pier, in one respect, was in the encouragement of sociability. It was impossible to avoid rubbing shoulders with fellow-promenaders in such a confined space. The Pier had, in addition, a prestige value as a very superior piece of engineering, seeing that Sir Charles Fox had also erected the Crystal Palace. But to young Arthur Smith, who was secretary to the Promenade Company, it represented the first stage in his plans for the further dignification of the resort. He had set himself up as an architect and surveyor at Aston House (later the *Hanover Hotel*) in the Steyne and was now preparing a scheme which, under the title of the Victoria Park Estate, was intended to bring about an ambitious extension of the town farther westward.

The effect of this scheme would have been rather like attaching a large piece of Hove to the small dwellings that then formed Bognor's western fringe. For the town petered out beyond West Street and the Rock Buildings, and from there on, except for the mill and coastguard cottages, fields stretched to the tree-hidden houses of Aldwick. Arthur Smith drew an astonishing bird's eye view of what he intended should occupy these fields. The influence of John Ruskin's *Stones of Venice* was strong upon him and he designed 351 buildings all in the Italian Renaissance style, with the exception of one church which was to be in English Gothic. Terraces, squares, villas, shops, all of them were generously embellished with the foreign finery of loggias, verandahs, tiled roofs, ironwork and coloured brickwork in patterns. Through the middle of the estate, an avenue swept in a fine curve up from the beach towards the distant railway station.

Arthur Smith's castles in the air had a little more substance than those of previous visionaries. Two terraces, one square and the avenue (Victoria Drive) eventually appeared by the mid-1880s, and that was all. But the grandeur of the original intention lingered in local minds and set the tone for those who were to continue the development of West Bognor.

With now a railway, a pier and these agreeable hints of architectural dignity to the west, it had become apparent to the Commissioners that their own status needed strengthening, especially in view of the national concern about health. The enquiry which followed a return of the dreaded cholera had emphasised that proper water supplies and drainage were still the missing factors in the fight against disease. At length, legislation made these services compulsory and Bognor adopted the new Act. The Commissioners re-organised themselves into a Local Government Board of 12 members and held their first meeting as such on 8 January 1867.

Before any step was taken to provide piped water, the new Board realised only too well that its main duty was to prevent the town suffering from an excess of sea water. The constant onslaught by the sea had to be checked. None of the old methods of defence was impregnable. Though the wooden groynes or break-waters, stretching like fences out to sea, certainly trapped the shingle and sand and banked it against the shore, the waves still had the power to remove the shingle between breakwaters in a single storm and attack the sea wall itself. In the very early days, the land had been protected by some timbering and also bundles of wood five feet long, called bavins, planted in the shingle. This form of 'sea wall' was then improved upon by using heavy posts inserted at short intervals with planks nailed on lengthwise, so that the frontage of Bognor from Nyewood Lane to Clarence Road presented a wooden wall to the sea, with 60 feet of beach between it and the normal high water mark. But the great gale-driven tides continued to pour over beach and barrier, flooding West Street, the Steyne and even High Street, piling shingle against the doors of houses on the sea front and inevitably flowing deep over the eastward lowlands, drowning pigs in Munday's little farm at the top of Gloucester Road, lapping against Felpham's White Mill and necessitating boats being sent to the rescue of those marooned in the bed-rooms of the cottages near Felpham Bridge.

A concrete sea wall seemed the only remedy and by 1870 this had been built by Robert Bushby of Littlehampton at a cost of £8,000. Now, in addition to its five-year-old pier, Bognor at long last had a proper promenade, paved with bricks, a place for the endless sauntering so essential to holidaymaking, somewhere on which to go so far and then come back again. And on the seaward side of it, the waves met their toughest resistance and broke with such force on the wall that columns of water, hurtling 30 feet high, added drama, spectacle and brine to the ordinary pleasures of a seaside stroll.

Another sign of progress was the building of Bognor's first police station in Dorset Gardens in 1867; and finally in this sequence of mid-Victorian improvements came the advent of the town's first successful newspaper, the *Bognor Observer*. There had been two previous attempts. Edward T. Prebble, a Tunbridge Wells man, had set up as a printer at 25 High Street in 1858 and published a short-lived sheet called the *Bognor Herald*. This was followed by his *Bognor Gazette*, edited for him by a fellow printer, Charles Henry Knight, who had brought a printing-plant over from Worthing where he had been co-founder of the *Worthing Intelligencer* in 1856. The *Gazette* began in 1870 and finished the following year, whereupon Knight sold his plant to William Oram, who was conducting the High Street Library & Bazaar. On to the scene then came Henry Lovett, who bought both the Library and the press, engaged Knight as editor and launched the *Bognor Observer & Visitors' List* on Wednesday, 1 May 1872. Mr. Lovett's reign, noisy with editorial thunder, lasted till 1898 and the *Observer* had no serious local competition until the founding of the *Bognor Post* in 1922. Edward Prebble, who was also the Postmaster, continued in business for a few more years, printing part of yet another paper, the *Bognor Express*, from 1871, but this was really only the local edition of a Lewes paper, the *Sussex Agricultural Express*. He died in 1874.

Meanwhile, the *Observer* was already making history in its first year by printing one special copy in gold for presentation to the town's most distinguished visitor that summer, the exiled Emperor Napoleon III.

Fig. 14. A Bognor Grocer's Bill-head, 1856.

Chapter XIV

MID-VICTORIAN VISITORS

THE SIGHT of Napoleon III standing on the new brick promenade and gazing stolidly out to sea rather in the manner of his celebrated uncle, must have appeared not a little strange even to Bognor, accustomed as it was to Royal patronage.

For it seemed only the other day that the Emperor of the French was engaged in trying to reorganise Europe while the glittering Paris of the Second Empire made merry to the new tunes of Offenbach and Waldteufel. Then, with startling suddenness in the summer of 1870, France had gone to war to remove what she regarded as the Prussian menace and had found Prussia a far more formidable opponent than she had anticipated. The clash of armies, the smoke, the bloodshed and the chaos of retreat had led in less than two months to Napoleon's surrender at Sedan, his imprisonment at Kassel and the end of a dynasty.

It was in March 1871 — while Paris was suffering the savage onslaught of yet another revolution — that the dethroned Emperor, released from captivity, had landed at Dover and taken the train to Chislehurst, where he rejoined his beautiful wife Eugénie. And now in September 1872, just two years after the disaster at Sedan, here was Napoleon himself at Bognor — the trimmed greying beard, the stocky build, the dull eyes, the inevitable cigarette — peering curiously at a string of black shapes that had appeared offshore as the tide receded.

'Tell me,' said the Emperor to fisherman Fred Crees, pointing at the broken line of the Rocks, 'what are all those boats doing?'

'Sir, they're Bognor Rocks.'

Napoleon had come down to Bognor to spend a few restful days at the *Royal Norfolk Hotel*, doubtless on the recommendation of Eugénie who had stayed there in previous years. Though he was a sick man his thoughts were still with France, pondering the possibility of a triumphant return and the future enthronement of his son. All his life he had been a believer in his star of destiny. After a few days he left the town, taking with him the golden copy of the *Bognor Observer* inscribed with his name, which had been specially printed for him.

His departure threw the Local Board into something of a flutter, for they had prepared an Address of Welcome to the distinguished visitor and now he was gone before they had time to present it. Instead, they had to write to him at Cowes, where he and the Empress had taken a house for a late summer holiday, and from there Napoleon replied in October: 'I enjoyed very much my sojourn in Bognor and I hope another time to stay longer in your town.' He had indeed been very comfortable at the *Royal Norfolk*, pleased with the attentions of John Naldrett, the hotel proprietor, and with his handsome copy of the *Observer*.

But there was to be no other time. He died at Chislehurst after an operation on 9 January 1873; and six years later his son the Prince Imperial, an officer in the British Army, was speared to death in the Zulu War.

In October 1965 distant memories of Napoleon's visit to Bognor were unexpectedly revived when two of his cigarettes came up for auction at Gosport, Hampshire. They were preserved in a glass phial which also contained a note: 'Cigarettes given to your Grandfather Newman by Emperor Napoleon at the Royal Norfolk Hotel, Bognor.' The phial had belonged to a Mr. Lapthorn of Gosport, recently deceased. It is possible that 'Grandfather Newman' may have been James Newman, the proprietor of Little Lansdowne, a lodging-house in West Street just across the road from the *Norfolk*. Perhaps one September day in 1872 Mr. Newman had gone out for a stroll on the promenade and had had a brief friendly encounter with an elderly bearded visitor who turned out to have been but recently the arbiter of Europe.

*   *   *

A sad emperor who mistook offshore rocks for fishing boats might well have found a place in the writings of Lewis Carroll; and the opportunity was there, for the author of *Alice* was also in the town in that same September of 1872. It was his third visit in three successive months, counting his one-night stay on 30 July 'to look for lodgings at Bognor'. He found them at No. 6 The Steyne (as had Sir Robert Peel nearly 30 years before), where he arrived for a three-week holiday on 3 August, bringing with him some friends from Surrey to enjoy the benefits of the seaside. 'Very eventless but very pleasant' was his verdict on three weeks in Bognor, where 'I made several very pleasant friends'. Excursions were made to Hastings and to the Aquarium at Brighton which 'gives one quite a new sensation, as if one were walking under water'.

The friends he made at Bognor included several parents of girls at St Michael's School in Hothamton Crescent. His introduction to St Michael's, whose pupils he found to be angelic, resulted in a return visit in September, following an invitation to attend the school's feast-day activities on the 29th, Michaelmas Day. These included a fancy-dress ball and a speech from the famous author to the girls, one of whom lived to a venerable age and never forgot the memory of his 'lovely dark hair'. On the previous day this connoisseur of seaside resorts 'went over to see Worthing'.

There is no mention in Carroll's diary of the Emperor Napoleon, whom he may well have passed unknowingly when taking a stroll on the promenade; though he did discover that his illustrator, John Tenniel, was also staying in the town that September. Nor, unfortunately, is there any record of Carroll taking any of his fine photographs of children during his visits to Bognor. He would have found some good subjects for his camera as this was the time when children were to be seen in full pursuit of seaside happiness and, having found it, were to establish the family custom of returning, generation after generation, to these wide smooth friendly sands. To come from the sultry inland to the sea, either by choir outing or Sunday school treat or with parents, was — just as it still is — a blissful adventure that held a special everlasting enchantment. No grown man today can put one foot on a beach without his mind whisking him back in a flash to sun-drenched childhood, and when he takes his shoes off and feels again the sensation of sand beneath his toes, the bitter-sweet flood of memories wipes every vestige of adult sophistication from him.

Such far-off days as these were recalled in detail by one man who came to Bognor as a boy. George Sturt (1863–1927) lived at Lower Bourne, near Farnham in Surrey. He had a wheelwright's business at Farnham, but was a writer by inclination. Arnold Bennett, who knew him well, described him as 'a dark man with regular features, fine benevolent eyes and an old-fashioned dark beard'. Of his many books, *The Wheelwright's Shop* has already established itself in English literature; and in another work, *A Small Boy in the Sixties*, published just after his death, he retraced his childhood and, by happy chance, discovered an entry in his first diary which read: 'June, 1874. Came to Bognor. Saw the sea for the 1st time'. This led him to look back at the mid-Victorian Bognor we have just reached, as well as to extend the period covered by the book into the Seventies; and there could be no better description of a boy's holiday than this:

'The next thing I remember is hearing a railway porter call out "Barnham! Change for Bognor", and then being in a little room at Bognor, looking across the road to the parade and a level blue horizon above it and wondering what that queer rattling noise could be from just beyond the parade. I soon found out that it was the scream of shingle drawn back by spent waves. Whether I had, that lovely summer afternoon, eyes to see, no doubt I had a nose to smell the bed of red carnations just under the open window in the front of our lodgings; but there was much else to look at. The parade was paved with pale bricks — pink and yellow; and on the further edge of it, near the beach, was a long row, stretching into the distance, of tarred wickerwork objects — lobster pots, I learnt. The pier, a little to the right, had whitewashed posts — or were they tarred? . . . It was prob-ably the next morning that, from far across the beach, I was aware of my mother calling. With my brother or my sister, I had followed down to watch the surf on that level sand; and my mother was in an agony of fear lest the tide should race back too hurriedly. How was she to know? Such things were possible on some shores. Once reassured, though, she never tired of watching the steady rise or fall of tide, as the waves, now here, now there, gained or perhaps lost more yards of the wide sand.

And that sand itself; what a wonder it was! To watch the innumerable ripple marks, or to look at the worm-casts dotted all over it, or to see round one's feet the dry surface grow wet and shiny and even squashy under one's weight! From the shingle, when the tide was high enough, one could make "ducks and drakes" out across the restless water. A flat stone could always be found. My fingers grew rough and my arm stiff with con-tinuous stone-throwing.

Wherever one turned, the sand was alive with tiny crabs, its own colour and no bigger than spiders, the month being June. And all along the beach, for miles perhaps, were the thin lines — "little windrows" as Walt Whitman called them — of seaweed, dainty and worth keeping an eye on for treasures to take home for my museum. Strange things the sea cast up: and a strange collection began to fill our chiffonier drawer, until soon the said drawer had a stale dry smell, like the hot shingle itself. Plentiful among the pebbles — the brown and sometimes grey pebbles — along with water-worn oyster shells and cockle shells and fragments of large scallops, were pretty little nut-brown and red spiral shells of the "netted dog-whelk". Their shape pleased me, and I did a careful drawing of one in my new diary. Moreover, under the drawing I wrote the name, and even the Latin name — *Nassa Reticulata*. Was that right? I never questioned it until now, but felt proudly learned . . . The seaweed was a joy in itself — branched, small, frondy, in brilliant pink or green or warm brown. I collected many different seaweeds, but could get no names for them, and lost interest; for, without names, how was I to make a show of knowledge?

As if my mother might otherwise be too free of care, my sister was taken ill with measles at Bognor. The water at Bognor was more briny than she could endure; and from Farnham some of the sweet home water was sent by Aunt Ann or brought by my father, who, if he did not travel with us, must have joined us later . . . One thing about my father comes back to my memory — one solitary thing during that Bognor holiday — his delight at finding that he still could swim . . . Not for twenty years, my father said, had he tried to swim and it gladdened him at Bognor to find that he still had the art.

We lodged in a little, sunny, very unpretentious place long ago gone, which was the home of a fisherman and his wife. The fisherman, unless my memory is quite wrong, was a large-faced sandy-haired old chap, with one peculiarity my brother and I noticed, though I rarely noticed such things. This old fisherman, bumbly, fumbly, had a queer way of wearing his ample trousers braced so low that there seemed no length of thigh above his knee. He looked all trousers. But he was a laughing, waddling, jolly old chap, and we liked him.'

*   *   *

Being on the edge of the sea, the parish was long used to the taste of salt water from its wells. Having so much salt in their blood may have kept the inhabitants healthy, but for visitors coming to Bognor in the hope of benefiting their health brine in the tea seemed too drastic a cure. Hence the spectacle of Sturt's father arriving at the station with a container of fresh water from Surrey; hardly the sort of freight that the Local Board wished to encourage.

In 1870, it fell to five men to promote a private Water Company, with a capital of £6,000. They were the Rev. A. Conder, appointed vicar of Middleton in 1866; Dr. Thompson; Mr. Long, the chemist; Mr. Lovett, proprietor of the *Bognor Observer*; and Mr. Yarnell, grocer and house agent. Four years later, in June 1874, the site for the well had been finally selected in a meadow opposite the villas in Dorset Gardens. That summer, visitors staying in that road — such as Barry Sullivan, the Shakespearean actor who was to play Benedict in *Much Ado About Nothing* at the opening of Stratford's Memorial Theatre in 1879 — looked out at the rising tower of the new waterworks and awaited the verdict of Mr. Edward Brown, busy sinking the well in the thick clay. At 330 feet a fissure in the chalk was struck, yielding 15,000 gallons a day — of slightly salty water.

At first this taint seemed of minor concern. The Directors declared the waterworks officially open on 25 June 1879, providing piped water to Bognor, Bersted and Felpham, and they sat down to a dinner at the Assembly Rooms. Likewise, the volunteer Fire Brigade — to whom the supply was not a matter of taste but of hydrants — dined heartily that evening at the *Crown Inn*. However, the unpalatable supply (though it was acceptable for household use) was soon exhausted and in 1882 the Directors had to sink three new wells in a field farther away from the sea at South Bersted. Here everything seemed satisfactory and Bersted was particularly proud that Bognor had come to it for fresh water. The vicar, the Rev. W. B. Philpot, saw in this an analogy with the Scriptures and seized his opportunity. 'Let our housemaids rejoice,' he thundered, 'that they have not to trudge backwards and forwards with their buckets to the well; nor any longer to pump up for family use the filthy soakings of a reeking surface'. Then, vividly comparing South Bersted with Jacob's Well, he went on to paraphrase the Lord's words to Rebecca: 'The words He said to that bad woman are said no less to us: "Those who drink of this Bersted water shall thirst again, but whosoever drinketh of the water that I shall give him shall never thirst ... ".'

This text was rather more apt than the vicar intended, for after a dry season the supply turned brackish and was pronounced to be impregnated with sea water. The Company was soon hovering near bankruptcy, but in 1893 it decided to follow up a recommendation of a site five miles inland at the foot of the Downs. Two hundred feet down, they found the pure water in the chalk. Later, only 20 feet away, another well was cut into a larger fissure, bringing the water gushing to within 40 feet of the surface to provide one of the main sources of supply ever since. This eventual success encouraged the town to try to buy out the Company in 1898, but the purchase did not come about until 1 April 1929 at a transfer price of £74,653. The last relic of the old Company, the water tower, was demolished in 1936, and nowadays the water supply extends over 65 square miles.

Main drainage began in March 1879, so that now, with everything piped and the town relieved of any criticism from visitors on that score, the Local Board felt a sense of accomplishment. Some lines by W. S. Gilbert who had stayed at Mrs. Good's lodgings in the Rock Gardens — where it seems quite likely that he wrote part of the libretto for *The Sorcerer* — might have been applied to Bognor's rulers:

> *And the culminating pleasure*
> *That we treasure beyond measure*
> *Is the gratifying feeling that our duty has been done.*

And H. S. Vaughan, author of *The Way About Sussex* in 1893, put Bognor at last in its proper Victorian perspective: 'It is,' he wrote, 'a quiet little place of eminent respectability and unimpeachable sanitary record.'

*   *   *

It was hard for Bognor, as it now grew gradually into a 'family resort', to throw off the various jibes about its sloth and lack of dash, for it lacked money. The town was poor. This was an age when almost everything was kept going by public subscription: and in a small community of less than 3,000 the gentry and traders could not always respond to the continual appeals for funds to supply the progressive needs of a modern town. But if one takes the year 1874 and selects a few items, they show at least the stirrings of local initiative.

The Volunteer Fire Brigade, formed in July 1873, was now fully organised under Captain R. Talmy Turner, head of the brewery in Mead Lane. They housed their engine in a yard at the rear of the *Beach Inn* and six of the Brigade raised funds for uniforms by canvassing the district in pairs. The evening of 18 May 1874 brought their first call to action, 1½ miles out to a blazing barn and cattle shed on the Chichester Road at Aldwick.

Local education made progress in 1874 with the opening of the £4,500 Board School in Lyon Street on 9 June. It was a sturdy Victorian–Gothic building designed by Arthur Smith in cream-coloured brick, a citadel of State education for the parish of South Bersted and shunned by 30 families within a few weeks of its opening. Their objection was to having to pay for education. Mrs. Clew of North Bersted, for instance, who had received notice to send three of her seven children to the school refused to do so because she said she could not send them on the 2½-mile journey unless they were properly clothed and shod. As all her husband's weekly earnings of 14s. went on rent and bread, she claimed that it was impossible to comply with the Board's demand. The non-attendance of her children was therefore permitted 'on account of the distance'. Parents who preferred to continue sending their children to small private schools in the town learned in July that they were legally responsible for the 'efficiency' of these schools — among which a particular favourite was Mr. Phillip Griffin's little academy in Bedford Street. The Board, however, had cast doubts on the efficiency of this establishment. Griffin, a retired coastguard, had 50 mixed pupils and taught them 'arithmetic, grammar, geography, a little navigation and some book-keeping'.

By the end of September, the Board School had enrolled 133 boys, a hundred of whom had never been to any school, and Mr. Freemantle, the headmaster, was hinting that, with such backward material, it might be two years before any examination at the school would do him credit. Some parents, meanwhile, continued to moan at the fees, to defy the Board's powers to order attendance and to object to the use of corporal punishment. One father, threatening to summon the headmaster on this last point, was told with Victorian firmness that 'if the boy deserved flogging, he would, no doubt, be flogged' and the parent could then choose his course of action.

Hardly less headmasterly in his treatment of the town as a whole was Henry Lovett, who, having founded the *Bognor Observer* in 1872, had thus provided himself with an authoritative platform from which to air his views on local affairs. To his fellow-townsmen, what Lovett wrote in his paper came alternately as a relief and a shock. The son of a Wiltshire solicitor, he came to Bognor in 1870 when he was 34, after spending 12 years with the Post Office and making 180 paddle-steamer trips across the Atlantic in charge of Canadian and American mails and government dispatches. One of the features of his 12-page newspaper was a list of visitors supplied by the various hotels and boarding establishments, an innovation that earned him the indignation of landladies if he mis-spelt a name or left one out. The tone of his weekly leading article was usually provocative and, for the 25 years that he remained proprietor, he withstood superbly the lash of the storms he had purposely created. Occasionally he received a body-blow, such as when he printed an apparently innocent contribution, *Ode to Selsey Bill*, discovering too late that the first letter of each line, read downwards, announced to all that 'Old Lovett is an ass'.

Among the early challenges that he made to his fellow residents was that they should wake up. In 1874 he was saying: 'It is quite according to precedent for the people of Bognor to bemoan over the dullness of their town and the scarcity of visitors in the month of July'. (He was referring to the weeks before the Goodwood races.) When the August visitors came, he goaded the town to greater efforts: 'Despond no longer, ye Bognor tradesmen and lodging-house keepers, but buckle on your harness of energy, promote the pleasure and satisfaction of the visitors, reap the harvest which is justly yours and help to extend the good name of Bognor.' Later in August he warned the lazy: 'The Bognor season, by reason of the comparatively few shops to supply the greater influx, brings a valuable profit; but it has to be waited for and lasts none too long'. More vigour was what he constantly calling for — 'The peaceful quiet of Bognor is delightful . . . but let us beware of becoming too drowsy' — and by December be curtly summed up the situation: 'Bognor does not do much in a year. Its people move slowly and are not very speculative; not over dashing.'

With this weekly whip cracking about them, however, the townspeople did appear to be stirring in the 1870s. For example, the Pier, so important an object of pride, was purchased by the Local Board just in time to prevent its being dismantled and removed to another resort. It had been a financial loss to the original company, who had sold it to a Rev. Gilbert. He grew weary of it and negotiations to take it away were in progress when 46 horrified ratepayers petitioned the Board in 1874 to take immediate action. By August 1875, and after a certain amount of friction with Whitehall, Bognor had borrowed £1,200 and bought the Pier, which became the property of the town on 6 December 1876.

Continuing our review of events in 1874, a Musical Society was started in September 'to supply a want of occupation during winter evenings'. The president was Lord Bingham, living at The Den, and the conductor was Mr. F. Helmore, described as 'Choirmaster to the late Prince Consort'. Already well into its stride, having been founded in 1872, was the Institute, a literary and dramatic society of 54 members which held fortnightly winter entertainments at the Assembly Rooms, as well as running a Reading Room there every day. The nature of the entertainment offered can be gathered from this report (March 1874):

> ' "A Domestic Episode, or a Night with a Baby" was the title of a reading given by the Honorary Secretary. The whole piece is of a very laughable character and the risible faculties of the audience were much exercised. A harmonium solo by Mr. A. E. Smith was next in the programme. It was, we believe, a selection from "The Grand Duchess" and was executed in a masterly manner.'

Amateur dramatic performances at the Assembly Rooms were being fostered by Mr. O'Brien Lomax, a talented artist and drawing-master who lived at Felpham. In November he presented and appeared with his company in two farces, *Poor Pillicoddy* and *Retained for the Defence*, the proceeds going to the relief of the poor. Meanwhile, the gentry were busy organising their private subscription balls, also at the Assembly Rooms, which were prettily decorated for those breathless evenings of white gloves, dance cards and fans, with impeccable etiquette preserved by a handsome array of stewards, including Mr. Graham of the 105th Regiment and Mr. Davenport of the 47th.

This was the town keeping itself going in the off-months, but by early summer 1875 funds were low and only £40 was subscribed, after a canvass, to provide the season's band at the end of the Pier. Mr. Lovett was incensed. He uttered strong words of warning in the *Observer*: 'You will not have visitors — at least, not any number to trouble you — in future years, even if you do get some who come in ignorance of your parsimony this Season; and such will not stop with you long. Band or no band? is a vital question.' He was not to know that it had all been said before, 50 years ago, by that anonymous 'Visitor' in the circular about the lack of a promenade: 'They will forsake you, they will come once, but only once'.

However, visitors by now were well aware of what Bognor could, and could not, offer. They had read their guidebooks. 'A thorough specimen of a respectable watering-place — very quiet, very clean and perhaps somewhat dull', opined the latest edition of Black's *Where Shall We Go*? But, dull or not, 973 families arrived during the May to October season in 1873; with the current average of four to a family, this meant nearly 4,000 visitors. If, on arrival, anyone asked 'What shall we do?', Mr. Lovett had a vigorous answer for them in his newly-published shilling *Illustrated Guide to Bognor and Its Vicinity*. One read it and felt guilty at harbouring even the tiniest thought of perhaps slinking out of the town by train for an evening's dissipation at Shoreham's Swiss Gardens.

> 'It is not indoor amusements that the visitor to Bognor most looks for,' stated the Guide with significant innuendo. 'He chooses the health-giving outdoor attractions. He loves to inhale the invigorating saline breezes of the shore, or to sniff the odours wafted from the rich pastures of the lovely country around. During the summer season, boating and fishing form a great feature in Bognor amusements. The morning dip in the splashing wave having been followed by a substantial breakfast, the strengthened and inspired visitor is ready for a personal "pull" or, if a fit of lassitude be on him, to lie listlessly in the stern while a brawny-armed, weather-beaten boatman of the coast impels through the glistening waters the light craft engaged. Perhaps an enlivening pull to Littlehampton or Selsey Point is enjoyed, or an hour or two may be agreeably spent over the rocks where whiting, red mullet, bream, etc., are known to be generally waiting to be hooked.'

A pull of 12 miles to Littlehampton and back may well have brought lassitude, if not decrepitude, but at any rate the visitor knew in advance that his pleasures at Bognor would be plain and healthy. This was no great change from the holiday-making there of 30 years before. Some hint of commercialism, a little more urbanity and a preoccupation with the resort's respectability might have been detected by old and regular patrons. If you booked accommodation through Mr. Frederick Hawkes, who had set up his High Street grocery in 1869, you were met at the station by his partner, Mr. Rusbridger, recognisable in a white tall hat, and escorted to your apartments. A cab would take four of you and 60 lbs. of luggage to any part of the town for 1s. 6d. The roads were still primitive, still a mass of loose shingle and flint, thrown down and left for the wheel traffic to press flat.

Vehicles kept to one side, which thereby became less bumpy, whereupon the Local Board erected barriers and forced the traffic to 'level' the parallel stretch.

As for sea-bathing, a byelaw of 1875 had tightened the regulations: 'A person of the female sex shall not while bathing approach within 100 yards of any place at which any person of the male sex above the age of ten years may be set down for the purpose of bathing.' This was the result of complaints the previous year regarding the indiscriminate use of bathing-machines. The Rev. G. W. Fishbourne, chairman of the Local Board, had steeled himself to reveal in August 1874 that he had actually seen a gentleman bathe from one of six machines standing together and clearly lettered 'For Ladies'.

Though on the wane – and finally to disappear about 1885 – the seaside sights of the beached coal boats and the mysterious little heaps of iron pyrites stacked along the promenade still aroused curiosity. The pyrites, or 'mine', had even become a local source of fun when visitors asked 'What's that?' and the poker-faced fishermen readily encouraged a chaotic conversation by replying 'That's mine'. Hunting for semi-precious stones on the beach remained a popular though often fruitless pastime, as young Sturt found out. There were elementary books on the subject, such as the attractive little best-seller, *Thoughts on a Pebble*, by the eminent and melancholy Sussex geologist, Dr. Gideon Mantell, but it was not easy to detect the pebble that would reward the visitor with – to quote the 1868 Bognor *Guide* – 'a relic of his marine wanderings and an heirloom for his family'. The general idea was to search for pebbles with holes, or with a blister on the surface, or with a surface resembling dirty pitted soap. Chipping carefully round the hole with a geologist's hammer, you might see a bubble-like mass, ranging from pale blue to black, which indicated chalcedony. If little cavities all over the pebble glittered, it sometimes denoted a pure agate, or if the hole, lined with sparkling quartz crystals, went deep into the pebble, there was hope of a beautiful combination of agate and chalcedony. The blister foretold a choanite, or miniature fossil sponge, embedded in the heart of the pebble and presenting a star-like pattern when split open. A fossil sponge in flint, cut and polished for use as an adornment or curio, was Bognor's own contribution to the lapidary's art and had first been tried and perfected by Richard Wyse at his shop in Waterloo Square in the 1830s.

When visitors had collected their stones, hoping they had found a rare 'landscape' agate, or the still rarer black moss-agate, they took them to Wyse for scrutiny and either received an unfavourable report, which meant discarding their load forthwith, or returned in a few days to collect those he had found worth polishing. Bognor's beach fortunately contained some of the finest pebbles on the Sussex coast, but this did not prevent tricks of the trade being practised. Mantell in 1837 had warned Brighton's visitors that the jewellers there were apt to sell water-worn fragments of bottle glass as 'Brighton emeralds' and that the moss-agates 'direct from the beach' had come from Germany. By the 1880s, this lucrative deception had been introduced to Bognor by a new 'lapidary' who studiously inspected your pebbles, retained some and sold you in due course what appeared to be the cut and polished result. These you took home delightedly, not suspecting that you had been sold some cheap German stones from work-shops in Oberstein and Idar, imported by the sackful. Not, of course, that the contented purchaser could tell the difference.

A stroll along the beach might yield other exciting discoveries — for example, the turtle which was washed ashore in 1860. It was immediately claimed by Mr. Newman, the proprietor of the *Claremont Hotel*, who took it back to the hotel, had it cooked and regaled his guests with steaming bowls of real Bognor turtle soup.

What to do of a summer's evening remained no particular problem as there was usually no choice, except a visit to the Assembly Rooms where there might be a lecture or a touring company playing a one-night stand. Ben-Yusuf, a Cam-bridge undergraduate in native dress and surrounded by Eastern objects, spoke on Arab life one July evening in 1874; and in August Mr. J. C. Buckmaster, of the Science and Art Department, came down from the South Kensington Museum to address and instruct residents and visitors on Cookery. On the lighter side, there was Bessie Melville's London Comedy Co. in *The Ticket-of-Leave Man* for a week on 1 July and the annual visit of the versatile comedian and singer, The Great Vance, on 19 August. Alfred Vance from London presented a very popular two-hour concert party in miniature, with a small band and a company of three: Miss Eunice Irvine (comedienne), Mr. Edgar Austin (lightning cartoonist) and Mr. David Wood (violinist and conductor). Seats cost 1s. to 3s. and a 'Family Ticket to admit 4' was 10s. September saw Arthur Sketchley delighting a good house with his female impersonation of 'Mrs. Brown', and that month there was also a visit from some acrobats billed as Tannaker's Dragon Troupe of Japanese Per-formers — who must have spent a frustrating evening as, according to the local paper, 'the room was too low for some of their best performances'.

Outdoor entertainment consisted of aquatic sports, a visiting circus and the annual Bognor Fair. The Fair was not to the liking of Mr. Lovett as it tended to introduce an unrefined element among Bognor's high-class clientèle and, in his view, Fair Week was 'simply one of the old-fashioned obnoxious periods of excitement for the young and giddy, with a strong tendency to harm'.

The aquatic sports were arranged by the piermaster, John Smith, and from vantage points on the Pier and promenade the visitor could watch the various events enlivening the sparkling sea by day or the calm warm water on Saturday evenings. Sometimes there were four-oared ¾-mile galley races by boys of Dr. Conder's school in Spencer Terrace competing against adult crews. Fishermen would join in the fun of a tub race for 5s., spinning and twisting all over the course. Walking the greasy pole for a leg of mutton or 15 lbs. of beef was usually a triumph for the boatman 'Scott' Ragless, thus reducing his butcher's bill for the season. At the Pier entrance, bread rolls dipped in treacle hung from a pole, and children with their hands tied behind them competed in snapping at the sticky target. Most of all, the visitors enjoyed the swimming displays by Bognor's two bathing-women, Ellen Ragless and Mary Wheatland, who had a repertoire of tricks, such as diving off the Pier and 'standing on their heads' in the water, waggling their toes at the fascinated spectators.

Mary was to become a Bognor institution as the years rolled on. Small, strong and reserved, agile as an eel, always in a heavy-skirted blue serge bathing-dress, with her hard, kind face peering out under a straw hat, she had her own bathing-machines on a pitch just east of the Pier, with a small white horse to draw them. She was a country girl, born a few miles inland at Aldingbourne in 1835, and came to Bognor in 1849 as assistant to the veteran bathing-woman, Mrs. Martha Mills. She taught herself to swim: 'I never cared how rough the sea was. I loved the big waves and when they came rolling in, I used to plunge into them.' Eventually she could stay in the water for 1½ hours and was the first woman to teach swimming in Bognor. Her clients put themselves in her care at all ages, so that, when she was 88, she could look back and say: 'I started bathing people when they were children, and I bathed them when they were grown up and married, and when they were grandmothers and grandfathers.' What they remembered in later life was the rough feel and the salty smell of Mary's thick blue dress as she took hold of them and perhaps ducked them for disobedience: 'When I went in with parties of children, I always stood in the deep water to prevent them coming out too far. "Now, my dears," I used to say, "if you come out here, you bob under with me." Many's the time have I had to duck and push back naughty children to safety.'

The first person she saved from drowning was the heavy wife of a London brewer in 1851. She never lost a life, saved 30 and won a bronze medal and two certificates from the Royal Humane Society. Those she rescued also rewarded her. A man whose heart gave out in deep water presented her with £20 on awakening in his hotel bed. One woman handed over 3d. A mother, whose five children were drowning in a batch till Mary swam seaward of them and brought them in one by one, sent her beef at Christmas and contributed £2 towards her back rent. For 62 years Mary was to be found on Bognor beach, always on the same pitch, which was never intruded upon by the fishermen. In 1906, at the age of 71, she gave up swimming. Rheumatism was crippling her, but she was still to be seen on the shore up to 1913, though her eldest daughter, Mary Collins, was in charge of the machines — on which the competition of bathing tents and huts was beginning to have an adverse effect. Old patrons sought her out, giving her a drive in a carriage-and-pair or calling to read the Bible to her. She would never accept the offer of an outing by car: 'You don't catch me in one of them things.' She died, aged 89, on 1 April 1923, and her coffin was borne to South Bersted churchyard on the shoulders of her fishermen friends.

*   *   *

One further outdoor entertainment in that season of 1874 was the band; that of the Royal Sussex Militia, duly subscribed for and playing three days a week on the Pier in a lean-to-shelter. To stroll along the Pier to hear the band, or to go boating and listen to the music across the water, are delights now lost to Bognor but once part of the legendary romance of a seaside holiday. There were, of course, occasional hazards. One evening in September, the wind suddenly got up with such force that the Pier shook and the music-lovers made a rush for the land. The Pier withstood the gale, but not so the ladies who as they emerged on to the promenade 'presented a sad plight with tattered garments and one was minus not only her hat but her hair'.

As for excursions beyond the town, they had become easier since Albert Florence established his coach business in 1859. Every day after lunch, for 2s. 6d. return, you could travel to see Arundel, Slindon, Chichester or Goodwood. It was in keeping with the town's dignified reputation to have these stately four-horse coaches still rumbling out over the rich countryside where the finest turnips in England were growing. Private mews, stables and coach-houses abounded in the town, for the habits of former days were still strong, and one's status was still measured by one's carriage and turn-out. Selling one's horses signified misfortune, except perhaps in the case of the sweet and high-principled spinster, Miss Teresa Mercer. Well beloved and most benevolent, she lived at 'Springfield' in South Bersted, and when her coachman became ill with palsy, the horses were sold so that she could support him and his aged father. It was a gesture typical of her. Her mother was a French-Canadian, Miss de Bathe, who married a British officer fighting in the War of American Independence. Teresa was born at Detroit in 1783, was brought to England, grew up unmarried and supported her widowed mother. For her income she depended on her writing and her first novel *Montbresil Abbey*, one of many, earned her £100. She lived at South Bersted from 1839 until her death in 1879 and left 2s. 6d. a week in her will for her two dogs, Toby and Sambo.

Thus, in these awakening days, with Disraeli as Prime Minister, the new Suez Canal under British control and the Queen proclaimed Empress of India, more and more visitors discovered Bognor, sampled its mild pleasures and returned in subsequent years, sometimes grateful that there was no great change in the somnolent scene. They came to Bognor to rest or recuperate. They came because it was hot and stifling in the cities, particularly in an over-clothed age, and Bognor was cooler. They came because the sands were ideal for children and because the place was select and yet quaint, with its rural–maritime flavour and the hint of the old-world and even of the romantic. The sea spell still held. Even as you stood on the beach the waves might deposit the name-board of a boat at your feet and an 18-gallon, or even a 100-gallon, cask of brandy. The battle between coast-guards and smugglers was still keen. Men of the eight watch-stations between Elmer to the east and Danner on Selsey Bill were kept on their toes by regular visits of inspection from the Admiral Superintendent, the Duke of Edinburgh, who arrived at Bognor by train and, with the Bognor coastguard captain, would be driven by Albert Florence in a carriage-and-pair to inspect each outpost of defence against 'the enemy' on this brandy-soaked coast.

The hint of the romantic could be extended, perhaps, beyond brandy smugglers to include Victorian drug addicts, one of whom might have been seen any time between October 1875 and July 1876 at the peak of his addiction, reeling moodily through Bognor en route for a studio in Belmont Street or clambering over the battered seaweedy groynes of Aldwick beach. He was Dante

Gabriel Rossetti, poet and painter, with seven years to live and suffering from loneliness, illness, financial worry and exhaustion. The blows of life had taken toll of him. The death of his wife, the beautiful model Elizabeth Siddal, in 1862; the exhumation of her body by his literary agent in 1869 to recover an unpublished manuscript of his poems which had been buried with her; and the attack on the sensual nature of his poetry in a London weekly in 1871; all these trials had finally reduced him to such depths of sleepless despair that only gigantic doses of chloral and whisky brought any relief.

Increasing debts and a consequent writ drove him from Chelsea to a rented house in Aldwick, probably on the suggestion of his close friend, the Methodist writer and painter James Smetham, who knew the district well. Here his mother and sister and various friends kept him company on and off through the nine months of partial recovery. He composed more poetry. Mrs. William Morris came down to pose for a new picture, 'Venus Astarte', and the lovely Alexa Wilding sat for 'The Blessed Damozel'. He got up at lunchtime, sunken-eyed, and took afternoon walks at a terrific pace over the beach with his secretary, George Hake. Everything was black to him. Even an elm falling across the lawn was seen as an omen which he put into a sonnet, *The Trees of the Garden*. Gaiety gone, brimful of Scotch and chloral, it is a wonder that he wrote and painted as much as he did. The winter winds that rocked Aldwick Lodge, the bad light and draughts, drove him at first to seek better painting facilities in Bognor itself, and for a while this creator of wonderful portraits and writer of passionate poetry found sanctuary in a converted stable in the garden of Belmont Lodge, in Belmont Street. The studio, which now serves as a private garage, belonged to a fellow artist, W. G. Burton, whose painting of Christ looking out through a prison window, entitled *The World's Gratitude*, was considered by Rossetti to be a masterpiece. In early July 1876 Rossetti went back to Chelsea; he died on Easter Sunday 1882 in a bungalow at Birchington.

*   *   *

The ebb and flow of visitors, ever since Hotham had created the resort, had always been difficult to predict. In the early days, there had been too many of them and not enough accommodation. In the last quarter of the century there was to be plenty of room, but with the bulk of visitors tending to hold off until Goodwood Week. Though this was the social peak of the Bognor year, the rocketing prices while the resort 'made hay' kept ordinary family visitors away until the racing was over. Thus there was one booming week in July and then the quieter influx of regulars in August.

Just before we take another look at Goodwood Week and what it now meant to the town, we might make a brief digression. The name of Bognor's founder crept in just now, so this is the moment to fit in a visit to South Bersted in order to see what was happening to the remains of Sir Richard Hotham.

At Bersted, the church was in need of repair. In 1866 Mr. Ewan Christian, architect to the Ecclesiastical Commissioners, had prepared a scheme for beautifying the building and in 1879–81 this was duly carried out. No alarming alteration was made to the structure, but Hotham's galleries were removed; and with the west gallery went the old hand-turned barrel organ of six tunes, used since 1840 in place of a fife which previously accompanied the singing. A new organ, embodying stops from the barrel organ, was built for £350 and it was decided to instal it in an organ chamber to be erected at the side of the chancel. This meant building on to part of the graveyard.

Outside the chancel wall, it will be remembered, were the stone steps leading up to the gallery entrance and the black tablet denoting Hotham's resting-place beneath the steps. Here on 17 June 1879, a workman's pick broke through the brick side of the staircase, revealing Hotham's coffin, the woodwork perished, the lead cist intact and on it a roughly incised plaque bearing his name and the dates of birth and death. During the work of restoration, the church floor was levelled, which meant disturbing the remains of those buried in the church. A large pit was dug outside and one night, in order to avoid involving the contractors in Home Office red tape as a result of an official application, the workmen unceremoniously dumped the parishioners' bones into this common grave.

Hotham, luckily, was spared such ignominy. Indeed, he was treated with considerable respect for there was a great deal of local interest at his re-appearance and Mr. Richard Talmy Turner, the brewer, immediately offered the use of his own empty family vault in the churchyard. One month later, at 6.30 on the evening of 18 July, the vicar — having impressed upon the workmen the solemnity of their duty on this occasion — supervised the removal of the coffin and led the procession of parishioners to the new grave. There, in the words of the parish magazine for that month, 'as the shades of evening were fast closing in, the remains of the parish patriarch were hidden from view'.

So, incidentally, was Hotham's memorial plaque. It remained *in situ* on the chancel wall, which was soon enclosed within the church as part of the new organ-chamber and was completely blocked from sight by the Dulciana pipes. In an unmarked grave and with his memorial masked, the 'parish patriarch' passed to an obscurity that was not lifted until the next century.

Fig. 15. Samuel Reynolds' first High Street shop in 1870.

Chapter XV

GOODWOOD WEEK AND COTSWOLD CRESCENT

'PRINCELY GOODWOOD' was a favourite title for the Duke of Richmond's race meeting in the early '80s, as a result of the Prince of Wales's patronage. By 1888 the newspaper world had popularised it as 'Glorious Goodwood', and glorious it remained for the traders of Bognor until the advent of motoring made rich patrons less dependent on hiring a house for the week.

The Duke, like his father before him, still regarded the meeting as an occasion for a happy annual house-party of old friends and comrades, with some good sport thrown in, and this informal mood caught the fancy of Society. From 1860, Goodwood became a far more aristocratic occasion than Ascot or Epsom. Jaded nobility made for the Sussex Downs and the sea in carefree spirits, despite the chalk dust of Downland lanes and the staggering cost of a bumpy bed in Bognor. Wealth rolled down to the coast and Bognor soaked it up in a brief period of magnificent extortion.

Other towns offered no serious rivalry. Worthing was too distant and secured only a small share of racegoers; Midhurst, Arundel and Littlehampton had not the accommodation; Chichester was chosen by the less rich; and so it was Bognor that received the patronage of the well-to-do in the four-horse drags. The long-awaited opportunity was grasped. Prices soared. The danger to future trade was ignored. Visitors already in the town found they had to leave their lodgings unless they were prepared to pay 'Goodwood' prices. Mr. Lovett, with the *Observer* as his platform, tried to talk some sense into local minds:

> 'Strangers and those who have honoured us before with their society and patronage alike should be fairly and justly treated. If all who let their apartments or houses for Goodwood realise this, it is well; but there are, we fear, some who do the whole of their fellow inhabitants harm by thinking the medium between £10 and £80 is somewhere from £60 to £75 — may such people have their Goodwood gains reduced to a minimum by frequent non-lets,'

Lovett's curse bore fruit. Guidebooks began to warn holidaymakers to steer clear: 'During race week the lodgings in Bognor are charged double, consequently few people go down till after the races' (Black's *Where Shall We Go?*, 1888 edition). Few people of ordinary means, that is; the well-to-do were there in force.

The four days of racing, beginning on the last Tuesday in July, spread their bounty over three weeks. As the houses filled up, residents found their town glittering with officers of the Life Guards and the Blues. Lord Lonsdale would be staying here, the Duke of Beaufort there and Lord Londesborough nearby. Private coaches poured in. Local transport was augmented by Mr. W. Cooke from

166

from London bringing his stud of ponies and horses to the *Norfolk Hotel* mews and running a coach daily to the course for 15s. return. It was not unusual to see thirty coaches career out of the town on those July mornings. James Smetham, the religious painter and writer, friend of Ruskin and Rossetti, stood with his children watching the exodus on the Wednesday morning of Race Week in 1869. Vividly he caught the scene in this letter to a friend:

> 'As I write, there pass coaches and four, half a dozen of them (one with postillion in blue), going to Goodwood races. That is a "swell young man" with a horn. The Honourable Somebody, no doubt. Coaches clean, not dusty as when we saw them return last evening; dresses clean and stylish; horses spanking and skittish. The drivers are swells: some young swells, others old swells, with white reins. As they pass, the Hon. Mr. Hornblower sees me standing at the toy shop door, and he thinks to himself — seeing one whom nature marked out for an aristocrat, but who is reduced to a perambulator and two little children to take care of at a toy shop door — "How that fellow envies us! How he wishes he were going to Goodwood, poor devil! I'll treat him to a taste of my horn" and so he holds it straight out and makes it say, Tootle-tootle-too-oo-oo-oo-oo! which was very kind of him, and may he never want a horn to blow, and an elegant middle-aged party to admire him, standing at a toy shop door.'

One could, of course, travel much of the way by train, but this was unenterprising and any racegoers in West Sussex who considered themselves gentry braved the turmoil of the hills and drove the whole distance in their own carriages. The hordes of Londoners who were 'vulgarising' Ascot in the 1870s still found Goodwood too inaccessible — to the relief of the old sporting men — despite the inducement of the railway station at Drayton, four miles south. It required a certain amount of stamina to make the train journey from the capital, and a writer in Charles Dicken's weekly magazine *All The Year Round* (29 July 1876) gave the reasons why:

> 'To run down to Goodwood and back in a day, in the hottest week of the entire year; to sit for hours in a stuffy railway carriage; to scramble for a fly; to drive through the dust whirlwind between the railway station and the park; and to go through all this again in the stifling heat of early evening — after having lost one's money — is a trial which none but the most determined turfites will undergo.'

But if you were already staying in Bognor or Chichester, there was none of this fatigue, only the excitement of taking part in what almost seemed a carnival. Flags hung over the streets. Yellow London omnibuses on holiday, curiously labelled *Old Ford* and *London Bridge* and *Hammersmith*, were marshalled at Chichester Cross. Carriages boarded in the early hours toiled in from Brighton and Portsmouth. Victorias, hansoms, waggonettes and high dog carts headed for the foot of the Downs where, despite the care of the Duke and the Railway Company in watering the approach roads, the hot white dust billowed over the beautiful silk dresses and lace parasols. Astute ladies avoided the 'millering' and wore dust coats. From Bognor some carriages would take the route past Goodwood House, for there was always a hope of meeting the Duke's guest of honour, the Prince of Wales, and receiving a bow directed towards your particular party. At the bottom of the 500-foot hill, wild and grimy gypsies waited with trace horses for the faltering coach or carriage.

Hitching on, they lashed their horses up the slope, then unhitched and galloped them down again, mad for more custom.

Up on the course, the cheerful informality of the scene remained unchanged. The fashion parade of the ladies on the lawn before the grandstand was still *the* subject for the Press artists. Parties having picnic lunch in their carriages found themselves surrounded, as always, by colourful and importunate hangers-on: gypsy women with their babies, children who had stolen a ride up from Bognor on the back-axle, ostlers, racecard men, showmen, stable helps, fortune-tellers. There were boxing booths among the sideshows and through the crowds stalked a man on stilts inviting you to hurl money up at him, which he caught in his cap. The Prince, when he became Edward VII, once tossed him a sovereign. Another familiar figure each season was the missioner, the Rev. William Izard, respected rector of Slindon.

The half-moon course, encircling the bowl of farmland below, was still the loveliest sight to those escaping from the duties of the London Season. The cool dark woods lining the course, the perfume of the Downland flowers, the green turf and the presence of so many friends and acquaintances combined in creating the unique Goodwood atmosphere. You felt for a few days that you really were a guest of His Grace, using his estate for your own sport; and even if you had no eye for a horse, there was Sussex to look at from the top of the Trundle. Below, in the Charlton and East Dean valley, the cattle browsed, the sheep bells tinkled and the blackberry bushes were blossoming. For a while, the dust was motionless down the lanes of those farms which old Cobbett had said were 'some of the finest in the world'.

When the day's racing was done, the hills emptied, calm fell over Goodwood and the coaches went swaying down to the coast, to be greeted at Bognor's level-crossing by hordes of children yelling 'Cart! The Races!' and scrambling for the flicked penny and occasional coconut. One race day, young Morton Booker was missing. Notices went up in the town, 'Lost at Goodwood . . .', but he turned up eventually. He had sneaked a return ride underneath a coach — but, instead of going to Bognor, it went to Portsmouth.

The warm, soft air of the promenade echoed in the evenings with the chatter and laughter of dinner parties, which could be seen through the open windows. James Smetham, in that same letter in which he depicted the departure of the coaches for Goodwood, also described the end of the day:

> 'In the twilight last evening, walking on the promenade, I heard a trumpet and a viol, and, looking across, saw windows open and a party of a dozen seated at dinner, attended by near a dozen liveried servants: white cravat, spotless linen, black dress, faces fresh and glowing, hair crisp and wavy and nicely parted, and brushed smoothly and clingingly to the smooth forehead. Every face, whether it were a fat face like Monsieur Jullien's or an Apollonic face like Byron's, was what we understand by an aristocratic face — not disturbed by cares of the petty and common kind, with a manner properly and gently restrained.'

The gently restrained mood became more relaxed after dinner when the promenade was thronged with people in evening dress, and the 'bloods' sought amusement. The Prince of Wales, following in his family's footsteps, discovered that Bognor was discreetly drilled in a tacit acceptance of Royalty. Goodwood Week often saw him visiting the town incognito with Lord Aylesford or the great boxing patron, the eighth Marquis of Queensberry. The Duke of Portland and Mr. J. W. Gladstone, one of the sons of the Prime Minister, were the Prince's hosts at a lunch party at 4 Park Terrace in 1880; and one evening there was an incident that typified the environment of jovial and even hearty familiarity, allied with due respect, in which the heir to the throne liked to move. While staying at Goodwood with the Duke of Richmond, he descended on Bognor with some Guards officers and they amused themselves by linking arms and marching down the promenade, holding up all the ladies they met. The local police sergeant interfered and unknowingly picked on the Prince as ringleader. He laid the arm of the law firmly on the royal collar. In a flash, the Prince wriggled out of his coat and the astonished policeman found himself seized by the Guards and slung into the sea.

Elsewhere in the town on these Race Week nights, the sound of the banjo was heard as 'Squash' made his seasonal appearance in white trousers and tail coat, serenading the wealthy bookmakers at the hotels. The *Bedford*, built at the west end of High Street in 1872, was popular with the bookies who stood like Caesars at the first-floor windows, eyeing the crowds of unemployed skilled men who gathered in hopes of coins being thrown down. Imperiously the bookies acted, heating a shovel full of pennies, hurling them out over the street and laughing at the discomfiture of those trying to pick them up.

By mid-August the racing fraternity had departed and the regular visitors began arriving. Goodwood's brief glory had set Bognor ticking into motion again, like a slap on an old grandfather clock, and the momentum had to last the year out. So it did, through the '80s and '90s and into the reign of King Edward. For the meeting became more and more popular, culminating in the Goodwood Week of 1904 when the new red-brick grandstand was opened and the King provoked a delighted gasp by appearing in a white top hat instead of the customary and more formal black silk. Between them, the King and the 7th Duke, who was in straw hat and flannels, completed Goodwood's revolution in dress and by 1906 frock coats and top hats were out, panamas and lounge-jackets were in. In the royal words, it had become 'a garden party with racing tacked on'. Three years later, in 1909, there was a more significant change. A car park appeared. The following year — 'the motor being one of the most popular means of getting to and from race meetings' — an additional motor enclosure was made. By 1921, the charabanc had arrived in force. Except on the course, the horse was almost eclipsed; and there was no need to rent a house within carriage range when you could so easily motor down from town. So Bognor lost its lords and their lobster dinners and was left at the post with nannies, children and penny ice-creams.

*   *   *

It would be easy, having just glimpsed ahead into the 1920s, to stay there, listening to *Avalon* on a gramophone on the sands or to the double click of a pogo-stick on the promenade. Some might say that Bognor looks little changed, except that the gaps in the front have been filled up and there are no meadows between High Street and the beach. But that is one reason why we should go back to where we were, to see how the fields were filled and to meet an old friend for the last time.

On the bright morning of Thursday, 8 July 1880, Bognor's oldest and most indefatigable patron left his London home at 34 Hans Place and was effusively welcomed aboard the 10.30 train at Victoria. He joined a high-spirited party of 40 friends and business associates in the two special saloon coaches and set off once more on his favourite maritime pursuit, the bolstering of Bognor. He was, of course, Lord William Pitt Lennox, 80 years old, game to the last, and not only a director of the Brighton Aquarium but now prepared to sink or swim as chairman of the board of what seemed the soundest investment south of Goodwood — the Bognor Residences and Hotel Co. Ltd.

The scheme this time was to build a crescent (to be called Cotswold Crescent) of thirty-one 13-roomed houses facing the sea in a field between the pier and Sam Beazley's New Crescent to the east. In the centre of the 600-foot crescent, and slightly forward of the houses on either side, would be the town's largest hotel (seven suites and 42 bedrooms). A subway beneath hotel and crescent would communicate with stables and cottages. In Lennox Street and York Road, which bounded the field on west and east, rows of eight houses were to be built. The architect, Mr. G. Gard Pye, estimated the total cost at £51,000. The Company proposed to let all the houses, either as residences or boarding-houses, and to run the hotel themselves. Rents from houses, stabling and cottages would bring in £4,000 a year; and, with the minimum profit from the hotel calculated at £3,000, the total revenue, less expenses, would be £6,000 at least. Prospects for shareholders in this £60,000 company were said to be unusually favourable.

It was the increasing popularity of Goodwood Races that had fired Lord William's enthusiasm. He knew that Bognor's shortage of accommodation in Race Week was notorious. He knew that people unwillingly paid the outrageous rent of £30 or £40 a week for a furnished house in late July and early August, that many had to put up with inferior lodgings and that some racegoers were forced to seek refuge as far away as Southsea or Worthing. It stood to reason that the crescent and hotel would be packed out in Goodwood Week and possibly for the whole season, and that the 47 beautiful new houses would appeal so strongly to would-be permanent residents that they were likely to be let before they were even completed. With such roseate thoughts in mind, Lord William and his party glided by railroad down to the lucrative coast.

In Bognor, of course, such a project was no novelty and there was an understandable air of scepticism until labourers began digging what appeared to be a curved canal across the field in May. For over fifty years, the three-acre field had belonged to the Cook family of London, with the Tates of Bognor acting for them and letting the land for grazing. Thirty years back, in June 1850, a momentary development mania had seized the family, and Fuller of Chichester had been engaged to survey the site and draw up plans for a crescent and 64 houses. Nothing happened, nor did Mr. Fuller receive his five-guinea fee. But in the late 1870s the idea was re-born. The land was cleared of allotment 'squatters' and Dr. Robert Cook of Wimpole Street leased the site for £200 a year to the Residences and Hotel Company — no doubt handing over the original 1850 plans, for the two projects were almost identical. Now the huge foundation trench was dug and on 8 July Bognor politely awaited the laying of the foundation stone.

Shortly after 1 o'clock the train from Victoria drew in and the distinguished arrivals made their way to the crowded promenade, where flags were flying along the line of the excavations. Lord William had brought his third wife, Maria Molyneux, and his four fellow-directors: Charles Minns, a civil engineer; Capt. T. Maude Roxby (late 55th) of Binfield House, Wimbledon; Frederick A. Pullen, who was also a director of the Portishead Waterworks; and A. J. Lewis who was to run the hotel, having spent 30 years in the trade, lately as manager of *The Cliftonville* at Margate.

Promptly at 1.30 Lord William performed the ceremony with a golden trowel. In a cavity were placed copies of *The Times* and the local papers, some coins and a prospectus of the Company on vellum. The upper stone was lowered amid loud cheers and then the directors and their guests stepped into a marquee for lunch, a convivial two-hour session with speeches coming thick and fast. The vicars of Bognor and South Bersted (the two parishes, as we shall see, were now separate) both grasped the opportunity to ask the Company for a contribution to their churches, a thrust which Lord William parried with a promise to accede when the dividends were large enough. A descendant of Sir Francis Drake's family, Capt. Thomas Drake, R.N. of the Dome House, replied to the toast of the Navy. Casting a wary eye towards the Channel, he admitted he did not much like the Navy's idea of discarding wooden ships in favour of these unproved iron vessels and hoped that the Company's new building would be carried to completion and not be knocked about by a French fleet off the coast. There was a sharp compressing of lips when Mr. Treeve Edgcombe of Fleet Street, replying on behalf of the Press, said that on being suddenly summoned to go to Bognor he had to search the map to find its whereabouts.

When finally Lord William rose to speak, he held his audience spellbound — and no wonder, for here was a figure from another age, godson of William Pitt, cousin of Charles James Fox, playmate of Princess Charlotte on Bognor sands. Never had the town received quite such a testimonial as it did now. The local air, said Lennox, had made him the man he was, and during his years in the House of Commons he had always come down here to re-invigorate himself. Many people had tried to improve Bognor and the attempts had failed because they had brains but no money. This new venture, he assured his listeners, was quite different in that men of sound sense and practical knowledge were engaged in the undertaking and would not mislead shareholders. The new accommodation would help to attract people to Bognor, for the town was superior to Brighton in health and comfort and had a prettier countryside for driving in; furthermore, in Bognor one could lounge about in any costume without drawing attention to oneself, as would be the case in Brighton. Brighton had been called the Queen of Watering-places. Bognor was the Princess Royal of Watering-places. He concluded by stating that the Company would bring great benefit to the town and he would devote all his energies to furthering its objects. It was hoped to have Cotswold Crescent and the hotel ready in a year. On this, three cordial cheers were given, the gathering broke up and the workmen, police and railway officials moved into the marquee to finish up what was left of the food.

Lord William had conferred on the town a new title, but by the time he died — which was in the following year, on 18 February — he had given it neither a new hotel nor a crescent. Despite the excellent lunch, the venture failed just as had its predecessors and only four of the houses were built. Two of them were inclined slightly, marking the start of the intended sweep of the crescent. The houses, a stern and solid pile of dark grey brick with continuous verandah and balcony, stood looking rather surprised and cut-off at the western end of the giant trough in the meadow.

In the winters that followed, the great seas that still poured over the promenade and into the town frequently flooded the excavations. Boys made rafts from the timber of breakwaters and voyaged over this new waterway or skated on it. The four houses (now the *Carlton Hotel*) were at least dignified by the name of Cotswold Crescent and, after 17 years, the abortive crescent was slightly extended, though to the design of another hand and another age. No attempt was made to match up, either in height or style. 'Seaside' architecture had come into play and the prevailing style in 1908 happened to be Flemish gabled. The additional houses became two hotels, the *Béaulieu* and the *Béaulieu Downs*.

A. FLORENCE, ESTABLISHED 1859.

LANDAUS, BRAKES, WAGGONETTES, DOG & RALLY CARTS & CARRIAGES
OF EVERY DESCRIPTION.
Lansdowne and Norfolk Mews, Bognor.

Good Saddle Horses.   Lessons in Riding and Driving.   Omnibuses to and
from the Station to n. .. &. Trains (in front of Station)
AGENT FOR THE L. B. & S. C. RAILWAY CO.

Fig. 16. Bill-head for 'A. Florence'.

31. (*left*) Bognor's first Town Hall and Assembly Rooms in Sudley Road, (now called the 'Bognor Club') was built in 1837, and used for various indoor entertainments.

32. (*below*) Laurel Cottage, Church Path, was where Mrs. Smith, of Bersted Lodge, founded her Charity School in the 1820s.

33. The *Norfolk Hotel*, before the balcony and Royal coat of arms were added in the late 1880s. Napoleon III stayed here in 1872.

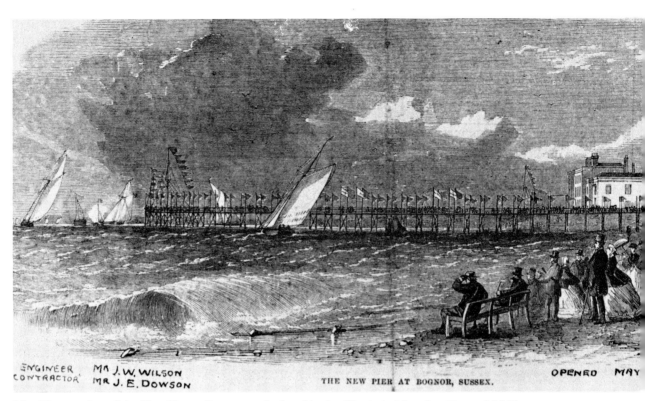

ENGINEER MR J.W. WILSON
CONTRACTOR MR J.E. DOWSON   THE NEW PIER AT BOGNOR, SUSSEX.   OPENED MAY

34.   The opening of the New Pier at Bognor, as depicted in the *Illustrated London News* of 1865.

35.   An early view of the Steyne, where Sir Robert Peel and Lewis Carroll once stayed. St John's chapel can be seen at the far end on the right.

6. Bath House in the Steyne (built in 1824), where James Smith, and later Richard Hillary, provided sea-water baths.

7. The Library, Waterloo Square, next to Manor Place, which was named after the Manor House which had housed Binstead's previous library (see pl. 30). Later it became Burgess's toy shop and was visited by Queen Mary in 1929.

38.   Waiting at Barnham Station is one of the first trains to use the newly-completed branch line to Bognor in 1864.

39.   The High Street in the 1850s. This was Bognor's 'first complete street'. On the right is Mr. Hounsome's library, now the Coffee House.

40. The Board School in Lyon Street was opened in 1874 and demolished in 1969.

41. A break from the 3 Rs for these Board School 'inmates' around the turn of the century.

2. A school treat (believed to be a celebration of a Royal event), in field on the east corner of London oad and High Street.

43. Lord Justice Field (in top hat, centre) turns on the new water supply in South Bersted in 1884.

44. The Water Tower, next door to St John's church in London Road, was opened in 1879 and demolished in 1936.

45. An early view of the beach, east of the pier. In the distance is Colebrook Terrace, and beyond, on the Brookland, are the buildings of Black Rock (p. 105), demolished in the late 1870s.

47. High tide on an Edwardian summer's day, west of the pier. Note the horse, used to pull the bathing machines, which is waiting on the shingle.

46. Mary Wheatland, Bognor's celebrated bathing woman, whose pitch was in front of the *Beach Inn*.

48. The old St John's chapel-of-ease in the Steyne, where the Rev. Edward Miller preached his fiery sermons. The clock tower survived the chapel's demolition in 1892.

49. The 'new' St John's church and vicarage, from Sudley Road.

9. The Roman Catholic church and priory in Clarence Road, designed by Joseph S. Hansom and opened in 1882. The priory was demolished 100 years later.

. The Primitive Methodist apel was demolished in 1976.

52.   The Wesleyan chapel and Sunday School on the north side of High Street was used as garage premises from the 1920s and replaced by shops in 1980.

53.   The stone-laying ceremony of the Wesleyan Sunday School in 1893. The magnificent lady seated at the front was Mrs. Euphemia Calder, of Culver Cottage, Aldwick Road.

4. Fitzleet House, formerly Hotham's East Row, became a convalescent home for the Merchant Taylors' Company 1870. The site is now occupied by Queensway.

. The Scott Memorial Home of Rest, Belmont Street, began as a cripples' home in 1880. It was replaced by a car rk in 1958.

. The Victoria and (on the left) the Princess ry Memorial Homes stood on the sea front tween Clarence Road and Albert Road until 80.

57. Bognor's leafiness was once praised by guidebook writers (pp. 194-5). Today this is a busy road junction at the entrance to Hotham Park, and the turreted lodge has been replaced by the present red brick building.

58. The Black Mill, at the foot of Nyewood Lane, produced 'Roman' cement for facing Bognor's Regency buildings.

. The choir of
John's church,
ondon Road. In
e picture are the
rate, the Rev.
T. Gill (front
w, fourth from
e right) and
son, Eric Gill
e sculptor, at
e back, below
e centre lancet
the middle
ndow.

60. A garden party at South Bersted
Vicarage, c. 1900, with the Bersted
Band in attendance at the rear.

61. A triumphal arch erected in
Station Road to welcome the Duke
and Duchess of York, who opened
the convalescent homes (pl. 56) on
9 July 1900. Beyond the arch is the
Roman Catholic School in London
Road, now replaced by Central
Buildings.

62. Lord Justice Field at his residence, No. 5 Marine Parade (see also pl. 43). On the left is Culver Cottage.

63. There was room to stand and chat in the High Street, as shown in this pre-1900 view, looking west.

65. Licensee Mr. Richard Sharpe, outside the *Stamp House*, North Bersted.

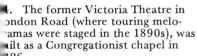

4. The former Victoria Theatre in ondon Road (where touring melo-amas were staged in the 1890s), was uilt as a Congregationist chapel in 326.

5. A bcflagged High Street. The occasion is not known, but the Post Office on the left dates the photograph between 387 and 1901.

67. (*above*) Crowd posing for the camera; Walter Howard was one of many entertainers who amused the crowds on Bognor's sands in the early 1900s.

68. (*right*) The first aeroplane on the sands, which landed on 26 May 1913, was piloted by the Pashley brothers from Shoreham.

69. The *Beaulieu Hote* built in 1908 next door to the *Carlton Hotel*, became a 'teen-hotel' fo a brief period in its hist

Chapter XVI

CHURCHES, CHILDREN, INVALIDS
AND CRITICS

THE FAILURE of the Bognor Residences and Hotel Company marked the last attempt ever to be made to give the town any suggestion of residential magnificence in the old style. In time, housing promoters retreated from any such sublime ambitions and concentrated on modest rows of villas. The perennial problem posed by Bognor — namely, was it little more than a seaside village with a brief summer season, a high-class residential town in embryo or a potentially grand health and pleasure resort? — was too much of a conundrum for speculators to bother their heads about any longer. It was wiser to play safe with a few bay fronts than to risk derision and disaster with crescents and colonnades.

Yet, in one respect at least Bognor had come up in the world for, as already briefly mentioned, it was now an independent ecclesiastical parish in its own right. It had at last severed itself from the mother parish of South Bersted on 11 February 1873, and the Rev. Edward Miller, who had reigned for 35 years as 'chaplain' of St John's Chapel in the Steyne, found himself created the first vicar of Bognor.

Mr. Miller in full-sleeved black gown, with his white hair, challenging eyes and Dundreary whiskers, was a powerful preacher who had been calling down the wrath of Heaven on Bognor for as long as anyone could remember. He appeared first in 1828–31 as curate to the original chaplain, Mr. Gauntlett, then left for a spell as curate in Lambeth and returned to take charge of St John's in 1838.

His chapel had a whitewashed ceiling, wide gallery, organ, reading-desk, pulpit and pews with doors. Pew rents provided him with a stipend of £100 with which to raise his nine children. Here, year in, year out, he built his reputation on his sermons and gave them to posterity in six printed volumes. He loved the richness of words. 'The Battle Axe of God' was the title of his discourse on the death of Wellington in 1852. One of his favourite sermons — and he had many which he would repeat annually to the amusement of those hearers who recognised a familiar striking phrase — was on 'Rizpah, the Daughter of Aiah', which was calculated to reduce his congregation to tears. His services were plain and simple in the Evangelical manner. Certain pews were allotted to children and when, for instance, the boys of Mr. Griffin's little school misbehaved, discipline was equally plain and simple. Mr. Griffin just leant over and caned them during the service. In the gallery, where 50 seats were monopolised by the girls of the Jubilee School, supervision was more difficult. One shocked visitor, forced to go upstairs because of overcrowding, reported to a resident that he 'heard one girl, old enough to know better, say to another, amidst smothered laughter and at the same time indicating a young man opposite, equally foolish, "He's winking at you", indicating a current of thought undesirable even in a less sacred place.'

There had been occasional weekday morning services at St John's neither regularly attended nor particularly punctual; and Mr. Miller often came to the chapel, wrote 'No congregation' in the service register and departed. But with the birth of the new parish and the arrival of an active curate, Mr. G. W. Jeudwine, weekday services increased; and finally, despite the vicar's opposition, the parishioners demanded and obtained Sunday evening services, which began in October 1874. On those evenings, a resident recalls, 'the clerk used to hand the preacher a lighted candle as he mounted the pulpit steps, a ceremony rather in the manner of a butler performing the last duties of the day as the household retired to rest'. The clerk was Mr. W. Smith of 33 High Street, a man of many parts, for he was hairdresser, stationer, perfumer, seller of prayer-books and hirer of pianos. Wild nights of storm, with a preacher in black vying with the elements, psalms and shadows on the ceiling from the flickering candles sometimes ended, as on one Sunday evening in 1878, with the sea bursting up the Steyne and the congregation being rescued by boat.

It had been hoped to repair and enlarge the chapel, but two arguments against this were given by an architect, John Oldrid Scott, in his report on 17 May 1876. The walls were too thin and, in any case, roads bounded the chapel on east and west. That heralded the end of old St John's and also the end of Mr. Miller who died the following year. He was succeeded by the Rev. R. B. Tritton, a reformer who introduced a surpliced choir and held a public meeting in 1878 to decide where to build a new church. A site in Dorset Gardens alongside the new water-works was purchased, Mr. (later Sir) Arthur W. Blomfield was appointed architect and on 25 August 1880, in the presence of the Bishop of Chichester, the founda-tion stone was laid by a distinguished resident, Lady Cecilia Bingham, the youngest sister of the Duke of Richmond and Gordon. (By now there was a 6th Duke at Goodwood, Charles having died in 1860 and been succeeded by his son — for whom that magnificent 21st birthday party was held in 1839. In 1876 the old dukedom of Gordon was revived for him.)

It was a happy ceremony and, at a luncheon afterwards, Lady Cecilia was told by Sir Walter Barttelot that she could not have laid the stone better if she had been born a mason. Also present, and telling everyone how kind they were to his niece and how he liked pretty Bognor with which he had been so intimately associated, was the familiar figure of Lord William Pitt Lennox, now earning a living as a lecturer. Only the previous month he had himself laid a foundation stone, that of Cotswold Crescent, and doubtless the excellence of Lady Cecilia's performance was partly due to her uncle's expert advice.

Two years later, the new St John's, handsomely built in red brick and Bognor flint, was ready, except for the octagonal spire which was not completed till 1895. The long delay started rumours; and when the Bishop returned to dedicate tower and spire, he may have gazed upwards more in apprehension than invoca-tion. For the vicar was being forced to deny publicly that the tower was cracked from top to bottom and that the whole thing would have to be pulled down;

that the church itself was crumbling to bits under its weight; and that, in any case, there was no place for the bells.

These unfounded rumours, typical of a little town, sprang from the resentment of the older die-hard residents who, with the fishermen who never set to sea on Sundays, preferred to worship at their old chapel in the Steyne. But this was finally denied them in 1891–92 when old St John's was pulled down, leaving only the clock tower as a landmark for seamen. When the chapel material was sold to a builder, Mr. Southerton, who used it to erect St John's Terrace in Highfield Road, the rumours turned to ominous prophecy regarding such profane use of consecrated material. Being Sussex and superstitious, the people said this act would bring woe and misfortune to Mr. Tritton and his successors and from that day, it is said, the vicars of Bognor have lived under a curse — though the demolition of the 'new' St John's in 1972 may have ended it.

Mention might be made at this point of the progress of some other religious denominations in the town. The Catholics, of whom there were barely a dozen in 1881, had no chapel up to that year. Slindon House, six miles to the north in the beechwoods, had been the centre of the old faith in West Sussex since penal times. Here, early in Elizabeth I's reign, Sir Garret Kempe had rebuilt the house and constructed a secret chapel in the roof, together with a hiding-hole for hunted priests and an escape route through the cellars. Through the centuries and the long, intermittent persecution which culminated in the Gordon Riots in London in 1780, the faithful trod the concealed staircase to the chapel, while even as late as the 1750s the Puirsuivants were searching the house to arrest the mission's priest, Fr. Molyneux. In 1814 the Earl of Newburgh, descendant of the Kempes, left £500 for a church to be built eventually at Slindon. Chichester had its Catholic church in 1855 and Slindon in 1865, with Archbishop Manning preaching the first sermon. It was to these churches, or to Arundel, that Bognor's Catholics then made their way, sometimes walking there and back to Mass on Sunday, until 1881 when a temporary chapel was opened on 26 July in a room above a grocer's shop in Steyne Street.

This new mission was founded by the Servite Fathers, with Fr. Alphonsus Coventry as priest-in-charge; and if the arrival of 'Romish monks' had first caused some alarm, it was nothing to the storm of religious intolerance that broke out in Bognor when it found a Catholic chapel in its midst. Public meetings were held; and when, six weeks after the chapel had opened, the first convert was received, the uproar almost developed into a 'No Popery' riot. The young convert, Miss Clara Allen, daughter of a gardener, had so much public abuse hurled at her that she was forced to leave the town. She obtained a job, which lasted 25 years, as nurse to the Rayner family of five boys; and six years later, when for some reason a proposed holiday at Southsea was being tearfully cancelled, she courageously suggested Bognor as an alternative. So the Rayners brought her back to her own town again. They enjoyed Bognor and continued to visit it for over 50 years; and when Clara married, she settled there. Her two daughters became nuns. In the meantime, the Servites had found a benefactress, Miss Susan Walker, to help them build a church and priory. The architect was

Joseph Stanislaus Hansom, second son of Joseph Aloysius Hansom who had designed Arundel's beautiful Catholic church (now the Cathedral) in 1873 and who invented the safety vehicle which was modified into the Hansom cab. On 16 August 1882, three days after St John's had been completed, the church of Our Lady of Seven Dolours was opened in Clarence Road, with the Duke of Norfolk at the head of the congregation. Also present was a young member of the Servite Order who, as Cardinal Lepicier, was to return from Rome 50 years later to participate in the celebrations marking the Golden Jubilee of the church.

The Methodists had already long been established in the town, having held their first meetings in a fisherman's thatched cottage on the shore, a site later occupied by the *Beach Inn*. An early mention is of a quarterly meeting at the cottage in 1819, and by 1824 the congregation had raised £288 3s. 7d. to build their first chapel at the northern end of what consequently became known as Chapel Street. In 1840, for £782 11s. 9d., they bought land in High Street and built a larger chapel to seat 200, enlarging it in 1862, adding a Sunday school in 1893 and eventually selling the site in 1924 to build a new church that year for £13,000 at the western end of the same street.

The Congregationalists began, in similar fashion, with a cottage meeting-place at South Bersted, provided for them in 1816 by one of the Hounsom family. A move to Bognor was made in 1826, when they built Hanover Chapel in Dorset Gardens, with the Rev. D. Evans as first minister. Moving farther down the road in 1869, they built a new church for £2,621 on some grazing land at the corner of High Street, retaining the old chapel as a Sunday school. It later became a lecture hall and was converted in 1897 into the Victoria Theatre. The increasing noise of traffic finally made the High Street church unsuitable for worship and the site was sold to Timothy White Ltd. in 1929 for £17,000. A year later, a new Congregational church and Sunday school were built in the quieter Linden Road, to the designs of Mr. S. T. Hennell, for £21,334.

*   *   *

In the accounts of other holiday towns, the period of the 1880s is usually described as one of 'rapid development'. In Bognor's case, the town stood still, apart from a few tentacles of brick stretching out into the perimeter of corn. Deep sleep descended over the development of the parish until the 1920s.

It was repose rather than stagnation, forty winks that lasted forty years, and when the sleeper awoke and looked around, much of the South Coast had become hideous and despoiled. Bognor, a town in a trance, had somehow saved itself.

Mr. Lovett and others had fought this torpor. In May 1879 a meeting was held in the Assembly Rooms to discuss the proposed advertising of Bognor. Though the current penny *Guide* issued by the L.B. & S.C. Railway Company ignored the town, the Company made amends — in June 1880 — with the first railway poster, a lithographic view which put Bognor in company with Brighton, Worthing, Southsea, Ryde and Littlehampton.

'We are now being advertised,' said the *Observer* on 8 July, 'so it is for all of us to do our best to maintain the character of the town as a desirable temporary residence.' Earlier in the year a challenge had been flung out by Mr. Lovett, who asked: 'How shall we make our town more attractive?' and he had characteristically shown how — by engaging at his own expense the Royal Hand-Bell Ringers of Poland Street, London, to perform twice on the pier on a fine, windy August day.

It was true that Bognor seemed to be catering for all tastes in entertainment in 1880. On 13 August there was Hutchinson & Tayleur's Grand American Circus, featuring Monsieur Edward Cristolle, the 'French Samson and Wonder of the Age', who fired a cannon from his shoulder, weighing 512 lbs. Aspects of strength in other fields could be observed at the Lecture Hall in London Road (as Dorset Gardens had now become), where on 30 August 'Miss Weston, the sailor's friend, has announced her intention of giving an account of her work among the sailors, ashore and afloat'.

But the leading attractions were still those which were so commonplace to the inhabitants that they ignored them just as they do today. These were the sea and the health-giving air, both of which sustained the town's reputation far more than any man-made amusement.

Bathing as a health cure had given way to the idea of bathing simply for pleasure, and for those who were new to this pastime there were popular handbooks which regularised one's pleasure into disciplined activity under such headings as: How Long to Bathe, How to Bathe, Bathing for Children, When and When Not to Bathe and How Often to Bathe. People needed such advice; and, instead of shivering after a cold dip in June, they learned that it was always best to take a run along the sands and that, after any bathe, a vigorous rub-down with a coarse towel brought a reaction that was a luxurious tonic to the system.

Hot sea-water baths, good for rheumatics, were still available at Bath House in the Steyne, under the control of its new proprietor, Mr. R. C. Hillary, a plumber. In 1884 he was charging 2s. for a hot bath and a guinea for twelve. Hot and cold sea water could be delivered for 4d. a hot pail, 2d. cold, and in the early mornings one might see this local trade in motion in the person of Mr. Alfred Baker cycling round to various households on his penny-farthing with a bucket of sea water suspended on each side of the 16½-inch handlebars.

Curatively speaking, however, the sea air had tended to become more important than the water itself, ever since 'ozone' had been discovered by the scientist Schönbein in 1858. It was said to be prevalent in air near the coast and, though no one knew quite what it meant, the word was fashionable in medical circles and of considerable advertising value to seaside resorts. The telegraphic address in 1886 of Frederick Yarnell, grocer and house agent of 23 High Street, was 'Ozone, Bognor'. But even without this mysterious quality, Bognor's soft and relaxing air was being increasingly recommended for chest complaints. 'The air is pure and balmy,' stated *The Medical Record* of 1 June 1885, 'and is recommended in all cases where the throat and lungs are affected. Bognor is specially suitable as a residence for invalids.'

Single and sometimes celebrated invalids had long been taken for granted in the town. Invalids in bulk were new, and the first influx took place when the Merchant Taylors Company of London purchased Fitzleet House (originally Hotham's East Row, facing Waterloo Square, and the former home of the Fitzpatrick family) and converted it into a convalescent home with 45 beds. The Company had a fund, originating from the will of Robert Dunkyn in 1570, which they utilised for the poor of London; and the Charity Commissioners approved the use of the fund for establishing a home at Bognor for men patients discharged from London hospitals. It was opened on 5 July 1870.

In 1880, a Cripples' Home was opened at Aberdeen Cottage, Belmont Street, by Miss Elizabeth Duncan-Scott of Chiswick; and in Wood Street three cottages had been converted into the Seaside Cottage Retreat, housing 25 beds for convalescent adults and children of the poorer classes, received there on a subscriber's order.

The number of convalescent homes was to increase swiftly. In fact, one reason given for the gradual disappearance of the gentry from Bognor in the pre-1914 period, and a consequent decline in the 'tone' of the town, was that these fastidious gentry found the sea front monopolised by the sick and they disliked sitting on the promenade in company with them. The town's magnetic attraction for convalescents certainly did not appeal to Arthur Smith. In 1891 he was engaged in promoting the Highfield Estate for small villas of £50 rental on either side of the railway and, championing the local climate in his prospectus, he wrote: 'The average death rate for the past four years has been about 14 in the 1000; if deduction were made of visitors who come down when past all hope of recovery, it would be very much less'.

If nothing else, the invalids behind the high flint walls of Fitzleet House gave the local boys something more to wonder about. A Bognor boy in the '80s and '90s found his fun in and around the town, not merely on the shore. The sea and beach had not for him the irresistible appeal that smote children from inland Chichester when they saw it.

'To experience the authentic thrill of sparkling waves,' wrote a Chichester boy, Wentworth France, in later life, 'one had to be at Bognor on a fine June morning. From the station we took a short cut over a rough field and squeezed under a railing, and then the old black windmill came in sight and, beyond it, the sea dancing and sparkling in the sunshine. That sparkle always made one gasp from sheer glee.'

Local boys, of course, might play cricket on the sands, using a breakwater for wicket. Sometimes they tried getting on the Pier for nothing. One boy would approach the pierkeeper in his kiosk and say: 'How much to go on, Mr. Smith?' On being told it was penny, he handed over the coin, and meanwhile eight of his friends had slithered over the railings unseen. Just west of the Pier, the refined girls from St Michael's School bathed from the machines, affording a pretty sight in their long skirted and trousered costumes. It was a free show for the boys as long as it lasted, which was seldom long, for a sudden raucous yell from Ellen Sumption, the bathing-woman, sent the 'peeping Toms' scattering.

Waterloo Square, too, had its attractions, being a three-acre grazing meadow in which sheep and cattle were penned by the town's butchers before slaughter.

A ewe was permanently retained there as a decoy to lead other sheep out of the field to the slaughter-houses in narrow Norfolk Street, or 'Blood Alley' as it was known to boys who watched the killings.

Forever cruel, some boys enjoyed chasing a little man nicknamed Jimmy-the-Bunch-of-Keys. He worked for Miss Loweth, a milliner, and carried a large wooden hat box which the boys would kick from under his arm. He had an impediment of speech and would scramble up from the gutter where he had slipped, dust his coat and yell strangely at his tormenters.

Yet, in different mood, the boys found pleasure in testing their knowledge. George Howick, a grainer and gilder, painted some shop shutters in imitation wood graining and cleverly worked into the graining the faces of four eminent men, Disraeli, Lord Randolph Churchill, Gladstone and Sir Charles Dilke. Boys in the know would take others along and challenge them to discover and name the faces.

Then there were the strange days when the town quietened and across Belmont Street the boys found hurdles barring the road. Smallpox had broken out at Alma Place. There was also the night the tramp died. He had sought warmth on top of a brick kiln and by morning the fumes had suffocated him. People who ordered bricks for their houses after that always requested that they should have none from where the tramp had slept.

There were noisy days, election times when the Liberals of South and North Bersted marched to meet Bognor's Conservatives in a free fight in High Street. Mr. Perry's donkey, kept in an orchard in Scott Street, was painted red, white and blue on these occasions. And there were particularly noisy nights, glorious for boys, when the town decided to give someone 'rough music'. This widespread custom — designed to show public disapproval of men who beat their wives, turned people out of their homes or got girls into trouble — took the form of an organised uproar outside the culprit's front door. Tin cans, baths, drums, bells, whistles and any other items that made a noise were used by the crowd, who marched to the house and kept up the din as long as they had strength. One victim, who lived at 58 High Street, received this effective treatment for three nights running up to 11 o'clock. His neighbours, far from being annoyed, joined in and lent the crowd more 'instruments'.

Anything well done by the boys brought forth the town's catch-phrase: 'Beautiful dripping!' It originated from an old woman who, accompanied by her lovely grand-daughter, paid a weekly visit by cart to sell dripping obtained from the Goodwood kitchen. Knocking at Bognor's doors, she asked how many penny-worth were wanted and always added: 'Beautiful dripping! Comes from the Duke's.' This phrase became the town's synonym for perfection. If a man raced for a train and just caught it, his fellow passengers remarked 'Beautiful dripping!' In Harfield's saw pit in High Street, if the sawyers cut off a plank neatly, the comment was 'Beautiful dripping!'

The fields provided boys with sport. In the Brookland towards Felpham they netted birds. To the west, where now are the trim lawns and municipal flowers of Marine Park Gardens, they caught pheasants and rabbits or else chased hares along the beach. As autumn and winter came, football, 'rumpy' (hockey) and skating claimed their time. The boys were poor. An owner of skates might have to lend his pair to about thirty others. For indoor entertainment they were allowed to go up into the small gallery in the Sudley Road Assembly Rooms to hear the concerts and the Bognor Minstrels. At Christmas, they gathered in the streets to watch the fantastic Tipteers.

The Bognor Tipteers, nine local men grotesquely costumed, were one of the many troupes who enjoyed performing the ancient English miracle play about St George and the Dragon. This consisted of some twenty minutes of traditional doggerel, old songs and weird mime by the four leading characters, Father Christmas, St (or King) George, the Turkish Knight and a Doctor. The play had a pagan origin and through the centuries had accumulated so many allusions that its verses were often incomprehensible. The words varied slightly from district to district, but the opening verse remained more or less the same:

> In comes I, old Father Christmas,
> Welcome or welcome not.
> I hope old Father Christmas
> Will never be forgot.

Standing in the gutter before Bognor's hotels and big houses, the Tipteers 'worked' the town for the two weeks each side of Christmas. It was customary to give them money, as with carol-singers today, and the usual sum was a halfpenny. Once in High Street a wealthy man gave them a sixpence. The players were so overcome that they stopped the performance to discuss the windfall. On Boxing Day they walked to Goodwood House, gave a show, were feasted in the servants' hall and then went on to Chichester to give the play several times before finishing up with celebrations and sleeping under whatever cover they could find. Next day they walked back to Bognor.

Crime did not enter often into the local boys' lives; the punishment was too severe. Stealing was almost unknown and the currants and raspberries grew untouched on the allotments. But when in 1874 two boys, habitual fowl thieves, were finally caught near the town, the penalties had a Dickensian flavour. One was given four months, the other two weeks in solitary confinement followed by five years in a reformatory. There is a distinct hint of Dickens, too, in the waif found on Bognor beach in 1871 by a Mr. Fegan. He adopted the boy, had him educated and trained and sent him to Canada. From finding this one child on the beach came a philanthropic idea that developed into Fegan's Homes and the assisting of thousands of boys to start life in Canada.

Food was what a boy enjoyed most, particularly if he was fortunate enough to be invited to one of Mrs. Anthony Trollope's parties at Nyewood Villa. Trollope and his wife were living apart, 18 miles apart — he at The Grange, South Harting, on the other side of the Downs, she in a small, cement-faced house in Bognor on the corner of Wood Street and Nyewood Lane. Trollope's vast literary labours over, he retired in the summer of 1880 to South Harting to enjoy his remaining two years in the company of visiting friends such as J. E.

Millais, the artist, and the poet Alfred Austin — the latter being so taken with the beauty of the grounds that he was inspired to write *The Garden That I Love*. Mrs. Trollope retired the same year to Bognor and enjoyed the company of 50 local children that September at her first party, giving them a superb tea and providing swings, games, cricket and a handsome toy for each guest to take home.

Lastly, in these skimmings of Bognor boyhood, there would always be a hope of fireworks, a brilliant, explosive finish to some great day like Queen Victoria's Golden Jubilee in 1887. This anniversary had special associations for Bognor, for some of the oldest inhabitants well remembered the Queen as a child at Bognor Lodge. Furthermore, her aide-de-camp for the last 10 years, Major-General Christopher Teesdale of South Bersted, was now Sir Christopher, one of her new Knights of the Garter. Teesdale, with his fine trim figure and white moustache, was the hero of the parish: the Crimean warrior who, so his general had announced in despatches, 'fought like a lion' in defending the fortress of Kars. His bravery won him the V.C., but when he was back in his home, 'The Ark', opposite South Bersted church, the neighbours liked to think that those initials also stood for his important parochial status as Vicar's Churchwarden.

Jubilee Day, 28 June, began with a band of the Royal Sussex Regiment leading a procession of the Local Board, Jubilee Committee, Fire Brigade and local Lodges, with the Bognor Drum & Fife Band in the rear, to a thanksgiving service at new St John's. At 1 o'clock, dinner was given to 400 people at the New Assembly Rooms which Arthur Smith had erected for a private company opposite the railway station in 1886. (The most prominent feature of the building was an octagonal lantern tower which made a picturesque contribution to the Bognor skyline; in later years it housed a revolving light which could be seen for miles.) Eight hundred children marched across the town at 3 p.m. to sing the National Anthem in a field where sports, horse-racing, tea and the presentation of Jubilee medals to the children kept everyone occupied until evening. At 9 o'clock both bands set off again, winding in and out of the streets in a torchlight procession which ended on the promenade. And here, at 10, the perfect climax was reached with 'A Grand Display of Fireworks from the Pier, the Band Playing Meanwhile'.

*   *   *

If you were neither child nor invalid, and thus deprived of the faculty of fully appreciating Bognor, it became a matter of sheer desperation for the guidebook writers to decide what you should do with your time. With heroic hopelessness, Black's *Guide* of 1889 suggested that a visit might be made to a mousetrap factory at Selsey.

Variance of opinion among these writers increased as the century came to an end. For some the resort remained forever dull, while another protested that 'the inhabitants are at pains to destroy the quiet retirement of the place to which it owed the presence of royalty' (1890). The flatness of the immediate landscape was resented by the more Gothically-minded, yet in 1912 another eye saw it as 'Holland-like and interesting. Residents here understand Turner's sunsets, because they see so many on the western horizon.' Against those who found Bognor featureless — 'possesses even less of interest than Littlehampton' (1893) — there were critics who recognised its species: 'Worthing's twin-sister', 'a sort of Sussex Broadstairs'.

Bognor, now a hundred years old, rode the waves of insult, proud of the late Lord William Lennox's valedictory praise and prouder still of a descriptive piece headed 'Breezy Bognor' which appeared in the *Daily Telegraph* on 16 September 1890: 'One thing is sure to strike anybody visiting Bognor for the first time, and that is the Dutch-like cleanliness of the town. The aspect of the houses and streets is essentially that of the proverbial new pin.' The local press seized upon the 'Dutch-like' label, cherished it, memorised it and were still using it 65 years later ('Bognor, on the whole, can still pride itself on its resemblance to "a little Dutch town"'*Bognor Regis Post*, 25 June 1955.)

Life in England was inevitably beginning to quicken. Even in Bognor, resistant to vulgar change, there was soon to be a little hastening, a jolly jog-trot into the reign of Edward VII, whose influence on social matters was already so strongly felt that his era had begun ten years before he took the throne in 1901.

Of the old Victorian Bognor, though, we can catch two final glimpses, two highly critical impressions by writers who saw the resort in the off-season of what now seems a remote age. In October 1880 along the coast from Bournemouth came Mr. Charles W. Wood. He had been writing articles about the New Forest for *The Argosy*, a magazine owned and edited by his mother, the novelist Mrs. Henry Wood, and he came to Bognor not primarily for 'copy' but to see a lady friend. He arrived in blinding rain and wind after a train journey of six hours, saw the girl that evening and then battled his way back along the front to the *Norfolk Hotel*:

'Not a creature was visible; the place might have been given up to the dead. Either there were no lamps, or they had been blown out by the gale, and the darkness might be felt. The water within a hundred yards surrounding the Norfolk Hotel was a foot high; in the darkness no path could be found, so that I kept going round and round and returning to the starting point.

'The next day the place looked dilapidated and dreary — the dreariness of a sea-side place out of season. Not that Bognor, as far as I could discover, is ever very much in season — and this, perhaps, forms one of its few attractions: the possibility of escaping a crowd. Added to this, it looked driven and tempest-tossed, washed out. It is a direct contrast to Bournemouth, being flat, unprotected, and almost on a level with the sea. This, so far — its level beach — makes it a favourable resort for children. It has a narrow, old-fashioned pier, with wide gaps between the boards, which are so many traps for canes and umbrellas, and have doubtless wrenched off many a lady's high-heeled shoe (so fashionable and so ugly) to be devoured by the hungry sea beneath. The sea itself was pleasant at Bognor, because it is pleasant everywhere: but it is especially so when it comes dashing in almost to your feet, so that at high water you may almost jump from the esplanade into the advancing waves. It rolls up over the pebbly beach with a drowsy, soothing, monotonous lull . . .

'"Horrid place"' said N.B. [the lady friend], as we patrolled the esplanade like sentinels unattached, while the sea splashed beside us and seemed to set her words to music; and the smallest and daintiest of feet, clad in the daintiest of shoes, and scarlet silken hose that set off a perfect instep and *ancles à merveille*, beat time to the waves.

"Horrid place!" she repeated with increasing emphasis. "You see we made the mistake of taking the house before seeing the place. I cannot think how we can have been so stupid!"

'And certainly, listening to her well-directed criticisms, I felt myself fortunate in having had an object in coming to Bognor apart from the place itself. One can hardly wonder that it has stood still, and that a century ago it might have looked very much as it looks to-day; though in these days of progress it would be rash to prophesy its aspect a cent iry hence.'

N. took Charlie for a carriage drive – her mother went, too – up to Slindon and over the Downs to Bury, and the three also explored Chichester, which he found quite depressing – so much so that, by contrast, 'even the dull, deadly-lively thoroughfares of Bognor had in them something almost pleasant.' After three days, he said good-bye to N. and her scarlet silk stockings and headed for St Leonards:

'My regret at leaving Bognor had nothing to do with the place itself. But it must be remembered that it was emphatically the "dead season" and at such times there is a certain air of stagnation about the liveliest place, which never fails to depress. The lodging-house keepers have reaped their harvest and retired into their shells; large windows, dirty and disrobed, stare you in the face with stony, unchanging aspect. Grass begins to grow in the streets, and few footsteps interfere with its progress. The little pleasure boats are all drawn up on the beach, high and dry for the winter; and if, on seeing an old boatman lounging about, he asks you if you would like a sail, he does it unconsciously, by the force of habit; just as a clock mechanically strikes the appointed hours through the night watches, though none are near to listen.'

The second critic came to Bognor by horse and trap with her husband at the end of June 1886. She was one of the strange new invaders of England whose accents and clothes were being imitated by the younger set in London, whose presence was not yet accepted socially and whose thrusting curiosity was considered past praying for. She was, in other words, an American tourist: young Mrs. Anna Bowman Dodd of Boston, who recorded her impressions of a six-weeks tour in an American-published book *Cathedral Days in Southern England*. With her husband, nicknamed 'Boston', she came by train from London to Arundel, hired a trap and set off westwards. It was hot summer, haying time, and they bowled down to the sea across across the plain, entering Bognor on a sleepy afternoon:

'We were in Bognor before we knew it. The fields led us directly into rows of neat, tidy little houses, and clean, well-swept streets. A man in knickerbockers with a tennis racket, and a lady wearing a thin white muslin gown and a thick fur cape, announced to us that the season at Bognor had already begun.

'Other signs of its activity greeted us as we proceeded on our way. Tennis was being played, with a zeal that made it appear to be a serious battle rather than a harmless contest about balls, in every square inch of green large enough to hold a court. The familiar London sign, "Apartments to Let", hung above the tiny, dazzlingly clean doors of the little houses. The number of these signs was conclusive proof that Bognor's season was not as yet at its height. So frequent were these modest appeals to the unlodged, as to prepare us for the comparative quiet we found brooding over the little town.

'At its best, however, Bognor could never, I think, have been anything but a dull little town. It was so decorous, so painfully clean, so oppressively self-conscious a prude, that dullness must have been as much a part of its being as were its demure little airs of conventional propriety. What has the sea to do with conventionality? Its merest ripplet is Nature's indignant protest against too clean and well-swept a beach. Here there was no beach at all. Instead there was a brick sea wall, which kept the sea at a proper offish distance. The waves broke a hundred yards out, as an English sea should do when it is to serve as the tame and tepid bath for an Englishman's wife and children.

'The houses that fronted the water might have been London houses, suburban London; there was no holiday air pervading them. There was nothing even of the flowery, pretty picturesqueness which had charmed us in some of the country inns and taverns we had passed along our road. These dull-brown and brick façades were the epitome of British decorum. Even when off on a holiday, it appears that the Englishman feels he must build him a prison in which he can lock himself in and others out.

'"The Englishman can't throw off his social straight-jacket even when he puts on his bathing-suit," I said in a fit of disgust to Boston. "Have you noticed the bathing-machines? The notices on the doors are little chapters of autobiography."

'"They are of a piece with all the rest," was Boston's answer. On the doors of several of the bathing-machines were signs in large printed letters of "Elizabeth Primrose, aged fifty, bather from Teignmouth, where she had been bather for over thirty-five years".

'"Even one's bath-woman must have a pedigree!" we said, and then we laughed.

'But we were the only laughers. No one else was gay. Holidaying at the seaside, it appears, is a serious amusement over here, to be enjoyed in a measured spirit of conscious dullness. Even the children, who with their governesses were gravely walking along the sea wall, were evidently far too well brought up to look upon the sea in the light of a playfellow. Other promenaders there were whose expression was familiar; it was the look we had grown to know in London, in the Row — that of being bored according to the most correct methods of a well-bred *ennui*. A few very upright young ladies were sitting alone or in pairs, under huge white parasols, on the little iron benches. They were looking out at the sea, staring at it as if they expected, if there was to be any conversation, the ocean would begin it. The only talking there was, was being done by several stately old ladies in bathchairs. They were each accompanied by their upright handsome husbands — or such we took them to be, from their air of indifference to the ladies' chatter and from their general air of command . . . These fine old gentlemen were pictures of blooming old age, with their pink cheeks, white hair and well-knit, erect and graceful figures . . .

'It was with but little regret that we passed out of the long, stiff, straight little streets, noting, as we passed, the fact of how cheerfully many of the houses gave up half their façade to the great business of proclaiming their names. Where else except in a land of of cockneys would a residence twelve by ten be dignified by a name, ostentatiously paraded, suitable only for a palatial dwelling? "The Elms", the "Albert Villa", the "Richmond Mansion" — such were the pretentious signs painted in great flaring letters over every other house-door which we passed. For a modest people the English break out into astonishing vagaries of vanity.'

And so, in the summer of 1886, Anne Dodd rattled off to inspect Chichester Cathedral, leaving vainglorious villas, melancholy maidens and only the hot passion of the grass courts to disturb the propriety of a seaside afternoon.

Chapter XVII

TURN OF THE CENTURY

THOUGH ANNE DODD was not to know it, she was witnessing in Bognor's nameplates the growth of tradition. That commemorative instinct which helps to form the character of towns was already evident in Bognor. Names of houses and streets proclaimed dignified associations, personal whims, reflected glory and pride of ancestry.

The ducal family at Goodwood was honoured by Richmond Villa (Mrs. Dodd surely betrayed her American origin by referring to Richmond *Mansion*) and by Lennox Street — and there was also Anglesey House in memory of the 5th Duke's comrade-in-arms. In Charlwood Villa there was an echo of the farmland in Hotham's day, in Lansdowne Place and Portland House the memory of aristo-cratic patrons, in Scott Street a reminder of the Colonel. Royal roads led to the sea: Gloucester, Clarence, Albert, York and Victoria (but not, surprisingly, Charlotte); Lord Strathmore's family connections were retained in Lyon Street, Strathmore Place, Glamis Street, Sidlaw Terrace; and the reign of Lord Arran was brought to mind by Sudley Lodge, Sudley Road and Arran Meadow. Each street had some narrow hall of fame with history gilded on the fanlight over the front door: Brunswick Villa, Hanover House, Nelson House, Gladstone Villas. Those who preferred Bognor as a tranquil, pastoral backwater were to be found under the sign of Lawn Villa, The Laurels or The Shrubbery. If you had rolled home from Chinese waters, like Captain Thomas Macey, you dropped anchor at Woosung Cottage or Yangtse Villa.

Visitors, staying at some noble address, were made further aware of the town's lineage by the various signs of royal favour in traders' advertisements, such as the claim to have been 'Patronised by the late Emperor Napoleon' used by James Cross in announcing carriages for hire. In Manor Place, off Waterloo Square, a large board bearing the arms of the Prince of Wales blocked the bedroom window above a tiny fish-shop owned by James Yeates, who had given the Prince a taste for Bognor prawns while at Goodwood and continued supplying him in London. Farther along the promenade, Mr. Carlisle Barber had taken over the *Norfolk Hotel* in 1886 and re-named it the *Royal Norfolk*. Two years later, he extended the building, adding a long balcony and erecting a large reproduction of the Royal Arms in artificial stone on the coping. No one questioned the propriety of this until 1917 when the Royal Warrant Holders Association, in a burst of patriotism, argued with the Home Office over the hotel's right to exhibit the arms, as there was no official record of a grant. The matter was settled in the hotel's favour, the arms having been in position for so long that the Home Office saw no reason to have them removed, provided that the royal insignia was used in no other connection, such as on the hotel notepaper, china and linen. That is still the situation today; it was reaffirmed when the hotel again changed hands in 1948 and the arms were picked out in colour.

Bognor's increasing tendency to regard itself as the well-connected 'elder statesman' of the district was not shared by neighbouring towns. To Chichester, the resort merely afforded an access to the beach by train; and after 27 August 1897, when a light railway was built from Chichester to Selsey, the Bognor journey became superfluous. At a Selsey luncheon on the opening day, the point was clearly made by the mayor of Chichester, Alderman Ballard, that it was now possible to get to the sea without waiting about at Barnham Junction for a connection to Bognor, whose inhabitants had always been rather 'stand-offish' and had opposed a direct line from Bognor to Chichester. From Littlehampton's point of view, Bognor was an upstart and in their *Visitors' Guide* of 1892 it was pointed out that, should anyone trouble to visit Bognor, 'there is a capital pier and a fairly good promenade. The rest of the local attractions are nil'.

With extended responsibilities bringing buoyancy to Bognor's Local Board, the members had sought better offices for transacting the town's business. Up to 1871 they had been using No. 7 Hothamton Place at the western end of High Street, but when this — like the neighbouring Fitzleet House — was sold to the Merchant Taylors Company for part of a second Convalescent Home (for ladies), the Board hired accommodation in the old Assembly Rooms in Sudley Road for £50 a year and let it be known that they were contemplating building a Town Hall. For some time now, the Jubilee Charity School in High Street had been closed and the Trustees had decided to sell. It was a site that seemed ideal for the Board's resplendent new offices as visualised by the town's surveyor, Mr. H. W. Stringfellow. On 4 June 1880 school and site were purchased for £500, whereupon a storm broke out among the ratepayers. Public opinion was rigidly against any grandiose schemes. There was to be no brand-new Town Hall, only an alteration of the existing school building. The surveyor put away his plans, transformed the school into offices for a further £559 and on 3 March 1882 the Board sat down to an inaugural lunch in the restricted comfort of their modest new premises.

If the Board had felt that they were then the truly humble servants of the town, their pride was restored in 1894 with the passing of the Local Government Act (Urban & Rural Councils) whereby the former Local Government Board became an Urban District Council of 12 members (including the irrepressible Henry Lovett) with Mr. Alfred T. Long, the chemist, as Chairman at the first Council meeting on 31 December.

The population of the Bognor town area in 1891 was 4,096. From 1874, the area of the Board's jurisdiction had comprised the new parish of Bognor and that part of South Bersted parish in which were the Dome House and Hotham's other mansions. Now, as a Council, their authority was strengthened and in 1896 the powers, duties and liabilities of the two parish Vestry Committees were transferred to them; and by 1900 more of South Bersted parish, including the old village and part of Pagham parish to the west, were added to the Urban District.

To mark the town's new status, someone had an apt thought and merged the arms of Sir Richard Hotham with those of the County of Sussex to create Bognor's own neat, if unregistered, coat-of-arms. It was at once put to use in the late 1890s to give tone to the cover of subscription concert programmes.

Of their many responsibilities, the U.D.C. found the upkeep of the Pier a continuing burden, although in 1900 they improved its attractions by building a small pavilion at the sea end in which the band played in summer and the local youth roller-skated in winter. What the Council really wanted to do with the Pier was to sell it, but prospective purchasers were deterred by being required to operate it under Board of Trade control; and in the meantime the structure deteriorated. Ladies' heels not only sank between the planks, but into the very planking. Just before Easter in 1908, in view of the coming holidays, the Local Government Board in London enquired very pointedly as to 'the intentions of the Bognor Council in connection with your Pier'. At a melodramatic meeting, Mr. Lovett, knowing that Bognor had something rotten in its sea, cried out in characteristic fashion to his fellow councillors: 'If the Council do not decide to shut that pier, I am going out tonight to wire to the Board that I wash my hands of anything that may happen.'

The Pier was thereupon closed, and a Southampton firm was asked to estimate the cost of repairs. The Local Government Board also sent down an inspector who made a tour along the Pier with various officials. In the party was a representative of the Bognor fishermen who wasted no time with words but simply took out his fishing-gear knife and drove it up to the handle into the woodwork. The inspector was rather impressed and returned to London. In due course the estimate arrived and, since it had been based more on rebuilding the Pier than on merely repairing it, the cost would be £11,000. The Council's request for Government permission to raise this money by loan was refused. It was hinted that enough money had already been wasted on a mismanaged pier.

The only course left was to be rid of it at once at any price, the only stipulation being that the purchaser had to repair it to the estimated cost. In August 1909 the condemned Pier was officially handed over to the private company which had accepted this condition. The price paid was purely nominal. It was ten shillings and sixpence.

The new owners, Messrs. Alfred Carter and W. M. Shanley, not only made the Pier serviceable again but in 1910–1911 spent nearly £30,000 in widening the shore end and erecting there a large block of buildings comprising a theatre, a cinema and an arcade of 12 shops, which effectively obstructed the clear view along the coast and promenade. Mr. Shanley, of Irish descent, was known as 'The Chair King', his father having introduced to Britain the Parisian system of hiring out chairs on the spot. He was the chief supplier of chairs for London parks, Royal occasions, bandstands and seaside resorts. He had a house at Felpham and was fond of recalling the day when the Pier was sold. 'One of my most profitable interests,' he said, 'is Bognor Pier, which I bought for 10s. 6d. What made it pay? Simply the building of an arcade on the shore end where people could shelter from the rain.'

If the foregoing has suggested that the new Council's life was not an easy one, there was compensation in the gala days, proud square-shouldered days when the town's elect could show the real measure of their worth. Out of this period, we might pick just one occasion – Monday, 9 July 1900, when the Duke and Duchess of York (the future King George V and Queen Mary) came to open two new convalescent homes.

These substantial buildings in dark red brick and terra cotta faced the sea at the eastern end of the front, filling up one more meadow; and both had been erected, at his own expense, by Mr. Max Waechter of Richmond, Surrey. The builder was William Tate of Bognor. The Duchess's mother, the late Princess Mary, Duchess of Teck, among her many charitable works had maintained a small summer rest-home for poor London women at Coombe, near Richmond, and when she died in 1898 it was decided to continue the work as a memorial to her and also to build the Princess Mary Memorial Home at Bognor. The year before she died – which was the Queen's Diamond Jubilee year – Princess Mary had herself become interested in a proposed seaside convalescent home for Surrey women to commemorate the Queen's long reign and to be administered by the County of Surrey. The Victoria Convalescent Home was being planned at Bognor when the Princess died and subsequently her own Memorial Home was built next door. Both were now officially to be opened on the same day.

The flurry of preparation included mustering a guard of honour by members of the 2nd Volunteer Battalion of the Royal Sussex Regiment, compiling the programme of music for the band (Flotow's *Jubel* overture, waltzes by Strauss and Gung'l, Godfrey's *Reminiscences of England*, excerpts from Sullivan's *The Rose of Persia*, etc.), the building of a stand for children on the waste where Lord William Lennox's Cotswold Crescent should have been, and the erection by the fishermen of a Bognor speciality, an elaborate arch of fishing nets, oars and lobster pots across the road near the Homes.

At 1.20 p.m., with the band playing and the Volunteers drawn up, Their Royal Highnesses were welcomed at the railway station by the Chairman and members of the Council. A procession then set off with the police and fire brigade leading, followed by four Council carriages and the three royal carriages with an escort of Hampshire Carabineer Yeomanry. It had been decided to show the royal couple the best of Bognor, so while the other guests and the public made their way direct to the promenade, the procession veered off into Hotham's leafy aristocratic quarter and made a roundabout approach to the Homes. It was, perhaps, not the wisest route. There was hardly a soul in sight in this quiet residential area and as the Council carriages passed two small boys standing on the pavement, the Town Clerk leaned out and hissed desperately at them: 'Cheer! Cheer!'

The hush lifted as the procession emerged on to the sea front. Crowds greeted the royal visitors and watched the Duke inspect the coastguards and saw the Duchess receive the key from Mr. Waechter and open her mother's Memorial Home. The Bishop of Rochester performed a dedicatory service in both buildings and then luncheon followed, prepared by Nuthalls of Kingston-on-Thames in a tent on the lawn. By 3 o'clock, the speeches and handshakes and private inspection of the Homes were over. Their Royal Highnesses re-entered their carriages and drove under the fishermen's arch, which delighted the Duke, and past the yelling children. Another circular route, via West Street and High Street, took them to the station for a final look at the rugged coastguards and the beaming councillors before departing for Portsmouth on the 3.45 p.m. train.

The town relaxed. The sun shone. The children gorged a free tea, the Volunteers, coastguards, police and firemen ate a hearty late lunch and the two matrons opened the Homes for sightseers. That evening at 7.30 p.m., as if the day's excitement was not enough, the Council brought fresh glory to the resort by opening the new £2,000 pavilion at the end of the Pier.

*   *   *

In most writers, as we have seen, Bognor evoked either pity or melancholia, and it is with relief that we come at last upon three men whose imaginations were set astir by contact with the town. They were Victor Whitechurch, Max Beerbohm and H. G. Wells.

In the meadowland where the convalescent homes were built, the red-jacketed Volunteers used to drill. Their first headquarters was an old malt-house in London Road and one of their most ardent members was Victor Lorenzo Whitechurch, who became an early N.C.O. in 'I' Coy. Born in 1868, he went to school at Chichester and spent his boyhood in Bognor, roaming the beach and coast with the fishing families, Ragless, Ide and Allen, who taught him to sail and fish. The railway also fascinated him and he would beg rides on the footplate to Barnham.

Out of these adventures grew his first story, a railway yarn which appeared in the *Strand Magazine* in 1894. By then he had joined the Church and of his 40 years of clerical life, 38 were spent in the diocese of Oxford. He became a canon of Christ Church and for 13 years was rural dean of Aylesbury and vicar of Hartwell-with-Stone. In 1931 ill-health brought him back to Bognor and retirement at 'The Halt' in Victoria Drive. He died in 1933.

To thousands of people, this handsome forthright man was not so much a clergyman as their favourite romantic novelist. His tales had wit and force and his heroines were frank modern girls who, however, had not forgotten how to blush deeply. For background, he used the neighbourhood he knew so well, though with disguised names for people and places. Bognor was 'Britford' or 'Selgate', Chichester was usually 'Frattenbury', Barnham was 'Foxby' and Pagham became 'Rundleham'. Pagham and its fishermen were his inspiration for *First and Last*, and 'Dad' and 'Neighbour' Allen of Bognor appeared in what he considered his best book, *Concerning Himself*. His most famous novel, *The Canon in Residence* (1904), earned him the fury of ecclesiastical Chichester and caused a minor sensation in West Sussex. The story dealt boldly with a new Canon at 'Frattenbury' Cathedral who rode roughshod over the etiquette laid down by a pompous Dean and Chapter and fought to right the wrongs of the townspeople. As the Dean and Mayor were the villains of the piece, with civic corruption and scandal in the Close vividly described in a city that could only be Chichester, it was no wonder that the book remained a best-seller for over 25 years. Yet Canon White-church considered there was little reward in novel-writing. He was at Bognor in January 1912, preaching at St John's, and a fellow clergyman asked how much he had made so far from *A Canon in Residence*. 'My publishers gave me £50 down,' he replied, 'but I have two friends who compiled a little book of devotions called *Helps to Worship* and they each net about £200 a year for it.'

On Sir Max Beerbohm, Bognor's allegedly depressing appearance in the off-season had a most stimulating effect. He preferred the grey deserted promenade in winter, though he did not object to the sedate summer season, and in August 1896, when staying in West Street at the *Berkeley Inn* (now No. 35), he wrote in a letter: 'Bognor is so placid a town . . . Really rather pretty and nice, mild air . . . and several quiet town-bands playing furtively round the quaint old corners.'

It became his favourite winter resort for many years, and in the opinion of his friend Logan Pearsall Smith, the American-born essayist who lived a few miles away at Ford Place, it was undoubtedly Bognor he was describing when he wrote about an un-named town in 'The Seaside in Winter', an essay in his volume entitled *More*, published in 1899. This essay has great charm and is full of obser-vations that had escaped others: a walk to the station to get the newspaper, the waves 'carrying up seaweed in their white teeth and arranging it in strips on the sand', the curious importance attached to a lone visitor and making him 'a dominant and most romantic personage'. And only Beerbohm could look at a file of orphan girls going down with spades to the wintry shore and observe: 'They are going down to the dreary task of building. If one of them tried to escape, I suppose she would be shot down like a Dartmoor convict.'

In 1919 there appeared his book of short stories, *Seven Men*, one of which, written in 1914, dealt with a neurotic fellow named Laider whom the narrator found at his seaside hotel in February. They were both recovering from influenza. According to Logan Smith, the setting is again Bognor; the hotel could easily be the *Royal Norfolk*. As for the story itself, its conclusion makes one gasp with laughter.

One wonders if the seaside air drew out some extra frivolities from that droll mind. Smith recalled an occasion at Bognor when Beerbohn decided to cheer up a fellow-writer:

> 'Once when the author of novels no one ever read was about to visit him, he engaged the unhappy local sandboy to inscribe broadly in large letters on the seashore the news: "The famous novelist Augustus Tubbs has arrived in Bognor". Max's walk the next morning on the sands with his friend was for him also a pleasant promenade.'

At the end of the Steyne there stands a smart little Regency building, then the *Steyne Cottage Hotel*, where in April 1926 Beerbohm was enjoying the off-season and from where he penned this reply to a lady who requested his autograph:

> Dear Miss Miles,
>   You say you 'will pay postage on' the arrival of my autograph. But really I do not think my autograph is worth so much as tuppence. So I affix to your already addressed

envelope a penny stamp. A penny is not too great a price for the pleasure I have in
complying with your request. All this is very graceful.
                                   Yours very truly,
                                   Max Beerbohm

H. G. Wells saw Bognor as the setting for the attempted seduction of Jessie
Milton in his early novel, *The Wheels of Chance* (1896). Jessie, aged 18, slender,
dark and full of spirit, has fled from her domineering stepmother in Surbiton and
set off on her bicycle to lead her own life. Her male cycling companion, an
unspeakable cad named Bechamel, has promised to help her but instead is luring
her south across Surrey and Sussex for his own purposes. Their route coincides
with that of little Mr. Hoopdriver, a draper's assistant on a cycling holiday, who
senses that something is wrong and pursues them in the rôle of amateur detective.
It is in a Bognor hotel that Jessie realises with beating heart that she is trapped.
'I have you,' sneers Bechamel. 'You are mine. Netted — caught. But mine.' He
goes for a stroll on the front, which gives Hoopdriver the chance to sneak in and
save the girl in a whirlwind rescue. They pedal madly off into the moonlit night
towards Chichester. The story ends in Hampshire, where Jessie's panting stepmother catches up with them and the reader is left with the tingle of hope that
Jessie will seek out her knight errant again when the fuss has died down.

There is an exhilarating freshness in this novel as one follows the three characters down the dusty, bumpy roads through Guildford, Midhurst and Chichester
to the exciting climax at Bognor. Wells knew every inch of this countryside from
his days at Midhurst Grammar School, and he placed the 'Vicuna Hotel' at 'the
very westernmost extremity of the seafront', which suggests that he was thinking
of the *Victoria Hotel*.

The book had immense topicality when it was published for it came out in the
midst of the cycling boom. The bicycle had freed the slaves of England from
behind the shop counter and many a real-life Hoopdriver was able to set off on
a cheap and novel adventure, comforted by the knowledge that the Bicycle
Touring Club was watching over his interests. The B.T.C. sign was already hanging
outside the *Claremont Hotel* at Bognor in 1882.

At the entrance to Bognor Lodge, the local boys used to watch Mr. George
Gatehouse's son wheel out his bicycle. It was the first one in the town to have
pneumatic tyres. Jessie and Bechamel in Wells's novel also had pneumatics and
Hoopdriver was able to follow the tyre-tracks till he lost them on the cobbles of
Chichester. Not until the evening did he find them again, one ribbed like a
shilling, the other chequered, printed in the dust on the road that led to Bognor.

In 1896, when *The Wheels of Chance* was published, the Bognor Cycling Club
organised a dozen runs during the season from May to October. They started from
the *Sussex Hotel*, their headquarters, at 6.10 p.m. and made trips to Worthing
via Arundel, to Emsworth, Eartham, Goodwood and such Downland haunts as
Singleton and Madehurst. Traders kept pace with the sport and at Mr. A. R.
Southerton's Cycle & Motor Engineering Works in Sudley Road his skilled workmen built cycles to order and cycling was taught 'by experienced instructors'.
Just on the market was Sargent's patent detachable handle-bar. One handle-bar

unscrewed from its fellow, thus making the machine unrideable and safe from theft, and its hollow interior formed a container for pump, oil-can, cleaner and spanner.

Each year, at the Club's cycling gymkhana, the girls competed in balancing the longest on their machines, in cycling with a lance and sticking a square of cardboard on the ground, or in manoeuvring in and out of a line of bottles. Men went in for the potato, egg & spoon and tortoise races, the prize in the latter going to the slowest competitor. Five members went on a long run in June 1897 to see the Diamond Jubilee Naval Review at Portsmouth, leaving at 3.30 p.m. and not getting back till after dawn. On the way home, one young man had fun chasing a couple on a tandem and cycling round them. He rejoined the main party later on, reporting that the couple had led him and themselves astray and had landed up in a saw-pit at Emsworth. Coming into Chichester, the Club members developed a thirst and saw lights in the *Dolphin* and the landlord standing outside, waiting for guests to return from the Review. He listened to the cyclists' entreaties, decided they were bona-fide travellers and served them with drinks as the dawn was breaking over the city.

Older folk in Bognor sometimes literally felt the impact of this new age as cyclists swerved from one side of the street to the other to find a more level surface. There was restlessness in the air. One new invention followed on another. At the High Street library they were now selling Bagnell's Magnetic Electric Pen Nibs, which would not corrode when left wet. At a Unionist smoking concert at the new Assembly Rooms in November 1898, four out of 14 items were listed as 'Gramophone . . . Mr. R. Gatehouse'.

With the advent of the cycle, even the Downs were being discovered. They had forever been remote, ignored by those holidaymakers who sought only rest and certainly never rambled over by mixed couples on a walking tour, an association on which people tended to frown. The hills were left to the artist and the student, the poet and the botanist. Thus, in August 1888, while London was being terrorised by Jack the Ripper, one would have found Tennyson and his son wandering among the gaunt yews in Kingley Vale and up the serene valley of the Lavant, where he was so transported by the beauty of it all that he leant on a gate and recited two of his own poems without a break.

It was a magic moment that might have been shattered by the Bognor Cycling Club. For Kingley Vale was often included in their runs and the silence of the Downs was liable to be broken by whistle blasts from their captain: one for slower, two for faster, three for single file, and a long blast for stop.

*   *   *

On 22 January 1901, Queen Victoria died at Osborne in the Isle of Wight and on 2 February her coffin was brought by train along the coast and thence to London, via Arundel. Bognor emptied as the townspeople made their way across the countryside to the main line to pay their last respects, standing at the level crossings at Woodgate and Yapton and on the platforms at Barnham Junction.

There was an awesome grandeur about the occasion, for the train had been eight minutes late in starting and was trying to pick up time. The purple-clad engine *Empress* came past the bareheaded crowds in a flash of heat and steam at 80 miles an hour — and arrived at Victoria two minutes early.

It was the town's brief moment of farewell to an age already gone. Bognor had already crossed the threshold of the new era and it was the Railway Company that had given it this sense of advancement. They had decided to rebuild the station.

Passengers to Bognor hitherto had alighted on a small platform among the allotments and stepped out through a wooden shanty containing waiting rooms, offices and a porter's room. In 1874, the Railway Company had made a gesture and added a porch to the station; and in 1892 they re-erected the building after it had collapsed in a gale. On Ash Wednesday, 3 March, 1897, another storm blew the platform roof off; and during the night of 29 September 1899 the station caught fire. A policeman saw the blaze and gave the alarm at 1.25 a.m. Twenty-seven minutes later, the fire engine arrived from its new headquarters in High Street, followed at short intervals by members of the Volunteer Brigade, but there was nothing left to save except the Company's safe standing among the ashes. The wooden station had been swiftly and completely destroyed and the heat had cracked the window of Knowles's furniture shop outside. A suggested cause of the fire was that a porter's coat, left drying in front of a fire, had caught alight.

A year's delay elapsed before rebuilding began in September 1900, but it was a pregnant pause and Bognor was finally presented in July 1902 with a brick station of such size and magnificence, in comparison with its predecessor, that it was said to be one of the finest in the country. The clairvoyance of the L.B. & S.C.R. thrilled the town, for the company had spent £68,000 in creating this imposing terminus and buying up the adjacent allotment for new yards, thus wisely creating 'accommodation for traffic almost beyond the dreams of the present generation'. The single line from Barnham was doubled on 16 January 1911.

As the town stirred slightly under the wind of development, the chance to create its missing civic hub and shopping centre on the land circling the railway station was ignored — in spite of the lead set by the New Assembly Rooms in 1886. Most of the new schemes were set afoot within a stone's throw of the sea. Very gradually, the meadows along the shore to east and west were being transformed into residential patches, with the promenade edging farther along every few years to give a uniform frontage to the scene.

Prominent among the pre-1914 builders was Mr. William Tate (1848–1931), grandson of Thomas Tate who had established the first furniture-making business in the town. His parents, Thomas and Anne Tate, had emigrated with their children to Australia in the *Flying Cloud* in 1869, becoming pioneer dairy-farmers at Ithaca Creek, Brisbane. William returned to Bognor in later years and, having built the two new convalescent homes, he brightened up the High Street with an attractive shopping arcade, opened in August 1902; and then immediately to the south, between Belmont Street and the sea front, erected a large complex building resplendent with copper domes and white woodwork. One part of it housed an excellent theatre, to whose main entrance the Arcade provided a convenient covered approach; while the seaward half, presenting a highly decorative façade to the Esplanade, housed a roller-skating rink a balconied tea room and an entertainment hall called Pierrotland. The whole edifice, designed by Mr. W. Tillot Barlow, was given the fashionable German name of The Kursaal and was opened in 1910.

The Council also had ambitions and in the early 1900s, farther west along the Esplanade on a triangular strip of grass that had once been part of the garden of Hotham's original Hotel, it spent £60 in erecting a small circular bandstand, enlarging it in 1910 to accommodate the girth of a full-sized military band. (An earlier addition to the amenities of this section of the promenade west of the Pier was Arthur Smith's *Royal Hotel*, built in the ebullient style of the late 1880s on the site of the old Manor House library — and so close to the beach that, from the upper windows, it seemed as if there was nothing between you and the sea.)

Another notable event in 1910 — rendered necessary because St John's, though less than 30 years old, was already becoming outgrown by its congregation — was the dedication of a new church, St Wilfrid's in Victoria Drive, which would, so the *Observer* piously hoped, 'prevent visitors and residents from becoming Sabbath breakers by roaming the sands through lack of accommodation for Divine worship.'

*   *   *

Thus the town reached its zenith as a select family watering-place, held in fond regard by its regular patrons, a little aware of its dignity, still small and still somewhat rural, with Welsh draught oxen bellowing in Baley's forge at South Bersted as they were tied and thrown for shoeing. Seemingly uninfluenced as yet by what was going on elsewhere along the coast, Bognor found itself still sought out for that unexpected reason — its tranquillity. As the century turned, even the guidebook writers now saw this as a virtue. The wealth of trees was one of the things that caught their fancy. Whereas to the townspeople the trees on each side of High Street were supports on which to hang Chinese lanterns and fairy lamps on gala days, to the author of *Heywood's Guide* of 1901, published in Manchester, they were indicative of the town's good taste:

> 'The High Street is one of the prettiest in the kingdom. It is wide and one side is composed of first-class shops which have a picturesque variety of frontages. The north side is primarily occupied with good houses which are set back from the road, permitting of long bright gardens in front. There is a large number of trees, which give a charm to the whole aspect of the road, without detracting from its appearance as a useful business thoroughfare.'

In fact, the time had now come for Bognor to be commended for assets lost to other resorts through the ravages of development:

> 'On all sides are evidences that Bognor has not grown out of its rural clothes entirely,' observed *Ward Lock's Guide* (1908), 'and great would be the pity if these should be

shorn for the purposes of township expansion; while the town itself is interesting, because
its main business thoroughfares have been allowed to retain the beauties of a country
road. Unlike most seaside resorts, Bognor gives its houses good gardens, and thick-foliaged
trees spread a welcome shade . . . Bognor has not been developed in the way that renders
many places unbearable to searchers after a true holiday . . . to the visitor who comes to
it from a busy city resounding with the almost ceaseless roar of traffic, this quiet, unpretentious, pretty Sussex town appeals in the same manner as would some secluded
village on a stretch of moorland.'

A likeness to a leafy village was not quite the impression that the Council
wished the town to convey. It was more desirable, in their view, that Bognor
should be recognised for its progressive outlook, and in the pre-1914 years the
Council conceived its main duties as fighting the fishermen and removing their
gear from the promenade, having a local Bench, providing the first Council houses
and allotments, extending the Urban District and demanding a better train service.
Bognor's prosperity, as various councillors saw it, depended on attracting a good
class of resident and assisting the individual tradesmen against the competition of
chain stores which took good money out of the town. Fewer shops and more
houses was a suggested line of development, and development in general — in spite
of the guidebooks' approval of its rural qualities — was aimed at making Bognor
as much like other resorts as possible. This trait was a common one in coastal
Councils and sometimes had the effect of destroying the very things that visitors
had come to see — and to which the local people were habitually blind. There
were visitors who liked a seaside town to retain its own character. They did not
wish to come on holiday to a reproduction of a city suburb, but preferred to
discover, like Beerbohm, the 'quaint old corners' and to enjoy the unaccustomed
sights of lobster pots and boats drawn up by the pier and the smell of nets and tar.

Fortunately, many of Bognor's characteristics were irremovable. Having grown
up piecemeal on each side of a lane, its irregularity of plan was now permanent
and in marked contrast to the monotony of straight-streeted resorts. The 'village-
like' label was to stick for years and was often, as we have seen, an enticement.
It was a period of emigration from London and the settling of families within
easy reach of the metropolis. They followed the railway lines out into Essex,
Kent, Surrey and Sussex until they found a pleasant spot. So, with the advent
of the new age, new faces were appearing in Bognor; and, though few of the
newcomers had riches, the town became both more homely and more lively.
The spirit of the times was reflected in a tennis club which opened in mid-May
1905 at the Nyewood Lane sports field. All four courts were occupied daily till
dusk and many of the men and girls wanted to continue playing on in the
moonlight.

Meanwhile, the type of the older Bognor resident had not changed and there
was still a doffing of hats as Lord Justice Field passed by either on foot, with his
manservant a few paces behind, or in his spotless landau with two dalmatians
running close to the rear wheels. Born in 1813, son of Thomas Field of Fielding,
Bedfordshire, he had been a High Court judge from 1875-90 and retired to
Bognor for his health. He lived at 5 Marine Parade and imparted distinction to
such ceremonies as turning on the town's Downland water supply in 1894.

At Sudley Lodge, one of Nelson's swords was to be seen: the property of Colonel Alexander Nelson Hood (1839–1924), who succeeded his father as Viscount Bridport in 1904. He was a descendant of Nelson's niece who had married into another great naval family, the Hoods. He also inherited the Sicilian title of Duke of Brontë and 15,000 acres on the slopes of Mount Etna, which had originally been conferred on Nelson in 1799 by the King of Naples. His wife, Lady Maria Georgiana Julia Fox-Strangways, was the sister of the fifth Earl of Ilchester and they had three children. Lord Bridport was a popular figure in Bognor, present at most local functions, very often in the rôle of performer. His favourite instrument was the könighorn (posthorn), sometimes combined in a duet with a corno di bassetto as at a smoking concert in 1898, but usually reserved for an expert solo turn. In November 1908, having formally presented medals to the Volunteers at the Assembly Rooms, he produced his könighorn and brought the evening to a roaring close with two fine solos. He left the town after the Great War and died in Guernsey.

Lord Bridport's next-door neighbour at The Den was Colonel Harman Grisewood, who had taken the house in the mid-1880s, following Lord and Lady Bingham's occupancy, and in whose family the old mansion remained for some 25 years. Grisewood's second cousin, Frederick, was to earn national fame as a broadcaster.

Opposite the gates of Sudley Lodge, on the south side of High Street, was Belvedere House, a valuable mid-Victorian addition to the mainly Georgian architecture of this eastern end of town. Built in the 1860s on land known as Arran Meadow, it presented a handsome if somewhat severe Renaissance façade to High Street and amply justified its name with a fine view of the beach, across still virgin grazing land, from its more characteristically Victorian south front. In 1890 the house was acquired by the Dominican Sisters from Shoreham-by-Sea, who opened it as St Dominic's preparatory school.

Farther to the east, where High Street joined Upper Bognor Road, the trees had matured into a woodland around Hotham's Chapel House, which had now undergone a second change of name. From being Bersted Lodge, it had become Aldwick Manor since William Fletcher, who had inherited the property from his father, was Lord of the Manor of Aldwick. His widowed mother still lived at the house, where she was joined by William and his wife Agnes. An air of mystery had long pervaded the estate as a result of William's intensive interest in arboriculture and his wife's preoccupation with reptiles. Her pets included pythons, boa-constrictors, small crocodiles and giant lizards, and her husband mildly associated himself with her interests and could pick up a handful of seven adders without harm. The naturalist W. H. Hudson was exploring the district in 1889–90, gathering impressions which included his famous denunciation of Chichester — a city of 70 pubs where 'the brewers . . . are determined that when a man staggers out of one tavern, he shall not be obliged to walk more than twenty yards before finding another' — and at Bognor he learned from Mr. Fletcher the art of handling Downland adders, from which he had hitherto usually fled, and how to tame them in five days and accustom them to the feel of the human hand.

A London solicitor from Mincing Lane, Mr. W. Ward-Higgs, was among the newcomers to the town and for six years (1901-7) he lived with his wife and children at 'Hollywood', South Bersted. He was a large jovial man who endured the occasional train journey to London for the pleasure of returning to Bognor to plunge into such delights as playing croquet – he won the men's singles at the local Club's 1905 tournament – and composing songs. In his robust friendly way, he was very much of the age and took his cue from Kipling's poems, setting to music seven of the *Barrack Room Ballads*, of which *Follow me 'Ome* became quite well known. But when Kipling's great poem on Sussex came out in 1902, there was his real inspiration; he felt that what one man could do for the county in verse, he could do in song. This he achieved and in the convivial atmosphere of Bognor's seaside life, among his friends in the Volunteers and Yeomanry and the local musical societies, he wrote the words and music of a marching song that was to become famous, *Sussex By The Sea*. That was in 1904. Soon the Royal Sussex Regiment were singing it at camp concerts and adopting it as their subsidiary regimental march, while in far corners of the globe gatherings of Sussex exiles gave voice to it, steeped in thoughts of summer breezes through green beech-woods and forgetful of the heat of outback and prairie.

It was from the beechwoods of Slindon in 1905 that a dog-cart would descend on the town, with a stout cob between the shafts and a formidable figure at the reins. This was Hilaire Belloc (1870-1953), then living with his wife and family at Court Hill farmhouse and already commanding a wide public as the author of *The Bad Child's Book of Beasts* and *The Path to Rome*. If Sussex may sometimes have been regarded as a remote and undistinguished county by the rest of Britain, it was soon to become exalted and hallowed at Belloc's hands and mankind was to be informed, among other dogma, that Sussex had been the Garden of Eden. It was the year before the dam broke and Belloc's surge of Sussex truths poured in a wave over the defenceless topography of other counties in the form of *Hills and the Sea* (1906), *Sussex* (1906) and *The Four Men* (1912).

Belloc had been brought up at Slindon from the age of eight and this was the first countryside that he had really known. In 1905, back in the village once more, he wrote and explored anew, looking at his old haunts, sometimes from a boat becalmed off Bognor where he could see the Nore Hill Folly white against the woods above Slindon, sometimes from the hilltops where he saw 'southward the sea plain and the sea standing up in a belt of light against the sky, and north-ward all the weald'. That summer, he renewed the pleasures of scything a field, of riding over the familiar chalk tracks on the cob Monster, his 'kind and honour-able horse', and of galloping home from Gumber to a supper of beer and bacon. In 1906 he moved to Shipley, near Horsham, to set up his permanent home, but returned now and then to Slindon to visit his mother and to descend once more on Bognor (by taxi in 1914) to see his two younger boys, Peter and Hilary, at St Dominic's School.

At 'Strathmore' in High Street lived the family of the Rev. A. T. Gill, whose eldest son Eric (1882-1940) had an eye for the beauty of clean-cut unhampered form. This led him to shock convention with his uninhibited sculpture and

drawings and to become recognised as a master-designer of lettering. In 1897, Mr.
Gill had brought his numerous family from Brighton to Chichester, where he
became curate at St Peter's for two years, and then moved to Bognor as curate
at St John's from 1899 to 1914. Eric had gone on from Chichester Art School to
London and came home at weekends, while his six brothers continued their
schooling in Bognor. Romney and MacDonald, the two next eldest boys, went to
the Royal Naval Academy in Victoria Drive. Romney in due course became
Archbishop of Papua, New Guinea; MacDonald was articled to a Bognor architect,
Lionel Pilkington, and continued in architectural practice in London, but he
became more widely known for his pictorial maps, attracting early attention with
one of London which he did for the Underground in 1913. While Mr. Gill busied
himself with parish affairs and became well liked in the town, his wife, a former
opera singer, spent most of her time at home, keeping the children neat and
respectable and maintaining strict discipline, to the extent that the boys were
allowed to bathe on Sundays but not the girls.

Enid, the eldest daughter, named after Tennyson's character, became the poetic
one, and Eric's first published wood-engravings were done for a volume of her
poems — a form of brotherly thanks, perhaps, for the high polish she used to put
on his boots when he visited home. In 1907, with the children spreading their
wings, the family moved to a smaller house, 32 Glamis Street, and then, in 1914,
left for West Wittering, where Mr. Gill remained as vicar until just before his death
in 1933. In later life, looking back on the Bognor of his youth, Eric was merciless:

> 'I was only a short time at that remarkable place (truly remarkable because it's so
> difficult to know why it exists — except for its sands and the amazing number of hair-
> pins which, in those days, were to be counted on the promenade).' (*Autobiography*.
> Jonathan Cape, 1940).

He didn't even mention the Rocks. Yet he had been sufficiently impressed by the
architectural qualities of St John's to make a suitably uncontroversial drawing of
the church — for the cover of the parish magazine.

*Fig. 17. Victoria Place (The Steyne Cottage Hotel
is on the right).*

Chapter XVIII

EDWARDIAN HOLIDAYS

BY NOW, the town had a fresh problem. As the number of nursing homes and children's homes increased, as the invalids took the air on the esplanade and the school treats spread themselves on the sands — as the big terrace houses became flats for families and the remaining pocket of gentry stood aloof from the visitors — it was difficult to decide whose claims were the most important.

Was Bognor, thanks to its beach, to be regarded primarily as a children's resort? The call of the sands was annually irresistible, as Miss J. C. Elmslie was aware when she took over the *Royal Clarence Hotel* in July 1905 and ran it exclusively as an hotel for children for 23 years. To this convenient establishment parents sent their children with governess or nurse for a seaside holiday, while children from abroad were looked after by a resident nurse. Yet the appeal of children *en masse* was somewhat limited and the *Bognor Observer* that year was asking caterers to combine against the incessant Sunday School parties which were of great annoyance to visitors.

A health resort, then? This indeed was what the town's reputation had been primarily built on and to which it owed Royal patronage. The various nursing and convalescent homes dotted over the parish showed that a considerable weight of opinion had already decided that this was Bognor's rôle among the resorts.

But was there not, nevertheless, a danger of the town developing into a go-as-you-please holiday resort, with considerable lowering of tone? There had been early signs of degeneracy. The *Daily Telegraph* correspondent in 1890 had noted that 'a stroller on the Pier is apt to be considerably startled by the apparition of a Venus Anadyomene whose flesh-coloured tunic of diaphanous material would assuredly not be tolerated by the London County Council on the boards of the Empire or Alhambra.' More recently and again on the Pier — at an Angling Festival in August 1905 — a local paper was distressed to notice, among the onlookers, 'girls and demoiselles who think it "form" to go about with that degree approaching almost the abandon, where slovenliness, to be minus hose and to have a headgear of panama clapped on an untidy head in the most freakish and rakish manner, however uncomfortable it may be to them, is considered the "correct thing" in Bognor.'

Of course, if Bognor had been wealthy and capable of attracting capital, a strong influencing mind would have decided the question — probably directing the town's destiny towards health by building a fashionable German-style hydro with resident doctors and every kind of treatment from massage to electropathy. Alternatively, a prosperous entertainment king might have decreed that Bognor should be the Southend of south-west Sussex, with switchbacks blocking the view of an insufficiently profitable sea, as was to be the fate of Littlehampton.

199

However, the problem remained unsolved and was handed on to future generations, while the town continued patching up the gaps in its lay-out left undeveloped by Hotham and his successors, and endeavouring to preserve some sense of seemliness in the face of increasingly jolly family visitors and hordes of noisy children.

The jollity of the Edwardian families grew from a sense of reunion, for the 'thing' about going on holiday to Bognor was the certainty of finding the same families staying there as last year. There was a feeling of welcome in the town during the season, fostered by traders such as Mr. Hawkes who stated in his advertisement (1903) that there was 'No advance in price to visitors' and that 'Visitors receive the same attention as residents'.

A certain air of distinction still survived. Yeates, the fishmonger, had kept pace with the times and altered his sign to read: 'By Appt. to H.M. The King'. One observed, too, that Wingate's Dairy in Aldwick Road was 'Patronised by the King of Siam' and that the *Royal Hotel* was under the 'Patronage of the Marchioness of Salisbury & Family'. If one was fortunate enough to have obtained lodgings at Bognor for Goodwood Week in 1905, there was the added pleasure of seeing and cheering Queen Alexandra as she motored through the town; and in 1911 the three pretty little sisters that one saw on the beach, collecting shells and burying each other in the sand, were princesses from Athens: by name Olga, Elizabeth and Marina.

It is doubtful if the regular visitor noticed much in the way of 'progress' in the town. A resident was naturally conscious of every little change; he had seen the old black mill and cricket field disappear in 1896 to make way for houses, had witnessed the first electric illumination at Mr. Southerton's shop in March 1905, followed by Mr. Tate's private plant to light the Arcade and Kursaal, and had benefited in 1913 from the first town supply by the new Gas & Electric Light Co. To a resident, progress was represented by such matters as Bognor's total of 1,443 inhabited houses in 1904, by the inauguration of a Salvation Army Corps in 1903 and by 60 flushed females gathering at 'Hazleden', Sylvan Way, in 1911 to listen to Miss Evelyn Sharp, authoress of *Rebel Women*, addressing them on Woman's Suffrage.

The visitors, however, preferred an annual reassurance that the seaside was still the same, that the yellow gravelly roads led down to a shore that had suffered no great change since they last saw it. Here they could renew acquaintance with Mr. Dick Neale's string of donkeys, the goat carts, the renowned local lobsters, the bearded fishermen and the linseed-soaked nets. It was true that the last of the clay cliff had disappeared when the seawall and promenade was extended westward from the Rock Gardens Terrace in 1898, but these improvements soon petered out into shingle beach and tamarisk hedge and cornfields sweeping down towards the Channel. This western beach, between the town and Aldwick village, had a gaiety that had caused visitors to liken Bognor to an English Trouville, for here was the continuous line of Mr. Charles Gray's bathing huts, painted white and cream and some with a broad scarlet stripe. His father, Captain Gray, had retired from the sea, built himself a fishing hut on this beach, and bathers paid him a few pence for the use of it to change in. In 1875, because they disturbed his fishing gear, he had built a second hut next door solely for bathers; and the idea was developed by his son, who was in the building trade and had been working on the new Baron's Hall at Arundel Castle. After supervising the huts for 50 years, Charles Gray died in 1939 at the age of 81, leaving the business to his sons.

Though the wheeled bathing-machines were still in use near the Pier, the huts (or 'boxes') were more comfortable; and there was novelty and a touch of daring in emerging from a hut and walking down a long plank laid on the pebbles and so into the sea. Women's bathing costumes had become less cumbersome and consequently more people were learning to swim at Mary Wheatland's hands instead of merely bobbing about in the shallows. In 1900 men could still bathe without a costume in the early morning at the extreme eastern end of the promenade, but the Council expected them to be covered after breakfast hours. On the rest of the beach, from 1900, mixed bathing was the rule, which made Bognor less restrictive in this respect than either Worthing, where even in 1908 mixed bathing was still permitted only at certain points, or Littlehampton where in 1908 it took place but was not yet officially recognised.

Though the coal now came in by rail, and the 'mine' collectors, the diggers of kidney rock and the agate hunters had disappeared, the sands and sea never ceased to fascinate. Even the Rocks now possessed a virtue, perhaps more psychological than medical, for the visitor could stand on the promenade and inhale the air 'abounding in ozone which is wafted into the town from the sea-weed on the Bognor Rocks' (*Heywood's Guide*, 1901). There were few prettier sights than on those late summer evenings when the Council and the fishermen called a temporary truce and staged an illuminated procession of boats, with two dozen vessels sailing out to sea, their shapes outlined in Chinese lanterns, and then engaging in a mock battle, using fireworks for shot and shell.

When, on 31 August 1905, the cartoonist of the *Daily Chronicle* visited the town to sketch this 'quiet, summer family resort', he, too, had eyes for nothing but the seashore: the lobster pots, the boats drawn up on the promenade, the waves beating up the sea wall, the sand castles and the riders and cricketers on the wide expanse of sands.

Firm on their bed of clay, the sands had lost the carriages of Dr. Davis's day, but in 1911 there was something faster: a sand 'yacht' on wheels, capable of 40 m.p.h., and on 8 May that same year, at 7 p.m., there came a strange noise over the quiet shore as an aeroplane appeared, heading west at 300 feet. It was the first aircraft seen over Bognor, a Henry Farman biplane piloted by Douglas Graham Gilmore. There would soon be many more.

Horses from the local livery stables or from nearby racing establishments paddled in the surf, joined by groups of children; the boys with boots laced together and slung round their necks, the girls clutching drenched knickers and rumpled frocks. Nearer the sea wall, within penny-throwing distance of the crowds above, were the various entertainers and the sand-artist, 'Scratcher' Mather, whose choice of pitch depended on which groyne was free of seaweed and stones; it was usually off the end of The Steyne. His sand-scratching was brilliant and he would draw the Houses of Parliament in half-an-hour, starting with a confusion of pinnacles and working down the building backwards towards the sea wall.

In among the earnest children, busily creating their fated fortresses of sand before the tide returned, one found sometimes a game of tennis in progress but more often a family cricket match. One father used to put pieces of white paper on the sand to encourage his son to bowl at them, so as to cultivate a good length. The boy's name was Arthur Gilligan and one summer day, after bowling a long time, he succeeded in hitting the same piece of paper six times and received a penny. The next step for this future Sussex and England captain — at the age of 12 in 1906 — was to bat for Bognor when the side was one short. Enthusiasm for the game once caused him to cycle 8½ miles, with his cricket bag across the handlebars, to play for Arundel. Finally, with his brother Harold, he won a regular place in the Bognor team, playing against the strong neighbouring clubs. In his book *Sussex Cricket* (Chapman & Hall, 1933), this outstanding sportsman looked back over his career and acknowledged his debt to Bognor sands and the early encouragement he received from A. J. Davis and Arthur Goodall, captain and secretary of the Bognor Club.

The exploring visitor could still see the countryside from the top of the four-horse coach which left the Pier daily at 2 o'clock for either Arundel, Selsey, Slindon or Goodwood; Bognor was to be one of the last holiday resorts in England to abandon this method of travel, retaining it up to about 1918. Solitary venturers who preferred travelling the byways alone, like the novelist George R. Sims, would hire one of Neale's donkey carts. For the more up-to-date minded, there were motorcar trips in 1908 to the same places as the coach, competing at the same price of 2s. 6d. for the round trip and offering additional runs to Little-hampton for 2s. and Worthing for 5s. A special car service on Sundays for 1s. 6d. return enabled visitors to attend service at Chichester Cathedral.

The wanderer along the shore westwards found little change at Aldwick. It retained its exclusive air, which was what the Council's *Official Guide* of 1912 meant to convey when it stated that at Aldwick 'there is a post office, an infants' school and an inn; it is here that most of the principal residents are found'. Of the residences near the shore, the pretty thatched cottage built by Sir Thomas Brooke-Pechell was burnt down on 18 April 1909; the Pavilion had been renamed Craigweil and was now a private mental home supervised by Dr. Alonzo Stocker; and West Cottage, where Knox the ornithologist had lived, was the summer retreat of the actor Beerbohm Tree, whose daughter Viola was a constant spectator of the Gilligan brothers' cricketing feats on the sands.

There were changes at Pagham, however, and anyone who sought the mysterious Hissing Pool was disappointed, because the harbour had been reclaimed. The harbour mouth, thrusting eastwards, had threatened Pagham village and a recla-mation syndicate — largely financed by Graftons, the Manchester calico printers — was formed in 1876. The mouth was blocked and the waters slowly receded from the long submerged land, leaving banks of shingle which was sold in thousands of loads to Bognor's building contractors. Between the reclaimed acres and the sea was a narrow spit of beach. Farming was resumed and for 34 years the spit held — until 10.30 a.m. on 16 December 1910. It was at the end of a week of violent gales, and suddenly the sea was through at a point a quarter of a mile south-west of the former mouth. Eight hundred acres went under deep water, breakers rolled over the fields and panic spread through Aldwick and Bognor. No further attempt was made to reclaim and since then the tidal wastes, green with cord grass, are again the haunt of wild fowl and the waters flow out on the tide through a more secure mouth — which, even so, is turning very slowly to the eastward.

Older Bognor habitués, revisiting Arundel, found a considerable change in the appearance of the castle, as a result of the 15th Duke's objection to living in what Augustus Hare had described as a 'miserable sham-gothic deformity'. Between 1879 and 1903, he and his architect, Buckler, with 200 men, completed the last great phase of reconstruction, removing and toning down all Duke Charles's excrescences in favour of a severe 13th-century style, so that the result resembled a fortress and no longer a wedding cake. The most marked addition was a tower, 130 feet high, at the south-west corner, which became known in Arundel as 'the Drainpipe' but which contributed most of all to the castle's new appeal to the imagination. Opinion varied at the time as to whether the castle had in fact been improved. Some felt that it was now too solemn and ecclesiastical and rather like a school or asylum. Some even preferred another example of the Duke's taste, the new Tudor-style post office in the town which, being on his land, he had leased to himself in his official capacity as Postmaster-General.

Within the castle keep, visitors found the famous owl 'Lord Thurlow', now stuffed (it died in 1859), and from the heights they looked down on the roof of the new Barons' Hall and the mass of ducal chimneys, perhaps wondering down which one the little chimney-sweep had lost himself. Charles Lamb long ago had told the tale: how the sooty child had emerged in a state bedroom by mistake, crept on to the bed and was discovered 'sleeping like a young Howard'. Out in the woods, paddocks and valleys of the Park, the public were entertained by a variety of sights, ranging from white fallow deer and red Highland deer to Indian humped cattle, llamas, South American ostriches and members of the 2nd Battalion of the Sussex Volunteeers in camp.

One minor sightseeing excursion from Bognor was to the *Rising Sun* public house at North Bersted, where there was established one of those local curiosities beloved of visitors. This was a room papered entirely with stamps. There were three million of them not only stuck on walls and ceiling but also on the picture frames, furniture, tablecloth and candlestick and even on a bust of the King. Surplus stamps had been threaded into paper-chains across the room, others hung in bundles and 'pictures' had been made of them, including representations of the late Queen, the Prince of Wales's feathers and the Bognor coat-of-arms.

Mr. Richard Sharpe, the licensee, had commenced his handiwork in 1882 and took five years over it, since when the philatelic decor had spread to his summer-house at the back and also to the hallway where one door, adorned with Swan

River stamps from Western Australia, was constantly bid for by stamp collectors. There was no entrance fee to the Stamp Room, but a pamphlet was on sale, written by the postmaster of Arundel who brought specialised knowledge to bear upon the visitors by reminding them of the amount of tongue moisture the work had necessitated. A hint then followed that ale and lemonade could be obtained on the premises.

By 1911, there were 600,000 signatures in the visitors' book and Mr. Sharpe, who was famous enough locally as founder and conductor of the Bersted Brass and Reed Band, had become the recipient of letters and parcels of stamps from all corners of the world. King Edward VII, when Prince of Wales and during one of his frequent visits to West Dean House near Singleton, called at the *Rising Sun* with his host, Mr. Willie James, and left £5 on the counter for the villagers to have a drink on him that evening. Mr. Sharpe died in 1930, aged 84; and when the *Rising Sun* (which had been a 'free house') was taken over by a brewery after the Second World War, the stamp collection was removed and dispersed to schoolboys. The inn was finally demolished in 1957.

*   *   *

Complaints about Bognor's lack of entertainment had now become fainter and the holiday mood was sustained by the sound of banjo and piano on the sands, band music on the pier, melodrama in the new Assembly Rooms and gaiety from the concert parties.

The first week of July saw the annual Fair arrive on its traditional pitch (now occupied by Bassett and Cavendish Roads), together with the drafting of extra police into the town. It was still a painful week for the gentry, for the uproar was full-blooded. Freak shows, beer booths, swings, shies and roundabouts contributed to the din, and the crowds swarmed about the stalls buying sticky gingerbread, winning a clock for 1d. at hoop-la and cheering local heroes who braved the Southampton bruiser, Joe Beckett, in the boxing booth.

Touring companies played at the Assembly Rooms, which seated 800, and also at the old Hanover Chapel in London Road which Mr. A. Adlington converted into the Victoria Theatre in 1897. His opening attraction was a melodrama, *Over The Indian Frontier*, followed by Ivy Rivers and L. E. B. Stephens in a 3-night stand, playing the comedy hit *Madcap Madge*. Mr. St. Aubyn Miller of Henry Irving's company was another early attraction in two comedies, *Our Boys* and *My Sweetheart*. There was some local prejudice against the use of the former Congregational chapel as a theatre and audiences were thin, sometimes causing companies to be stranded in the town without funds. Reception, also, was mixed and once when a substitute went on to read a part, a coffee-stall proprietor in the audience rose up, hammered on the footlights and shouted out:! 'We've been done, we've been done!'

Both these early halls were outclassed by the opening of the Kursaal Theatre in 1910 and of the Pier Theatre (with *The Belle of New York*) in 1912. The Kursaal, which in a few years became the Theatre Royal, once booked a farce,

Oh, I Say!, with A. E. Matthews in the cast, and on the opening night one of the actors was missing and was replaced by an understudy. It was discovered later that the actor had walked into the sea and cut his throat, which considerably annoyed the touring company's London office. 'Why didn't he do it in London instead of waiting till he got to Bognor?' was their exasperated query.

To many holidaymakers, the real breath of the seaside was in its bands. Both the Council and residents realised that without music a resort lost face, and this danger was averted for some 12 seasons by raising a subscription, amounting to £200, to engage the Blue Hungarian Band. These talented musicians, who were Austrian and German, had been left behind in Bognor by a circus and had adopted the town as their home. They made their living with odd jobs, street playing and performances at functions. Some seasons, having failed to raise the necessary money in time, Bognor lost them to better offers from Littlehampton.

Summer music in the pavilion at the sea-end of the Pier was the responsibility of the Council until the Pier changed hands in 1909, and considerable success was achieved by engaging a 10-piece ladies' orchestra in July 1905. The *Bognor Observer* reporter, a susceptible lad, was overcome by their beauty and floated back to his desk to pen the following:

> 'O, listen to the Band! Please do. I am referring to the Blue Zouave Ladies' Orchestra. Their season is young yet, but I say without hesitation that it is the best Orchestra I have heard at the Pier for several years. Comparisons are odious, but give me a ladies' orchestra. Here you have not to look at a double-bass player with an 'Ally Sloper' nose of a ruddy hue, or a bleary-eyed flautist, but the eye as well as the ear is charmed by the curved lip of a fair (it may be brunette) musician using her sweet breath to produce melodious notes from the flute, while cornet blowing can only serve to round the soft curves of a lady's face.'

On the sands, on pitches in the High Street or in the garden of the *Victoria Hotel*, one came across small groups of entertainers, such as the Red Coat Singers and the Top Hat Boys, but of them all the best-known to the visitors were The Thespians who arrived on the beach opposite the *Royal Hotel* in 1897. Their leader, August Sears ('Uncle George'), had been a London clerk who sang at his firm's concerts and enacted scenes from Dickens. For seven seasons he was a comedian on Margate sands before settling at Bognor where his troupe rapidly became popular, singing and entertaining to the last minute as the tide came in and then scrambling to rescue their 'fit-up' stage and piano from the waves. Their costume was blazer, straw hat and white flannels and they gave afternoon and evening performances with a song-and-dance competition for children every week.

As the seasons went by, Uncle George's former employers in London never lost sight of him, contributing to his needs for 40 years. He became a lone performer, playing a portable harmonium, and was adored by children and hailed by every theatrical and sporting celebrity who leaned over the promenade railings. He died in January 1928, and if he had lived three more years he could have seen himself portrayed on the Drury Lane stage. For it was Bognor beach and the Thespians that were adapted for the purposes of the famous Brighton seaside scene in Noel Coward's *Cavalcade*.

Coward had remembered Uncle George with tenderness from a childhood holiday at Bognor in about 1904. Rather against his mother's wishes, he entered the weekly song competition and lined up on the beach one evening with his fellow aspirants. In his autobiography *Present Indicative* (Heinemann, 1937), he describes the occasion:

> 'When my turn came I sang "Come along with me to the Zoo, dear" and "Liza Ann" from *The Orchid*. I also danced violently. The applause was highly gratifying, and even Mother forgot her distaste of Uncle George's vulgarity somewhat and permitted herself to bridle. At the end of the performance Uncle George made a speech and presented me with the first prize, a large box of chocolates which, when opened in our lodgings, proved to be three parts shavings.'

Coward and Gertrude Lawrence first met as pupils at Italia Conti's stage school, not realising they might have seen each other before, for she herself was at Bognor in August 1904 and earning a better prize than Coward at a rival concert party in the Olympian Gardens, just east of the Pier. In her case, a motherly shove sent her up on the stage the moment volunteers were asked for. Her song was 'It ain't all honey and it ain't all jam' and the award for this skinny Cockney six-year old in a pink frock was a gold sovereign.

Her main Bognor adventure, recorded in *A Star Danced* (W. H. Allen, 1945), was her first bicycle ride, which took place in the Steyne:

> 'I had never been on a bicycle before, but I had no doubt of my ability to ride one. I leaned it against the railing, mounted it, and, holding on to the railings with one hand, managed to pedal round the crescent. It was thrilling, like riding a circus horse around the ring, and there was always the possibility that the people were watching me from the windows of the houses. I fell off several times, skinned my knee, while the side of my frock nearest the railings became ornamented with stripes of green paint, but I kept at it, getting better with each lap. I had forgotten Dad and Mother, even the words of the man at the bicycle-stand to be back within an hour.'

The railing around the garden in the Steyne has long since been replaced by a low wall.

Among other aspirants to fame who collected seaside prizes at Bognor were Leslie Henson and A. P. Herbert. Henson in 1909 won half-a-guinea for singing a comic song in an open competition and Herbert at the age of 12 won a copy of *Black Beauty* for writing an extra verse for a pierrot song, a verse which dealt with a remedy for Mrs. Pankhurst, the militant Suffragette.

The Olympian Gardens, scene of these triumphs, had grown from the patch of land at the foot of Lennox Street on which the town's coal had been dumped from the boats. In the 1890s it was roughly fenced and was regarded as Mr. F. Osborn's coal yard; and here, using a coal cart for a stage, early pierrot shows were presented by Tom Foss. His entertainment included apple and treacle-eating competitions, with conjuring by Paul Valladon, who later made a name for himself in South Africa, and piano-entertaining by a pianist who was subsequently shot in Texas by a disgruntled listener.

In 1900, the coal yard was neatly boarded in, roofed with canvas and christened the Olympian Gardens by the shrewd summer show king, Wallis

Arthur, who with his partner Paul Mill was presenting pierrots at Lowestoft, Cromer, Westcliff-on-Sea, Hastings, Eastbourne and Weston-super-Mare.

His first season of 'Al Fresco Concerts', with Fred Rome at the head of the company, did not draw. For three more seasons he lost money, until in 1905 he went into the programme himself and helped to make his first profit. Gradually Bognor's residents and visitors took to the pierrots, supporting their Benefit Nights (one third of the receipts to the beneficiary) and making favourites of the vivacious Doris Lee and Carrie Herwin, the attractive contralto whom Arthur considered the greatest artiste that concert party had ever known. Members of his companies were interchanged and during the years Bognor saw many young performers on their way to fame: Winnie Melville, Olive Fox, Gillie Potter, W. H. Berry, Whit Cunliffe, Ernest Sewell and his marionettes, Malcolm Scott and the sophisticated Milton Hayes with his original and unusual monologues, such as 'The Green Eye of the Little Yellow God'.

Wallis Arthur clearly had the knack of assessing ability, but he admitted to a lack of judgment once when a short, good-looking youth in a rather shabby blue suit and straw hat came to see him: 'He wanted to be one of my pierrots. While he was talking he seemed extremely nervous, pressing his light cane into the sand and causing it to flick up into the air, rapidly catching it across his body. In response to his request, I told him I needed a light comedian – not a low one. Subsequently, he drifted out to the Pacific coast and the cinema gained what the pierrots lost.' It was some loss, for the man who wasn't quite good enough to get a job at Bognor was Charlie Chaplin.

The Olympian Gardens lasted for 30 years, closing on 27 September 1930 with the final performance of Leonard Henry and his Little Show. The Council had refused to renew the entertainment licence of the premises in their present form; and in the following year over a thousand residents protested unsuccessfully against official permission being granted to a Mr. Butlin to erect a fun fair on the site.

Films first came to the town in the form of travelling cinemas, such as a Church Army mission van in 1904 at the corner of Longford and London Roads. Some idea of what 'the pictures' meant had already been gathered by those residents who had attended the annual week's visit of Poole's Myriorama to the New Assembly Rooms. Here they had seen live actors performing before a moving scenic background which was revolved on rollers. On August Bank Holiday, 1909, the Bognor Pier Company turned the sea-end pavilion into the town's first cinema, with Mr. Claude Flude, the Pier manager, as projectionist; and at Easter 1911 the new wonder was transferred to the recently built hall at the shore end, which was named the Electric Palace.

In 1909 the town had the additional thrill of actually seeing films being made by Cecil Hepworth's company, who spent six months on location at Bognor producing short comedies and thrillers and using local men as 'extras'. *Painting the Pier* was a slapstick comedy and *Animal Sagacity* dealt with a clever dog that found its master murdered on the Bognor–Pagham road and helped to hunt down the murderer in a chase round the Rock Gardens. The wrecked hull of the

Brixham ketch *Foundling* which had gone ashore at Aldwick in 1906, was used for a drama, *Fire At Sea*, with Bognor's 'actors' leaping for their lives through the smoke produced from burning straw.

Such films provided a novel means of publicity for the resort; and equally novel was the illuminated poster displayed at the Electric Exhibition held at Olympia, London, in 1911, at which the Credenda Signs Company of Birmingham demonstrated their latest bright idea for night-time advertising. Having obtained a poster of Bognor from the railway company, they mounted it on a metal sheet in which holes were punched, and filled with glass beads, so as to outline the illustration and the lettering. The poster was then passed in front of a box containing a mass of electric bulbs so that, when the lights were switched on, visitors to the Exhibition were regaled with a glittering picture of children riding a donkey on the beach, accompanied by the words 'On the Sands at Bognor, the Popular South Coast Family Resort'. As a result, quite a few families may have decided to spend their Coronation Year seaside holiday at a place which, if this brand-new method of advertising was anything to go by, must be right in the van of progress.

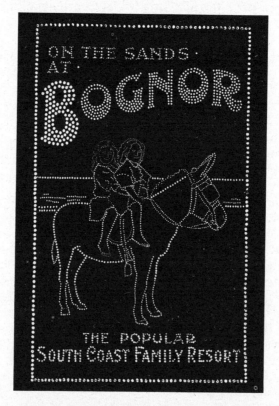

Fig. 18. Advertising Bognor in lights at Olympia, 1911 Electrical Exhibition.

Chapter XIX

PEACE AND WAR

KING EDWARD died in 1910, and triumphal arches representing castle gateways went up in High Street and London Road to celebrate the Coronation of George V. It was the traditional thing to do and by now Bognor was well set in its ways. Its character was formed and its individuality could now be remarked upon. It had 'a certain air becoming its old distinction of princely patronage', observed Black's *Guide* in 1911; and Ian Hannah, author of *The Sussex Coast* (1912), was also influenced by echoes of the past: 'The Early Victorian atmosphere still pervades the little place; the cemented houses that we deem ugly now would form an exactly suitable setting to some of the scenes of Dickens and Thackeray.'

It was this air of primness that endeared the town to certain visitors and sometimes gave them the urge to play jokes. A mood of mild revelry as if at a large house party, was seldom absent in the season, especially if Lord Charles Beresford, a prince of practical jokers, had come over from Portsmouth. There was hardly a corner in Portsmouth that had not some association with the escapades of this popular and distinguished admiral. The renowned 'Charlie', when in Bognor, held a ceremony before a statue of Neptune which stood in front of Marine Parade Terrace and then took it out to sea and sank it. It was eventually restored to land and stayed put till 1940.

It was such a mood, or else the ozone, that made some visitors take a donkey up to their bedrooms in the Rock Gardens Terrace, inspired Alfred Baker to drive a cab down the beach into the sea, and caused Solly Joel, the 'Diamond King', to keep his sober fellow-guests at the *Royal Norfolk* awake all night. He engaged 'Uncle George' and his troupe, provided them with umbrellas, agreed to insure their instruments and told them to stand outside and serenade the hotel. The performance began shortly after 10 p.m., jugs of water descended, the umbrellas went up, Joel's party thoroughly enjoyed themselves and dawn broke in the summer sky before Uncle George was allowed to pack up.

'Frivolity with Dignity' might have been Bognor's motto in the years just before the Great War. Clean, neat and leafy, with a population of 8,387 in 1912, it mixed those two qualities with an engaging lack of self-consciousness. It aimed its local advertising lightheartedly at the ignorant visitor rather than the resident, telling him to buy photographic supplies at the shop 'Under the Big Clock in High Street', or neckwear from the draper's 'Opposite Church with High Steeple'. For a souvenir you took home a 1s. 4d. bottle of scent entitled Bognor Breezes Bouquet from the chemist who had supplied you during your visit with the new glycerine jelly for sunburn or a 6½d. bottle of sunburn lotion.

Yet each week the stately Visitors' List continued to be published and guests at the *Royal Norfolk* vied discreetly to retrieve as a memento a cigarette-end left by the chain-smoking Princess Victoria, the late King's daughter, who was staying there with her ladies and her father's favourite pet dog, Caesar. Whenever the famous came to the hotel — Queen Alexandra, Prince George of Greece, ex-Empress Maud of Russia — Bognor revived its one unforgettable sight, and on the promenade the evening crowds gathered to watch the elegantly guests swaying past the lit-up windows as Royalty danced by the seaside.

Between seasons, the resort became a village again. The giant seas returned and the waves broke high in the winter sunlight, pouring over the promenade, flooding York Road at Christmas 1912, and affording another chance for Mr. W. P. Marsh to take some of his celebrated photographs. Marsh had set up his studio in Waterloo Square as long ago as 1875 and made a substantial profit out of Bognor's natural enemy. His pictures of spectacular waves dwarfing the houses had won him the Royal Photographic Society's medal and were in demand in America and on the Continent — particularly in Belgium where they were palmed off to tourists as being sea studies on the Dutch coast.

To spread the impression that the town was being pounded to bits by the sea was hardly the Council's idea of good advertising, but the photographs were very much to the visitors' liking and their sale was enormous. 'At Bognor,' wrote the editor of the *Practical Photographer* in January 1897, 'it is recognised as quite the thing for visitors to take a "breaking-wave picture" home as a souvenir, or to send one as a present to friends at a distance. Just as Edinburgh is famous for its "rock", Doncaster for butterscotch, Dublin for pigs of bog oak, or Ormskirk for gingerbread, so Bognor is noted for its seascape photographs, certainly a more cultured reputation.' He then described Mr. Marsh out on stormy pier and promenade taking his pictures:

> 'Often the wind is too strong for a tripod to be used, and the camera is placed on the floor of the pier, to be held down by a firm hand while, with quick eye, the photographer releases the shutter just at the moment when a green column of water dashes into white spray and foam on the hard concrete of the promemade.'

In 1914, the Council's Surveyor, Oswald Bridges, curbed the power of the sea and the scope of photographers by strengthening the eastern seawall of 1870 and curving the top outwards towards the beach in a bullnose of ferro-concrete, which effectively snuffed the waves and stopped the accustomed floods.

*   *   *

'Much booming has been done for Bognor and the town does its best to live up to it', opined the *Sussex County Handbook* for 1912, and this aptly summarised the situation. The old days had gone, the new ones had come and the resort grappled with the thursting demands of the modern competitive age.

Traders saw the necessity of impressing on potential residents, emigrating from London, that Bognor supplied goods 'at lowest London prices'. Leverett & Fry, the High Street grocers, stressed that their emporium had 'all the advantages of a London store close to your home'. Newcomers and week-enders were to find that in Bognor a tailor-made suit could be had for 38s. 6d., whisky was 24s. a gallon and a cottage could be 'completely and tastefully furnished from £50'. The day visitors cheerfully ate their lobster teas and their ices ('in season') and paid 1s. for joint and two veg., 5d. for pot of tea and roll and butter, and 2½d. for a pint of beer. In the shops there is Bognor gingerbread for sale, and you can find hand-made cigarettes for 7d. an ounce, free dark rooms for amateur photographers, tea at 1s. 6d. per lb. and the latest in tea gowns at Madame Nunn's.

Yet all this was really a finale, a burst of seaside sunshine before war darkened the world. The beach is crowded, and there are plays and concert parties at the Kursaal. Appearing at the new Pier Theatre are stars like Vesta Victoria and Violet Vanbrugh — and also a captivating young Danish dancer called Karina. Among those she captivated was a small boy, Patrick Kay, who was born at Slinfold, near Horsham, in 1904 and whose family were now living in a house they had built close to the seashore at Felpham, Shamrock Cottage in Admiralty Road. One day they went along to Bognor Pier to see the show in which Karina was appearing, and she made such an impression on Patrick that he resolved there and then to follow her example and become a dancer himself. This resolution was strengthened when he watched the little daughter of friends of theirs performing graceful pirouettes with enviable ease in their drawing-room at Felpham. His parents were beset with entreaties to allow him to take dancing lessons; and he was granted his wish when the family moved to Brighton in 1914.

It was as a pupil of a dancing-school in Hove that Patrick made his first stage appearance — at the Theatre Royal, Worthing — and after embarking on his professional career in London he adopted the name by which, before long, he was known all over the world. But though he became one of the greatest dancers of the century, Sir Anton Dolin never forgot that his first steps towards international fame were inspired by that childhood visit to the theatre on Bognor Pier.

At the Kursaal's Pierrotland in 1914, 'Pierrotania' was being presented by Matt Melrose, little guessing that some of his pierrots would soon be exchanging their traditional dress for Army khaki. So, while peace still lingers, we will leave the pre-war holiday scene, with the sea lapping the promenade on which Ellen Terry is strolling, as are Hall Caine and Conan Doyle, and Marie Lloyd with Alec Hurley. George Edwardes of Daly's Theatre, London, has his horses stabled for Goodwood at the back of the still small and compact town, near Herrington's smithy. The farmlands stretch right from the hills to the sea, just opening a little on the shore to allow room for Bognor. The town is ringed with sheep and cows; and when the tide is out the racehorses move on to the sands for the glory of a two-mile gallop to Middleton.

But at Middleton, eastward along the coast, the new era that lay ahead was already proclaiming itself. There were strange and harsh sights on the clay cliffs that Constable had painted: the hangars and slipways of the aircraft works established in 1910 by Norman Thompson, an electrical engineer. At Middleton he produced a 75 m.p.h. two-seater aeroplane with aluminium wings and a

seaplane designed to compete in the *Daily Mail* 'Round England' race which was
due to be held on 10 August 1914.

Meanwhile, the inhabitants of Bognor had the thrill of seeing an aircraft land
for the first time on their own familiar sands. This was on 26 May 1913, when the
famous Pashley brothers, Cecil and Eric, chose Bognor for the first of the series
of air displays which they organised at resorts on the South Coast and which gave
many people their first experience of flying (the Pashleys took you up for five-
minute 'flips' at two guineas a time). The plane developed trouble shortly after
setting off on its return to base at Shoreham, so it landed on the beach at
Middleton and spent the night on one of Mr. Thompson's slipways under the
protection of police and coastguards.

Eric was killed in the war and Cecil became chief flying instructor of the
Southern Aero Club at Shoreham. Late in life (he died in 1969) 'Pash' recalled
that Bognor was not only the first venue of the brothers' flying displays but also
their favourite — 'we always looked forward to our visits to the town'.

*   *   *

The Great War really began for Bognor several hours before the official declaration
of hostilities. At 2.30 a.m. on 4 August 1914 orders came through to the Sussex
Yeomanry to comandeer horses immediately for military service and every stable
in the town was instructed to send its inmates to Waterloo Square. Even Osborne's
coal cart lost its horses; and Lord and Lady Whiffen, driving in from Aldwick in
their brougham, were stopped and asked to surrender their high-steppers. By
mid-morning a long line of horses and ponies was tethered on the grass immediately opposite the Pier entrance, while the August holidaymakers strolled past in
the sunshine and the cows and sheeps still grazed as usual at the northern end of
the Square. After being vetted, the selected horses were taken to the railway
station and entrained for the mobilisation centre at Canterbury.

Volunteers for 'Kitchener's Army' were sworn in at the Drill Hall in Bedford
Street and many of them joined the 11th Battalion of the Royal Sussex
Regiment, which was commanded by Colonel Grisewood of The Den. The Royal
Sussex adopted William Ward-Higgs's *Sussex by the Sea* as its marching song;
and quite a few of the Bognor men who sang it on the long and weary treks to
the trenches would have been surprised to know that it was written so close
to their own homes — at South Bersted.

Bognor's military connections, however, were not limited to Sussex, for a
battalion from a neighbouring county — the 9th Hampshires — set up its headquarters in the town. Young Gussie Forbes, who later became secretary of the
Beckley branch of Toc H, recalled arriving at Bognor one evening in 1916 to
join the Hampshires. The recruits were met by a lance-corporal who escorted
them across the road to the Queen's Hall, as the New Assembly Rooms had now
become. There 'we were ushered into the main hall where an endless vista of
plank beds and swarming figures led up to a stage.' Early next morning they
were taken to the battalion headquarters in the commandeered Princess Mary

Convalescent Home, where they were given breakfast — 'a civilised meal served on the crested plates of the Hampshires. This was plainly no ordinary regiment!'

There followed a spell of coastal duty and, half a century later, Mr. Forbes remembered some of the excitements that broke the monotony — an unexploded torpedo, a floating mine, a cargo vessel which was blown up shortly after leaving Littlehampton harbour: 'There's a full cargo of motor-cycles on the sea bottom if anyone fancies a bit of skin-diving.'

To Norman Thompson at the Middleton aircraft works the outbreak of war brought a bitter disappointment — the cancellation of the 'Round England' air race which he had set his heart on winning with his specially designed seaplane. But there was compensation when the Admiralty, having commandeered and tested his machine for coastal duties, placed an initial order for six more. The works were enlarged and each morning cars and lorries left Bognor with employees, who had the satisfaction of knowing that the aircraft they were constructing were the first to provide effective action against enemy submarines. The Thompson seaplane had won through after all.

By the end of the war a quite different type of aircraft had become as familiar a sight in the Bognor sky as the seaplanes from Middleton — probably even more familiar, for in 1918 the airships of the Royal Naval Air Service maintained a continuous submarine-spotting control over the Solent and adjacent waters. The great grey shapes emerged mysteriously from the depths of the countryside and vanished no less mysteriously at the end of their turn of duty. They were, in fact, swallowed up by the dense trees around the hillside village of Slindon, where the R.N.A.S. concealed them in bays cut out of the woodland just to the north of Nore Hill. The old stone 'folly' still to be seen on Nore Hill was used as a wireless station.

Meanwhile, visitors were still coming to Bognor for a breath of the sea air, and one March day in 1915 the novelist D. H. Lawrence and his wife Frieda took a stroll on the pier. They were spending the winter with Wilfred Meynell at Greatham, near Pulborough, where Lawrence was haunted and depressed by the as yet unaccustomed slaughter of the war.

> 'Today,' he wrote to Lady Ottoline Morrell, 'we drove to Bognor. It was strange at Bognor — a white, vague, powerful sea with long waves falling heavily with a crash of frosty white out of the pearly whiteness of the day. And the small boats that were out in the distance heaved and seemed to glisten shadowily. Strange the sea was, so strong.
> 'I saw a soldier on the pier with only one leg . . . [The women] look at him with eyes of longing and then want to talk to him.
> 'It seemed to me that anything might come out of that white, silent, opalescent sea . . . I cannot tell you why, but I was afraid. I was afraid of the ghosts of the dead. They seem to come marching home over the white silent sea . . . '

One cannot imagine any visitor to Bognor during the Napoleonic campaigns of a century earlier writing in this strain. In those days war added a spice of adventure to seaside life; and an attempted invasion by the enemy would, one feels, have been welcomed as providing some extra spice. The sea was scanned

almost hopefully for the approach of Napoleon's ships, not fearfully for ghosts
of the fallen. But to Bognor, as to every other town in the country, the Great
War brought personal loss and tragedy on a scale unmarked by any previous conflict; and though its end was greeted by the expected jollification, one of the
town's first official decisions after the Armistice was to set up a War Memorial in
honour of those who did not return from across the sea. A temporary memorial
was erected in 1919 opposite the *Bedford Hotel* in High Street; its permanent
successor now stands in front of the Town Hall in Clarence Road.

But already the changing pattern of life which was to characterise the post-war
era was beginning to establish itself. Only seven months after the Armistice the
Queen's Hall, having obliterated all traces of its wartime career as a military
reception centre, became a full-time cinema. Renamed (for a second time) the
Picturedrome, its inaugural programme on 5 June 1919 featured Alma Taylor
and Gerald Ames in *Boundary House* ('shown before release date by courtesy of
Moss Empires Ltd.'), several short comedies, the latest issue of 'Pathé's Gazette'
and a film of the Victory Derby which had just been run at Epsom.

Released from wartime duty, Bognor looked forward to a decade that seemed
full of the promise of prosperity. Whether that promise would be fulfilled
depended, as for generations past and as with every other holiday resort, on
successful publicity and promotion. In that respect, at least, nothing much had
changed since the time of Hotham.

Fig. 19. Bognor lobster boat and herring lugger.

Chapter XX

THE TWENTIES –
AND THE COMING OF THE KING

THE LINE taken by Bognor to promote itself in the 1920s was not a new one. It was that of Dr. Davis in 1807 – and much the same phraseology was used. This is not surprising, for the doctor's observations on the benefits of the climate had been adapted by Richard Dally for inclusion in his 1828 guidebook and had been echoed in every successive guide since then. The new *Bognor Directory* of 1920 was therefore unwittingly following tradition when it stated, in early 19th-century phraseology, that the Downs were sufficiently distant from the town to 'allow a free circulation of the air'.

The post-war visitor was informed, just as his father had been in 1890, that storm-clouds followed the hills, leaving Bognor dry, and that while fog-bound Londoners were 'wrapped in murky gloom', Bognor's visitors could sit for hours in the bright warmth of promenade shelters. 'The mildness of the temperature is visible in the luxuriance of the trees and shrubs,' wrote Dally in 1828 – an observation which was confirmed a century later, and in slightly fewer words, by the 1928 *Directory*: 'The mildness of the climate is shown by the luxuriance of the vegetation.'

This was probably the best line to adopt, because it was true. Whatever the fate of the coastal towns – and Belloc was to mourn them: 'You would not find Sussex there any more ... It is but a string of London outposts from Selsey to Rye ...' (*The County of Sussex*, 1936) – there was always the sunshine. The L.B. & S.C. Railway did not have to invent 'The Sunny South' for its great advertising campaign in the early '20s. The Sunny South was a fact, as any engine driver on the Bognor line could testify, coming through the cold clinging mists of the Weald to Amberley tunnel and suddenly, after a few yards of darkness, emerging into the sunny warmth of the sea plain.

Sea, sands and sunshine were sufficient for most family holidaymakers, but Bognor was still determined to catch up with modern times. 'The primitive little Bognor, beloved of those in search of a restful holiday of the "Sleepy Hollow" kind,' announced the 1920 *Directory*, 'has been left far behind, and though its progress was temporarily arrested by the devastating war, there is very little doubt that it will continue to grow in popularity. A Winter Garden and other improvements are planned for the near future.'

Things started to move quite quickly. In 1921 Waterloo Square, for so long a rented grazing meadow providing the town with meat and mushrooms, became town property for £1,000 and was transformed into gardens and bowling greens by 1925. Hothamton Place, which overlooked the Square, was also bought by the Council in 1921, the price being £6,600; and behind this stately old terrace was erected one of Mr. Thompson's seaplane assembly sheds from Middleton to serve as a substitute 'Winter Garden'.

This was deemed to be cheaper than building a Winter Garden on the sea front, but the idea of transplanting a portion of an aircraft factory, 173 by 145 feet, into the centre of Bognor was horrifying to many townspeople — particularly Mr. Lovett, now aged 86 and no longer a newspaper proprietor but 'Father' of the Urban District Council. 'A monkey house in a back street' was his description of the proposal at an historic Council meeting on 1 April 1921. It was the last of his many colourful pronouncements and he died the following May, at Southend. Nevertheless, his fellow councillors proceeded with their plan, the cost of which was estimated at £22,388. Their decision was regarded as a form of post-war madness by the Ratepayers' Association, who promptly called upon the Council to resign. 'Glorified impudence', was the Council Chairman's retort and the scheme went ahead, though trimmed by Government intervention to £16,500, which meant a more modest design. The assembly shed, camouflaged by a lath-and-plaster façade of twin towers and surrounded by gardens, was opened to the public in the summer of 1922, with The Co-Optimists concert party among the early attractions. Finally named the Pavilion, it held 3,000 and proved quite suitable for dances, plays, congresses and exhibitions. It also had other uses and in 1925 the town's first magistrates' court was installed in a side section, with the ladies' cloakroom serving during court sessions as a 'cell' for prisoners. The dancing craze of the 1920s gave the Pavilion an initial popularity and the surrounding gardens were a much appreciated asset.

*   *   *

In the 20 years between 1901 and 1921, Bognor's population had increased slowly by 5,000 so that the total of natives and newcomers now stood at 11,490 and a penny rate brought in the sum of £250. The town was quietly on the move towards a more expansive age.

There were daily films at the Picturedrome and the arty vogue of 'ye olde' crept in in 1920 with the opening of Ye Needlework Shoppe in West Street. One of the minor outcomes of the recent war was a change of name for the Kursaal, whose theatre became the Theatre Royal in 1919. By about 1922 the rest of the complex had followed suit and dropped its original name, the Kursaal Skating Rink being now the Theatre Royal Skating Rink. The entertainment hall, however, was still Pierrotland and concert parties were back there almost as soon as the war ended. A poster advertising one of them in 1919 listed among the performers 'Jack Hylton, pianist' and 'Tom Handley, comedian'. These two young men, who contributed a songs-at-the-piano act, took digs at Barnham for their Pierrot-land season: and, as they could not afford the train fare, they did the journey to and fro on bicycles.

In 1923 the skating rink bowed to changing tastes and emerged in the more fashionable guise of a 'Palais de Danse'. And on the beach in 1925 a girl correspondent of the *Daily Express* noticed how the holidaymakers lived in their 'bathing costumes' all day and that the Continental cult of sun-bathing was becoming a feature of Bognor's summer life. 'At Bognor,' she observed, 'children follow the advice of a famous sunbath exponent. By the time the holidays are at an end, their skins have pigmented and they are more likely to be immune from contagious disease.' While the beach remained a 'children's paradise' and on the promenade the invalids strolled or were propelled or merely reclined in recuperative calm — like the rotund G. K. Chesterton, who praised the strength of Bognor's deck-chairs — the civic balloon swelled to such proportions that in 1926 the Lord Lieutenant of Sussex (Lord Leconfield) and the mayors of Brighton, Hove, Arundel, Chichester and Worthing took part in a procession to open the new Post Office in High Street.

This prestigious gathering of notabilities assembled in Bognor at the invitation of the Chairman of the Council, Mr. Henry Staffurth, who was determined to use every opportunity to make Bognor cut a dash in the world. He certainly did not share the view, expressed in a good many quarters, that it made the town look ridiculous to open a Post Office with such grandiose ceremony — but, in one respect at least, he could claim to have the last laugh over his critics. For the colourful inauguration of Bognor's new Post Office earned front-page picture coverage in one of the national newspapers — the *Daily Mirror*, no less. And the *Daily Sketch*, perhaps with its tongue in its cheek, informed its readers that 'the burgesses of Bognor nearly burst with pride when the Lord Lieutenant bought the first penny stamp' and that Lord Leconfield had expressed the hope that the day would come when Henry Staffurth would become Bognor's first Mayor.

Mr. Staffurth was, in fact, already widely regarded as the current 'King' of Bognor. Born in Huntingdonshire in 1857, he arrived in Bognor in 1882 and opened a solicitor's practice in High Street. Within three months of his arrival he was appointed Clerk to the local Board and remained as Clerk to the Urban District Council until 1911. He entered local politics as a councillor in 1913 and in 1924 was elected Chairman. On his death in 1931, his long-established practice was taken over by a colleague, Reginald Bray. But as a tribute to the 'strong and dominating personality . . . with a very kindly heart' (as Mr. Bray described him) who had started it almost half a century earlier, the founder's name was retained in the firm's new title — Staffurth & Bray.

Still standing when the new Post Office was opened, only about a couple of hundred of yards away at the corner of High Street and Lyon Street, was Derby House, a picturesque gabled building believed to have been Bognor's first Post Office. (In 1811 William Hayley had cause to complain about its failure to deliver his letters promptly, because of the postman's habit of 'carrying them round Bognor in his pocket'.) Derby House — which was succeeded by several other post offices in and around High Street — was demolished in 1939 for road-widening purposes; but its two neighbours, a charming pair of Regency villas known rather grandly as 'Valhalla' and 'Manora', have fortunately survived.

*   *   *

Even in the mid-1920s, Bognor still possessed a certain quality of remoteness and for some visitors it was still a minor adventure to discover the town after following those winding country roads down to the sea. And when they got there it was quite a surprise to find a civilised little community with a very lively new paper, the *Bognor Post* (1922), pretty Chinese lanterns glowing in Waterloo Square and plenty of attractive shops. 'A girl who comes to Bognor without a dance dress need not fear that she will not be able to buy one in the town', remarked the *Daily Express* explorer in 1925.

If nostalgic older visitors sought the solitude of a walk along the shore, there were unexpected changes as they approached Felpham. Here a curious bungalow colony confronted them, consisting of inhabited railway coaches raised on brick stilts in the Brookland, the legacy of a housing shortage dating from 1916. Farther east, near Middleton, the spirit of Hotham had seized Sir Walter Blount who had decided to create what he termed The New City out of what remained of the derelict aeroplane works. By building bungalows and flats and converting the great assembly sheds into dance hall, garage, tennis courts and dining hall, he completed in 1922–23 what was, in fact, one of Britain's pioneer holiday camps — dubbed 'The Town of Never-Mind' by one of his first guests, the poet Leopold Spero.

West of Bognor, the half-moon of Pagham beach had also undergone a change, such a severe change that Canon Whitechurch was moved to describe it in a novel, *First and Last* (Collins, 1929), bringing his leading character back to this haunt of the author's boyhood to observe:

> 'How changed was that beach. Where it had been bordered on the shoreward side by a great broad strip of open land, rough with tussocks of grass, sea poppies and a hedge of tamarisk separating it from cornfields, stood, in a medley of confusion, two score or more of dwelling places. Old railway carriages converted into "bungalows", wooden erections of all shapes and sizes, refreshment huts and a row of bathing cabins.'

Visitors to the shore also noticed the absence of the coastguards, disbanded in the national economy cuts of 1922 and their stations closed down and sold. The flat sea beaches and the creeks of Chichester Harbour were now undefended, save for a customs official with binoculars and motor-cycle; so it was no wonder that the old smuggling trade quickly revived, more streamlined than previously, with ex-Army officers bringing the contraband over in yachts and cars waiting in the deserted thread of lanes to carry it to London. Nightclubs were the new ready market for smuggled goods, not only cigars and spirits but a more dangerous cargo — drugs.

In all this minor flurry of change, alarming to some, indicative of the optimism of the age to others, there were those who remained oblivious of everything except the most exciting things in their lives, which were rock pools, shrimping, paddling, shells, sand and seaweed. To be young and happy by the sea, safe in a family atmosphere, living in houses on the front, looked after by expert nurses, this was the lot of many children at Bognor and particularly those who had been brought there by Mrs. Emily Ward. The opinion of Dr. Davis in 1807 that this was the resort in which to rear rosy children was echoed in 1907 by Mrs. Ward when she opened the seaside branch of the Norland Institute and Nurseries of which she was the foundress.

She was a magnificent martinet, short, stout, with the glance of an empress and a temperament that mingled deep kindness with terrifying scorn. 'You're known all over Bognor,' said one of her charwomen meanfully, when giving notice. 'I am not known all over Bognor, but I *am* known all over the world,' was the reply.

She was born Emily Mary Jane Lord at Derby on 13 August 1850, and grew up on Lavender Hill, Battersea, where her father was a local landowner. As a young mistress at Notting Hill Gate High School, she was worried at the lack of special training for infants and saw the obvious advantages of Froebel's kindergarten system in developing a child's mental, moral and physical resources. When the Froebel Society was inaugurated in Britain in 1874, she became a member; and in 1876, with money from her grandmother, she opened her own kindergarten, the Norland Place School at 164 Holland Park Avenue, to prepare small children for the High School at Notting Hill. Soon her school was the foremost kindergarten in London but this, in her opinion, was not enough and she opened a training school for kindergarten teachers under the same roof in 1882. There she demonstrated to her students the art of story-telling and the playing of children's games and taught them the practical side of home and school life, from carving joints to folding tablecloths in the proper creases.

Her zeal fought her health, and in 1880 she recuperated at Bognor after a serious illness. Back in London, another scheme took shape in her mind. There were many bright and industrious girls who were devoted to children but were unsuccessful in attaining the intellectual standards required for teachers. The solution was to train them not as teachers but as the finest possible nurses for children; and in 1892, with five probationers, the Norland Institute was inaugurated.

Good nursery training was, in Mrs. Ward's view, the only sure foundation for a child's future development at school. She worked hard at her new project, giving courses of lectures, introducing dress-making, arranging menus, criticising the cooking and going the rounds to ensure that work in every department was thorough. By now she had married Walter Ward, a quiet retiring man who had been an Eastern merchant and was brother-in-law to Mrs. Humphrey Ward, the novelist.

New premises for the Institute were set up at 10 Pembridge Square, and in 1904 another house was acquired for yet another venture, the Norland Nurseries, where training was perfected in the handling of children and nurses made fully acquainted with the living standards of the homes where they were to be employed. The name 'Norland Nurse' was now a hall-mark. So great was the number of applicants for training that a third property in the Square was leased, and in 1907 the Institute reached Bognor in the form of a house — 4 Field Row, Gloucester Road — where the children from the Nurseries spent holidays in relays.

Mrs. Ward and her husband settled in Bognor, and her great plan now was to build a block of flats, with housekeeper and cook in charge, to which parties of

her trainee nurses and children could come for a holiday. Flats could also be let
to families who employed Norland nurses. In 1909 Field House flats were opened
at the eastern end of the promenade, to be filled almost continually with parties,
including – in the summer of 1911 – the three Greek princesses mentioned in
a previous chapter.

The Royal children were brought from Greece by their own Norland nurse,
Miss Kate Fox, who had firmly organised the palace nursery at Athens on English
lines, including the scrubbing of baths with Monkey Brand soap and opening the
windows at night. The youngest child, the six-year-old Princess Marina, said her
prayers in English before she learnt to do so in Greek; and her first ambition was
to become a Norland nurse herself, having made her own cap and apron (and
imitation medals) for performing such duties as arranging her doll's bed strictly
according to Norland rules. She didn't, in fact, become a Norland nurse; instead
she became a Princess of Great Britain, as well as of Greece, for she married Prince
George, Duke of Kent and son of King George V, in 1934. Princess Marina always
remembered her happy holiday on those wide smooth sands, and she was to send
her own children to play on them in the years to come.

The industry of Mrs. Ward never flagged. Field House grew with additions and
annexes during the 1920s, while she resided at Sudley Lodge with her husband
who installed an organ there and enjoyed playing light melodies. In January 1926
she bought The Den next door in order to save the estate (though only temporarily) from speculators and opened it as a children's school and a training centre
for domestic science students. It was then that her health began to fail at last.
Her heart weakened, and on 5 June 1930 her doctor forbade her to drive to
London for the At Home day of the Norland Institute. Thwarted, she walked
down Gloucester Road to the promenade for the last time. On 15 June this
remarkable woman died. In London a boy of six in the Nurseries was told that
God had taken her. 'Then there will be no more Bognor and the sea,' was his
sad reply.

But Mrs. Ward's achievements lived on and the highly trained nurse that she
created still goes out into the families of the world from the Norland Nursery
Training College.

*   *   *

It was nothing new to laugh at Bognor and such jibes were still the fashion in the
1920s. Some verses by Edith Boodle in the *Sussex County Magazine* for January
1928 told of a Worthing policeman being asked why people flocked to that
resort:

> *He raised his head with simple pride;*
> *'We are not Bognor!' he replied.*

And at a convention of holiday organisers that June, Beverley Nichols, pained
beyond measure, informed his audience that 'Bognor is the most agonisingly
hideous creation of Man on the earth.'

Consequently, a gasp of incredulity swept through the council chambers of the South Coast in January 1929, when it was announced from Buckingham Palace that King George V was to be moved to *Bognor*, of all places, to facilitate his recovery from his serious illness. The subsequent four months, during which the eyes of the world were focused on the town, was a period of baffled envy for rival resorts which considered themselves far better qualified for the honour.

George V, who had visited Goodwood the previous summer, had caught a chill in November which affected his right lung; and at the beginning of December the nation was told that his heart was weakening and that the Prince of Wales had been summoned home from East Africa. The King became unconscious and there was a hush of foreboding tragedy, but after a lung operation on 12 December he began a determined struggle for life. Hopes revived throughout the Empire. People prayed for him by day and night in the churches and gradually the carefully-worded bulletins became less grave. Finally, at noon on 22 January, came the glad news: 'The time is approaching when his Majesty's removal to sea air will be advantageous'. On the same day a further statement was issued from the Palace:

> It has been realised by the King's medical advisers that, prior to the establishment of convalescence, there would arrive a time when sea air would be necessary in order to secure the continuation of his Majesty's progress.
>
> With that knowledge, careful search was made for a residence not only suitable in itself but possessing the necessary attributes of close proximity to the sea, southern exposure, protection from wind, privacy and reasonable access to London.
>
> The residence selected is Craigweil House, Bognor, placed at his Majesty's disposal by Sir Arthur du Cros, Baronet.

The secret had been well kept. Though Post Office engineers had been working for the past week installing private lines at the house and a small domestic staff had been making preparations, the reason for the activity in the groves of pines and firs along the shore was not generally suspected. If anything, attention had been drawn eastward to Clymping, where Bailiffscourt was thought to be a possible residence during the preliminary search before the announcement was made.

But now the great news was out and though Craigweil House stood in Aldwick in the parish of Pagham, then nearly a mile beyond the Urban District boundary, Buckingham Palace had clearly stated 'Craigweil House, Bognor' and the newspapers of the world followed the lead. Some redress was made by the *Daily Telegraph*, which mentioned that Aldwick was 'an old-world Sussex village with quaint shops and winding streets about a mile and a half to the west of Bognor'. Excusably, perhaps, Fleet Street was not familiar with the geography of the area and the same newspaper informed its readers that 'the King will see to westward the massive head of Selsey Bill thrusting far into the sea. In another direction he will get a distant view of the Isle of Wight.'

Bognor took the news with comparative composure. After all Royalty had long favoured the neighbourhood, and there were numerous well-known doctors who had recommended the coast for lung complaints. Everyone was quite sure sure that the King would enjoy peace, privacy and healthful air among a community who respected these assets themselves.

Sir Arthur du Cros (1871-1955), who bought Craigweil House (formerly called the Pavilion) in 1915, had been given a baronetcy in 1916 for his war work, which included initiating the Motor Ambulance Service. At 12s. 6d. a week, he had started life in the Irish Civil Service; and then, turning to commerce, became a founder and later president of the Dunlop Rubber Company, as well as a founder-director of the Austin Motor Company. As a pioneer of pneumatic tyres, he fitted them to the cycle he rode at Queen's College sports, Belfast, in 1889 — the first occasion on which pneumatic tyres were used in cycle racing. For 14 years he was a Conservative M.P., representing Hastings (1908–18) and Clapham (1918–22); and in 1919 he reconstructed Craigweil in sumptuous style, adding a wing to east and west so that every bedroom had a sea view and the principal rooms overlooked a terrace and lawn that led straight on to a private promenade, 200 yards long, above the shingle beach. Seawater was piped to every bathroom, a lift served three floors and there was a music room equipped with stage, film projector and an electric organ whose strains could be relayed throughout the house. Here among his treasures, his rare furniture, old masters, glass paintings and Spanish and Italian objets d'art, his guests — who included two Prime Ministers, Bonar Law and the Earl of Oxford & Asquith — enjoyed recuperative holidays, hidden away at the end of a half-mile carriage drive in a wooded estate of some 30 acres.

It so happened that the house was on the market in 1929, but when the search began Sir Arthur — through the King's doctor, Lord Dawson of Penn — offered Craigweil for as long as the King should need it. Royal protocol demanded that only his Majesty could give assent to such an offer from a subject; but, as the King's health did not permit his being consulted, a formal tenancy agreement at a nominal rent was entered into between Sir Arthur and Sir Frederick Ponsonby of the Royal Household, in which it was put on record that Sir Arthur had voluntarily and freely placed Craigweil at the disposal of the King.

On 23 January, the day after the announcement was made, a cordon of Bognor police discouraged sightseers from trying to penetrate the grounds. Photographers were also forbidden entry, and only the local knowledge of Mr. E. J. Cleeve of Bognor enabled him to secure photographs of the house from the seashore before guards were stationed at this convenient loophole. On 29 January Queen Mary, accompanied by her daughter Princess Mary, paid her first visit and spent three hours inspecting the house, while at Bognor arrangements were made for guests during the Royal visit to stay at a private hotel — No. 3 Goodman Drive. The King was to travel from London by ambulance and in order to discover the least bumpy of the rural roads in the vicinity of Craigweil, Lord Dawson conducted the trial runs himself. London photographers, avid for pictures, were massed at the main gate to take a shot of Lord Dawson's ambulance leaving the estate, but the vehicle emerged from the back entrance straight into the lens of the fortunate Mr. Cleeve, whose exclusive picture once again caught the London train.

At the end of the following week, at 12.30 p.m. on Saturday, 9 February, Queen Mary arrived to await the King. Exactly one hour later there came the memorable moment, of which the *Bognor Post* has this description of the scene at Aldwick crossroads:

> Round the bend of the road came the ambulance at a speed that could not have exceeded 10 miles' per hour. The blinds of the Royal vehicle were raised and the assembled multitude could see the long couch and the reclining figure against a billow of white pillows. For a brief moment there was sympathetic silence, although men's hats were removed and handkerchiefs were waving wildly. Then a thing happened that unlocked the flood gates of the crowd's emotion. The King waved back a greeting and the cheers would not be denied.'

Three days later the King was allowed his first cigarette for two and a half months.

Their Majesties were in residence for just over 13 weeks. It was not a mild winter and during that time at least three Royal Standards were whipped to shreds by the south-westerly wind. There was still anxiety among the doctors and a feeling of tension in the district.

However, the sight of Queen Mary driving forth on her numerous excursions and visits, or walking round Aldwick village, began to encourage local confidence. A glow of pride suffused the parish on Sunday, 17 February, when the Queen attended service at Pagham church and it was a happy day for her, exactly a month later, when she returned from the same church in time to see the King walking unaided for the first time. He walked 50 yards.

By late February the Queen had already begun to shop in Bognor. The familiar royal car moved slowly along the streets with the stern yet beloved occupant gazing out shrewdly for a glimpse of an antique shop. Not that she patronised only this trade. Many a shop assistant was put at ease by a few kind and gracious words as she came to buy thrillers for the King or toys at Burgess's; and shoppers in Woolworths were delighted by the memorable sight of a royal progress advancing slowly down the aisles in search of trinkets.

Everyone wanted to get a glimpse of Her Majesty. One day a crowded fish-shop quickly emptied when the fishmonger suddenly shouted 'The Queen!' But it was not the royal Daimler that the shoppers saw approaching but a 'Silver Queen' country bus whose conductor had ordered a parcel of kippers to be all ready to be picked up as he passed by.

The Queen's afternoon car drives kept West Sussex in a constant state of expectancy and dealers in curios rooted to their premises. Her journeys took her out to local beauty spots, such as Amberley, and to Arundel Castle and the great houses of Goodwood and Petworth. At Chichester she twice attended Sunday morning service at the Cathedral, visited Archdeacon Hoskyns and his wife and, typically, made a preliminary inspection of the articles to be auctioned at Wyke Lodge. At Portsmouth she paid a call on the Commander-in-Chief and did a round of antique shops at Southsea and Cosham. She visited Hove and Brighton, inspecting Hove Museum and the Royal Pavilion and calling on friends.

March was a month of real progress for the King, who on the 27th was well enough to grant an audience to the Prime Minister, Stanley Baldwin. And, at Easter, Bognor's residents and visitors were able to see with their own eyes the rapid improvement in the King's health. The holiday attraction at the Pavilion was the Kneller Hall Band and as the King enjoyed light music (one of his favourite pieces was the Indian Love Call from *Rose Marie*) it was arranged for the band to give two concerts, on Easter Saturday and Monday, in the grounds of Craigweil House. Hundreds of people made their way along the sands to listen to the music with the King, who afterwards walked down to the sea wall to greet his subjects and express the hope that they too had enjoyed the concert.

On Easter Monday, too, a garden fête was held at Colebrook House, Aldwick, the home of Mrs. Emily Ricardo, a friend of Queen Mary. The Queen looked in at the fête and a bunch of primroses which she had held in her hand was put up for auction. As a result, the funds of Pagham church benefited by an extra £6 10s.

On 19 April one of the heroes of the day, Major Henry Seagrave, holder of the world's land and water speed records, came to Craigweil to receive the accolade of knighthood — entering the house by the tradesmen's entrance to avoid the crowds gathered outside the main gate. After the ceremony Sir Henry had a long chat with the King, who wanted to know just what it felt like to travel at such terrific speeds.

Of royal visitors there was, of course, a constant succession. They included the Prince of Wales and the Duke of York (the future Edward VIII and George VI), their sister Princess Mary, Queen Maud and Prince (later King) Olaf of Norway — and on 17 March, for a two-week stay, the King's three-year-old grand-daughter, Princess Elizabeth. So once again, after an interval of just over a hundred years, a child who was destined to become Queen of Britain came on holiday to this stretch of the Sussex coast. She spent much of her time playing in a sandpit specially made for her at Queen Mary's request in the Craigweil grounds, where the Queen enjoyed helping her in the task of making sandpies. The little Princess was the apple of the King's eye and her fortnight's stay probably did him as much good as the combined effect of his doctors and the sea air.

In a few weeks he was a different man. On 15 May, with a healthy glow in his cheeks and his old sense of humour fully restored, he was ready to return to Windsor — not in an ambulance, as he had arrived, but sitting beside the Queen in the royal car. The streets of Bognor through which he was to pass were decorated with flags and bunting. A banner bearing the words 'God Speed' was displayed near the Western Bandstand, where the car stopped for the Chairman of the Council, Canon A. J. Sacre, to convey to the King the good wishes of the townspeople. The King chatted with him for a few moments, raised his hat to the cheering crowds and then went on his way. Bognor was no longer the focal point of the British Empire, but it had done what had been expected of it. It had restored the King-Emperor to health — to reign for seven more years.

*   *   *

A few weeks later Bognor had its reward, and it was a lasting one. At the May meeting of the Urban District Council it was decided, in commemoration of the King's visit, to apply for royal approval to change the name of the town by appending the word 'Regis'. At the June meeting it was announced that his

Majesty had approved the application, thereby conferring on the town what the *Post* described as 'the very greatest honour that, as a southern watering-place, it could hope to attain'.

It was not, as we know, the first time that Bognor had changed its name, but 'Hothamton' had been quietly dropped after a couple of decades and never revived. This time the new name was to stick — doubtless to the mild chagrin of larger resorts which may have considered that lowly Bognor had allowed its unaccustomed dose of international limelight to go to its head.

Anyway, the deed was done and it was now Bognor Regis . . . The King's Bognor. And it would be hard to maintain that the title was undeserved, for in the brief period between February and May the Bognor area had been honoured not only by the presence of the reigning monarch but of three future British sovereigns as well. This was a record probably unrivalled in the annals of any other coastal resort, however highly patronised; it was a distinction to which not even Sir Richard Hotham would have dared to aspire, not in his wildest dreams.

SEA AIR CURE AT BOGNOR
FOR
THE KING.

—◆—

HOUSE CHOSEN.

———

TREATMENT "PRIOR TO CONVALESCENCE."

———

AID TO PROGRESS.

Fig. 20. The news breaks, Daily Telegraph, *23 January 1929.*

Chapter XXI

ROYAL ACCOLADE – AND THE
BATTLE OF THE CABBAGE PATCH

OF COURSE, it took some getting used to. The Bognor Regis Urban District Council. The Bognor Regis Ratepayers' Association. The *Bognor Regis Observer*. The *Bognor Regis Post*. Bognor Regis on the railway tickets and on the destination boards of the green-and-cream Southdown buses. Inevitably, the more conservative residents had their doubts. Lyme Regis was all very well, but somehow or other *Bognor* Regis seemed to strike a quite different note. It sounded like a combination of dignity and impudence — especially in the ears of those who regarded the adoption of the regal suffix as 'a piece of unnecessary presumption' and as a highly unsuitable attempt to cash in on the publicity value of the King's convalescence.

But in most quarters the honour was gratefully received and the new name savoured with unconcealed enjoyment. The *Post* obviously could not have enough of it:

> 'The years may come and go, but it will be long before 1929 will be forgotten in the annals of Bognor Regis. The change is not yet apparent and even yet the future of Bognor Regis has to be considered in a judicious and long-sighted manner; but there is no doubt that, fired by the worthy example of His Majesty, the better-class visitor will in future be attracted to Bognor Regis, always provided that the amenities of Bognor Regis are such as to cater adequately for his needs while on holiday.'

One could almost imagine that a stern edict had gone out to the editorial staff to the effect that anyone caught referring to the town simply as Bognor would be faced with instant dismissal.

In its review of the events of the year, the *Post* reflected the sudden mood of euphoria which pervaded Bognor (Regis) during that glorious summer of 1929. There was a feeling that, along with its new name, the town was on the threshold of a new chapter in its history, a chapter in which the self-styled 'Cinderella' of South Coast resorts could, at long last, take its place among the leaders. Things were on the move and even the Urban District Council seemed to be eyeing the future with an unaccustomed confidence. At midnight on 31 March, while the royal invalid was still at Craigweil, the Council assumed control of the Bognor Water Company; and on 22 May, a week after the King's departure, a crowd gathered in Clarence Road to watch the laying of the foundation stone of nothing less than a new Town Hall. Hearts swelled with pride when the artist's impressions revealed a dignified building in the fashionable neo-Georgian style: a worthy civic headquarters at last, from which to guide Bognor (due to receive its royal accolade the following month) into the glittering future which had so

226

unexpectedly opened up before it. Truly 1929, like 1787, was proving itself an *annus mirabilis* – and in the golden weeks of the first 'Regis' summer, while the holidaymakers basked on the sands and the walls of the Town Hall gradually approached shoulder height, anything seemed possible.

There were solid grounds, quite apart from the weather, for this mood of confidence and optimism. Publicity is the lifeblood of any holiday resort and Bognor had just received a massive transfusion. The beneficial effects, though they might take a little time to become apparent, were bound to show themselves in due course – as, in fact, they did one December day in the following year, 1930. The occasion was an official visit by 30 doctors from various parts of the Commonwealth who wanted to see for themselves the place where the King had recovered from his illness. Bognor, to them, was an object of curiosity – and understandably so. Previous monarchs, notably the King's father and grandmother, had been accustomed to go abroad for their health, a habit which had brought as much benefit to places like Nice and Biarritz as to themselves. But it was a British resort – and in winter, too – which had restored King George to health, and the visiting doctors were eager to cast a professional eye on this salubrious spot.

As luck would have it, Bognor greeted them with cloudless skies and brilliant sunshine; and after the visitors had dutifully inspected schools and sewage works, Dr. Ayres, the local medical officer of health, took them for an enjoyable walk along the sands, where they marvelled at a climate that permitted children to play on the beach in mid-December.

Lunch, in the words of the *Post* report, was partaken of at the Pavilion; and the distinguished guests also had time to partake of tea at the *Royal Norfolk* before catching the train back to London. After which, it is safe to assume, the members of the Bognor Regis Publicity Committee, who had been largely responsible for the arrangements, spent a self-congratulatory evening. The visit had been a complete success, the doctors had clearly been most favourably impressed and there could be little doubt that, when they returned home, they would prove valuable allies in the task of spreading publicity for Bognor throughout the Commonwealth.

In 1931 the town received a further gift – in fact, a sheer windfall – of international publicity in the unlooked-for shape of a best-selling novel by one of the most talked-about writers of the day. R. C. Sherriff had won world fame following the triumphant success of his play *Journey's End*, first produced in London in 1929 and afterwards in numerous countries abroad. The comparative failure of his next two plays convinced him (mistakenly, as it turned out) that his career as a dramatist was finished and he and his mother took a consolatory holiday at Bognor. He still had a strong urge to write, though not for the theatre, and it was while they were sitting on the Esplanade watching the crowds go by that the idea for a book suddenly came to him. He would take a typical London suburban family and write a story about what they did on their annual holiday at Bognor. He started on the first chapter of *The Fortnight in September* that same evening in his hotel bedroom, with no idea of what would have happened to the family by the end of their two-week holiday. He was, as he recalled years later in his autobiography, 'writing for my eyes alone', with no intention of submitting the result to a publisher. After all, it was a very simple theme on which to base a novel.

But the story progressed so well (he had the advantage of being surrounded by his raw material every time he stepped out of his hotel) that, when he finished it, he decided to sent it to Victor Gollancz, the publisher of *Journey's End* — and, to Sherriff's genuine amazement, they leapt at it. Enthusiastic reviews greeted the book when it came from the printers and the first edition was sold out in a week.

From Bognor's point of view, the great thing about *The Fortnight in September* was that Sherriff (unlike Jane Austen in *Sanditon*!) had made no attempt to disguise its setting under a fictional name. It was a story about a family holiday at Bognor and nowhere else; you could find your way about the town in its pages, and it was easy to identify 'St Matthews Road' (where the Stevens family was lodged in a house 'halfway down on the right-hand side') with the real-life Gloucester Road. For as the family, after arriving at the station, made their way along High Street searching for their destination, they eventually found that it was the third turning on the right after passing Clarence Road. And since the September holiday was such an enjoyable affair, both for the family in the book and for the reader, the Local Publicity Committee had further good reason to feel pleased with life — though in this particular case they could take none of the credit.

Even better was to follow, for Sherriff's novel was published in several European countries and in America, and enjoyed as great a success abroad as in Britain. From New York an American girl wrote to Sherriff to tell him that she read his book every morning on the ferry that took her across the Hudson River on her way to work and it made her feel 'so warm, free and happy'. Did she, one wonders, ever cross the Atlantic to experience those feelings at first hand in the place that had engendered them?

Sherriff himself amply repaid Bognor for inspiring his second great success as an author. He proved himself to be the sort of visitor on whom Hotham had always set his sights: a rich and famous man who spent his holidays at Bognor and then decided to build a house there. Sherriff's house, white-walled with a green-tiled roof, was in a choice part of the town — in King's Parade, facing Marine Park Gardens.

The Fortnight in September was a wonderful boost to Bognor as a summer resort, but perhaps the publicity expected to accrue from the visit of the Commonwealth doctors would fill a greater need. For the doctors had seen and admired the town on a winter's day: and it would be Bognor's reputation as a winter resort, and as a healthy place for all-the-year-round residence, that would lift it into the high-class category to which it aspired — the category long occupied by places like Torquay and Bournemouth.

'Any seaside resort,' as the *Post* remarked, 'can attract visitors during the summer-time, but there can be no doubt that it is the more wealthy and influential visitors who ultimately confer upon a town the most lasting benefit.' It might almost have been Sir Richard Hotham himself speaking! Bognor may have begun a new chapter in its history, but it could not allow itself to forget the dictum pronounced — and acted upon — by its founder from the very beginning: to aim primarily at attracting the well-to-do and socially prominent in the hope that, having spent a holiday at Bognor, they would then decide to take up permanent residence.

Hitherto, as we have seen, this had proved an elusive ambition; but in the late 1920s and early 1930s there were increasing grounds for optimism. For the Bognor neighbourhood had succeeded in capturing a prestigious prize after Hotham's own heart — none other than the beautiful Lady Diana Cooper, the darling of London society. The Duff Coopers had taken West House at Aldwick, little knowing that they would soon have the King as one of their neighbours; and in her autobiography, published in 1959, Lady Diana painted a nostalgic picture of life in what she described as 'Duff's terrestrial paradise'.

Those were the days when her big cream-coloured car was a familiar sight in the Bognor streets, especially in the vicinity of the Pier where she used to stop at a stall run by Billy Welfare, a well-known local fisherman, to buy lobsters and prawns. Years later, Mr. Welfare recalled that 'she treated me very kindly. It was Billy this and Billy that, no side at all. When it came to lobsters, you couldn't push her off with anything. The stuff had to be good and alive and always on the small side and sweeter. She knew, you see.'

Weekend parties were a regular feature at West House. An assortment of celebrities, such as the Earl of Oxford & Asquith, the Duke of Rutland and Maurice Baring, would be met at Bognor station and whisked off to Aldwick — a sight to warm the heart of any resident ambitious for the social status of the district. Sea-bathing on Sunday mornings would be followed by sustenance in the shape of Billy Welfare's freshly-cooked prawns, washed down by tots of rum. Lazy afternoons were succeeded by evening visits to the Shell House, a romantic 'folly' in the park of Goodwood House. There were picnics under the moon or in the candlelit shell-encrusted interior; Hilaire Belloc would burst into song; Duff Cooper would intone the sonnets of Shakespeare and Keats; and, when the candles guttered, 'we would go home to the garden and at last to bed to the sound of the eternal waves'.

Such was the idyllic existence made possible by the possession of a house at Aldwick — an asset which, before long, many other people would be able to share with the Duff Coopers. Inevitably the King's visit had drawn the attention of property developers to the rich potentialities of the farmlands surrounding Craigweil House; and one of the most significant events of that eventful year of 1929 — possibly more significant even than the start of the new Town Hall, though it attracted far less attention — was the birth of the West Bognor Estates Company, whose object was the development of Aldwick and Pagham.

Sir Richard Hotham had established the east end of Bognor as the fashionable part of the town, but the Felpham brookland had prevented further residential expansion in that direction. Bognor's future as a developing place of residence clearly lay in the west — and in the early 1930s nowhere on the South Coast was more 'ripe for development' than Aldwick, still basking in the blaze of publicity reflected from Craigweil House. True, Craigweil itself did not long survive its few months of glory, for it was demolished in 1932; but in some ways this was an advantage. The disappearance of the mansion cleared the way for the builders, and prospective buyers could now be offered the alluring prospect of a home of their own on the very estate where the King had regained his health.

The developers, knowing they were on to a sellers' market, wasted no time and within a few years the Aldwick that the King had known was transformed. Across the virgin farmlands the surveyors plotted the courses of avenues with exclusive-sounding names like The Drive, Wychwood Close, Craigweil Lane and the inevitable Kingsway; and before long, as Lady Diana Cooper recalled with a twinge of sadness, 'cornfields gave way to villadom'. But it was a superior brand of villadom. Opulent mock-Tudor gables rose among the trees, tasteful mock-Georgian windows surveyed expansive lawns; and seldom, in those early days of development, was the eye affronted by anything semi-detached.

Clearly the new Aldwick was just what was needed to improve the social standing of the Bognor area as a place of residence, but desirable homes and leafy avenues were not in themselves sufficient. The developers having played their part, the town itself must make its own contribution. As the *Post* had warned, it was vital, in order to attract the 'better-class' visitor and resident that 'the amenities of Bognor Regis are such as to cater adequately for his needs'. One amenity within easy reach of the new residents of Aldwick had already been provided for by the Council's praiseworthy purchase in 1926 of a stretch of land fronting the foreshore a few hundred yards west of the Western Lawns. This was part of the far-spread estate of Mr. William Fletcher of Aldwick Manor. By their prompt action, the Council rescued this valuable site from the hands of the builders who had already had their speculative eyes on it and by the early 1930s it had been handsomely laid out as the Marine Park Gardens, bounded on the north by the suitably named King's Parade.

It was, however, now generally accepted that it was only by the provision of *winter* amenities that the town would gain the sort of reputation to which it aspired ('any seaside resort can attract summer visitors'). The King, by his own winter visit, had laid the foundations for such a reputation, and it was for Bognor to carry on from there. And if there was one amenity common to Britain's 'better-class' resorts, it was the provision of music, light or symphonic, at all seasons of the year. Places like Bournemouth, Scarborough, Brighton, Worthing, Folkestone and Eastbourne all had orchestras and, what was equally important, suitable halls in which one could listen to them in winter as well as summer. Bournemouth had its Winter Garden, Scarborough its Spa, Folkestone its Leas Cliff Hall, Worthing its Pavilion, and so on. Bognor, it is true, also had a Pavilion, but the ex-seaplane assembly shed from Middleton was too large and cavernous to provide the right atmosphere for daily concerts of light music, though it served well enough as a dance hall and entertainments centre and as a venue for occasional 'celebrity' concerts.

The lack both of a permanent orchestra and of a suitable venue for its performances was perhaps the most serious obstacle to Bognor's chances of joining the select company of established winter resorts and thereby consolidating its claim to recognition as a desirable year-round place of residence for the well-to-do. It was not, however, until 1936 that the Council – now in occupation of its new headquarters in Clarence Road – got down to considering a project for removing the obstacle. This was nothing less than a scheme to equip Bognor, on the august example of Bournemouth, with a Winter Garden designed primarily as a concert hall. It would be built on the site of the Western Bandstand which had stood on the lawns near the *Royal Norfolk Hotel* since 1901.

The Winter Garden scheme had much to commend it. It envisaged a concert hall flanked by open-air terraces and equipped on either side with sliding glass doors which would be closed in winter and in bad weather. On fine summer days the doors would remain open so that the terraces became part of the auditorium. The terraces themselves would be surrounded by raised promenades which would serve as windshields, and there would be a café overlooking the sea.

According to the prospectus, this ingenious and well-planned structure would 'give an impression of gaiety and cheerfulness in keeping with the character of Bognor Regis'. But far more important than any impression it might give was the fact that it would enable orchestral music to be enjoyed throughout the year, and in all weather conditions, in a pleasant setting within a few yards of the beach. Here at last was the sort of asset which would attract the winter visitor and perhaps persuade him, once he had taken a look at the type of property becoming available at Aldwick, to become a permanent resident. The cost was estimated at £38,000.

Perhaps if the scheme had been produced early enough to catch the mood of sunny confidence that prevailed in the period immediately following the King's visit, the plans might have been given the go-ahead. But by 1936 (the much-loved old King died in January that year) the mood had sobered down and the Council, characteristically shying away from the Winter Garden, opted instead for an open-air – and therefore summer-only – music enclosure, with shelters surrounding a central lawn, at less than one-tenth of the cost. Thus the brief hope that Bognor would soon be diverting autumn and winter visitors from Bournemouth in the west and from Worthing in the east began to fade; and all for a saving of £35,000. To many it seemed a short-sighted economy.

But all was not yet lost, for one part at least of the original conception had been preserved. The Winter Garden had been intended primarily for orchestral music – and when the substitute Western Band Enclosure, as it was named, was opened in June 1937 the stage was occupied not by one of the usual military bands (for which the Eastern Bandstand, built in 1910, was still available when required) but by nothing less than the newly-formed Bognor Regis Municipal Orchestra under Walter Collins.

The revolutionary step of equipping Bognor with its own orchestra had not been taken without the customary fireworks in the Council Chamber and it was doubtless with the idea of mollifying the opposition that the inaugural concert

at the Pavilion on Sunday, 29 May was a private function for the councillors and
their guests. Next day it was the turn of the public to assess the qualities of the
orchestra and of its 'dark, dynamic' conductor, as the *Observer* promisingly
described him; and the assessment was universally favourable. The opening item
of that Sunday evening concert was *Comrades All*, a piece specially composed for
Bognor by Mr. Collins and thereafter heard regularly as the orchestra's signature
tune. Collins, incidentally, was fortunate in having a useful stand-in in the
unexpected shape of Bognor's Entertainments Manager, J. R. (Joe) Cunningham,
who happened to be a quite accomplished conductor in his own right.

On 19 June the Band Enclosure — which had taken only 14 weeks to erect —
was formally opened, and the rows of green deckchairs neatly arranged on the
enclosed lawn were filled with appreciative occupants listening to Mr. Collins and
his players for the first time in what was to be their principal home. So it was
that Bognor suddenly found itself among the élite company of resorts which
possessed orchestras of their own. Admittedly the Bognor orchestra was not to be
an all-year attraction, as it would have been if the Winter Garden scheme had been
adopted, but it was a big step in the right direction. And if there were still any
philistine doubts as to the importance of music to a seaside town seeking to make
its name better known, they were swept away the very next month when, in an
atmosphere of what the *Observer* described as 'hushed expectancy', a packed
audience in the Pavilion awaited the first broadcast concert of Britain's newest
municipal orchestra. The programme opened with another Collins composition,
Pride of the South — and as this presumably referred to Bognor, the Publicity
Committee must have spent a happy day. Nor was that all, for the B.B.C. broadcast two further concerts from Bognor that summer.

Surely never had so small an investment yielded such speedy and handsome
dividends. The publicity and prestige value of those three broadcasts must alone
have justified the initial cost of the Western Enclosure (the main reason for the
existence of the orchestra), so that one cannot help speculating on the long-term
benefit to the town if the Council had persuaded itself to complement what the
builders were achieving at Aldwick by investing in the Winter Garden. For less
than £40,000, Bognor's long hoped-for reputation as a high-class winter resort
and residential town might have been clinched once and for all.

But now that elusive reputation was faced with a threat from another quarter.
West of the Pier, with the strains of the Municipal Orchestra wafting over the
lawns, with strollers admiring the flower-beds in the new Marine Park Gardens
and with a plentiful supply of the right sort of houses available at Aldwick for
would-be neighbours of the Duff Coopers, there was no denying that considerable progress had been made in the last few years. East of the Pier, however, the
picture was very different. In fact, it could be said that the main feature of the
Bognor scene in the 1930s was the running battle between East and West to
decide which of the two would wield the major influence in moulding the future
character of the town. It is time for us to leave the peaceful avenues of Aldwick
and the serenity of the Western Lawns and to plunge into the conflict.

*   *   *

The crucial battleground lay a few hundred yards east of the Pier: a stretch of vacant land which had been used for allotments during the war and had been known ever since as the Cabbage Patch. To explain why such a prominent site on the sea front was still undeveloped, we must go back into comparatively ancient history – as far back as 1881, when (as described in Chapter XV) the over-ambitious scheme to build Cotswold Crescent, an edifice designed to occupy a 600-foot frontage between Lennox Street and York Road, collapsed after only four of the houses had been completed. These, forming the west wing and the beginning of the western curve of the Crescent, survived – and, as the *Carlton Hotel*, survive to this day – as a curious truncated memorial to what would have been the largest building ever erected in Bognor.

At the time the Cotswold scheme was abandoned, trenches had already been dug and excavations made for the foundations and basements of the next stage of the work. These quickly filled with sea water, which may well have stayed the hands of future potential developers owing to doubts as to the suitability of the subsoil. Local boys, however, found the site ideal as an aquatic playground; and it also came in useful for the erection of spectators' stands when the Duke and Duchess of York came to Bognor in 1900 to open the two convalescent homes to the east of Clarence Road – 29 years before they returned as King and Queen for the royal convalescence at Craigweil House.

With the outbreak of the Great War, the excavations were filled in to enable the Crescent site to 'do its bit' for the war effort by becoming the Cabbage Patch. Possibly it was the spectacle of vegetable allotments occupying this prime position of the Esplanade that finally woke people up to the realisation that the site could not be left undeveloped for much longer and that after the war something more appropriate to the sea front must take the place of the cabbages and potatoes.

There was, of course, no question of completing the Crescent, even in a modified form. The day of crescents had long past; and in any case the water-logging of the original Cotswold foundations had proclaimed the unsuitability of the site for extensive building development. Moreover, there was a fairly general opinion that this stretch of land, having managed to escape the developers for so long, should remain free of buildings and be laid out as public gardens. These would not only enhance the appearance of the Esplanade east of the Pier but would raise the tone of that rather plebeian section of the sea front by providing it with a counterpart to the Western Lawns.

It did not go unremarked in Bognor that Worthing, too, had a Cabbage Patch on its sea front. The Worthing Council, however, had got to work on the site in 1923 and by the following year had transformed it by widening Montague Place into an attractive thoroughfare with broad tiled pavements and ornamental gardens on either side. In 1925, possibly with this example in mind, the owners of the Cotswold Crescent site, Mr. Hills and Mr. Salmon, offered it to the Bognor Council. The price asked was £22 10s. per foot of frontage; and the Council, then far more interested in its dreams of a new Town Hall a short distance to the east, turned it down – with what far-reaching effects on Bognor's future we shall see later on. Though it can hardly have been realised at the time, the Council's decision was of tremendous significance and the effects were to be felt for decades and even generations to come. (A year later, as we have already seen, when the Council was presented with the opportunity to purchase a similar vacant site west of the Pier it took the opposite decision and the site became the Marine Park Gardens.)

*   *   *

Faced with a negative reply from the civic authorities and with no prospect of using the land for large-scale building development, Messrs. Hills and Salmon had no alternative but to sell off the Cabbage Patch in lots. They found no lack of willing purchasers eager to set up a business on such promising territory. Among the first-comers were a Mr. Cass, who opened a tobacconist's shop; a Mr. Davis, who built a garage; and a Mr. Cheer, whose Esplanade Restaurant with its adjoining tea garden provided holiday-makers with a rendezvous tailor-made to the tastes of the 1920s.

The 1920s, however, were coming to an end, tastes and fashions were moving with the times and a new type of enterprise was about to make its appearance — that of the seaside amusement caterer and fun fair proprietor. Mr. Cheer's business did not long survive the change of decade, for by 1931 the restaurant had been converted into an amusement arcade and the tea garden had become an Auto-Car track. And this was just at the time when high hopes were being entertained that Bognor would start to match its new title of Regis by making a serious effort to attract the 'better-class visitor'.

It was a notable victory for the East over the more decorous West, and people now began to appreciate the full significance of the Council's rejection of the purchase offer six years before. Had the 1925 decision gone otherwise, there would have been lawns and flower-beds (and perhaps even a municipal tea garden) instead of the raucous amusements ushered in by the new decade.

The opposition, however, were not yet prepared to accept defeat, and there were plenty of protesting voices. The most heartfelt of these came from the Free Church Council, who were concerned with the effect the amusements were having on Bognor's Sunday observance. They made a 'respectful request' to the Town Hall to issue no further seven-day amusement licences and not to renew those already granted. The sea front east of the Pier, they claimed, 'is now spoilt for those who have regard for the Lord's Day'.

The Free Church Council might well have saved their breath, for in issuing their protest they had unwittingly taken on the most formidable of adversaries. They had challenged the man whose name, in the annals of Bognor, was destined to rank alongside that of Sir Richard Hotham himself as an arbiter of the town's fortunes and as a moulder of its character. In fact, a prophet might have foretold that his influence on Bognor in the mid-20th century was to prove even greater and more lasting than Hotham's at the end of the 18th. Yet it is doubtful whether the Free Church protesters even knew his name. They cannot be blamed on that account — for how many people in the Bognor of 1931 had ever hear of Billy Butlin?

He was, of course, already well known in the world of amusement catering and had progressed far in the 10 years since, with five pounds to his name, he had set himself up as a travelling hoop-la proprietor. Moving from one country fair to another, he did so well that he was able to open an amusement park at Skegness and from there he was now beginning to extend his empire to other holiday towns. No doubt it was the publicity arising from the King's visit that first brought Bognor to the attention of Mr. Butlin's appraising eye, and he was never one to be left behind when it came to jumping on a band-waggon – as he did when, after the departure of Leonard Henry's Little Show in 1930, he turned the Olympian Gardens into the Esplanade's first fun fair. The nearby Cabbage Patch lured him with its opportunities for more ambitious development, and negotiations for the purchase of the Esplanade Restaurant and Tea Garden were speedily concluded. Thus it was that, by ironical coincidence, Mr. Cheer was replaced on the Cabbage Patch by the man who would soon be widely publicised as 'Mr. Happiness'.

Publicity was inseparable from Billy Butlin, and now that he had become part of the local scene it was inevitable that Bognor would come in for a goodly share of that valuable commodity. It did not have long to wait. 'Mr. Happiness', confident of overcoming the opposition of the Free Church Council and other objectors, saw Bognor as an expanding market; and in 1933, two years after he had converted the restaurant and tea garden into 'amusements', he acquired Mr. Davis's garage. This he planned to transform into a zoo, with a plasterwork Alpine Range as its main scenic feature – rather to the alarm, one imagines, of the neighbouring *Carlton*, *Beaulieu* and *Beaulieu Downs* hotels.

Billy Butlin's Zoo was the immediate cause of the biggest dose of high-powered newspaper publicity Bognor had received since the King's visit and it also finally established Butlin himself as a household name throughout Britain. The opening of his latest attraction was fixed for Wednesday, 5 July 1933, and on that very morning one of the national papers, the *News Chronicle*, came out with a sensational report that a lion, destined for the new zoo, had escaped at midnight in the vicinity of Bognor while being conveyed from Butlin's other zoo at Skegness – and that Butlin and his lion-tamer were scouring the neighbourhood in search of it.

People locked their doors against the ferocious beast, the opening of the zoo was hastily postponed and the police began enquiries; and then in the middle of the morning came an alarming development. It was announced that a sheep had been found dead and badly mauled on a farm near Pagham, presumably a victim of the escaped lion. Fleet Street could have asked for nothing more and a small army of reporters and photographers descended on West Sussex to join in the hunt. Next day Bognor woke up to find that its lion was no longer a *News Chronicle* exclusive; it was front-page news everywhere.

Meanwhile, Butlin was facing up to the unwelcome realisation that, through no fault of his own, he had been landed in an extremely tricky situation. A telephone call to Skegness had revealed that the consignment of animals had not, after all, included a lion, and the news must certainly have come as a great relief. But what was he to do now? To deny the existence of the Bognor Lion at this stage, when the newspapers had told everyone that it was on the prowl, presumably seeking what — or whom — it might devour, would do nothing to end the search. It would merely look like a rather feeble attempt at a cover-up. And, even supposing his denial was believed, wouldn't it be widely assumed that the whole story had been a put-up affair, a discreditable hoax perpetrated by an acknowledged master of publicity to secure the maximum press coverage for the opening of his new zoo?

In danger of losing out either way, Butlin had to think fast and his natural resourcefulness did not fail him. Not for the first time in his life, he had an inspiration. The only way to end the panic once and for all would be to exhibit a lion — any lion — safely in its cage, so he telephoned a circus at Maidstone with an urgent request for them to send him one of theirs. Secrecy was essential, and the substitute lion arrived at the Bognor zoo under cover of darkness at 2 a.m. on the Thursday morning. A few hours later, when papers all over the country were regaling their readers' breakfast-tables with the sensational details of the Bognor Lion Hunt, Butlin announced that the escaped animal had been recaptured and that the press were invited to send reporters to view it with their own eyes.

The 24-hour scare was over and the postponed opening of the zoo, now well bolstered by the unexpected advance publicity, took place the following week; but the police were not going to leave it at that. The outcome of their enquiries was the trial at Lewes in December of an enterprising free-lance journalist who was accused of 'putting the public in fear by circulating false statements about an escaped lion and of arranging for a sheep to appear as if it had been mauled by a predator'. Also appearing in court were Butlin himself and the farmer on whose land the dead sheep had been found, both suspected of being a party to the plot. The journalist (whose father, it interestingly transpired, was on the staff of the News Chronicle) was fined £30, the farmer's penalty for aiding him was £10 — but Butlin was found innocent and acquitted. Far from being party to the hoax, he could claim to have been one of its chief victims. Yet paradoxically, as we shall see, it was to bring him the final triumph in the Battle of the Cabbage Patch. He had, of course, already won the first round by defeating local opposition to the spread of fun fairs on the Eastern Esplanade, with the result that the disputed stretch of land, instead of being transformed into the hoped-for public gardens, was now occupied by Auto-Cars, plastic Alps and somnolent jungle beasts yawning the hours away in an excess of ozone. But the ultimate prize would be greater by far than this initial success.

For though the Bognor Lion Hunt may seem, for all its intriguing and even mysterious aspects, a classic example of a non-event, its real significance lies in the fact that for the first time the names of Butlin and Bognor were linked together in the national newspapers and thus in the national consciousness. The hoax itself soon faded into history, but the link did not. For at least a couple of generations, and probably far longer, it would prove indissoluble; and in due course the day would come when to countless people all over the country Bognor would mean, first and foremost, Butlin.

Such were the spoils of victory.

10. An 'English Trouville' (p. 200)—the Tamarisk walk and Gray's bathing huts at the western end of the promenade.

11. Part of the local scene for centuries—Bognor fishermen and lobster pots.

72.   Summertime paddlers—a postcard view of 1915. In the background is the Kursaal, and Colebrook Terrace to the right.

73.   (*above*) The promenade with the Kursaal, built by William Tate in 1910.

74.   (*right*) The Picturedrome Cinema was built as the New Assembly Rooms in 1886, and first screened silent films in 1919.

5. King George V at Craigweil, with Queen Mary and his grand-daughter, the present Queen.

6. Craigweil House, c.1900, where Bognor became 'the focal point of the British Empire'. (pp. 221-224)

77. Seafront attractions in the 1930s, west of York Road.

78. At the foot of Gloucester Road: Winchelsea House, on the right, was later used by the Butlin camp for staff accommodation.

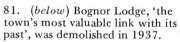

79. (*above*) The Western Bandstand site, where the chance of a Winter Garden for Bognor was lost in the 1930s.

80. (*left*) Hothamton Place, at the north end of Waterloo Square, was the first piece of Hotham's architectural legacy to become a casualty in 1935.

81. (*below*) Bognor Lodge, 'the town's most valuable link with its past', was demolished in 1937.

82. A German Junkers 88 brought down in the sea of Aldwick, 9 September 1940.

83. A War Savings Parade in the High Street in 1942.

84. The chapel of the Merchant Taylors' Convalescent Home. (*Photo: Les O'Brennan*)

85. Den Lodge, built of cleft flints, is the former lodge to 'the Den', where Claude Bowes-Lyon, great-grandfather of the present Queen, once lived.

88. (*overleaf*) Brookland, from the north-west, before the arrival of Billy Butlin. Hotham Park House is amongst the trees in the foreground, with Gloucester Road on the right.

87. (*right*) The 'Polly Anne' Restaurant, (No. 74 High Street) which made way for a supermarket extension in 1963. On the left is the flint wall surrounding the Merchant Taylors' Convalescent Home.

86. (*below*) Derby House, on the corner of High Street and Lyon Street, was a Post Office in Hotham's day, and the home of the Bognor Handweaving Industry before demolition in 1939.

89. These cottages in Chapel Street (demolished in 1970) were known to generations of Bognor fishermen. Beyond is the clock tower of St John's chapel.

90. The destruction of the tower of old St John's in 1961.

91. 'New' St John's suffers a similar fate in 1972.

92. The Theatre Royal and Rex complex, on the corner of York Road and Belmont Street. The Regis Centre now occupies the site.

93. The Theatre Royal auditorium during demolition in 1975.

94. Spencer Terrace, Upper Bognor Road, used continually for education since 1852, and described by Nairn and Pevsner as 'a very nice building to have in a town'.

95. Sudley Lodge was designed by John Shaw the Younger in 1827. It is shown here before conversion to flats in 1972.

6. Where a future Queen Victoria bought a pair of boots; the Tuck Shop stood at the top of Gloucester Road. It ʼas demolished in 1968.

7. St Dominic's School, the former Belvedere House, from the south. Gloucester House now occupies the site.

98. William Holland Ballett Fletcher, last of the local 'squires'; the private estate he helped to beautify is now Hotham Park.

99. William's wife, Agnes, with the family pet.

00. Hotham Park House, once the home of Bognor's founder, during the 'reign' of the Fletcher family.

101. The seafront at Bognor, 1983.

Chapter XXII

BREAKING WITH THE PAST

BY THE MID-1930s, with Billy Butlin undisputed King of the Cabbage Patch, a somewhat strident element had not only entered Bognor life but had obviously come to stay — at any rate, east of that great divide, the Pier. However, as we know, the West was soon to counter-attack with its new Band Enclosure, complete with Municipal Orchestra; and one can imagine that the anti-Butlinites may have been temporarily heartened by the result of a poll organised in 1937 to determine the relative popularity of the town's attractions. Top honours were predictably won by the sands and the sea air; and the next three places all went west of the Pier, the Marine Park Gardens in third place being followed by the Band Enclosure and the Municipal Orchestra, then both enjoying all the plaudits and publicity of their opening season. The Pavilion and the Pier, without the benefit of novelty, couldn't rise higher than No. 12 and No. 16 respectively; but even so they were way above Butlin's Fun Fair, beaten into 27th place by the recent extension of the promenade eastward to Felpham at No. 25 and, at No. 26, the joys of horse-riding on the sands.

Not, of course, that his lowly position in the poll had the slightest effect on the irrepressible spirits of Mr. Happiness, who had just scored yet another triumph by his successful appeal against the Council's refusal to renew his fun-fair licence for his original Olympian Gardens site and whose ebullient advertisements ('Hurrah! Its Butlin's') continued to appear with unfailing regularity in the local Press. Indeed, even at that early date, the extension of the promenade to Felpham, by which he had been narrowly defeated in the popularity poll, may quite possibly have sown in his fertile mind the first seed of a certain ambitious scheme which, if fortune favoured him (as it usually did), might well be brought to reality before many years had passed. Were his thoughts already following the new promenade eastward to the flat green Brookland which separated Bognor from Felpham?

Meanwhile, many people still clung to the hope that the future would see Bognor living up to its title of Regis by achieving that longed-for reputation as a high-class resort which so recently had seemed within its grasp. The King's Silver Jubilee, which had been celebrated in May 1935 with an open-air service in High Street, a two-mile carnival procession and a spell of glorious weather, may have revived something of the spirit of 1929; though the only tangible legacy of that year of optimism, now that Craigweil House had disappeared, was the extension to the hospital, planned to commemorate the King's visit. But within a year the King was dead. It was the end of one short sunlit chapter, which had seemed to promise so much, and the beginning of a very different one.

As if to emphasise the difference, the celebrations in honour of the coronation of King George VI in 1937 were in marked contrast to those of his father's sun-blessed Jubilee. For the rain dampened everything, including the temporary building erected for the Grand Fire-Fighting Display which was to be the highlight of the afternoon's festivities. As a result, the firemen had no chance of demonstrating what they could do with their hoses as the building failed to go up in flames as planned — and, before long, flashes of lightning presaged an extra heavy downpour which caused the rest of the programme to be abandoned.

1929 suddenly seemed a long time ago. It was already two reigns back in history, times had changed and the mood now was for severing what seemed to be unnecessary links with the past.

The demolition of Craigweil House within three years of its becoming a temporary royal residence had set the pattern, and in 1935 the destroyers had turned their attention for the first time to the architectural legacy of Sir Richard Hotham. That legacy had managed to survive almost intact since the Founder's death at the end of the 18th century, but now the bell was about to toll for Hothamton Place.

This, the earliest of Hotham's terraces, with a long well-proportioned frontage in his favourite red brick, occupied a commanding situation in the centre of the town, facing southwards down the length of Waterloo Square to the Pier entrance. The Pier, of course, was not there when it was built in 1789, so the sea-bathing visitors whom the terrace was designed to accommodate had merely to glance out of their windows to check whether or not the English Channel was in a mood to welcome swimmers.

Immediately to the east of Hothamton Place, and almost contemporaneous with it, stood Fitzleet House (originally East Row); and viewed from Waterloo Square the pair of terraces formed an 18th-century townscape of which any resort could have been proud, especially as there was an element of contrast. Fitzleet House was faced with white-painted stucco (the cement was manufactured in Nyewood Lane) which gave it a handsomer — or, at any rate, more opulent — appearance than its plain brick neighbour. In 1870, it will be recalled, Fitzleet House was opened by the Merchant Taylors Company as a convalescent home for men, and its lucky patients derived such benefit from Bognor's health-giving air that the Merchant Taylors extended their charitable activities to the neighbouring terrace, which became a convalescent home for women.

In 1921 Hothamton Place was sold to the Urban District Council for conversion into flats. By the 1930s it presented a somewhat seedy appearance, though that was no good reason for demolition. The only compensation, such as it was, for the Council's decision was that there was no intention of replacing the terrace with a new building. The plan was to use the site to provide a more spacious setting for the Pavilion (just to the rear) by extending its gardens and car park, with the additional bonus of opening up a quite picturesque view of the turreted Pavilion which had hitherto been concealed behind Hotham's red brick. In that respect the demolition — though depriving Fitzleet House of its complementary companion — could be regarded as an urban 'improvement' which might well have won the understanding, if not necessarily the approval, of Hotham himself.

One of the features of the extended Pavilion Gardens was a children's boating pool in the shape of an outline map of England and Wales, which was opened by one of Aldwick's most prominent householders, the Marchioness of Cambridge, in April 1937. It is doubtful, though, whether this new amenity can have provided much consolation for the fervid supporters of the recently defeated scheme to construct a tidal bathing pool on the beach. In 1936 this was the subject of one of the longest and hottest battles ever fought in the Council Chamber. It ended with the Ministry turning down Bognor's application to borrow £51,000 to finance the construction of the pool; and at the Council's September meeting the irascible Chairman, Captain H. C. Pocock R.N., created a sensation by announcing his decision to resign in protest the very next day. As he had a tendency to preside over the Council's deliberations with the same salty brusqueness that he had doubtless employed on the quarterdeck, it is possible that some of the polite expressions of regret at the Captain's departure were laced with sighs of relief.

*   *   *

Hothamton Place had scarcely been razed to the ground when the demolition squad moved in on another prominent landmark, the Water Tower of 1874. In 1929 Bognor's water supply had become a Council responsibility and the advance of progress had rendered the old tower in London Road superfluous; but as a familiar feature of the Bognor skyline, where it provided an effective counterpoise to the neighbouring spire of St John's church, it was regarded with a good deal of affection.

It was, of course, asking too much of the Council to spare the Water Tower merely on sentimental grounds and it duly disappeared from the skyline in 1936. There was, however, an infinitely stronger case for preserving the next item on the demolition list. For the chosen victim in Coronation Year, 1937, was none other than the most historic building in the town — Bognor Lodge, Hotham's first home in Bognor. It was now exactly 150 years since he had begun the work of transforming the original farmhouse into a dignified residence, complete with domed ceilings and decorations in the Adam style.

Since Hotham's day, the house had passed through a long succession of owners and many notable people had stayed there — most notably the future Queen Victoria, as a little princess, accompanied by her mother. Its owner in 1937 was a Mr. A. H. Winham; but Mr. Winham had not purchased Bognor Lodge in order to live in it. Quite the contrary. A speculative builder with an eye for development values, he had earmarked the Lodge and its grounds as a site for a block of flats — presumably on the lines of the curiously named Kyoto Court which he had erected in Nyewood Lane. Some of the proposed flats would enjoy spacious views through the trees of the green and empty Brookland stretching eastwards to Felpham, while others would overlook the adjacent grounds of Hotham's second and last home, the former Chapel House, which was still occupied by William Fletcher, now 85 years old.

A lone Bognor resident, hearing of this alarming plan, wrote to the Council urging them to purchase the Lodge in order to ensure the preservation of the town's most valuable link with its past. He was rewarded by a polite letter thanking him for his interest; and shortly afterwards the demolition squad set about the job of getting rid of the house where Bognor might be said to have begun.

As things turned out, they could have spared their energies, for a second edition of Kyoto Court (would it have been proudly named Coronation Court?) was not destined to take the place of the Lodge. Mr. Winham, having apparently allowed his ambitions to overrun his resources, went bankrupt and had to abandon the scheme before a brick had been laid — much to the relief, one imagines, of old Mr. and Mrs. Fletcher next door, who could continue to enjoy their garden without being observed by a set of brand-new neighbours.

Of course, the Lodge estate was still ripe for development by other hands, but it did not remain so for long. In 1939 the outbreak of the Second World War put a stop to speculative building and soon the vacant site with its fertile soil was making its contribution to the war effort by helping out with the vegetables.

Fig. 21. Waterloo Square in the 1850s.

Chapter XXIII

IN THE FRONT LINE AGAIN

AS IN 1914, war came in the midst of the holiday season. Bognor was thronged with summer visitors, whose choice of diversions included the Municipal Orchestra, now well established at the Western Enclosure; dancing at the Pavilion; the comedy *Spring Meeting* at the Theatre Royal, featuring Zena Dare and enjoying, as the *Post* reminded its readers, 'the inestimable advantage of being directed by John Gielgud'; and several concert parties, ranging from 'Revuettes of 1939' at the Pier's Roof Garden Theatre to 'Dazzle' at Pierrotland – part of the former Kursaal, whose name had already been conveniently dropped after the First World War, thereby saving the management the trouble of doing so at the outbreak of the Second.

To all intents, it was just like any other summer season of the 1930s. Those familiar figures, the Duff Coopers, were down at Aldwick as usual, and on the last day of August they set out for what proved to be their final pre-war picnic. The chosen spot was the summit of Halnaker Hill, where the lonely ruined windmill seemed to Lady Diana like a gaunt omen of the desolation that was threatening Europe.

Next day, the first of September, the threat became reality. Lady Diana and her son John Julius were buying sweets in High Street when from a radio in a car parked nearby they heard the announcement that Germany had invaded Poland. Duff, meanwhile, was playing a round of golf at Goodwood and was told the news in the club bar after he had finished his game. He drove home immediately. That afternoon, after hastily packing up, the Duff Coopers returned to London, where they dined the same evening with Winston Churchill. It was good-bye at last to those long idyllic summers in the 'terrestrial paradise' they had found at Aldwick.

Bognor had just over a year to wait for its first taste of active warfare. By the summer of 1940 France had fallen and the monotonous rows of concrete anti-invasion blocks which had sprung up along the foreshore were evidence that the town, like other South Coast resorts, was again in the front line, as it had been in Napoleonic days. Trouble could therefore be expected before long and it duly arrived on 14 September. Eight or nine bombs were dropped on Bognor that Saturday afternoon – and, with supreme irony, the first of them landed in the grounds of Sudley Lodge which was doing duty as an Air Raid Precautions control post. It suffered only minor damage, but its neighbour (originally Sudley Cottage) was less fortunate, for it received a direct hit from the second bomb of the raid. This was the charming house which, as mentioned in Chapter X, was acquired by Claude Bowes-Lyon, Earl of Strathmore, who renamed it The

(Lyon's) Den. Later it became successively a hotel, Mrs. Ward's school and, in 1939, a hostel for blind evacuees. Only the top floor was seriously damaged and miraculously there were no casualties; but the house was allowed to fall into decay and was demolished after the war when the estate was 'developed'. The Victorian Gothic Lodge at the entrance gate was, however, permitted to survive; and Bowes-Lyon's pun lives on in the name of Den Avenue, a road built across the lawns where once it was the height of social distinction to be seen playing croquet as the guest of the Strathmores.

So, with its very first raid on Bognor, the Luftwaffe had demonstrated its ability to take over the task of trying to rid the town of its aristocratic old houses, which had been temporarily interrupted by the outbreak of the war. A few months later a bomb just missed Hotham's masterpiece, the Dome House, to which some of the blind people had been moved when The Den was hit.

Altogether, between September 1940 and October 1944, about a thousand bombs were dropped on the town (24 of them in the Good Friday raid of 1941), demolishing 58 houses and killing 33 people. A favourite target was the gasworks which was repeatedly attacked and in 1942 was hit by the bomber itself, a Dornier crippled by anti-aircraft fire. Bognor's single flying-bomb, in August 1944, damaged hundreds of houses, though there was only one fatality.

The Esplanade lost only one prominent landmark during the war: the Eastern Bandstand which had ornamented the sea front, near the foot of Clarence Road, since 1910. Its disappearance was due not to enemy action but to an order for demolition — presumably because it could not be fitted into the anti-invasion defences. However, it was satisfactorily replaced a few years later by a very decorative bandstand bought from Cheltenham for £175 in 1948.

Compared with 1914–18, life in Bognor during the Second World War assumed a distinctly cosmopolitan flavour. On one side of the town, at Middleton, there were the Canadians, many of whom took part in the sea-borne raid on Dieppe in 1942 (soon afterwards the Luftwaffe dropped picture leaflets on Bognor in order to show that the raid had not achieved the hoped-for success); while Pagham, to the west, was host to the Free Norwegians. One of them, Crown Prince Olaf, was no stranger to the area, as he had visited George V at Craigweil House — so there was no need for him to enquire why the *King's Beach Hotel* at Pagham was so named. This friendly hostelry was such a favourite gathering-place with the Norwegian forces that it quickly became known as 'Little Norway'.

Bognor's last air raid was on 1 October 1944. By then the Allies were deep into France and, with the threat of invasion removed, the South Coast resorts were no longer in the front line. For the first time since 1939 they could look forward to a summer which would bring an influx of visitors — though, as it happened, the most important visitors to Bognor in 1945 did not wait for summer. They came in February.

*   *   *

The Duchess of Kent's three children — nine-year-old Prince Edward, who had succeeded to the dukedom on the death of his father on active service; Princess

Alexandra, aged eight; and Prince Michael, aged three — all went down with 'flu that winter. This automatically meant being sent to the seaside to recuperate and the Duchess decided on Bognor. It was an obvious choice. Not only was it the place where her father-in-law had regained his health, but she herself, as Princess Marina, had spent a childhood holiday there and could personally vouch for the excellence of Bognor's sands. So the children, in the charge of their French governess, were packed off to the *Carlton Hotel*.

The *Post* dutifully regretted that Bognor, after five years of war, had not much to offer them, 'though it has at least an air of tranquillity that was lacking in the days when the East Promenade was more or less devoted to the blare of fun fairs and amusement palaces'. Given a choice, the young visitors might willingly have swapped the tranquillity for Mr. Butlin's temporarily silenced blare, but even so they found plenty to do. For one thing, the beach was no longer out of bounds, though the anti-invasion defences were still in place and available for climbing practice. Every day, after the obligatory French lesson, they were down on the sands, where Edward rode his bicycle and Alexandra rode a pony borrowed from a local stable, while Michael doubtless tried his hand at construction work with bucket and spade. The two elder children went to the cinema to see *Lassie Comes Home*, and one weekend their mother came down to check their progress and take them to morning service at St John's.

The trio returned home after nearly a month at Bognor, all the better for an enjoyable convalescence which had provided them with as much sea air and healthy exercise as any doctor could have prescribed. 'Good advertisement for the town', remarked the *Observer*, thereby suddenly reviving a favourite topic of the 1930s which had lain dormant since the outbreak of war. For the royal children playing on the sands had provided a reminder that, with the end of hostilities at last in sight, Bognor would soon be back in its normal business of attracting visitors, for which the right sort of publicity and advertisement would be as vital as ever. (Meanwhile, the local Rotarians had boldly led the way back to normality by resuscitating a pre-war social function that had been in abeyance for half a decade. That same February they held their first Ladies' Night since 1939.)

The Council, to its credit, needed no prompting to prepare for a back-to-normal season. So quickly did the entertainment scene get into its stride that a returning visitor might almost have imagined that the war had been but a brief interlude and that the 1945 season was merely picking up where 1939 had left off. Already by Easter the Municipal Orchestra (now directed by Joe Cunningham, Walter Collins's pre-war deputy) was back in action at the Western Enclosure; and the summer programme at the Pavilion included a succession of well-known dance bands — starting off with a nostalgic reminder of the 1920s in the shape of the Savoy Havana Band. Any idea that Bognor had little to offer but 'tranquillity' would not have been shared by the summer crowds; and even the rather selfish fear, inhospitably voiced in some quarters, that the influx of visitors might result in residents going short of food, proved completely groundless. Nobody starved.

Chapter XXIV

PREPARATIONS FOR THE FUTURE

GREATLY ENCOURAGED by the success of what could be regarded as the first post-war season (though the war in the Far East did not end until the latter half of August), the Town Hall was brimming over with plans for enhancing Bognor's holiday attractions. Once again priority was claimed by the Western Band Enclosure, for which great improvements were envisaged after the war was over. But before anything could be done it was considered advisable to purchase the freehold of the site, which belonged to the nearby *Royal Norfolk Hotel*; so in 1944 the Council had taken the bold step of buying the hotel and its surrounding land for £28,000. Having thus achieved its purpose in respect of the Band Enclosure site, it then put the hotel up for sale again — in the teeth of bitter opposition from a body calling themselves the Municipal Electors' Association, who distributed a strictly rationed number of handbills ('Please pass this on — paper is scarce') convening what they confidently described as a Mass Meeting at the Pavilion one Monday evening in December 1945.

What ensued was rather like a rehearsal for the far more prolonged campaign which, in the decades to come, would rage over the future of the Eastern Esplanade. Indeed, if the Association had won this particular skirmish, it is quite possible that events east of the Pier might have taken a very different course. For in each case, both west and east, the battles were principally concerned with the provision of an entertainments centre. Many of the Municipal Electors had never ceased to regret the abandonment of the 1936 Winter Garden scheme in favour of what they regarded as an inadequate substitute in the form of the Band Enclosure — and now the Council was threatening to dispose of the ideal site on which to build the entertainments centre that Bognor needed if it was ever to join the ranks of the top-class resorts. Significantly the Association's precious handbills were headed 'The Royal Norfolk Hotel *Site*'. It was not the hotel but the potentiality of its site — and the danger of selling it to the wrong sort of developer — which was all-important to the conveners of the meeting: 'This central site is the keystone to the town's future. It is the property of the people of this town' — and, in words evocative of the 1914–18 War and *Keep the Home Fires Burning*, 'we demand that it be not sold until the boys who have fought for it come back and have their say . . . Never mind the dark or the rain. The boys abroad put up with more than that for you.' The challenge was irresistible, and a goodly number of Association members showed their mettle by leaving their cosy homesteads and boldly venturing forth into the December night to protest, albeit in vain, against the proposed sale.

What the boys said when, after allegedly fighting the Second World War in defence of the Royal Norfolk site, they returned home to find that the Council

244

had betrayed them by selling it while their backs were turned is, perhaps fortunately, not recorded. However, the buyer was not, as the Association had feared, a certain well-known proprietor of fun fairs and holiday camps; there was, after all, to be no take-over of the dignified Western Esplanade by the rip-roaring East. The new owners were a perfectly respectable hotel group who reopened the *Royal Norfolk* in 1948.

Meanwhile, the Council, now in possession of the freehold of the Western Band Enclosure, was going ahead with its improvement plans. The central grass area had already been tiled over in time for the 1945 season; and the next step, completed in the following year, was to provide the Enclosure with a canvas roof — though by 1946 there was no longer a Municipal Orchestra to benefit from it. Instead there were a number of well-known soloists and also a brief appearance by what was called the Bognor Regis Concert Orchestra under the direction of John Bath. One September evening if gave the 'world première' of Mr. Bath's suite *Flansham Sketches*, inspired by a series of books on life in that secluded hamlet near Felpham, and a good proportion of Flansham's handful of inhabitants turned up to listen to themselves in music.

But the Council was still not satisfied. It seemed as if they had at last realised what Bognor had lost in 1936 by the decision to abandon the scheme for an all-purpose, all-season Winter Garden in favour of an open-air enclosure; and now, in a new mood of post-war buoyancy, it was determined to do all it could to make the best of an ill-advised job. So in 1947 the stage was enlarged and the short-lived canvas roof was replaced by a more solid one of asbestos; and any relationship with the original band enclosure was finally dispelled by giving the building a new name. It was now the Esplanade Concert Hall and, as such, it was reopened in May 1947 — not with a concert but with a concert party called 'Funshine'.

As luck would have it, however, a good deal of the thunder of this piece of municipal initiative was stolen by the simultaneous completion, to the east of the Pier, of a rival scheme undertaken by private enterprise. This was the extensive refurbishment of the former Kursaal, which now emerged as the Rex Entertainment Centre, comprising a restaurant, a ballroom and the Rex Theatre. The latter, designed for light entertainment (the adjacent Theatre Royal, part of the Kursaal complex, had gone over to films), opened in May with 'Dazzle', presumably a descendant of the concert party which had graced the Pierrotland boards in 1939 — so the Esplanade Concert Hall, with 'Funshine', was faced with formidable competition from the very beginning of its career. Moreover, since the Rex retained the ornate domed façade of the original Kursaal, it presented a far more cheerful and attractive appearance than its municipal counterpart, whose plain exterior was compared in the local Press to that of a swimming bath or alternatively a large public lavatory.

*   *   *

Still, no one could have accused the Pavilion, still the Council's principal entertainment hall, of resembling either of these public utilities. It didn't even look too much like the aircraft assembly hangar that it once was, for the twin towers of the main façade — surmounted by oriental cupolas as if in emulation of that other Pavilion along the coast at Brighton — provided it with a commendably exotic disguise, especially when viewed across the flower-beds and rockeries of the surrounding gardens. The gardens, which now extended over the site once occupied by Hothamton Place (and could perhaps be considered a reasonable compensation for its demolition), held romantic memories for the Canadian and Norwegian soldiers stationed in the area, quite a number of whom met their future wives at the Pavilion dances and took them for strolls across the lawns in the intervals.

The Pavilion had served Bognor well since it was opened in 1922, but it had always been a source of controversy. In view of its origins, it was hardly likely to prove a perfect venue for all the types of entertainment it was called upon to house, though it did make a good dance hall and exhibition centre; and it had its fair share of detractors among the councillors and other residents who failed to see why they should have to continue to put up with what was, after all, a makeshift.

They did not have to put up with it for much longer. At about 3.30 in the afternoon of 14 July 1948 the Entertainments Manager, Howard Cotterell, was sitting at his desk in the Pavilion when he smelt something burning and, looking up, saw that the paint on his office wall was beginning to blister. He discovered that a fire had broken out at the base of the eastern tower and summoned the brigade. After about half an hour the whole tower collapsed in flames, watched by excited crowds who trampled mercilessly over the flower-beds and shrubberies.

The local firemen, assisted by brigades from as far away as Worthing, managed to save most of the building. Not that they encountered universal gratitude for doing so. As the flames died down, one disappointed resident was heard to remark: 'There we go again, always doing things by halves!'

In spite of its spectacular moments, the fire could hardly be described as disastrous and it was taken for granted that the damage would soon be repaired. By the end of the year the Council had approved a £76,000 reconstruction scheme under which the whole building would be encased in brick. In accordance with the dictates of a determinedly unpicturesque age, there were to be no towers; in fact, the published plan was reminiscent of the Esplanade Concert Hall on, of course, a much larger scale. The façade would, however, be relieved by a projecting first-floor restaurant with a semi-circle of windows overlooking the gardens. The Council, it appeared, had at last woken up to the importance of providing visitors with a pleasant view to accompany their morning coffee and afternoon tea.

The Chairman of the Entertainments Committee estimated that it would take at least a year for the building to be reconstructed and reopened. Actually it took a good deal less than a year for the Council to execute a complete reversal of its decision, resolving instead that the Pavilion must go. Tenders for demolition were invited in September 1949 and within a few months the vast cavernous hall, which could hold 3,000 people, was merely a memory.

The empty space where it had stood seemed enormous. What was to be done with it? There was a rush of suggestions: a swimming bath, a sports hall, Turkish baths, even a circus. The ratepayers held their breath, but the suspense was short-lived. The Council made up its mind with almost breakneck speed and by the autumn of 1950 the Pavilion had already been replaced. Occupying its site were three hard tennis courts and a little wooden chalet for the use of the players. It was perhaps the most shattering anti-climax in Bognor's history.

*   *   *

With the demolition of its two most prominent neighbours, Hothamton Place in 1935 and the Pavilion in 1949, Hotham's splendid Fitzleet House may have counted itself lucky to be still standing and still serving as a convalescent home for the needy, as it had since 1870. But in 1954, as a result of difficulties created by the inauguration of the National Health Service, the Merchant Taylors Company decided to close it and place it on the market. This news aroused considerable fears as to the possible fate of one of the finest 18th-century buildings on the South Coast and there was a vain attempt to persuade the Council to buy it for the town and put it to good use. The fears proved fully justified when, in February 1955, it was announced that the house with its extensive and beautiful grounds had been acquired for development by Mr. H. H. Murray, a London surveyor who lived at Pagham; and by the end of August Fitzleet House was already a ruin.

The chapel which the Merchant Taylors had erected in the grounds of the convalescent home survived the house itself for a few years until its own turn came in 1959. However it was not without honour in the manner of its going, as the hammer which struck the first blow on its Victorian stonework was wielded by no less a dignitary than the Chairman of the Urban District Council, Mr. Frank Phillips.

> 'What Mr. Murray has in mind for the future of these five acres in the heart of the town,' wrote the *Observer* after Fitzleet House had gone, 'we do not know. Whether he will prove himself a worthy successor to Sir Richard Hotham remains to be seen. However that may be, nothing can give us back the historical value to the town that the Merchant Taylors so zealously guarded during their long tenure of Fitzleet. And those of us who are jealous of the little history Bognor can boast are sad at heart.'

The shock at seeing Fitzleet House reduced to rubble was all the more acute because it had been a 'listed' building and had therefore been considered safe from demolition. But since neither the Council nor its new owner was prepared to shoulder the burden of its upkeep, it lost the protection of the law. This opened up an alarming prospect for the surviving treasures of Hotham's architectural legacy — and the *Post*, with an almost perceptible shiver of anticipation as to what the future might bring, asked the question that was forming in many people's minds: '*How safe are the Dome and Hotham House?*' (Aldwick Manor, the former Chapel House, had been renamed Hotham Park House.)

Once the Fitzleet site, its beautiful trees and all, was cleared, the Council moved into action with a proposal to purchase a considerable area of it — for the provision of nothing more exciting than yet another car park. The landlord of the neighbouring *Bedford Hotel* countered this idea with the hope that this key site might be used to provide the town with the amenity that had eluded it for decades. 'What good would a car park do for Bognor Regis?' he asked. 'The position is ideally suited for a Winter Garden, complete with concert hall, dance floor and other facilities. Bognor would then become an all-the-year-round resort.'

How often had those selfsame sentiments been voiced in the past and how often they would be repeated in the future!

Needless to say, no Winter Garden arose from the ruins of Fitzleet. Instead, Bognor was given its first taste of high-rise living in the stark shape of a 15-storey block of flats which appropriated the name of the mansion it had replaced. When the Duke of Richmond unveiled its marble 'foundation stone' in June 1960, he confidently predicted that he would have a clear view of the completed building from as far away as his own home, Goodwood House. There was ample space, too, for a new shopping street, Queensway, linking High Street with Crescent Road; and, of course, the Council also got its car park. One might well ask why the Council took no action to build a new entertainment centre to replace the Pavilion either on its old site or on that of Fitzleet — and, for that matter, why it had so suddenly reversed its decision to repair the Pavilion after the fire and voted instead for demolition.

What made the Council change its mind? The official reason was that there was no hope, for the time being, of the Government sanctioning a loan for the reconstruction scheme. But since this objection was presumably no less valid when the scheme was temporarily approved, it looks like a simple case of second thoughts. It seems fairly clear that the Council's heart was not in the Pavilion nor even in its site. It was the sea front that was beginning to dominate the Town Hall's view of Bognor's future and it was there, not in the Pavilion Gardens, that the municipal planners envisaged their principal showplace. So the Pavilion had to go. Why pour money into refurbishing the much-derided 'makeshift' when one day Bognor might possess the entertainments centre of the Council's dreams? — the gleaming purpose-built eldorado by the sea that would at last place the town firmly in the top league of Britain's resorts. And to think that this dream palace might already have been a reality if the chance had not been thrown away before the war. Quite a few councillors must have found their thoughts harking back wistfully to the defeat of the Winter Garden scheme in the mid-1930s.

Well, the chance might come again.

*　　　*　　　*

'I am very surprised to see the lot gone,' was the regretful comment of one of Bognor's visitors in the summer of 1947, duly quoted in the *Post*. His surprise and regret were understandable, for 'the lot' was none other than Colebrook Terrace, originally the New Crescent designed by Samuel Beazley in 1826.

Comprising a shallow crescent of four separate houses, or rather mansions, it formed the most important example of pre-Victorian architecture on the sea front. Its visual effect was enhanced rather than otherwise when in 1910 the multi-domed Kursaal arose immediately to the west — but while the latter was being restored and embellished for its new lease of life as the Rex, a very different fate was befalling its much older neighbour. For Colebrook Terrace had suffered the misfortune of being bought by the Urban District Council (the price was £48,000), and nobody needed the aid of second sight to predict that its days were thereby numbered. It was not the Terrace that the Council wanted but its site.

In December 1946 the Highways Committee recommended demolition and the laying out of the area with putting-greens, reinforced by other attractions such as sun parlours and deck-chairs. This struck some of the councillors as a waste of a prime site: could it not be put to better use by building a hotel or hydropathic establishment? (Or even a Winter Garden!) In reply, it was pointed out that in 1945 as many as 7,000 people had used the putting-greens at the western end of the promenade and that the advocates of the scheme had specially borne in mind the disappointment of the numerous visitors who had been crowded off the greens.

At this touching appeal to sentiment, the opposition seems to have crumbled and the Council formally approved the demolition of Beazley's four stately mansions. No time was lost (a precedent which, as we have seen, was followed three years later with the Pavilion) and by the early summer of 1947 'the lot' had gone. But by then the sad plight of the frustrated putters seems to have been forgotten. No putting greens were laid out on the levelled site, no sun parlours were erected and even the promised deckchairs were conspicuous by their absence. In any case, it had never been intended that these delights were to be other than temporary. The putting-green and so on were to be merely stop-gaps until such time as the Council's visions of the future could be realised.

If asked what exactly those visions were, what form they took, it is doubtful whether any member of the Council could have given a specific answer. It was still too early for that, but in 1947 everyone knew that, with the acquisition and clearing of this strategic Esplanade site, the first step had been taken along the road to a new Bognor in which outdated relics such as Colebrook Terrace, the Pavilion and the like would have no place. Colebrook Terrace had gone, the Pavilion would be gone before long, other links with the past would follow. But before the town could grasp the glittering prize that lay ahead — a redeveloped sea front which would be the wonder and envy of every other resort in the kingdom — there was still a serious obstacle to be overcome.

Once again that fateful piece of land known to an earlier generation as the Cabbage Patch was moving back into the centre of the stage; and still on it, still apparently holding the key to Bognor's future, stood the cheerful, irrepressible and inescapable figure of Billy Butlin.

Chapter XXV

BUTLIN REGIS

AT THE BEGINNING of the 1950s the Rex — which, with the disappearance of the Pavilion, had some claim to be regarded as Bognor's principal place of entertainment, at any rate potentially — presented a strangely isolated appearance. Both to the east, where Colebrook Terrace had stood, and to the west, where long ago it had been intended to build Cotswold Crescent, stretched wide expanses of undeveloped land, so that, seen from the beach, the Rex looked almost as lonely as if it were situated somewhere on the outskirts of the town. Yet it stood right in the centre of the sea front of a popular holiday resort.

Visitors strolling along the Esplanade must have wondered however much longer those two surprising gaps on either side of the Rex would be allowed to mar the attractiveness of Bognor's 'shopwindow' — particularly the western site which, with its rash of fun-fair amusements, had become the biggest eyesore on the sea front. Why didn't the Council get moving with some sort of comprehensive plan for this seedy section of the Esplanade? To be fair to the Council, it was only too anxious to get moving, but for the time being its hands and feet were tied. Though it owned the Colebrook site, the fairground belonged to someone else — that most immovable of obstacles, Mr. Butlin.

It is very probable that Butlin did not regard himself quite in that light. Indeed he could have argued with some justice that, far from standing in the way of the Council's still nebulous redevelopment scheme, he was its main inspiration. It was a case of one thing leading to another. For having determined, way back in the 1930s, that eventually Butlin must somehow be persuaded to remove the noisy and unsightly 'amusements' which were lowering the tone of the Eastern Esplanade, the Town Hall then had to accept the fact that, if Butlin did go, the empty spaces he left behind him would be almost as detrimental to the town's prestige as the fun fairs themselves. What could be done with them? It was while the planners were pondering this future problem during the war years that the seed of an ambitious idea implanted itself in their minds — a far-reaching scheme which, going far beyond the mere piecemeal patching-up of the Butlin sites, envisaged nothing less than the complete transformation of the sea front east of the Pier. But, as Butlin could have pointed out, had it not been for the spur provided by necessity of getting rid of the fun fairs, it is doubtful whether the scheme would ever have been born.

It was to this great idea that, with the return of peace, Colebrook Terrace and (indirectly, as we have seen) the Pavilion were duly sacrificed; but it still seemed likely that years would pass before the wondrous scheme for the Bognor of the future reached the drawing-board. For the planners could not get to work on it until the ground had been prepared by moving Mr. Butlin.

The Council had hoped to do this by the simple process of buying him out, but the Cabbage Patch was to prove a far tougher proposition than the Colebrook site. The snag was that not only was Butlin in possession but he had no intention of selling up and leaving Bognor, for which he had developed a lasting affection. The Council, though, had a valuable ace up its sleeve. In 1946, by what in hindsight seems to have been a remarkable piece of foresight, it had purchased the 39 acres of low-lying Brookland which separated Bognor from Felpham — though the extension of the promenade eastward to Felpham in the 1930s now provided a convenient pedestrian link between the two neighbours. In fact, the purchase of the Brookland can be seen as a natural corollary of the extension, for the new promenade had opened up the possibility of developing this hitherto virgin territory. Virgin, that is to say, apart from a wooden hut on stilts which was erected during a smallpox scare in the 1890s to serve as an isolation hospital. The scare died down before any patients were admitted, but in 1913 the Colebrook House School (which occupied one of the houses in Colebrook Terrace) took over part of the Brookland as a playing-field and used the hut, for a brief pre-war period, as a sports pavilion.

However, once the Council had finally set its sights on an overall rebuilding of the Eastern Esplanade, the development potential of the Brookland became, as it were, surplus to its needs. Instead of providing building land for houses, those 39 acres could be called upon to play a vital rôle in the long drawn-out negotiations with Billy Butlin. They could be used as bait.

It is important to emphasise that there was no wish on the part of Bognor's rulers for Butlin to leave the town; they merely wanted him to leave the Esplanade. And if his fun fairs were considered out of place on the Esplanade, that did not necessarily mean that they would be unacceptable elsewhere — on the Brookland, for example. So when the Town Hall had to concede defeat in its attempt at direct purchase of the Butlin sites, it decided to try its hand at horse-trading. There was even an idea of the Council setting up its own amusement park on the Brookland and then offering it on lease to Butlin in exchange for his Esplanade sites. Understandably, this suggestion made no appeal to a man who was acknowledged as the leading expert in his field and was not in the habit of leasing other people's fun fairs. Besides, his ambitions were spurring him on to bigger things — bigger and better by far than fun fairs or amusement parks.

Nevertheless, the Council was 'getting warm'. Playing the Brookland card had put it on the right track; and on 24 September 1958 it was announced to a slightly incredulous Bognor that a deal had at last been concluded with Billy Butlin. The ratepayers were not, after all, to be called upon to buy the Esplanade sites; instead, Mr. Butlin had agreed to *give* them to the town. In return, he was to take a 99-year lease of the Brookland for the purpose of running not a fun fair but a big-scale holiday camp. He would, of course, pay rent for the site and, in addition, there would be an annual rates bill estimated at £12,000.

Both parties could congratulate themselves on the deal. The Council had not only cleared the way for the redevelopment of the Eastern Esplanade without the necessity of purchase but in doing so had acquired a useful source of income. As for Butlin, he had achieved his ambition of building a prestigious holiday camp in his beloved Bognor Regis and he was overjoyed: 'I intend to make this camp the best thing I have ever done.'

There was only one dissentient voice in the Council, that of Mr. Norman Lewis who pointed out, with absolute truth, that what was being proposed was concerned 'not only with today or tomorrow, but with generations yet to come'. He went on: 'The town is going to be associated with Butlin holiday camps and members of the Council should reflect before approving a plan that will cast a stigma on Bognor Regis. We have heard about the wonderful money we are going to make, but what good is this money if we are going to drive off the people who come to settle in the town and the long-period visitor?' It was like an echo for the battle for the 'right type of visitor' of nearly 30 years earlier. 'Is it money we should be after,' demanded Councillor Lewis, 'or a town to live in? – not a town for which one has to apologise and about which people will say: Bognor, let me see, Bognor is where Butlin's is!'

He must have felt his fears confirmed when the *Evening Argus* came out with a headline: 'What People Think of Butlin Regis'. One of the people interviewed was a Felpham resident who was haunted by a ghastly vision of 'hundreds of people walking about with fish-and-chips'. There was also a nostalgic article in the *Post* about the birdlife of the Brookland which was soon to disappear. Yet, on the whole, there is little doubt that the Council's vote (17–1 in favour of the deal) was a fair reflection of public opinion; and, since the fun fairs could not be removed until the holiday camp was built, public opinion was getting a little restive when in the early months of 1959 there were still no signs of a start on building operations. Meanwhile, the birds of the Brookland were enjoying the bonus of another undisturbed springtime.

The cause of the delay was a final little flurry over the rife or stream which wandered through the low-lying site. Before work could begin on the camp it would be necessary to erect a concrete raft over the rife and to provide an adequate drainage system. When the Council requested Butlin to meet the cost of this work, he promptly replied with an ultimatum. Unless the Council agreed by 15 September to pay the bill, he would pull out of the deal. Seeing its cherished Esplanade redevelopment plan suddenly slipping from its grasp, the Town Hall had no option but to surrender and pay up; and, having won his point, Butlin wasted no further time. To the accompaniment of sighs of relief from the Esplanade planners, work started on the Brookland site in October with a view to completion the following summer.

Butlin and his wife rented a flat in Bognor for the winter of 1959–60 so that he could personally supervise the work; and Norah Butlin, speaking at a local Conservative dinner, told her appreciative listeners that 'this is the first time my husband has had a chance to build a camp in the way he wants it.' That, however, did not soothe the fears of the residents of Felpham, as they watched the vast holiday complex rising on their doorstep — the 39-acre doorstep which had hitherto preserved them from the fish-and-chips and candy floss of Bognor. Three of them, led by a retired major, took space in the local papers to launch a campaign against the unwelcome intruder, providing a form to be filled in by objectors. 'Butlin's,' ran the advertisement, 'have agreed to remove their unsightly fun fairs from the middle of the promenade if they can create a sprawling camp half a mile to the east. What will the buildings look like in 20 years' time? Why should the Council give way to this form of bargaining?' (Clearly the whispers about the tie-up between the building of the camp and the redevelopment of the Esplanade — a tie-up which the Council itself had devised — had not yet percolated to Felpham.)

The Felpham campaign was hardly likely to succeed, now that work on the camp had already started; but a Mr. Fraser, in a letter to the *Post*, rose up to praise Butlin's concern for the architectural qualities of his latest creation: 'I am sure that if Sir Christopher Wren had been available, Billy Butlin would have hired him to draw up the plans of his new holiday camp.'

To which Felpham's Major Linton, his fighting spirit apparently unimpaired by his retirement, replied: 'I think that Mr. Fraser is wrong in imagining that Sir Christopher Wren would have allowed himself to be "hired" by Mr. Butlin. Both aesthetically and architecturally there is a great deal of difference between Butlin's holiday camp and St Paul's Cathedral.'

Butlin had always thrived on opposition, confident of his powers to dispel it. In February 1960, by which time 500 bookings per day were being received from holidaymakers ambitious to sample the new camp in its first season, he addressed a meeting of ratepayers at the Rex and proceeded to charm their cares away. As the Council itself had long ago discovered, it was hard to maintain a firm line with such a friendly and likeable man; and when he disarmingly told the meeting that he had come prepared to collect a few sticks and stones from objectors, he had the ratepayers completely on his side and roaring with laughter at his sallies. It was a notable personal triumph and he clinched it with the promise that, for a nominal charge, residents would be able to use the swimming-pool, theatre and other camp facilities during the off-season.

Admittedly a few eyebrows were raised in March when a full-page Butlin advertisement in the London *Evening Standard* used the word 'resort' instead of holiday camp; it sounded rather as if the camp was intended to be a rival resort to Bognor itself. And a reference in the *Argus* to the forthcoming opening as 'B-Day, the day on which Bognor Regis becomes Butlin Regis' seemed to carry a threat that Butlin's was not merely going to rival Bognor but take it over.

B-Day was 2 July 1960 — barely nine months after operations had begun on the site. Workmen were still applying the finishing touches when the camp opened its doors (rather surprisingly without any official ceremony) to the 3,000 visitors who had booked for the first historic week; and frantic efforts were going on to clear up the effects of a minor disaster in the shape of a burst water pipe the previous night. Some of the new arrivals, finding their chalets dirty and surrounded by mud, decided to leave for other Butlin camps ('I'm off to Clacton!'

declared one exasperated but still loyal camper); but the stouthearts who braved the mud were consoled in typical Butlin fashion — free champagne on the house.

The promenade between Bognor and Felpham was crowded with sightseers who came to feast their eyes on what was undoubtedly the finest holiday camp in Britain and by far the largest building in the town. Though, as Major Linton had prophesied, it bore little resemblance to St Paul's Cathedral, it was neither so unsightly nor so garish as some had feared. With its fluttering flags, its panoramic windows, lawns and flower-beds, it exuded an air of cheerfulness rather than the anticipated raucousness; and its lavish array of amenities — especially the indoor swimming pool, one side of which was of glass and thus provided the adjacent ballroom with a transparent wall and a view of underwater swimmers — was soon being prominently featured in the national newspapers and magazines. Once again Mr. Butlin had garnered a rich harvest of publicity; and whether it would be the camp or the town itself that would reap the main benefit was really beside the point, for in most people's minds Bognor and Butlin's had become interchangeable terms . . . 'Bognor is where Butlin's is.'

Yet only a few hundred yards to the west of the vast holiday camp, gazing at it over the trees like the forlorn ghost of a forgotten past, rose the clock tower of Aldwick Manor, the Chapel House. It was in this house, now in a state of decay after being commandeered for military purposes during the war, that Sir Richard Hotham had planned a future for Bognor very different from the one that had suddenly materialised outside his front gates — but who in 1960 had time to spare a thought for Bognor's founder? Who remembered that the town now popularly rechristened Butlin Regis had once, for a brief spell, borne the name of Hothamton?

In that triumphant summer of 1960, Bognor had become Butlin's town just as long ago it had been Hotham's; and soon Butlin himself, like the man whose mantle he appeared to have assumed, would be a knight. In 1964 he became Sir William — thanks mainly, as everyone in the town was convinced, to his crowning achievement at Bognor.

Characteristically, he far preferred to be known as Sir Billy.

Fig. 22.   1975, Butlinland Bognor.

Chapter XXVI

A NEW BOGNOR?

BUTLIN WAS TRUE to his word. After the summer campers had departed (there had been 30,000 of them — a figure which would rise in 15 years to 125,000), the local residents were invited to enjoy all that the camp had to offer, as members of what was called the Bognor Regis Winter Social Club (president: Billy Butlin). Considering the lavishness of the facilities made available by the low-priced subscription, it is not surprising that by the end of the year the Club had attracted as many as 12,000 members. For a mere two guineas they had the freedom of what was probably the best-equipped sports-and-entertainments complex on the South Coast — and Butlin, moreover, was paying a sizable rent to the town for the privilege of providing it.

But to the Council, though it was duly appreciative of all these benefits, the Butlin camp was, as we have seen, primarily a means to an end: the means of realising the long-cherished dream of a grand new Esplanade, free of fun fairs and full of impressive buildings. The chief visionary was Councillor James Earle, Chairman of the Special Purposes Committee, who had voiced his hopes publicly for the first time when the deal with Butlin came up for approval in September 1958:

> 'Tall modern buildings in the style of Basil Spence, Corbusier or the many other gifted architects practising today are what I hope to see . . . We must not tolerate drab brick boxes. This is our chance to have beautiful architecture reflecting our own day and age, and we must seize it with both hands. Fine hotels, luxury flats, a solarium, shops, theatres, conference halls and civic buildings can and should arise, fronted by a broad impressive seaway . . . .'

In the face of this alluring prospect, approval of the resolution was a foregone conclusion; and so the Council was assured of the possession of the fun fair sites and the additional Butlin property on the east side of Waterloo Square. There were still, of course, other properties to be acquired if the Esplanade redevelopment was to be truly comprehensive; and in the autumn of the following year a headline in the *Observer* announced: 'First Steps in the Development of the New Bognor'. These historic first steps were the acquisition of the two adjacent Edwardian hotels, the *Beaulieu* and the *Beaulieu Downs* immediately to the east of the *Carlton Hotel*, and the inviting of tenders for the demolition of the Garden Café, one of the small buildings on the main Butlin site. The journey into the future had begun at last!

That was in October 1959, the selfsame month in which the Esplanade scheme was given its go-ahead by the start of construction work on the camp. Thus, on the eve of the 1960s, all was set for a scene change neatly coinciding with the change of decade. Just as the main theme of the 1950s had been the tug-of-war with Butlin, so the 1960s were to be dominated throughout by the Sea Front Redevelopment Scheme. And that, too, was to take on the character of a tug-of-war, in which the Council would find itself pitted against a challenger even weightier than Billy Butlin: a combination of the considerable local opposition to the scheme, especially among the older residents, and the fluctuating economic condition of the country.

For the time being, however, the Council was in command, and in April 1960 – as if to mark the start of the decade which, it was fondly believed, would bring to reality the dream of a new sea front – the plans for the Esplanade were placed on public exhibition. James Earle had already given an inkling of what the planners had in mind, but this was the first time that the ratepayers had been presented with specific details. They were amazed at the heights to which the Council's ambitions had soared. The whole area between the Pier and Clarence Road was to be transformed by 18-storey blocks of flats, a towering 960-room hotel, a civic centre (to replace the Town Hall), a theatre (to replace the Rex and Theatre Royal), a conference centre, a multi-storey car park, a traffic-free Esplanade – and not a fun fair in sight. The *Observer* had called it 'the New Bognor', but to many flabbergasted residents it didn't seem to be Bognor at all.

Councillor Earle, taking a leaf out of Butlin's book, addressed a public meeting at which he gave his enthusiasm full rein. It was certain, he said, that the rates income from the redevelopment 'will put the town in a position where we can be a really outstanding resort. We are creating a town that will make other places boggle at us.'

Waxing eloquent on the proposed exclusion of traffic from the sea front east of the Pier, he emphasised that it was absolutely essential that this part of the Esplanade should be reserved for pedestrians, 'for Bognor Regis is to become a town of such beauty that men, women and children walking along the Esplanade will be glad of the opportunity to stop and admire the buildings without fear of traffic.'

Possibly some of Mr. Earle's listeners may have found it rather hard to swallow the idea of family parties forsaking the sands in order to stand and gaze in undisturbed delight at the new blocks of flats; but, on the whole, comment on the proposals was favourable. The prospect of those cloud-capped towers rising on the Esplanade, perhaps within the next two or three years, was an exciting one – and, even if they didn't happen to be designed by Corbusier or Spence, they would be a vast improvement on Mr. Butlin's amusement parlours.

Unfortunately for Mr. Earle, his triumph was short-lived, for in the very next month after the plans were exhibited the Council elections were held and he lost his seat. What made the blow all the harder to take was that he was ousted by a lady, Mrs. Freda Moore, who did not attach quite the same importance to Esplanade Redevelopment. Top of Mrs. Moore's priority list was a new maternity hospital.

Deprived of the eloquent advocacy of its chief enthusiast, the Redevelopment Scheme seemed quickly to lose its initial thrust. The summers of 1961 and 1962 went by without any sign of progress – and, in spite of the much-trumpeted *quid pro quo* with Billy Butlin, his fun fairs were still blithely occupying their valuable sites on the Esplanade. With his holiday camp in full swing (and cornering most of the town's publicity), Mr. Butlin seemed to have done very well out of the deal. With his usual aplomb, he was enjoying the best of both worlds.

'What has happened?' demanded a *Post* leader in October 1962. 'The holiday camp is completed, yet the fun fairs remain — still in the hands of Mr. Butlin . . . The position should be clarified at the earliest possible moment.' If the Council had not maintained such secrecy about its negotiations there would have been no need for the *Post* to seek clarification, for there was a perfectly simple answer to its query. The agreement with Butlin had stated that the hand-over of his Esplanade sites would take place 'three full seasons' after the completion of the holiday camp, so that he was entitled to remain in possession until after the summer of 1963. However, possibly influenced by the growing impatience of public opinion as evidenced by the *Post* leader, the date was suddenly brought forward to November 1962.

So the seemingly interminable battle of the Cabbage Patch (and the other Butlin sites) was over and at long last the Council could claim them as its own. But anyone who imagined that the fun fairs would be swept away overnight to make way for the developers was quickly disillusioned. For it was revealed that, though the Council now possessed the sites, there was an agreement that Butlin could continue to rent them on a year-to-year basis, subject to six months' notice on either side. This made it only too clear that there was no question of an immediate start on Redevelopment and that other resorts wouldn't be boggling at Bognor for quite a while yet.

The *Post* expressed its frustration with a terse headline: 'Jam Tomorrow'. This was meant to sound pessimistic, but it veered heavily on the side of optimism. If the *Post* had only known it, there would be no jam until well into the next decade; and when it finally arrived it would be of a very different flavour from that envisaged in the early 1960s.

One of the reasons for the hold-up was the proposal in the 1960 plan to exclude traffic from the Esplanade — for where else would it go? However, with James Earle re-elected to the Council and back in charge of the Redevelopment Committee, that little difficulty was quickly disposed of — by the simple process of bringing out a new plan, passed by the Council in October 1963 and vastly different from the one it had approved three years earlier. Under this latest of the long series of plans which punctuated Bognor's progress through the 1960s (and perhaps helped to veil the fact that very little actual progress was being made), traffic would be allowed on the Esplanade but there would be pedestrian bridges spanning the roadway to a raised promenade 20 feet above the beach. So it would still be possible to gaze in contemplation at the architectural wonders of the New Bognor without disturbance from passing cars. A series of escalators would provide access to the sands — and Bognor, it was proudly claimed, would be ' the only resort in the country, almost certainly in Europe, with a decked sea front'.

The Ocean Liner Look, as it was called, was not only the most ambitious scheme so far produced but also the most expensive. What chance had the raised promenade of ever getting off the ground? Chatting informally with journalists in January 1965, the Clerk to the Council, Mr. Paul Smith, said he thought there would be a considerable delay before the start of building operations — a remark which, when duly reported in a local television programme, landed him in hot water with some members of the Council. One councillor, who described himself as shattered by the Clerk's comments, denounced them as 'utter rubbish'. There was, he said, no question of the development being postponed.

Perhaps he spoke too soon, for two months later an event occurred which appeared completely to justify Mr. Smith's assessment of the situation. This was the sudden start of work on the *Beaulieu* and *Beaulieu Downs Hotels* which, it will be remembered, had been purchased by the Council in 1959 for demolition and site clearance. But the workmen had not moved in on these two Edwardian neighbours in order to demolish them as a necessary prelude to redevelopment; on the contrary, the buildings were about to be refurbished! They were to be given a new lease of life as a single hotel, the *Caribbean*, designed for teenage holidaymakers. And meanwhile the Butlin fun fairs were carrying on undisturbed. Once again, mystified residents were asking what exactly the Council was up to.

The Council was, in fact, behaving quite sensibly. Even though it had officially approved the 'Ocean Liner Look', many time-consuming stages would have to be passed through before the contract for a scheme of this magnitude could be signed with the developers. Pending that happy event, by leasing out its Esplanade properties (which also included the Rex and the Theatre Royal, purchased in 1960 for £65,000) the town would be assured of a useful source of income until such time as building operations could begin. But by adopting this sound financial policy the Council had played right into the hands of the anti-development lobby. For the start of conversion work on the *Caribbean Hotel* was the surest indication yet that it would be years rather than months before operations could begin on the new Esplanade. This was a sheer gift to the opponents of the scheme, who were now assured of ample time in which to muster their arguments and prepare for attack.

The attack came in the following year, 1966, which could be said to mark the watershed between the mounting enthusiasm of the early 1960s and the sober second thoughts which pervaded the latter half of the decade. It was the year when even keen supporters of the Redevelopment Scheme began publicly to question the wisdom of the Council's ambitions.

'Is the Sea Front Development Really Necessary?' ran one of the headlines in March. It was a sure sign of the changing times. No headline would have dared to raise such a wet blanket of a query in the early 1960s, but the long delays — and, more important, the continuing lack of information as to the progress or otherwise of the great plan — had taken the initial enthusiasm off the boil. What produced the headline was the report of a study group appointed by the Ratepayers' Association: 'We have been shown suggested solutions for building developments on an immense scale, running into millions of pounds, for some imaginary need that remains unexplained'.

A few weeks later the local Hotel and Restaurants Association, equally incensed by the veil of official secrecy, entered the fray with a letter from its Chairman to the Council which seemed to strike the nail firmly on its head: 'It may be that the magnitude of the project is the chief reason for the hold-up'. The Chairman therefore 'respectfully submitted' a smaller and less costly scheme under which the Town Hall — whose replacement by a grandiose civic centre had been regarded by the Council as 'crucial' to the redevelopment — would be retained. The longed-for Winter Garden would at last materialise on the Colebrook site, and the promenade, though losing its extravagant 'Ocean Liner' upper deck, would in compensation be paved with multi-coloured flagstones — which, so the hoteliers maintained, 'would have a favourable psychological effect on visitors walking along the Esplanade'. (They would presumably have the reverse effect on the ratepayers who had to pay for them.)

Finally, as an adventurous concession to those still set on giving rival resorts something to boggle at, there would be a monorail passenger service all the way along the sea front from Gloucester Road to Marine Park Gardens. Not even Councillor Earle had aspired to anything like this, and it made his proposed escalators seem small beer in comparison.

Undaunted — or spurred on — by the existence of a rival scheme, the Council went ahead with the preparation for what was threatening to become an annual event, the public exhibition of its latest Esplanade plan. This one, unveiled in January 1967, turned out to be on a more human scale than its predecessors. Though the promenade was still up in the air, complete with escalators, the towering skyscrapers of yesteryear had disappeared and the Council had reluctantly given up its dream of a new Town Hall in deference to likely objections from the Government. Still, the Rex and the Theatre Royal were to be replaced by a conference centre and the *Carlton* and *Caribbean* hotels by an enormous S-shaped motel. There would be the inevitable flats and multi-storey car park — and also, rather daringly, a casino on an ex-Butlin site just to the east of Waterloo Square. Of course, it was possible that the Government would raise disapproving eyebrows at anything so inessential as a casino — in which case, suggested the *Post*, 'we could do with a shelter there instead'.

Neither a casino nor even a shelter, however, appeared in the Council's next plan, exhibited in April 1968. By then the *Caribbean* had been demolished, after its brief three-year career among the teenagers, and — wonder of wonders — the Butlin fun fairs had been removed from the Esplanade, 10 years after the original deal with the Council. So it looked as if things were at last on the move, though it was obvious from the new proposals that, after the futuristic visions of the early years of the decade, inflation had finally caught up with the planners. A moderate-sized hotel replaced the vast serpentine motel of 1967 and the conference centre gave way to what was termed a multi-purpose leisure complex. The net result was that redevelopment was now far more of a practical proposition than ever before. 'The Scheme WILL Start', ran a confident headline in July 1969; but it was not until early 1970 that the Development Committee expressed a fairly sanguine hope that by the end of that year a start would be made on Phase I of the scheme. This comprised nothing more exciting than three blocks of flats and a multi-storey car park on the Colebrook site.

Flats and a car park indeed! The Ratepayers' Association, beside itself with indignation, issued a heartfelt protest:

> 'Bognor seriously lacks leisure amenities and therefore we could not accept the proposed building of a multi-storey car park and blocks of flats as a first priority ... We are told that, after 35 years, the Council are about to put Bognor Regis on the map. What with? A car park swept by winter gales, plus some flats. They must be joking.'

*   *   *

The ratepayers, of course, were still hankering after that elusive will o' the wisp, an all-seasons Winter Garden or whatever it might be called in the 1970s. They were acutely aware that the only municipally-run place of entertainment on the sea front was the Esplanade Theatre (as it had been renamed), a makeshift conversion from the original Western Band Enclosure; and their frustration at the Council's wrong-headed sense of priorities was intensified by the sad state of the town's most prominent holiday attraction, the Pier.

In 1965 the Pier was exactly one hundred years old and was feeling its age. The lessees resolved that the most appropriate way of celebrating the centenary would be to raise money from the public for some much-needed restorative work; but the forces of nature decreed their own way of marking the anniversary. On a stormy Wednesday night in March, a terrific gale and tumultuous waves combined to sweep away the pretty little sea-end pavilion which was a popular venue for children's entertainments. Discovered among the debris washed ashore next morning was a large collection box bearing the words 'Please help the Pier'.

A whole array of collection boxes would not have made much of a dent in the amount required for repairs, though the whole structure might have collapsed if the sea end had not been severed from the main deck the previous autumn — a wise precaution now proved to have been fully justified. The Pier had to be closed, but a brave face was put on the situation by Mrs. E. W. Panton, Managing Director of the Bognor Pier Company — whose 81-year-old Entertainments Manager, Mr. Claude Flude, had retired the previous autumn after having held office since the Company took over control of the Pier in 1909. Mrs. Panton declared: 'It is going to be quite a job ... but we are as anxious as anyone to restore the Pier to its full length as soon as practicable'. The *Post*, doubtless with its eyes on the current architectural plans for the Esplanade, expressed the hope that the new sea-end Pavilion 'will not have the uncomely shape of much of to-day's design'.

Unfortunately, difficulties arose over the insurance cover; and at the end of 1966 Mrs. Panton's company sold the lease to another concern, the British American Novelty Pier Company, who quickly asked the Council to make a substantial contribution to the cost of repairs. With the Council up to its neck in the financial morass of Esplanade Redevelopment, it was perhaps not the most propitious moment for such a request.

In September 1969 the *West Sussex Gazette*, under the headline 'Bognor Pier to be Scuttled', came out with an alarming story announcing that the Pier was to be demolished: 'All that will remain is the stump of the landward end which holds the former theatre and other buildings'. (The Pier Theatre, like the Theatre Royal, had long since gone over to films.) Apparently the Council, though anxious to help the Pier, had ruled that the town could not afford the necessary financial assistance and the new lessees had therefore decided to pull out.

'A seaside town without a pier is daft,' snorted one councillor, presumably an opponent of the Esplanade scheme. And one of his colleagues, on seeing the *Gazette* report, remarked sadly: 'I thought I was reading the obituary of an old friend.' (But the Pier was not dead yet. In 1976 it was taken over by a local family firm, the Harrisons, who in the early 1980s would embark on the task of gradually repairing the main deck.)

Seen against this background of the threatened loss of one of Bognor's best-loved assets, the vehemence of the protest by the Ratepayers' Association at the Council's policy is understandable. Though the Town Hall maintained that it had no funds to help save the Pier, it was prepared to sink vast sums into the new Esplanade and to give priority to the erection of flats and car parks which — compared with a rejuvenated Pier — would do little to enhance Bognor's appeal as a holiday resort.

In the event, the Council's hope that work would start on the Colebrook site by the end of 1970 was not realised. The change of decade brought no change to the static Esplanade scene, and the only apparent activity was in the planners' office where they were, as usual, busily preparing yet another revised scheme. This one took quite a time to produce and it was not until January 1973 that the plans were exhibited at the Town Hall. The members of the Ratepayers' Association then had the pleasant surprise of discovering that the protest they had made to the Council in 1969 had not, after all, fallen on deaf ears. Instead of priority being given to blocks of flats, Phase I of the new scheme consisted of the entertainments complex they had been hoping for. This was to be built on the site of the Rex and the Theatre Royal.

On 28 March 1974 the historic event for which the town had been waiting for so long at last took place: the Council actually signed a contract with the developers. This was practically the last thing it did. For only four days later the Urban District Council, which had governed the town since 1894, ceased to exist.

Fig. 23. Bognor's Pier Pavilion, pre-1965.

Chapter XXVII

REDEVELOPMENT – THE FINAL OUTCOME

URBAN DISTRICT COUNCILS had no place in the Government's reorganisation of local administration, which came into force in 1974 on what struck some disapproving citizens as an appropriate date: 1 April. On that day the municipalities of Bognor Regis, Littlehampton and Arundel were merged to form the Arun District Council, whose headquarters were to be at Littlehampton. This had the effect of reducing Bognor's Town Hall to the status of a branch office, though its dignified oak-panelled Council Chamber would still be used for meetings of the new authority in rotation with the civic headquarters of the other two towns in the District. So it was just as well that the much larger and grander Town Hall, which the planners had regarded as a 'crucial' feature of the Redevelopment Scheme, had never got further than the drawing-board.

The expiring Bognor Council, which held its final meeting on 24 March, could at any rate congratulate itself that its 80-year career was ending on a note of triumph, with the long-awaited signing of the contract for the first stage of the Esplanade scheme – though one cannot help feeling that the sherry party with which the councillors celebrated this culminating achievement must have taken on something of the character of a funeral wake. Moreover there were doubts as to whether the new local authority could be relied upon to devote quite the same effort and enthusiasm to Bognor's Esplanade as the Council it had supplanted. There might be equally pressing matters in Littlehampton or Arundel requiring its attention.

There was also a fleeting financial worry. In 1963 the Bognor Council had purchased 200 acres of agricultural land to the north of Middleton, known as the Flansham estate, as a 'reservoir' to be sold off eventually for residential development. The proceeds of this sound piece of investment were to be earmarked as cash in hand for the Esplanade scheme; and such was the increase in the value of the land that by 1974 the property had produced well over a million pounds. But what would happen to this nest-egg now that it had been inherited by the Arun District Council? The new authority might well decide to scrap the plans for the Esplanade and use the money for some other purpose in its area – for example, though heaven forbid, a rival sea front improvement at Littlehampton!

Such fears quickly proved groundless, for the Arun Council proved itself to be, if anything, even more eager than its predecessor to get the Esplanade scheme moving. A cynic might have observed that the eagerness was due to the fact that the first item on the schedule – site clearance for the projected entertainments centre – involved the destruction of two of Bognor's most distinguished architectural survivals from the early years of the century, the Rex and the

adjacent Theatre Royal. However that may be, the demolition of the Rex –
whose clustered domes and balconied façade had lent an air of Edwardian gaiety
to the sea front for nearly 65 years – began in May 1975.

Meanwhile, an unexpected obstacle had arisen in the shape of a 'Save the
Theatre Royal' preservation group, determined on a last-ditch effort to rescue
from a similar fate the fine old playhouse whose stage had been graced by so
many famous 'names' – including George Robey, Marie Lloyd, Gertrude
Lawrence, Gracie Fields and the youthful Ronald Colman (who was too poor to
afford lodgings while playing at the theatre, so he slept under the Pier). Instead
of pulling down and replacing the Theatre Royal, people asked, why not spend
the money on modernising and refurbishing it? It could even form part of the
projected entertainments centre. Among the well-known actors who joined in the
fight to preserve the theatre was Marius Goring who visited the town and appealed
to the Council to save the 'pivot of a splendid Edwardian sea resort'.

The preservation campaign won sufficient support to justify the holding of an
official public enquiry in June, a step which aroused hopes of an 11th-hour
reprieve. But the hopes faded when the Inspector announced his findings:

> 'I appreciate that some members of the public will be sorry to see the Theatre Royal
> demolished, but in my opinion the appearance of the building is not sufficiently out-
> standing to justify the considerable restriction upon development which its retention
> would involve.'

Presumably the Inspector was referring to the external appearance of the theatre,
which admittedly was nothing like so ornamental as that of its steadily disappear-
ing neighbour, the Rex. It was the charming and typically Edwardian interior
that the preservationists were fighting to save, but there was no place for
Edwardian charm in the redevelopment plans.

Demolition of the theatre started in the first week of September and was
actually in progress when, by a supremely ironical stroke of fate, the great
Esplanade Redevelopment Scheme was itself completely demolished. 'Scheme
Scrapped!' screamed the front page of the Post on 13 September – and reproduced alongside the headline was an artist's impression of the promised new
double-deck Esplanade peremptorily crossed out as by an editor's blue pencil.

What had happened was that the spectre of inflation which had been looming
over the Town Hall for the last few years had at last struck; and only five days
after the bulldozers had moved in on the Theatre Royal an urgent planning
meeting was summoned by the Arun Council to face a sudden and serious financial
crisis. There was only one way of dealing with it – by bold, immediate and drastic
action. The whole concept of Esplanade Redevelopment was abandoned there
and then, and the town had to brace itself to the realisation that there wasn't
going to be a New Bognor after all.

*   *   *

Immediately a tumultuous storm burst from the ratepayers. Not only had all the
hopes and promises of the past 15 years come to nothing, but the town had just

lost the Rex and was in process of losing the Theatre Royal. The Council knew it would have to explain everything and wisely called a public meeting at the Esplanade Theatre. Braving a turmoil of jeering and heckling from the 750 angry residents who packed the auditorium, the Council's spokesman endeavoured to convince the crowd of the crippling effect of inflation; and things calmed down somewhat when it was emphasised that, though the scheme for the comprehensive redevelopment of the Eastern Esplanade had been sunk beyond recovery, the Council was none the less determined to build an entertainments complex. Plans for the new building and the landscaping of its surroundings, as well as a couple of modest blocks of flats, were to be prepared as a matter of urgency. The empty spaces left by the demolition of two perfectly viable places of entertainment within the past few months were already a source of embarrassment to the Council and the sooner they were filled the better.

The plans for the new Regis Centre, as it was to be called, were unveiled to the public in January 1977. They were greeted by the *Post* with a headline ('So This Is It!') capable of different shades of interpretation, and by many of the ratepayers with expressions of baffled perplexity. Could this really be 'it'? One of the stated aims governing the design of the Centre was that it should be 'memorable and distinctive'; and distinctive, at least, it certainly promised to be. The building revealed in the plans – brick-walled, slate-roofed, rigidly utilitarian – could safely claim to resemble no other seaside entertainments centre in Britain. 'It looks like a load of cattlesheds', commented one disgruntled resident.

Still, whatever it looked like, it wasn't going to cost the ratepayers a penny, thanks to the Council's investment in the Flansham estate (now being built up and bearing the inappropriately aristocratic name of Flansham Park); and in spite of its uninviting exterior the Centre would provide the town with a modern well-equipped theatre, a multi-purpose hall, a clubroom and a cafeteria where, it was said, 'people could look out over the sea'.

The hall was to be known as the Royal Hall, and in choosing a name for the theatre the Council seized the opportunity to pay tribute to the town's best-loved visitor. Ever since that childhood holiday in 1945, Princess Alexandra – like Princess Charlotte in the early years of the 19th century – had occupied a special place in Bognor's affections. She had visited the town again in 1967 to open a holiday hotel for blind people, returning in the following year to inaugurate a scented garden for the blind just opposite the hotel in Marine Park Gardens; and it was decided that the best possible name for the new theatre would be the Alexandra.

Bognor had another opportunity of welcoming its favourite princess in June 1977, when she accepted an invitation to unveil a commemorative plaque on the site of the Centre, on which building operations had still not yet begun. The plaque, bearing the uninformative inscription 'Princess Alexandra, 13 June 1977', was affixed to a small section of brick walling specially erected to receive it; and two days after the Princess had performed the unveiling ceremony, with a graceful little speech in which she recalled happy memories of playing on the Bognor sands as a child, the wall was demolished. This caused a minor sensation in the

London papers, for it seemed as if the Princess had been invited to Bognor merely to waste her time – until it was explained that, though the wall had disappeared, the unveiled plaque had been removed for safe keeping to the Town Hall, pending its incorporation in the completed Centre.

A possible explanation of this strange little affair, very much a case of the cart being put before the horse, is that it had been anticipated (as so often before) that building operations would begin earlier than they did and that by June there would be a permanent wall ready to receive the plaque. The temporary wall may have been a way out of the embarrassment of having to ask the Princess to post-pone her visit.

Work on the site began in October and, after the inevitable delays, the building – now renamed the *Bognor* Regis Centre – was formally opened by the Duke of Norfolk on 11 March 1980. After unveiling a plaque bearing his name and the date, alongside Princess Alexandra's resited plaque, he drew the first pint of beer in the bar and proposed a toast to the success of the Centre.

Bognor's residents now took the opportunity to inspect their new possession for the first time – the all-seasons entertainments complex for which they had waited for decades. No doubt there was resentment in some conservative breasts at the absence of the domes, pillars, terraces and balconies of the traditional winter garden; and it was disappointing that from nowhere in the building was there a view of the sea, except a ground-level glimpse from the cafeteria. Both in its style of architecture, which would have looked more at home on the industrial estate at the back of the town, and in its failure to provide windows or balconies overlooking the beach, the design of Bognor's latest asset appeared almost deliberatcly to ignore its prime position of the Esplanade. However, the great thing was that its doors were open at last and the Alexandra Theatre and the Royal Hall were all ready to stage the attractions announced on the posters outside – jazz, wrestling, country music, a Bavarian evening. The days of concert parties and municipal orchestras were over.

The main entrance was approached across a paved area occupying what had until recently been the seaward half of York Road. It was shortly to be named Place St Maur des Fossés in honour of the French town with which Bognor had become 'twinned' and whose Mayor came over to plant a tree outside the Centre in June. Inside the main foyer there was an unexpected feature: a number of cases of stuffed birds, clearly the work of an expert taxidermist. He was Henry Leopold Guermonprez (1858–1924), a self-taught naturalist who in 1892 left London with his invalid parents to settle in Bognor for the benefit of their health. He took a house for them in Albert Road and it remained his home for the rest of his life.

From 1906 until his death this impressive bearded figure wrote a weekly nature column, 'Selborne Notes', for the *West Sussex Gazette*; and the house in Albert Road became filled with examples of his skill as a taxidermist, including some magnificent specimens of birds in flight. Mr. Guermonprez had always hoped that his collection would eventually form part of a local museum; and in 1943 his family presented it to the West Sussex Council. After the war it joined

Bognor's own museum collection which, under the curatorship of Mr. E. M. Venables, was housed first in the disused Lyon Street School and then, when the school was demolished in 1969 to make way for a new Fire Station, in a house in Chichester Road.

These were purely temporary expedients until such time as (to quote the *Post*) 'the town is adult enough to build a proper Museum'. When in 1972 adulthood still appeared as far away as ever, the Guermonprez Collection was moved to Portsmouth where it was provided with a suitable setting at the City Museum. However, the Portsmouth authorities allowed a representative selection of the exhibits to return to Bognor for display to the public in the newly-opened Centre.

*   *   *

The Bognor Regis Centre, for which the Theatre Royal and the Rex had been sacrificed, now proceeded to claim another victim. The opening of the Centre had made the Esplanade Theatre redundant and the Council hastened to get rid of it. Within a few weeks, springtime strollers on the sea front were once again treated to the familiar sight and sound of bulldozers in action; and by the end of May there was nothing left of the theatre except its café, which was permitted to survive. (It provided a far better view of the sea than its counterpart at the Centre.)

Architecturally, of course, the disappearance of the Esplanade Theatre was no great loss to the town — in this respect it could claim to be unique among the various public buildings demolished during the past 30 years — but there was naturally some regret at the passing of a popular rendezvous which held nostalgic memories of the countless shows it had accommodated since it was opened in 1948. The local Operatic Society, too, were rather concerned at the prospect of having to switch their annual productions to the Centre's Alexandra Theatre which, though far better equipped, had only about half the seating capacity of their former venue. However, this meant that they were assured of full houses for their 1980 show, Ivor Novello's *The Dancing Years*, with which they made their inaugural appearance at the Alexandra in May.

By then there had been ample opportunity for residents and visitors to become acquainted with the new public gardens which had been laid out alongside the Centre and were soon to be backed by moderate-sized blocks of flats — the only other buildings to survive the collapse of the Redevelopment Scheme. Public gardens, it will be recalled, had been envisaged for this site (the historic Cabbage Patch) as far back as the 1920s, but it is safe to say that no one had ever envisaged anything quite like the eventual reality. There were no lawns or flower-beds or ornamental pools; instead, in a determined effort to avoid the conventional, the layout consisted mainly of a series of strange grassy hillocks planted with shrubs, punctuated at intervals by even stranger and rather unsightly wooden barriers — and if you wanted to do anything so thoroughly conventional as to sit down and rest awhile in the sun, you sat on a hard plank. The whole conception was guaranteed to puzzle anyone who hadn't been informed that it took its inspiration from the sea and the beach. The curious hillocks, reminiscent of bunkers on a golf course, were intended to call to mind the rolling waves, while the timber barriers represented the breakwaters. This struck some people as a waste of good wood, considering that the real breakwaters, like the real waves, could be seen a few yards away.

Anyone, therefore, with an urge to relax amid well-kept lawns and flower-beds, with comfortable seats from which to admire them, had to go elsewhere – to the very different world on the other side of the Pier, where a walk along the Western Esplanade would bring you to the Marine Park Gardens. These were as yet untouched by progress and therefore gave you all you hoped to find.

*　　*　　*

It was indeed a different world beyond the Pier. The Pier itself, except for the amusement arcade and other diversions at the shore end, had remained unrepaired and closed to the public since the disastrous storm of 1965; and the pier head, bereft of its pavilion and cut off from the main structure, showed every sign of settling down to a permanent existence as an uninhabited offshore island. But, though no longer what it was, the Pier still served as the dividing line between the two contrasting aspects of Bognor as represented by the Eastern and Western Esplanades.

We noticed earlier on, back in the 1930s, the striking change in character between the garishness of the Eastern Esplanade and the decorous atmosphere of the West. True, the East had now lost the Butlin fun fairs which were mainly responsible for the contrast (though it had actually succeeded in pushing its frontier forward a few yards by infiltrating a few 'amusements' into the central space of Waterloo Square), but it had also lost almost everything of architectural merit that it once possessed – and it was soon to lose the best of its surviving buildings, the Victoria Convalescent Home of 1900. Whereas immediately west of the Pier you entered a Bognor that had remained true to the architectural traditions of the seaside: a friendly Georgian and Victorian medley of bay-windows and balconies, of primness and exuberance, where the only echo of the destruction wrought elsewhere in the interests of Redevelopment was the empty space where the Esplanade Theatre had stood – and that, of course, had only stood there for just over 30 years.

Still presiding over the scene as it had done for exactly a century and half was the stately white-painted *Royal Norfolk Hotel*, from whose windows such distant historical figures as Napoleon III and the Empress Eugenie, Queen Alexandra and her sister the Empress of Russia, had gazed out over the sea. The hotel, having safely survived that brief threat to its existence at the end of the war, now had more windows than ever before, for in 1971 its frontage had been almost doubled in length by the addition of wings on either side. But just as in the 1890s, when a single small wing had been added, the new extensions were so completely in accord with the original 1830 building that they might have been designed by the same architect.

Meanwhile, its eastern neighbour, the *Royal Hotel* (built in the 1880s on the site of Richard Dalley's pre-1820 Manor House, which later became Binstead's Library) had also been doing some expanding. The chief feature of the new extension, opened in 1960, was a wide-windowed lounge which, though modern in style, harmonised surprisingly well with the Royal's typically ebullient late Victorian façade. And even though the *Rock Gardens Hotel*, just to the west of the *Royal Norfolk*, had closed in the early 1960s, following the death of Reginald Pullin who opened it in 1917, the Georgian terrace of which it formed part still survived, having escaped being replaced by a block of flats in 1965.

It was an unusually precious survival, for it was the oldest building on the sea front; it dated from before the battle of Trafalgar and its windows once reflected the glow of the fire which destroyed Bognor's first hotel in 1826. The future of this simple white-washed terrace was, of course, doubtful (it would be gone by 1982), but for the time being it was still there to provide a tangible link with Bognor's earliest days as a seaside resort. Moreover, just beyond it, the pleasant little early Victorian terrace known as Countland Court, whose dilapidated condition had for years seemed to offer an irresistible invitation to the bulldozers, had been admirably restored and its bow-windows were no longer curtainless.

To take a stroll west of the Pier in 1980, therefore, was to see Bognor as it had been known to past generations of holidaymakers. Even the ornamental fountain commemorating Queen Victoria's Diamond Jubilee was back on view. It originally stood on the sea front opposite the Steyne but had been moved to Waterloo Square in 1928. There it remained until 1956, when it was dismantled to make way for a temporary entertainment marquee, and its various components deposited under a shrubbery in Hotham Park. There they lay concealed, and apparently forgotten, until Mr. Jim Seymour — whose father, as a 14-year-old apprentice, had helped to erect the fountain in 1898 — started a fund to restore it. (The Council, in the thick of its plans for Esplanade Redevelopment, told him that no public money was available for this purpose.) The money flowed in, mainly in shillings and sixpences, and in April 1969 the fountain was re-erected at the southern end of the Steyne Garden, a few yards inland from its original site. The unveiling ceremony — attended by an enthusiastic crowd who welcomed this rare opportunity to watch something from Bognor's past being re-instated instead of destroyed — was performed by Captain Douglas Miller, who had been present at the original unveiling when he was one year old; and the honour of downing the first glass of water from the fountain fell to the Chairman of the Council, Mr. A. G. Anderson. This was in accordance with precedent, for in 1898 the same refreshing duty had been performed by his predecessor as Chairman, Mr. Curwen Sisterson.

The re-erection of the Jubilee Fountain in the Steyne provided some compensation for the disappearance a few years earlier of the most prominent of the Steyne's landmarks, the clock tower of St John's Chapel. The chapel itself (1822) was, as we know, demolished in the 1890s after the new St John's in London Road succeeded it as Bognor's parish church; but the tower survived until 1960. The Council had leased it from the parish in 1919, on the understanding that the town would become responsible for its maintenance; but little or no maintenance was undertaken and the tower was allowed to fall into a dangerous state of disrepair. No funds were allocated to restore it — and, in any case, the Council had other plans for the site, as was revealed by the notice published in August 1960 which stated that application had been made for the compulsory purchase of the tower 'for the purpose of providing a parking-place for vehicles'. So this well-loved landmark was demolished and with it went the clock and bell which had been warning Esplanade strollers of the approach of lunchtime ever since they were installed in 1833.

For a brief period it was hoped that the clock might be transferred to the tower of the 'new' St John's in London Road, but that tower was itself soon to suffer the same fate as its predecessor in the Steyne. For in the mid-1960s St John's was faced with a sudden financial crisis, all the more unexpected because a new parish hall, with flint-faced walls to blend with those of the church, had been opened as recently as 1955. It was a double-edged crisis of a diminishing congregation (which meant falling collections) and a heavy bill, estimated at £20,000, for necessary repairs to the spacious Blomfield church. Moreover, London Road was becoming increasingly important as a shopping centre and the market value of the church site was put at £200,000.

In February 1971, the Bishop of Chichester approved the Diocesan Pastoral Committee's view that St John's should be declared redundant, its site sold and the status of parish church conferred on St Wilfrid's in Victoria Drive. The final service at St John's, which happened to coincide with the Patronal Festival, was held on the last Sunday in June. The sermon was preached by the vicar (the Rev. W. G. Sinclair Snow), who then moved to St Wilfrid's.

In contrast to the shops and business premises which had grown up around St John's, St Wilfrid's — Bognor's third parish church in just under a century — was situated in one of the town's most desirable residential areas. It had started life as a tin chapel-of-ease, erected in 1896 to relieve the overcrowding in St John's, but its own overcrowding problem soon became so acute, especially in summer, that the only solution was to build a proper church. The foundation stone was laid by Mr. William Fletcher of Aldwick Manor in 1908, and the splendid new St Wilfrid's — conceived in a free 14th-century style by Mr. G. H. Fellowes Prynn, who was later to design a cathedral in Colombo — was dedicated two years later. As it still lacked its 140-foot copper spire, consecration would have to wait until the building was completed; and no one can have anticipated that the wait would last nearly half a century. In 1955, since there still seemed to be little prospect of the spire being erected in the foreseeable future, the Bishop decided to delay matters no longer. So although St Wilfrid's was still spireless when it became the parish church in 1971, it had at any rate been duly consecrated. Little time was now lost in demolishing St John's, with its 157-foot spire, and replacing this handsome ecclesiastical redundancy with a large store. The main section of London Road was now, for the first time, solid with shops and offices, lacking the trees and shrubs of the churchyard which had provided a break in the line of shop fronts on the east side. It was similar to the effect created in 1902 when High Street lost its patch of greenery as a result of the Arcade being constructed through the grounds of York House.

The loss of the two St John's spires, old and new, within a period of 12 years left Bognor's solitary example of high-rise flats in undisputed command of the central skyline. This 15-storey tower block, together with the new shopping street Queensway, was what the town got in exchange for permitting the demolition in 1955 of Hotham's Fitzleet House. Fitzleet was a 'listed' building and had therefore been assumed to be safe from destruction; and it will be recalled that the *Post*, on viewing its fate, had cast an anxious thought in the direction of Hotham's remaining architectural treasures: 'How safe are the Dome and Hotham Park House?'

To find out we must return to the eastern edge of the town, where Sir Richard Hotham started to build Bognor and where this story began.

Fig. 24.   St John's church, by Eric Gill.

Chapter XXVIII

EDUCATION TO THE RESCUE

SIR RICHARD had provided Bognor with what was possibly the most attractive entry of any of the Sussex resorts, and by the mid-1930s it had remained virtually unscathed by the passing of the years. As you approached from the east, there were still no sprawling suburbs to be ploughed through before reaching the town; instead, after leaving Felpham, you caught your first sight of the buildings of Bognor rising out of the green meadowland in a frame of mature trees: the same stately 18th-century houses on which the future George IV, that man of architectural taste, must have cast an approving eye when he drove over from Brighton to visit Princess Charlotte. All were built by Hotham: Bognor Lodge, his first home; the Chapel House (now Aldwick Manor), where he died; Hothamton Crescent, with the Dome House as its centrepiece; and, just beyond, the plain but dignified Spencer Terrace.

Turning left at the entrance to Aldwick Manor, the road to the town centre wound its way past the entrance gates of Sudley Lodge, the Earl of Arran's principal architectural legacy, and Belvedere House, a comparative newcomer of the 1860s; and then, with surprising suddenness you found yourself amid the shops of High Street, only a few hundred yards after leaving the open country. Few other towns of this size – if indeed any – could offer, as late as the 1930s, such a rapid transition from fields and hedges to main street shops and offices.

But the mid-1930s, as we know only too well, marked the start of that spate of demolitions which resulted in the loss of many of Bognor's historic buildings. It is time, therefore, to see what happened to the group of fine houses which conferred such distinction on Bognor's eastern fringe ('the real heart of Hothamton', as someone once described it) and to their extensive grounds on which many a speculative builder must have cast longing eyes.

All this remained superbly intact until 1937, when both the oldest and the youngest houses in the group disappeared within the space of a few months. It was in that year, as related in Chapter XXII, that Bognor Lodge was demolished, though by a merciful quirk of fate the site had not been developed. A far happier fate awaited it, for in 1950 it was acquired by the nearby Villa Maria Convent School (opened in 1918 and taken over by the sisters of the Servite Order in 1923) for use as a playing-field. On the opposite side of High Street, at the corner of Gloucester Road, stood a little old building which made its own contribution to the charm of this part of Bognor and was doubtless much appreciated by the Villa Maria girls, if not necessarily for its architectural qualities. This was the Tuck Shop, whose window displayed a tempting array of the sort of sweets to which one's thoughts tend to wander halfway through the morning's lessons. There were also, less interestingly, newspapers and cigarettes.

The Tuck Shop occupied the surviving remnant of a farmhouse which was erected about the middle of the 18th century and was the only building in the vicinity of that other farmhouse where Hotham and Blanchard found accommodation when they first came to Bognor. The shop had not always sold sweets, for it was once owned by a cobbler, Mr. Munday, and its chief claim to fame was that it was here, as mentioned earlier, that Queen Victoria, as a young girl staying at Bognor Lodge with her mother, was reputed to have bought her first pair of boots.

It was appropriate that this part of the town should possess a tuck shop, for although the eastern end of Bognor was originally renowned for its distinguished residents it was now more noted for its educational establishments — a process which had begun as far back as the middle of the 19th century. The Tuck Shop therefore enjoyed an enviable supply of potential customers, the nearest to hand being the boys of St Dominic's School, which occupied Belvedere House a few yards away on the opposite corner of High Street and Gloucester Road.

In 1937 St Dominic's, in need of larger premises, moved to St Leonards. The building was sold to the Government, who demolished it with the intention of erecting a new telephone exchange and Inland Revenue offices on the site. Owing to the war and the subsequent austerity era, however, it was not until 30 years later that the new block of Government offices was erected; and a contributor to the *Post* wrote scathingly:

> 'Apart from having a gallows at the entrance to Bognor Regis, I can't think of anything more conducive to the lowering of holiday spirits than the sight of an office block devoted to the grim work of the Inland Revenue. What a jolly welcome to a seaside resort!'

Admittedly the appearance of the building did not entirely reflect the alleged grimness of the purpose for which it was erected, but it was the first serious incursion of modern architecture into an area which had hitherto preserved its mainly Georgian (and partly Victorian) aspect almost intact. And, as luck would have it, the completion of the office block and telephone exchange coincided with the disappearance of the old and much-loved landmark just across the road. In 1966 came the dread news that the Tuck Shop had been bought by the Council, from which it was safe to assume that its days were numbered. 'Queen Victoria Shop May Go', ran the headline; and in 1968, as the finishing touches were being applied to the Government complex, go it did — thereby revealing a hitherto unseen view of the western façade of the eight-year-old Butlin Camp beyond the line of trees. The Council got on with the job of road-widening, the reason for purchasing the site, and the Villa Maria girls no longer had a sweet shop within sight of their playing-field.

Just to the west stood the elegant bow-windowed Sudley Lodge which by now had lost its neighbour, Arran's charming Sudley Cottage (later The Den), as a result of war damage. The Lodge continued to be requisitioned for Government purposes following its war-time service as an A.R.P. post; and then, in 1960, a headline with an all-too-familiar ring about it announced 'Threat to

Sudley Lodge'. The extensive grounds surrounding the Lodge had become irresistibly ripe for residential development and the application for the necessary permit also included the house itself.

The customary preservation campaign ensued, during which the Ancient Monuments Society played an active part in persuading the County Council to withhold permission for the demolition of what was now Bognor's sole remaining architectural link with Lord Arran; and success came in 1970. Sudley Lodge was to be preserved by being converted into flats and a maisonette and thus took its place among the small and reasonably attractive blocks of flats being built in its grounds — a rare example of a pre-Victorian, Regency-style villa forming part of a modern housing estate.

We turn now to the houses built by Hotham himself, of which so far only Bognor Lodge had gone. The Dome House, in contrast, seems never to have been in serious danger, despite the fears expressed by the *Post*. The sheer grandeur of Hotham's masterpiece was itself a form of protection and its importance was enhanced by its rôle as the keystone of Hothamton Crescent, flanked deferentially by east and west wings known respectively as St Michael's and Mordington. Like Bognor Lodge, or at any rate its site, all three components of the Crescent were destined to serve in the field of education.

St Michael's was the first to show scholastic leanings. Originally called East Lodge, it was renamed Arran Lodge when in 1809 it was occupied by Lord Arran. On his death in 1837, Lord George Lennox moved into what now predictably became Lennox Lodge; and in 1856 the house underwent a further name-change as the new home of St Michael's School for girls, which had begun life at Hove 12 years earlier. It later joined the group of schools founded on Christian principles by Canon Nathaniel Woodard, of which Lancing College is the crowning glory.

For a brief spell there were actually two girls' schools in Hothamton Crescent, the other being Miss Barnard's Ladies School which occupied the Dome House from 1870 to 1881. After that the Dome reverted to its original function as a private residence and for nearly half a century (1881–1924) was the home of Alfred Lloyd. Mr. Lloyd was an ardent naturalist who planted his grounds with flowers known to have a special attraction for particular species of butterfly.

Meanwhile, St Michael's was enjoying a prosperous existence, so much so that after Mr. Lloyd's death it took over part of the Dome House; and in 1936 it was still further extended to include the west wing of the Crescent, so that now Mordington, too, echoed to the clatter of schoolgirl feet. But not for long. On the outbreak of war in 1939, the school hastily packed up and retreated inland to the safe seclusion of Burton Park in the wooded countryside south of Petworth. Its new surroundings suited it so well that it has remained there ever since. But its example in converting almost the whole of Hothamton Crescent into a single educational establishment was not lost on the County authorities, for during the war — when, as we have seen, the Dome House served as a home for the blind and narrowly escaped being hit by a bomb — plans were already being prepared for converting the Crescent into a training college for teachers.

The Bognor Regis Training College (later the College of Education), opened in October 1946, was warmly welcomed not only as a valuable asset to the life of the town, which it quickly proved to be, but as a virtual guarantee that Bognor's finest group of Georgian buildings would be preserved for the benefit of posterity. It was not until 1970 that it began to appear that the guarantee was not as water-tight as had been imagined. Twenty-four years of college life had exposed structural weaknesses in the three buildings forming the Crescent, which were now nearly two centuries old; and in any case it had been found difficult to adapt the interior lay-out of these 18th-century residences to the requirements of the West Sussex educational authorities. There could, of course, be no question of demolishing a building of such outstanding merit as the Dome House, but for a time the future of St Michael's and Mordington looked highly doubtful. A deter-mined pressure group at Chichester's County Hall favoured pulling them down and erecting purpose-built replacements, but fortunately the County Council, conscious of its responsibility towards listed buildings, decided to consult public opinion before condemning them. The outcome was an overwhelming response in favour of the rehabilitation of all three buildings — strongly supported, to its credit, by the Bognor Council.

Thus Hothamton Crescent was saved in its entirety — though the Dome House, in particular, underwent extensive internal reconstruction — and so also was another prized item in the Hotham legacy, Spencer Terrace immediately to the west. Built in the 1790s, it was originally intended to house the retinue of George III when, as Hotham fondly hoped, the King decided to make the Dome House his seaside holiday residence. The terrace continued to provide accommodation for visitors until 1852, when Mr. Bevan's Hope House Academy for Young Gentlemen moved there from Chichester. Mr. Bevan could therefore claim pioneer status, for his was the first of the several educational institutions which were to establish themselves in Bognor's most distinguished residential district, beating St Michael's for the honour by four years. Mr. Bevan, however, did not stay long, for in 1866 his young gentlemen were succeeded by those of Middleton House School, and they in turn were followed by the boys of Northcliffe School, which moved to Bognor from Cliftonville in 1913.

Northcliffe — among whose pupils was David Sheppard, the Sussex and England cricketer and later Anglican Bishop of Liverpool — just failed to achieve a half-century in the terrace, as falling numbers and increasing costs forced it to leave Bognor at the end of the summer term of 1962. Having first moved from Kent to Sussex, the school now resumed its westward progress to Hampshire, where it settled in an Elizabethan country mansion near Romsey. It left behind it a memorial in the shape of its own name, for few people now referred to Spencer Terrace. Though the school was no longer there, the terrace continued to be known as Northcliffe — just as the east wing of Hothamton Crescent still bore the name of the departed St Michael's.

From the point of view of the College of Education next door, Northcliffe School could not have chosen a better moment at which to vacate its premises, for there was now a desperate need of additional living accommodation for the increasing numbers of College students. Since taking over the Crescent, the College had built a lecture theatre and was now, in 1962, engaged in a comprehensive programme to provide such essential facilities as a large and splendidly equipped library, a gymnasium, an art studio and science laboratories. The work schedule did not include additional students' rooms — which was perhaps just as well, for when Northcliffe School moved to Hampshire the College found a ready-built answer to its problem. The threat of demolition, which had almost automatically hovered over Spencer Terrace when the school announced its departure, was quickly dispelled by the County Council's decision to incorporate the terrace into the College and convert it into a students' hostel — even though the conversion would be a major undertaking. As the Principal, Mr. Roy Macklin, pointed out, 'one can hardly expect students aged 19 to 40 to live in dormitories designed for prep schoolboys'. After the work was completed, Spencer Terrace — like the Dome House after its own restoration — looked sprucer than it had done for decades.

It was, therefore, entirely due to the advance of further education that the complete range of Hotham buildings in Upper Bognor Road was now safe for the foreseeable future. Indeed, considering the changes which had taken place — and were still taking place — elsewhere in Bognor, the 'real heart of Hothamton' cannot be said to have fared badly. Though the late 1930s had seen the disappearance of Bognor Lodge and Belvedere House (St Dominic's) and there were the later losses of The Den and the Tuck Shop, the post-war period could be credited with the preservation of the Dome House, St Michael's, Mordington, Spencer Terrace and Sudley Lodge. It was a satisfactory balance sheet as far as it went, but the account was not yet closed. One item of the Hotham inheritance had still to be dealt with, and over its fate loomed an ominous question mark. Yet there is little doubt that, if forced to make a choice, many Bognor residents would have opted to sacrifice any other of Hotham's buildings — even, perhaps, the Dome House — if they could be assured of the safety of the one which had the closest personal links with the Founder. For if the Chapel House were to go, and its future looked black indeed, not only historic Hothamton but Bognor itself would lose its heart.

Fig. 25. St Michael's School, Upper Bognor, in 1869.

Chapter XXIX

THE REDISCOVERY OF HOTHAM

WHEN WILLIAM FLETCHER, the last private owner of the Chapel House, died in 1941 at the age of 89, the name of Hotham was virtually unknown in the town he had created. When all who had known Sir Richard had finally gone, his memory had become buried under the layers of local history, the long sequence of events and personalities which had brought Bognor into the middle of the 20th century. There were streets named after royalty, dukes and lesser mortals associated with the town, but not one commemorated its founder.

It was the same with the house where he had lived and died. There the memory of his own occupancy had been obscured by the succession of families who came after him: the Troubridges, the Smiths, the Mayos and especially the Fletchers, who had owned the property since 1857 and had long been inseparable from it in the public mind. Who could remember, or indeed imagine, anyone else living there? Even the name of the house had not long survived the man for whom it was built. Soon after his death, the Chapel House became Bersted Lodge; and it had now been Aldwick Manor for as long as anyone had lived in Bognor, except perhaps for a few of the oldest inhabitants. In any case, the name which Hotham had given to the house had lost its point, for his chapel was demolished by J. B. Fletcher shortly after he took possession.

William Fletcher was only 11 when his father died in 1863 and for many years the estate was ruled by his widowed mother. It was not until 1900 that William and his wife Agnes moved from Worthing to take up permanent residence in the family home. Both of them — like Alfred Lloyd and his butterflies over at the Dome House — were enthusiastic nature-lovers. Arboriculture was William's special interest and the 20-acre estate surrounding the house gave him ample opportunity for indulging it. He spent a fortune on laying out the grounds and planting them with a magnificent collection of rare trees and shrubs. The lawn in front of the house — created by the Rev. Thomas Smith when he had the public highway realigned farther away from his front door (the present south drive follows the original course of the road)—was mown by a horse-drawn machine whose motive power, named Nobby, wore leather shoes on his hoofs to protect the grass. William's lay-out also included a lake in which flourished a variety of water-lilies and also some very large goldfish, which their owner enjoyed feeding. Wearing his deerstalker hat and with his Airedale at his side, he would stand at the edge of the pond scattering bread and calling out 'Fish, fish, fish!' The goldfish would almost leap out of the water in their eagerness to obey the summons.

Agnes, who came from Louth in Lincolnshire, was somewhat more alarming in her tastes. As we noted earlier on, she was fascinated by reptiles, particularly

276

snakes, and unsuspecting callers would sometimes discover her with a young python slung comfortably around her neck. The billiard-room was used as a reptile house in order to accommodate her pets; and in cold weather the maids had to brace themselves to an additional household duty: filling hot-water bottles, wrapping them in blankets and distributing them among the denizens of the billiard-room.

William Fletcher, who owned many acres of farmland to the west of Bognor, was Lord of the Manor of Aldwick and a respected figure of considerable importance in local affairs. His name was given to the William Fletcher Secondary School, though this commemoration disappeared in 1967 when the Secondary School was amalgamated with the new Bognor Regis Grammar School, opened in 1960. Towards the end of his life, William's public appearances became rarer, for he and his wife preferred the privacy of their estate, sunning themselves on the lawn, following the winding paths through the woodland and admiring the trees in the fullness of their maturity. By now the name of Fletcher had acquired a certain aura, similar to that which had long ago surrounded that of Hotham, and to catch an occasional sight of the elderly couple was rather like being accorded a brief glimpse of royalty.

Agnes died in 1939, aged 84, and William survived her by two years. The contents of the house were sold in August 1941 (the reptiles had already gone to a zoo for safe keeping), but the house and grounds were requisitioned by the Army. Eventually, towards the end of the war, the property came on the market and hopes were expressed that it would be bought for the town. Not for the first time such hopes were dashed; and in February 1945 the *Post* commissioned an author who had done much research into Bognor's history to write an article chastising the Council for its faint-heartedness in failing to secure the prize available to them.

The three-column article was headed 'Glories of the Fletcher Estate', an indication of how exclusively the property was associated with its last owners. Had Hotham's name appeared in the headline, few would have known to whom the *Post* was referring. But when the reader reached as far as the foot of the first column, he had his initial introduction to someone he had probably never heard of before:

> 'Historically it is a notable house, for here lived and died Sir Richard Hotham, the man who founded the town as a resort. He came to Bognor in 1784 for his health. Returning each summer, he decided in 1787 to live here and develop the fishing village. He built Bognor Lodge (now demolished) as his first home and then moved next door to Aldwick Manor, which he built in 1792. He called it the Chapel House because of the fine chapel he added in 1793. He died in 1799 . . .'

In later years this would have struck the average reader of the *Post* as a rather unnecessary recapitulation of a familiar item of local history, but in 1945 there was nothing familiar about it. At the time, these few lines may not have made much impression on the public consciousness but they had sown the seed.

The article itself, however, made a deep and immediate impression. 'If Aldwick Manor estate is now lost to the town,' it thundered, 'it will be lost for ever.

The estate is for sale. Soon speculators will descend upon it . . . and what is now one of the most beautiful approaches to any seaside town may become the usual dirty sprawl of petrol stations, advertisements and cafés.' And, the writer might have added, bungalows.

After describing the beauties of the estate ('most of us know it only from a bus top, admiring the glimpse of the gracious lawns, the superb trees and the dignified old house'), the article concluded with a direct appeal to its readers: 'The future of the Aldwick Manor estate now lies in the hands of the towns-people. If you want the estate for Bognor, your hands must be strong: strong enough to crack the whip and bring the Council to heel. Into battle, Bognor!'

This clarion call to arms not only succeeded in its hoped-for effect but perhaps even more quickly than had been expected. The Council — seemingly determined to wipe out any suggestion of faint-heartedness — started negotiations for the purchase of the property; and early in 1946, the very next year, it was announced that the mansion and the whole of its estate had been purchased by the town from Mr. Fletcher's executors for £40,000. Although it was estimated that this would mean an additional 6d. on the rates for the next five years, the Council vote was unanimous.

The town was now the possessor of a splendid wooded park extending from the eastern extremity of High Street as far west as London Road. In anticipation of it being opened to the public in the near future, the Council's Publicity Manager, Mr. Howard Cotterell, decided that such an outstanding attraction for visitors could not be omitted from the forthcoming 1947 Town Guide and he asked the writer of the original *Post* article to contribute a piece about it. The park had not yet been named, so the chance was seized to add to the Founder's still meagre store of fame by referring to it in the guidebook as the Hotham Woodlands. Thus by the time the park was opened to the public Hotham's name had already been linked with it in print in an official Council publication. This considerably weakened the case for the various other suggested names — one of which, almost inevitably, was Regis Park.

The great day came on 23 May 1947, when the Chairman of the Council (Captain W. J. Corbishley) presided over the opening ceremony and duly announced the chosen name: Hotham Park. It was the first time that anything in Bognor had been named after the man to whom the town owed its existence; and in his speech Captain Corbishley took advantage of the opportunity to tell the assembled spectators a good deal more about Hotham and his achievements than what little they already knew. It looked as if Sir Richard was at last on the way to reassuming his rightful place in the life of the town after well over a century of obscurity.

Naturally the Chairman also paid tribute to William Fletcher, to whom the Park owned its 'luxuriant growth of rare trees and shrubs collected from all over the world'. And the people of Bognor would no longer have to content themselves with merely glimpsing them over the wall from the top of a passing bus. This leafy domain, hitherto so strictly private and so tantalisingly mysterious, was now theirs and they could enter its gates as often as they pleased.

In due course, Hotham Park was provided with other attractions besides those with which nature and Mr. Fletcher had endowed it. They included a zoo (on whose reptile house Agnes would have cast an approving and even envious eye), a miniature railway through the woodland, a café, a bandstand, tennis and putting; and William's goldfish pond became a boating lake. Fortunately the Park was able to absorb these 'improvements' without too much adverse effect on its natural beauty — which, if the Council had failed to act when it did, might have been lost for ever.

At the western end of the estate, where it bordered London Road, two small buildings had survived from Hotham's time. One was a farmhouse, now converted into two cottages, which proceeded to solve a problem that had been worrying the County library authorities for years. There had been a public library service in Bognor since 1926, but so far it had endured a somewhat pillar-to-post existence. The library, first housed in part of the Lyon Street School (which later became a temporary home for the Museum Collection), moved in 1930 to the old Water Tower which stood next to St John's church in London Road. Five years later, when it became clear that the Tower's days were numbered, the books were transferred farther down the road to the former Congregational Sunday School. A final solution to the accommodation problem came when the Council purchased Hotham Park, including the unwanted farmhouse. This was demolished in 1963 and replaced by the town's first built-to-order Public Library, which was officially opened in October 1964.

The other Hotham building at the London Road end of the Park was much smaller but rather more interesting. This was Sir Richard's ice house, an igloo-like structure with a partially underground chamber, about twelve feet in diameter, in which winter ice was stored until it was needed for making ice cream and for other cooling purposes the following summer. Mr. Fletcher continued to use it for preserving ice up to about 1914, and to the time of his death it was still performing a useful function as an apple store. In 1966 the Council decided to preserve it as a relic of the past and, though it was in remarkably good condition, voted a few hundred pounds for the necessary refurbishment. (It was a good deal cheaper than repairing the recently damaged Pier.)

*   *   *

After the estate had been renamed Hotham Park, it did not take long for the mansion itself, as a natural consequence, to become known as Hotham Park House. The Army had vacated it, but it was still on lease to the Government for use as offices by the Ministry of Pensions and National Insurance. The lease was not due to expire until 1968; and as that date approached the future of the house became a widely talked-about issue. It was town property, so the town must decide what was to be done with it. It could, for instance, join all the other Hotham buildings in the vicinity by becoming part of the College of Education; but the most popular idea — to which the Council gave general approval — was that it should provide a temporary home for the Guermonprez birds and the various items in the Museum Collection. Then when the town got round to erecting a permanent building, as had recently been done in the case of the Public Library, a local writer envisaged 'Hotham Park House restored to its original Georgian splendour, like a Brighton Pavilion in miniature, with rooms devoted to the English seaside, to Hotham the Founder and to little Princess Charlotte, the Prince Regent's daughter, whose holidays here have led children Bognorwards ever since'.

It was an enticing dream: a museum of the seaside in the home of the 18th-century pioneer who had created Britain's first purpose-built seaside resort. But a mere glance at Hotham Park House as it appeared in the late 1960s was sufficient to relegate any such dreams to the far distant future. Nearly thirty years of occupation for Government purposes, both military and civilian, had left their mark and the gracious old house was a sad sight to behold. It was in a state of decay, and clearly no decision as to its future could be taken until it had been thoroughly surveyed. The surveyors – under the direction of Mr. R. T. James, who had been responsible for the restoration of the Nash terraces in Regent's Park, London – began their work in April 1969.

Public concern at the possible fate of the house was now intense. Other Hotham buildings, even Bognor Lodge, had been swept away with little more than the raising of an eyebrow, for few people then had ever heard of Hotham, let alone the part he had played in the history of the town. And even when, with the opening of Hotham Park, his name had emerged from the mists of time, there were stronger competitors for the limelight in the shape of Billy Butlin, with his promised holiday camp, and the Esplanade Redevelopment Scheme with its more nebulous promise of a New Bognor. But by the time the 1960s were nearing their end, the situation had undergone a complete change. The Butlin Camp, after the novelty and excitement of its inaugural seasons, was now taken for granted as a familiar feature of the Bognor scene, into which it had become thoroughly assimilated (people no longer talked of Butlin Regis); and as for the Redevelopment Scheme, that had passed its peak period and was becoming a bit of a bore. It was Hotham Park House, with its future under active discussion, which now moved into the centre of the stage. Suddenly people had become alive to its importance; and this was not primarily for its architectural qualities but for its unique historical value as the home of Bognor's founder. Hotham had not only been rediscovered but, by a remarkable transformation of public opinion, was at last receiving the full recognition that was his due.

A sign that such recognition was on its way had come in 1967 when a group of Hotham's admirers were reminded that 18 January was the anniversary of the day in 1787 when Sir Richard embarked on the task of building a town specific-ally planned as a seaside resort – starting, naturally enough, with his own house, Bognor Lodge. 18 January could therefore be regarded as Bognor's birthday, and what better way of celebrating it than by going along to South Bersted church-yard and laying an appreciative wreath on the Founder's grave? This pleasant little ceremony duly took place and was repeated annually for the next ten years or so.

Sir Richard's reinstatement, belated but all the more welcome for that, took a great stride forward early in 1969 with the publication of *Sovereign's Key*, an historical romance by Rosalind Laker. The novel is set in the Bognor of Hotham's time, and its real-life characters include both Hotham himself and his friend Captain Blanchard. Not only that, but the dust-cover carried an illustration of the Chapel House — where the hero and heroine of the story, Andrew and Theresa, meet at a masked ball.

And now that same house was the property of the people of Bognor who, at the time of the publication of the novel, were anxiously awaiting the verdict of the surveyors (and none more anxiously, one imagines, than Mr. Venables, the curator of the Museum Collection). The surveyors' report, when it arrived later in the year, made depressing, if not entirely unexpected, reading: deathwatch beetle, dry-rot, weakness of floor timbers which should be replaced by steel beams, and the necessity for a comprehensive strengthening of the ground floor and basement before the house could be used for public purposes. The estimate for a complete restoration of the building was about £110,000, while the cost of bringing it to a state suitable for housing the museum exhibits would be £85,000.

Was the Council able or willing to find the money? That was the question over which battles were to rage in the Town Hall and in the columns of the local newspapers over the next few decisive years. An early shot was fired by Councillor L. E. Walwin:

> 'I would not like it to be thought that the Council was parsimonious, but we haven't any money at all. If we are going to ask for a huge loan from the County allocation, it could mean the postponement of other projects.' (A reference, presumably, to the ever-present and inescapable Esplanade Redevelopment.)

And Councillor D. W. Hansford stressed that if the house were to be converted into a museum at the ratepayers' expense, 'it would be like a noose round our necks'. He did not think it was a very admirable building — it was 'something of a hotch-potch' — but it was 'part of Bognor Regis and we must endeavour to preserve it in such a way that it does not become a burden on the public'.

On the other hand, there were those who considered that the house should be pulled down and replaced by a new museum, a solarium or a restaurant — or even that always elusive Winter Garden. In reply, a letter from a lady architect in the local press asked pointedly: 'If Hotham Park House is pulled down and a restaurant built in its stead, shall we be given another Esplanade Theatre? — an example of Bognor's civic building and an eyesore if ever there was one'. Another letter urged that there should be an appeal for funds to save the house, and an old-age pensioner promised that 'if there is a public collection for Hotham Park House, I and my mate will give a pound each'.

In 1970 the *Post* ran a public opinion poll on whether or not the mansion should be restored as a home for the Museum Collection. The count was 608 in favour and 253 against; and within a few weeks a resolution reflecting the result of the poll was unanimously adopted by the Council as a 'firm policy'. Applications for grants would be made to interested bodies such as the Pilgrim

Trust and the Georgian Society; and in any case there was now the possibility of the public rallying round with contributions.

One of the councillors, Mrs. Culver, had in fact already decided that, if the Council agreed in principle to the restoration of the house, she would form a society to launch an appeal fund to help towards the cost of the work. She thought of the idea when acting as Treasurer of the fund for restoring the Jubilee Fountain in the Steyne; and a few days after the Council had passed its resolution she announced the formation of the Friends of Hotham Park House. They aimed to raise money by annual subscriptions, public appeals and the holding of Coffee Mornings and other functions. The principal speaker at their inaugural general meeting at the Esplanade Theatre in February 1971 was Rosalind Laker whose *Sovereign's Key*, by arousing wide interest in Hotham and his old home, had proved a valuable asset in the preservation campaign.

But the house, no longer in use, was deteriorating rapidly and the estimate for restoration was moving correspondingly upward. The Council was therefore urged to adopt a policy of partial, even piecemeal, restoration aimed at keeping further deterioration at bay. At a vital Council meeting in July, Councillor W. G. Rhys-Parry addressed his colleagues thus:

> 'Let us not forget that if Sir Richard Hotham had not spent his *own money* on Bognor, none of us Councillors would be in our Town Hall tonight, as there would have been no Bognor to administer . . . Let the heart of Bognor start beating again — Bognor has too many demolition sites and too many unfulfilled "dream-schemes".'

This appeal doubtless found a sympathetic response in the hearts of its hearers, but partial restoration was considered impracticable. There would be little point in spending money to restore one room and then going off and leaving the rest of the house to continue to decay until further money was available. As the Clerk of the Council (Mr. R. J. Sheppard) remarked, 'You can't do a half-job. It's either all or nothing'.

All or nothing: these were the stark alternatives. The Council had already agreed to shoulder half the cost of a complete restoration, providing that the other half came from grants and public contributions. There had been a grant of £2,500 from the Pilgrim Trust and promises from other sources, including an interest-free loan from the County Council; and the Friends, after an enthusiastic first year, had collected £1,500. But the total so far raised was still far short of the amount, now about £55,000, required to meet half the cost of the work; and the Council was determined not to be inveigled into paying more than its half-share. It was equally, if reluctantly, resolved not to wait any longer for further contributions from societies and individuals, for further delay would mean further deterioration of the fabric of the house and thus raise the cost of restoration.

The Council therefore decided on 20 July 1971, in the face of a vehement protest from Mrs. Culver (now Chairman of the Amenities Committee), that the house where Bognor's Founder had lived and died would have to be razed to the ground. The town reacted with an almost audible gasp of dismay.

*   *   *

The campaign to save Hotham Park House had been fought and lost, yet there was still a vestige of hope — shared by probably a majority of the Council — that its almost certain fate might still be averted. The house could not be demolished right away, for the Council had first to apply for and obtain Government consent to remove it from the list of protected buildings, inevitably a fairly length process. This might give time for the public to delve deeper into their pockets and also for the various 'interested bodies' to come forward with practical support — especially as the Friends had won a valuable ally in the Earl of Bessborough, a highly influential figure in the field of preservation. Meanwhile the Town Hall was doing its best to rebut the attacks made on it by putting the blame for its fateful decision on the lack of public support ('As the ratepayers are not interested, then the Council cannot justify the very large cost involved'); but in September it received a letter from the Department of the Environment regretting that 'this highly-graded building' should be allowed to decay and advising that emergency repairs should be undertaken 'as soon as possible'. It was therefore agreed, pending the Government's decision on the Council's application, to make an annual allocation of up to about £500 for partial repair work.

These developments, such as they were, may have temporarily revived hopes; but over the next few years, during which everyone had something to say but nothing seemed to alter the situation, any tendency to optimism steadily evaporated. The Friends — who by now had raised over £15,000 — were still carrying on the fight in spite of the gathering gloom, and their Chairman, Mrs. Jean Rose, admitted to being 'furious' at a speech by one of the councillors who said he was 'looking forward to driving into the house on a bulldozer'. He was, no doubt, getting impatient at having to wait so long for his joy-ride.

Both the Government and the new Arun Council may have been playing for time in the hope of something turning up, but time was not on the side of Hotham Park House. It had now become something of an eyesore; and many a former preservationist, on casting his eyes over its crumbling façade and glancing at the appeal for funds set up by the Friends near the front door, must have shrugged his shoulders and asked himself 'What's the good?'

After what had seemed an interminable wait, the Government decided that the final outcome could be delayed no longer and announced that the customary Public Enquiry into an application to demolish a scheduled building would be convened early in 1977. There was little doubt in anyone's mind that this meant that Hotham's house would be gone in a matter of months for, in spite of having been given about six years' grace in which to save it for posterity, the town had let the opportunity slip through its fingers. If six years had proved insufficient to achieve the great aim of preservation, what hope was there of doing so in the course of a few hours at the Enquiry? It was a heart-breaking prospect for Hotham's now numerous army of admirers, but they had no alternative but to steel themselves to face the inevitable verdict. And then, as if out of the blue, came the news that the date of the Enquiry had suddenly been postponed. Rumours flew around, and the Friends decided to defer the annual January wreath-laying at Hotham's grave in the expectation of an important announcement.

Mr. Abraham Singer was a retired Buckinghamshire businessman who loved old houses, particularly if they were in a state of neglect and in need of care and attention. One of his greatest satisfactions was to find such a house and bring it back to life by making it habitable once again – and, having been trained in electrical engineering, he often carried out the rewiring himself. The first of the nine houses lucky enough to be saved by him was in Norfolk, built in 1485 and surrounded by gardens and orchards. After the work had been completed, the Singers lived there for many years. Later restorations included a large Victorian house in Buckinghamshire – similar to the one in which Mr. Singer had been brought up as the youngest of 11 children – and this too became the family home.

He first heard of Hotham Park House through the Department of the Environment, where he was informed by one of the inspectors that the building had probably deteriorated beyond the point where it could be preserved. 'It was a challenge,' Mr. Singer later told the *Observer*, 'and as I had never seen the place I came down to have a look at it. I called in an architect and a quantity surveyor, and we agreed that it was just marginally viable to save it.' Its association with Sir Richard Hotham aroused his keen interest, and he made up his mind to accept the challenge and to open negotiations with the Council – which resulted in the postponement of the Public Enquiry. The Enquiry was in fact never held, for it was announced that there was now no question of the house being demolished. Mr. Singer had taken it on a 99-year lease.

*   *   *

So, in the end, victory was seized from the very jaws of defeat. One man, however, seemed coolly unaffected by the general mood of rejoicing. Abraham Singer, never a lover of the limelight, had a job of work to tackle and all he wanted to do was to get down to it. After all, not only was he eager to see a handsome old house restored to its former glory but he and his wife intended to live there. The work started shortly after the lease was signed, and soon the people of Bognor were treated to a heart-warming sight: the whole of the house encased in scaffolding, right up to the cupola surmounting the clock tower, as a prelude to the thorough restoration of its flaking exterior. When, one wondered, had it last been given a coat of paint?

Even more exciting was the work going on inside. As always, Mr. Singer's object was to restore the rooms as far as possible to their original appearance. Small details like brass doorhandles were copied by craftsmen from those already existing, as were the classical fireplaces and the plasterwork on ceilings and walls. Layers of paintwork were stripped to reveal Hotham's colour schemes, which were then reproduced by the modern decorators. Once again the domed ceiling of the staircase glowed with the warm coral pink which Hotham had chosen for it, and in the principal rooms pastel shades – pale green in the drawing-room – contrasted with white mouldings or columns to produce the Wedgwood effect so fashionable at the end of the 18th century.

These embellishments, of course, had to wait until after the major structural work, such as the replacement of decayed timbers by steel beams; but Mr. and Mrs. Singer did not wait for the completion of the whole project before moving into their new home. They 'camped out' in a few of the rooms as soon as the workmen had rendered them just about habitable. However, all was ready by the latter half of 1978; and soon there would be other people moving in, for the restoration programme also included the conversion of part of the building into separate flats.

Naturally the idea that the house might become Bognor's Museum had long been abandoned, but the search for suitable premises for the Collection (which had had to vacate its temporary resting-place in Chichester Road) continued in a more hopeful mood. One of the welcome fruits of the rapidly increasing interest in the town's past, sparked off by the prolonged battle to save Hotham Park House, was the formation in 1979 of the Bognor Regis Local History Society, whose stated aims included the establishment of a museum in the town; and four years later the Society achieved its objective. It succeeded in obtaining from the Council a rent-free lease of the gabled lodge at the main entrance to Hotham Park and thus it was that in 1983 the Museum Collection ended its peregrinations in an appropriate home — if not in Sir Richard's mansion, at any rate on his estate.

Mr. Singer can have been left in no doubt as to the feelings of gratitude he had inspired by his last-minute rescue of Bognor's most prized possession. He had probably never thought of himself as a benefactor, but when he and his wife took a walk in the Park people would come up to them and, to their surprise and pleasure, thank them warmly for what they had done for the town. The Singers also caused much delight by bringing their grandchild with them — probably the first child to live in the house since the boyhood days of William Fletcher.

When he strolled round the scaffolded house watching the work being done on the exterior, Mr. Singer may perhaps have realised that he was following in the footsteps of someone who was doing exactly the same thing in the last decade of the 18th century — and who, like him, was eagerly awaiting the day when he could move in and take up residence. Then, too, the walls were encased in scaffolding, but the house was not merely being repaired and restored. It was being built; and one can picture Sir Richard Hotham walking over from Bognor Lodge on one of his frequent tours of inspection to see how the work on his new home was progressing.

It is tempting, also, to imagine Sir Richard paying a return visit today in order to take a look at his Chapel House after the passing of nearly 200 years. The first thing he notices is the disappearance of the chapel, though its tower has survived; and standing outside the front door — the same door where long ago he was accustomed to welcome the Prince of Wales, Richard Sheridan and other notabilities — he looks up on hearing a well-known sound which once provided a regular accompaniment to his everyday life: the clock in the chapel tower striking the hour. He smiles with satisfaction at this reassuring evidence that the clock, installed for him by John Thwaites of Clerkenwell in 1794, is still in working order. As for the house itself, newly restored and refurbished by his 20th-century successor, he would be agreeably surprised to find it looking just as he remembered it, except that the graceful canopy over the balcony had not yet been replaced. Of course, it was no longer the Chapel House; but its new name, in honouring and preserving his own, he would surely regard as adequate compensation for the discovery that the town he created has long ceased to be known as Hothamton.

After contemplating with a mingling of pride and amusement the plaque to his memory presented by the Friends in 1978, he would probably spend a little time admiring the fine trees which had been planted and come to maturity since his day — some of them, like the Chinese handkerchief tree, quite unknown to him. From the beginning, he had envisaged Hothamton as an exemplification of *rus in urbe*, the country coming into the town; and his enquiring eye is therefore well rewarded as he looks north and sees his Dome House and its neighbours embowered in trees as if they were set in some Arcadian landscape. This was just the effect he had dreamed of when he started planning his ideal seaside resort.

The dense growth of trees and shrubs obscures the view from the house to the east, so he would glimpse little or nothing of the strange complex of buildings (what did Bognor's founder know of holiday camps?) which spreads itself over the Brookland — nor, turning south, would he be met by the once familiar sight of the very first house he built here. All the other houses in this 'heart of Hothamton' had survived to greet him on his return, but in the place of Bognor Lodge there was simply an expanse of well-tended grass. The spot where Bognor began was now a school playing-field.

The shade of Sir Richard Hotham would, one feels, view this change of scene not with regret but with approval and satisfaction, all the more so if at the time of his imagined visit the Villa Maria pupils were enjoying a hard-fought game of netball, cricket or rounders. Nor would the shouts and laughter of the children, echoing through the trees, disturb his peace of mind or cause him any annoyance. On the contrary, he would consider that there could be no better or more appropriate use for this particular site, the historic plot of land where he had embarked on his crowning achievement. Children held a special importance for him, for he knew it was on them that the advancement and prosperity of his resort would depend in the years to come. He always looked to the future.

*   *   *

And what did the future hold as Bognor approached its bicentenary, the 200th anniversary of the start of work on Hotham's great project? Towards the end of 1982 an exciting possibility sent an anticipatory flutter through the town. In the past, a succession of royal children had spent happy holidays on this stretch of coast; and among them were two future Queens, Victoria and Elizabeth II. But so far the young visitors had not included a future King. Then came the news that Earl Spencer, the father of the Princess of Wales, had purchased two adjacent houses on the seashore at Aldwick — primarily, it was believed, to enable his grandchildren to enjoy carefree hours with buckets and spades on a secluded sandy beach. This aroused a sudden hope that soon, holidaying on the sands with his cousins, would be a little boy who was destined one day to ascend the throne as King.

Casting his first fascinated glances at the glistening sands and dancing waves, Prince William would be blissfully unaware of his significant rôle in the continuing history of Hotham's town. Yet his presence on the beach would mark the completion of Bognor's first two centuries as a seaside resort in just the way its Founder and its present-day inhabitants would have wished — by filling, at long last, that all-important gap in its gallery of royal childhood stretching back through the years to the distant but beloved figure of Princess Charlotte.

Fig. 26. Garden approach to Bognor's High Street.

BIBLIOGRAPHY

Anon, *Memoirs of Mr. Sheridan*, 1840.

Austen, Jane, *Sanditon* (completed by 'another lady'), 1975.

Bartlett, William, *History and Antiquities of the Parish of Wimbledon*, 1865.

Beerbohm, Max, *More*, 1899,

Berry, Mary and Agnes, *Correspondence*, 1863.

Bettany, L. ed., *Edward Jerningham and his Friends*, 1919.

Bishop, M., *Blake's Hayley*, 1951.

Bognor Directories and Guides.

Burney, Frances (Fanny), *Diaries and Letters*, 1842.

Carey, George, *The Balnea: a History of all the Popular Watering Places of England*, 1801.

Chamberlain, W. H., *Reminiscences of Old Merton*, 1925.

Clayton, William, *Tales and Recollections of the Southern Coast*, 1861.

Cook, A. A., *Old Wimbledon*, 1927.

Cooper, Lady Diana, *The Light of Common Day*, 1959.

Coward, Noel, *Present Indicative*, 1937.

Davis, John, *Origin and Description of Bognor or Hothampton*, 1807.

Dodd, Anne, *Cathedral Days in Southern England*, 1888 (U.S.A.).

Doughty, Oswald, *A Victorian Romantic: D. G. Rossetti*, 1949.

Eustace, G. W., *Arundel: Borough and Castle*, 1922.

Fleming, Lindsay, *History of Pagham*, 1959.

Gamlin, Hilda, *George Romney and his Art*, 1894.

Gilchrist, Alexander, *Life of William Blake*, 1863.

Gill, Eric, *Autobiography*, 1940.

Gilligan, A. E., *Sussex Cricket*, 1933.

Glover, Peter and Jackson, Graham, *Staffurth & Bray: The Centenary of a Sussex Practice*, 1982.

Granville, A. B., *The Spas of England*, 1841.

Green, Roger Lancelyn, ed., *The Diaries of Lewis Carroll*, 1953.

Green, Thomas, *Memoirs of Princess Charlotte*, 1818.

Hack, Maria, *Geological Sketches and Glimpses of the Ancient Earth*, 1831.

Hardcastle, Hon. Mrs., *The Life of John, Lord Campbell*, 1881.

Hay, Alexander, *Hay's Guide to Chichester*, 1794.

Hayley, William, *Life and Letters of William Cowper Esq.*, 1809.

Hayley, William, *Life of George Romney*, 1809.

Hayley, William, *Memoirs of the Life and Letters of William Hayley Esq.*, 1823.

Hobhouse, John, *Recollections of a Long Life*, (2nd edn.), 1910.

Hotham, Sir Richard, *Reflections on East India Shipping*, 1773.

Hotham, Sir Richard, *A Candid State of Affairs relative to East India Shipping for the Year 1773*, 1774.

Kegan, C., *William Godwin, His Friends and Contemporaries*, 1876.
Kent, John, *Records and Reminiscences of Goodwood and the Dukes of Richmond*, 1891.
Lawrence, D. H., *Letters*, 1932.
Lawrence, Gertrude, *A Star Danced*, 1945.
Lennox, Lord William Pitt, *Fifty Years' Biographical Reminiscences*, 1863.
Lennox, Lord William Pitt, *Celebrities I Have Known*, 1876.
Melville, Lewis, ed., *The Berry Papers*, 1913.
Newdigate, Lady, *The Cheverels of Cheverel Manor*, 1898.
Parry, J. D., *The Coast of Sussex*, 1833.
Project, Peregrine, *A Tour through the Southern Counties of England*, 1804.
Sermonetta, Duchess of, *The Locks of Norbury*, 1940.
Sharpe, W., ed., *Recollections of Samuel Rogers*, 1859.
Sheridan, G. G., Account of R. B. Sheridan's life in *The Dramatic Works of Richard Sheridan*, 1874.
Sherriff, R. C., *The Fortnight in September*, 1931.
Sherriff, R. C., *No Leading Lady*, 1968.
Sturt, George, *A Small Boy in the Sixties*, 1932.
Trench, Melesina, *The Leadbeater Papers*, 1862.
Wells, H. G., *The Wheels of Chance*, 1896.
Whitechurch, Victor, *First and Last*, 1929.
Young, Arthur, *A General View of Agriculture in Sussex*, 1793.

Records and Documents
Abstract of Title to the Property of John Dudman Esq.
Chapel Register, Royal Hospital, Chelsea.
English Law Reports: Hotham and two others v East India Co. (1779); Hotham v East India Co. (1787).
The Flaxman Papers (British Museum).
Parish Registers, Holy Trinity, York.
Parish Registers, South Bersted.
Proceedings of the East India Company (British Museum).
Prospectus of the Bognor New Town Company, 1825 (British Museum).
Vestry Books, St Mary's, Wimbledon.
Vestry Books, South Bersted.

Newspapers and Periodicals
Argosy Magazine
Bognor (Regis) Observer
Bognor (Regis) Post
Brighton Gazette
Brighton Herald
County Mirror and Chichester Magazine
Daily Express
Daily Mirror
Dodley's Annual Register

The Gentleman's Magazine
London Magazine
Morning Advertiser
Morning Herald
Notes and Queries
South Bersted Parish Magazine
Sussex County Magazine
Sussex Weekly Advertiser
West Sussex Gazette

INDEX

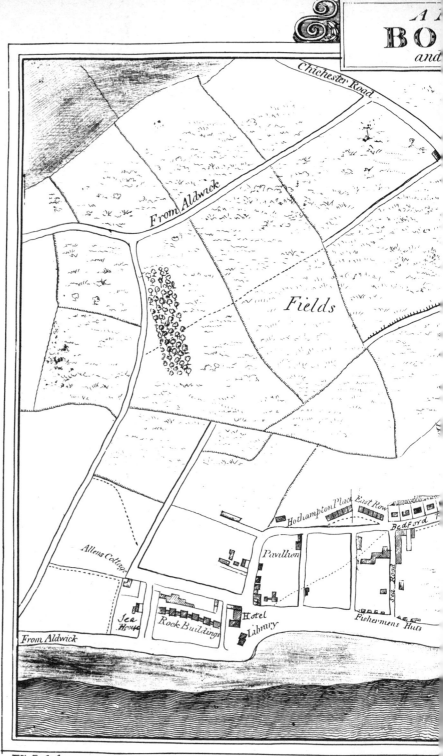

A
BO
and

Chichester Road

From Aldwick

Fields

Hothampton Place East Row

Bedford

Pavillion

Allens Cottage

Sea Road

Sea
House

Rock Buildings

Hotel
Library

Fishermens Huts

From Aldwick

I.M. del

Scale of ha

Published Sep. 16. 1817 and to be had